SONG HONGBING

CURRENCY WARS V
The Coming Rain

Song Hongbing

Song Hongbing (born in 1968) is a young economic researcher who emigrated to the United States. He worked there as a consultant for the American pension funds Freddie Mac and Fanny Mae that will disappear during the financial crisis of 2008.

货币战争⑤山雨欲来

CURRENCY WARS V
The Coming Rain

Translated from Chinese and published by
Omnia Veritas Limited

www.omnia-veritas.com

© Omnia Veritas Ltd – 2021

All rights reserved. No part of this publication may be reproduced by any means without the prior permission of the publisher. The intellectual property code prohibits copies or reproductions for collective use. Any representation or reproduction in whole or in part by any means whatsoever, without the consent of the publisher, is unlawful and constitutes an infringement punishable by copyright laws.

PREFACE 13

CHAPTER I 16

Gold Beheaded, the Battle for the Dollar 16
- April 12 gold massacre 17
- April 15, a once-in-a-million years horror 20
- "Chinese Auntie" is going up against Wall Street. 21
- London Gold: noble birth, private ways 24
- Swiss gold: the heart of a lady, the life of a maid 28
- U.S. QE3: One Stone Stirs a Thousand Waves, Dollar Confidence Shakes 36
- Echoing each other: developed countries come together, devaluation war drums heard 38
- Chain Reaction: Her Majesty the Queen as a prop, the Bank of England as a showstopper 48
- Fears escalate: EU robberies busy, Cypriot depositors panic 49
- COMEX gold inventory pulls a red alert 51
- Inventory cloud 55
- Gold ETF, Wall Street's "little vault" 58
- Insider disclosure 61
- How long will the red flag fight? Is there a future for gold and silver? ... 66
- Expound 70

CHAPTER II 72

The Truth Tunnel, Through the Space of the Bubble 72
- The black vulture in the stock market 73
- Bernanke's shock 76
- Stock market boom, or stock market puffiness? 78
- What is a share buyback like? 81
- Buy stocks by borrowing, God knows what 86
- "Ageing" of corporate assets 88
- Can the stock market still bounce after unplugging the QE ventilator? . 91
- A raucous bond market 93
- Corporate bond inventory shrinks, market makers fail to adjust 98
- Junk bonds, "subprime" in corporate bonds 102
- Expound 105

CHAPTER III 109

The Money Scare, The Sleepwalking Shadow Party 109
- Syria crisis, timely rain for Wall Street? 110
- A buyback is a pawn on a bond 115
- The June Surprise of the Repo Market 119
- Traditional currency creation 121
- Shadow money: a new law of money creation 125
- A sub-mortgage, a couple of bottles with a cap for acrobatics 129

"Buyback expiry" deals: a new way for financial magicians to play 132
The "fantasy drift" of junk debt 134
Shadow money and shadow banking 139
How much of the shadow currency was created by the repo mortgage?
.... 143
Why is there a money crisis in June? 144
Expound 148

CHAPTER IV 151

INTEREST RATE VOLCANO, THE FINAL DAY OF RECKONING 151

Federal Reserve suddenly "impotence", Bernanke unexpectedly changed
his mind 152
QE's Titanic, headlong into the repo iceberg 154
Collateral shortage worsens as regulatory chill hits 158
How shadow banks can kill off the competition 161
Twisting interest rates, the Fed acts as both referee and goalkeeper ... 164
Interest rate volcano, the ultimate killer of asset bubbles 167
Interest rate swaps, New Yorkers can't afford to be hurt 169
Interest rate swaps between governments and banks 170
The interest rate swap hacks behind the Detroit bankruptcy case 173
From interest rate swaps to interest rate "drop traps" 175
The origin of Libor 177
Who's manipulating interest rates? 181
Ultra-low interest rates blow up the biggest financial bubble in history
.... 185
To quit QE is to seek death, to continue QE is to wait for death 188
Expound 193

CHAPTER V 195

WALL STREET SPECULATORS IN ACTION 195

The Wounds of Bleeding Home Prices: Foreclosed Homes 196
Foreclosure blockage, house prices stabilize 199
Wall Street Speculation, the Rhythm of Home Price Reversal 202
Phoenix, the first test of the speculators 204
The Vegas Bounty 207
Turn to Southern California 208
Black Rock, the largest landowner in the United States 211
Who are the victims of the Wall Street speculation? 214
Is real estate awake or sleepwalking? 217
A new trend for young people: moving back home to "eat the old" 219
Interest rate volcano will burn real estate 222
The Deadly Trap of "Tenant Empire" 224
Roadmap to the Great Escape for Victory 227
The second battleground of escape: rent-backed securities 230

  Expound... 233

CHAPTER VI **236**

Wealth Divided, Broken Wings of Dreams 236
  On Wall Street, the president ate behind closed doors 237
  "The Volcker Rule" 240
  The demise of London Whale 243
  Lawlessness and lawlessness 248
  Sinking middle and lower classes 253
  The truth about the job market.. 256
  The division of wealth broke the wings of the American dream 267
  Greed and Dream Stealing 269
  Asset fragmentation is far more severe than income fragmentation... 276
  Expound... 281

CHAPTER VII **284**

Rome's Rise and Fall, Bloodthirsty Path of Greed 284
  Death of the Civil Protector Gracchus 285
  Gracchus's upbringing... 287
  The Gracchus Brothers' land change law... 289
  Hard work built Rome, greed destroyed the republic 292
  The big twist: inward exploitation to outward expansion 299
  The imperial age of the monetary economy 303
  Fragile monetary cycles... 308
  The economic crisis in dormancy... 312
  The economic nature of military dictatorship 317
  Currency devaluation and hyperinflation... 321
  The collapse of the currency sounded the death knell for the empire .. 326

CHAPTER VIII **331**

The Rise and Fall of the Northern Song Dynasty 331
  The Northern Song Dynasty, the pinnacle of mankind's second monetary civilization 332
  Currency overshoot and inflation.. 338
  The rise of the banker.. 341
  The fight between gold and power 346
  6-7% of the wealthy have annexed 60%-70% of the land 348
  The destruction of the Song Dynasty dream 351
  The "money shortage" is worsened by the snow............................... 356
  Why did Wang Anshi change his ways and why did he fail?................ 359
  The final madness of greed 363
  The world's first paper currency... 367
  Sovereign credit, greed as usual 370
  Expound... 374

CHAPTER IX **376**
    WHAT'S NOT THE CHINESE DREAM? 376
        "The Roman Dream," "The Song Dream," "The American Dream" is broken. 377
        The Second Wealth Merger in the United States *381*
        What is not the Chinese Dream? *386*
        Real estate and wealth distribution *390*
        The key to urbanization is job creation *397*
        Land transfer and farmers' income *400*
        Only with boundless strength can you let your dreams fly *405*
POSTSCRIPT **409**
OTHER TITLES **413**

PREFACE

People's ability to think is often paralyzed in the face of overwhelming information and a myriad of opinions. Critical data is drowned out by noise data, important details are confused by minutiae, deeper pathologies are confused by superficial pathologies, core reasoning is tied up in trivial logic, analysis loses its bearings and judgment goes astray. Ultimately, the illusion displaces the truth.

This is particularly true in the economic sphere.

Five years after the end of the financial crisis in 2008, views on the future course of the world economy are still divided. Has the U.S. quantitative easing been effective or not? Is the global currency overshoot a blessing or a curse? Are financial markets becoming safer, or more dangerous? Has the economic recovery been steady or short-lived? In short, is the world gradually moving away from the last recession, or is it accelerating its slide to the next crisis?

Conflicting market performance, conflicting economic data, absurd interpretations, mixed attitudes, controversial policy measures, welcome to the chaotic and noisy scene of recovery in today's world!

The lack of a deeper understanding of the nature of economic activity stems from the lack of a deeper, unified logical framework. Instead of participating in the economy in a highly rational state, human beings chase wealth in the midst of intense emotions filled with desire. Human nature, and especially the inherent greed in human nature, has always been the fundamental force that drives the economy.

All the activities that mankind has ever engaged in have always revolved around two most basic tasks, one of which is the creation of wealth and the other is the distribution of wealth, from which all other activities are derived. Whether creating wealth or distributing it, human greed has been the source of their ultimate energy since the beginning.

The "good in greed" drives technological advances that save energy, reduce time, reduce intensity, and increase pleasure, resulting in a continuous increase in productivity and more prosperous wealth creation. However, insatiable greed can inspire trickery, speculation, fraud, quick gains and extravagance, which in turn stifle productivity progress, lead to a distorted distribution of wealth and reduce the economic vitality of society.

The focus of this book is to use wealth distribution as a scalpel to dissect economic activities, to compare the American Dream of today with the Roman Dream and the Song Dynasty Dream in history, and to provide a historical reference for the Chinese Dream of the future.

The first six chapters of the book are a microscopic look at the current state of the U.S. economy, looking at the dollar from the gold market, analyzing the economy from the stock market, understanding capital from the bond market, exploring finance from the repo market, peering into the crisis from the interest rate market, insight into the bubble from the housing market, identifying the recovery from the job market, and ultimately, greed from the distribution of wealth.

The plunge in gold prices in April 2013 was interpreted as a good recovery of the U.S. economy, and thus the decline of gold's risk aversion demand; and the evidence of a good economy is the stock market record highs, but if we analyze the root cause of the stock market rally momentum, we will find that the stock buyback behavior of listed companies, in fact, is the dominant force pushing up stock prices; stock buyback funds are in turn from the bond market financing, and the bond market fire is the result of monetary quantitative easing. As a result, the abnormal boom in financial markets is due to the ultra-low interest rate environment created by the QE policy.

Has the monetary flood caused by QE really spurred a recovery in the real economy? The answer is no.

The company's sales growth rate is decreasing, after deducting inflation, has actually fallen into negative growth; enterprise capital expenditure is shrinking, which explains the long-term difficulties of the job market, leading to the real economy's core assets show serious "aging" symptoms, followed by a rapid decline in labor productivity; real estate price recovery is nothing more than the masterpiece of Wall Street speculation in real estate, the reduction of employment opportunities, resulting in a large number of the younger generation was squeezed out of the potential housing purchase team, the real estate success has been determined; the United States mainstream middle-class high-paying jobs recovery is slow, before 2025 are difficult to restore to the 2000 level.

QE policies have failed to save the real economy, in fact, cheap money is not promoting economic growth, but destroying capital formation.

If QE has been proven to be a failed policy by five years of economic practice, the path out of QE is by no means a smooth one. Exiting QE will trigger an interest rate volcano, while continuing QE will hit the repo iceberg head-on, with both paths ending in the re-emergence of the financial crisis. The Federal Reserve in QE between the wandering and hesitation, both in the real economy in a hopeless situation, but also put the financial markets in the edge of danger.

Whether or not interest rates can be infinitely suppressed is the windsock to judge the next round of the financial crisis!

The United States has embarked on a path that has benefited only a few but has affected the vast majority of the population, rooted in the excessive greed of the powerful and the rich, which has made it difficult to reverse the worsening trend of wealth mergers, which in turn has exacerbated the economic woes.

The last three chapters of the book expand the scope of observation to the year 2000, from a close look at the U.S. economy, to an examination of the historical context; from the inflection point of the rise and fall of the Roman and Northern Song prosperity, to gradually show a slow-motion shot of a highly approximate process of decline: greed rises, annexation arises; land accumulation, taxation is deformed; the treasury is empty, the currency is depreciated; the people's power is depleted, internal strife is born and external trouble is caused!

The collapse of the American Dream, the Roman Dream and the Song Dynasty Dream does not tell us what the Chinese Dream is, but it can remind us what is not the Chinese Dream.

If a future China can avoid repeating these lessons of history, no power can prevent it from realizing its dream of rejuvenation as a powerful country rich in people.

CHAPTER I

Gold Beheaded, the Battle for the Dollar

In April 2013, the gold market took a sudden turn for the worse, with the plunge in gold prices shocking the world. "Gold is dead," "gold is useless," "the bull market is over," "the bubble is bursting," "the gold price will fall to $500," and so on, are all the rhetoric. Gold has become a "pariah" overnight from a high-profile investment star to a "pariah" that public opinion is vying to deride.

People began to doubt the validity of the belief of "hiding gold in a troubled world", confidence in the investment value of gold and silver was fundamentally shaken, pessimism was widespread, and the chanting was widespread, and even the basic logic that over-issued currencies will eventually lead to inflation became ambiguous. Market sentiment is severely disconnected from rational logic, and price signals and wealth intuition are misaligned. Suffice it to say that the perception of gold has fallen into an unprecedented funk.

Is there really no hope for gold? That is absolutely not the case!

In 2013, the U.S. government and Wall Street hit the gold market with a ferocity not seen in 30 years; which in turn illustrates another problem, such madness and such intense behavior means that the dollar's fear of gold is also unprecedented in 30 years!

Weak confidence in the dollar is exactly what is hitting gold!

This chapter will provide an in-depth analysis of the behind-the-scenes and behind-the-scenes aspects of the United States gold crackdown on April 12 and the root causes of the dollar's plight. From a historical point of view, gold has always been the wealth of "Noah's Ark"; to the reality of the market analysis, the production cost of gold is the bottom of the market; looking at the future trend, gold must be the biggest beneficiary of the dollar crisis.

April 12 gold massacre

> *"For Americans, a financial and economic disaster may be close at hand. The Fed and the financial institutions it relies on have joined forces to crack down on gold and silver prices as a deterrent to investors is evidence of this."*
> Paul Roberts, former Assistant Secretary of the United States Treasury, 4 April 2013

> *"It's true that the (US) government loathes the skyrocketing gold price, especially as they pursue the largest currency devaluation policy in history ... (whether or not the April 12 gold plunge was manipulated) we will never know (the truth)."*
> Bipa Magellan, former Special Assistant to the President of the United States for Economic Policy, 7 June 2013

April 12, 2013, was the darkest day in the history of gold.

Since the beginning of the year, gold has oscillated downward from around $1,700 to the edge of a huge abyss by April 11, and on April 12, at 8:30 p.m. EDT, gold was set at $1,542, the last moment of calm before the cataclysm.

This day coincided with Friday, the New York gold futures market just opened on the black clouds, thunder and lightning, 100 tons of gold selling orders fell from the sky, this sudden heavy sell-off like a huge wave generally smashed into the unprepared market, the long head hastily under the battle, gold prices plunged. For the next two hours, the panicked market breathed a little. Traders were dazed by an unsuspecting air ambush, and for a while, rumors abounded and people panicked. However, the huge sell-off suddenly fizzled out and calm returned to the market.

It was the characteristic silence that preceded the great earthquake, and a strong sense of ominousness enveloped the market.

At 10:30, the real catastrophe finally struck when the 300-tonne gold sell-off raged, the size of 11% of global gold production in 2012! The dumbfounded traders saw no longer a 10-meter high swell, but a 30-meter high tsunami! Fear freezes everyone's heart to the freezing point, and moments later, the madness burns everyone's brain to bursting, taking the road and fleeing is like a survival instinct that dictates all behavior. Market dynamics reversed in an instant and the cries of short selling were deafening.

The key support point of $1525 was instantly pierced and the direction of the gold bull market since 2000 turned around. All the long buyers who set automatic stop loss at this bull-bear demarcation point were like mummy warriors awakened by a spell, suddenly joined the short army and turned to kill their own camp.

At this time, when the New York market is at its most liquid, London and Europe's major gold markets are opening, so that the extreme horror of the gold price avalanche can be fully felt, the time of the short sale is pinpointed to every minute!

The shockwave of the gold plunge instantly spread around the world, and the London market was simultaneously blasted. However, London is more inclined to trade physical gold relative to the New York gold futures market, and for clients ready to withdraw spot gold, the New York futures plunge has somewhat given them the opportunity to buy at a discount. However, as buyers in the London market were preparing to take a dive, they suddenly discovered that their computer trading system had an extremely rare "malfunction" and that no one could buy or sell. While they can still place orders over the phone, there can be a shortage of spot gold in London at a time when market conditions are changing rapidly, making it difficult to fully realize their trades.

Panic-stricken buyers of physical gold in London wonder what is really going on in the market. Meanwhile, gold prices in the New York market remain in an avalanche. If gold prices continue to plummet, then the vast majority of long positions will be busted and the gold market is bound to accelerate. In order to hedge the risk of holding physical gold, buyers in London, unable to buy in the London spot gold market to spread the cost, had to sell short in the New York futures gold market to cover their losses. They had to make the most of it, and the instinct to escape once again dominated.

Short sale first, then ask questions!

Traders in London also jumped on the empty chariot, crushing the corpses of the long ones as they continued their mad dash.

The downward trend of New York futures gold, in the London physical gold market, which should have been counterattacked, not only swept through the past without any bloodshed, but also successfully disarmed London buyers who held physical gold and forced them to join the army of shorting gold.

The unprecedented strength of the short attack, after the $1525 stop loss point was broken, triggered a large-scale long stop loss of the backsliding, and then forced the London market of physical gold buyers to join the mutiny, for a time as if into no man's land.

Short sale! Short sale! Short sale!

From New York to London, from Singapore to Hong Kong, from Shanghai to Tokyo, terrified gold investors were slaughtered and the markets were bloodied.

The Wall Street media excitedly commented that gold's plunge was like a freefall, and that the shorts had "a sharp blade like a soft cream".

The psychological defenses of the gold market have completely collapsed. Electronic trading continues after the end of the in-floor public call. By 5:07 p.m., the gold price had plunged to $1476.1, the biggest drop of the day at $88.8!

This heralds a greater disaster still to come!

In the gold futures market, both long and short sides use margin trading, with small funds to leverage the way to pry large transactions, the leverage ratio can be as high as 1:20. When the price falls, the long margin will bear the same multiple of the loss. The magnitude of the day's plunge in gold prices was bound to knock out a large number of long margin accounts. Throughout the weekend, banks and brokerage firms didn't take breaks, but rather spun up at high speed, working overtime to count accounts one by one. Immediately afterwards, the large amount of margin call "ultimatum", was quickly served to the stunned long clients, they only have 24 hours to either surrender, by the exchange forced to close the position; or before Sunday to take out a large amount of cash to cover the margin.

Gold futures market has been subjected to two rounds of fierce "air raids"

At the moment, the painful long, not only suffered a heavy loss of funds, but also suffered great psychological anguish. The weekend all media machines are in full swing, short-selling gold news and comments are all over the place, "gold price collapse," "bull market end," "bubble burst," "ridiculous gold cried," "burst," "wild dump," and other extremely powerful headlines flooded television, radio, newspapers and the Internet, the atmosphere of terror in the media under the exaggerated magnification, rapid spread, large-scale infection. Desperation, after a weekend of psychological fermentation, pushed the gold market into a "species extinction-level" catastrophe on Monday, 15 April.

April 15, a once-in-a-million years horror

A once in 10 years misfortune is called a disaster, a once in 50 years misfortune is called a major disaster, a once in 100 years misfortune is called a major disaster, and a once in 2 million years misfortune? I'm afraid it can only be called an "extinction-level" disaster.

What happened to the gold market on April 15, 2013 was an extinction-level disaster!

In the whole weekend, the call sheet of margin call as snow flakes generally filled the global gold market, high times the leverage under the gold long has faced the end of the disaster. On Monday, the Asian markets just opened, the people who were desperate to escape trampled on each other, and there were numerous deaths and injuries, thus opening up the biggest rout in the history of gold.

The London market plunged, the United States market collapsed, the television news of the gold price show has not kept pace with the gold plunge, the world was dumbfounded to witness the people's hearts of the wealth "Noah's Ark", actually in just a few hours to sink.

On the day, New York futures gold prices closed in free fall at $1361 from $1501 on Friday, a wild $140 drop of 9.3%, the largest single-day drop in 30 years!

In terms of market volatility, intraday trading was even more thrilling that day. Britain's *Daily Telegraph* on April 16 exclaimed,

> "Using the theory of normal distribution as a basis for your calculations, you'll see volatility on Mondays (in the gold

market) that only happens once in 500 million trading days, or once in 2 million years."[1]

When disaster of this magnitude strikes, the dinosaurs will also become extinct. Wall Street's media cheerleaders ripped their voices out and chanted: Gold is finished!

"Chinese Auntie" is going up against Wall Street.

However, the gold investors were not "exterminated" and what happened next surprised the world!

April 16, just in the futures gold prices plummeted in the waves, in the silence of a thunderstorm!

The physical gold snappers all over the world, as if they had heard the firing gun, suddenly killed from all corners almost at the same moment. They stormed the gold shops and banks of the major cities violently and without warning, and a gold rush that had not been seen for half a century swept the world!

In mainland China, the first to be heard of is the "Chinese big mom". They do not understand the Wall Street Journal, nor do they know the technical graphs of New York gold futures, seeing the price of gold fall, just like hearing that the price of Beijing's Third Ring Road has fallen from 50,000 yuan (per square meter) to 30,000 yuan, where is the reason not to rob? They only care about value and not value, and they don't care about futures. The people's thinking is simple: gold is more valuable than paper, and earth is more solid than money!

Not only have first-tier cities such as Beijing, Shanghai, Guangzhou and Shenzhen seen a massive gold rush, but almost every provincial capital city has seen reports of gold selling out of stock.

How big of a purchase is that, exactly? The data from the Shanghai Gold Exchange says it all.

The Shanghai Gold Exchange is the central hub for all legal spot gold trading in China. All domestic mineral gold, recovered gold, and

---

[1] Thomas Pascoe, The Gold Price Crash is Further Evidence of Market Rigging, The Telegraph Blogs, 2013-04-16.

imported gold from overseas must first enter the Shanghai Gold Exchange before it can be legally traded and sent to the country. In the retail market, the ultimate source of all gold products comes from the Shanghai Gold Exchange. The members of the Shanghai Gold Exchange include financial institutions, production, smelting, processing, wholesale and import and export trade of precious metal products such as gold, silver and platinum. In a nutshell, the Shanghai Gold Exchange's exit volume.

Chinese Auntie" buys gold in droves on April 16, 2013 is the total volume of all legal gold traded in the Chinese market.

In April 2013, the Shanghai Gold Exchange's outbound volume soared 182% year-on-year to a staggering 236 tons! The Institute's full year 2012 depot volume was 1,138 tons, and the April 2013 depot volume is close to the first quarter of 2012 total!

By the end of April, the domestic gold market has been basically out of stock, the Shanghai Gold Exchange's spot gold premium than the international market per gram higher than nearly 10 yuan, while the normal situation is generally not more than 1 yuan, which means that to buy gold at home than to buy gold abroad per ounce expensive $50! Such a high premium reflects the fact that physical gold is already in extreme shortage in the Chinese market.

Because the domestic price of gold is too expensive, a large number of "Chinese mothers" have rushed to Hong Kong to sweep the goods, directly leading to the Hong Kong gold and silver trading floor inventory was "ransacked", the total transaction amount reached a record 160 billion Hong Kong dollars, equivalent to 400 tons of gold trading volume! By 24 April, Hong Kong's physical gold stocks were on the verge of depletion and had to be restocked urgently from London and Switzerland, with orders four times higher than usual!

At the end of April, with the approach of the domestic "May Day" long holiday, a large number of "Chinese amah" again with a large amount of money "bombed" Hong Kong, Hong Kong's gold stores once again made a full bowl of money. According to Hong Kong media reports, from April 29 to May 2, the territory's 1,200 jewelry stores gold sales soared 50% year-on-year, selling 40 tons of gold in 4 days!

"China's big mothers" became famous in the war, they in the international gold futures price plummeted, gold market popularity collapse crisis, swept the mainland China and Hong Kong gold, shocked the international financial market, but also shook the Wall Street bigwigs.

On April 10, Goldman Sachs released a report that was strongly bearish on gold and advised clients to short gold on a large scale. Just 13 days later, in front of the world's physical gold rush, Goldman Sachs had to change the word and declare that while continuing to be bearish on gold, it does not recommend that clients continue to short gold.

In fact, the rush to buy gold is not only breaking out in China, the enthusiasm for investing in physical gold and silver around the world is also like a prairie fire, spreading.

Immediately after the plunge in New York futures gold prices, U.S. physical gold and silver investors began a massive swoop.

On April 16, Amark and CNT, the largest U.S. precious metals dealers, announced that their silver inventories were out of stock and that they were also designated by the U.S. Treasury Department as raw material suppliers for the manufacture of gold and silver coins. As a result, SD BULLION, an important US precious metals ordering website, put up the words "Out of stock!" on its home page that day. ("SOLD OUT!") for the notable reminder that "Due to the unprecedented scale of physical sales today, order delivery will be delayed by 20 days."

Bill Hayne, who has 41 years of experience in the precious metals industry, could not help but lament:

> *"Never seen such a large-scale shortage of gold and silver, many of the U.S. precious metals wholesalers have been out of stock, order pickup was delayed 4 weeks to 6 weeks processing. The ratio of buyers to sellers of physical gold and silver has reached a staggering 50:1, causing fees for all precious metal purchases to skyrocket."*

On April 17, a report released by the U.S. Treasury Mint, the world's largest provider of gold and silver coins, showed that Americans went on a buying spree that day, buying a record 635,000 ounces of gold, or two tons of gold! And the "Chinese Auntie" in the "May Day" sweeping the Hong Kong market, the scale of the sale of 10 tons per day!

On April 24, just as Hong Kong gold was sold out, the U.S. Mint announced that 1/10 ounce gold coins were also sold out, with the supply disrupted for more than a month. 1/10 ounce gold coins are the most popular gold coin investment in the United States, with sales soaring 118% year-on-year since 2013. Throughout April, the U.S. Mint sold nearly 210,000 ounces (6.8 tons) of gold for $311 million, the highest amount ever sold at the Mint.

India, the world's largest gold consumer, imported 142.5 tonnes of gold in April, up a whopping 66% from the average of the previous three months; in Australia, Perth Mint gold sales hit a record high of 112,000 ounces (3.6 tonnes) in April, up a whopping 534.4% year-on-year; and in Japan, there were long lines of Japanese people waiting patiently for three hours to buy gold in gold shops in the Ginza business district of Tokyo.

From Istanbul to Abu Dhabi, from Mumbai to Dubai, from North America to Europe, from Australia to Switzerland, from Singapore to Hong Kong, from Beijing to Tokyo, physical gold investors around the world have been buying physical gold in a big way during the two weeks of the futures gold confidence collapse.

There's a miracle of ice and fire in the gold market! The futures gold market is cold to the extent of "extinction", while the physical gold market is hot to the "hot" market!

One wonders, are we talking about the same thing? Why is the world's physical gold so highly sought after, but futures gold "keeps on plunging"? Which market really calls the price of gold?

To understand the rationale behind this, it's necessary to look back at the history of the world gold market.

London Gold: noble birth, private ways

In the early 19th century, Britain was the first in the world to establish a gold standard, with one ounce of gold set by law at £3.17 shillings and 10.5 pence. Simply put, it was the Bank of England that promised to buy all gold at any time at the price of £3.17 shillings and 9 pence, and to sell it to the market in unlimited quantities at the legal price of £3.17 shillings and 10.5 pence. The Bank of England was the largest market maker in the world gold market at that time, its main duty is to defend the gold price and ensure that the gold standard system is safe and secure.

Of course, the Bank of England is not personally going bareback, calling in the market to buy and sell, but relying on the five major

London goldsmiths for wholesale business, who in turn rely on their own powerful channels for retail. In fact, the essence of finance is also the channel is king, but the channel in circulation is financial products.

London's five major gold merchants are almost two or three hundred years old, the most famous is the Rothschild family, they not only control the European countries of the public debt market, but also the world's gold market is their hegemon, in the 19th century is known as the "sixth largest power in Europe. Apart from the Rothschild family, the Mocatta family is the second oldest and has been running a gold business in London for nine generations, even older than the Rothschild family's qualifications. The other three include Johnson Matthey, Sharps Pixley and Samuel Montagu, who began gold and silver inspection as early as 1750.[2]

Since the nineteenth century, Britain has held the pre-eminence of the birthplace of the industrial revolution, backed by maritime hegemony and leveraged by financial strength, established a colonial empire spanning Europe, the United States, Asia, Africa and Oceania, monopolized the global supply of raw materials and energy, controlled the division of the world market, held the channel of ocean trade, and controlled the flow of international capital. The world's gold from South Africa, Canada, the United States, Russia, Brazil, Australia and other places of gold mines to London pooled, the Bank of England based on gold reserves to create the pound to pass through the world, then the pound capital and industrial products from Britain to all corners of the world market, and finally, the huge profits wrapped up in more gold back to London, complete the great circle of international capital.

The classic gold standard monetary system laid a solid foundation for British prosperity and hegemony until latecomer Germany began to challenge this mechanism of wealth creation under British rule.

The outbreak of the First World War broke the world gold cycle, centered in London, and the countries involved in the war had to suspend the exchange of paper money and gold. In a wartime state, the gold output of British colonies such as South Africa went directly into

---

[2] Timothy Green, *The New World of Gold*, George Weidenfeldand Nicolson, London, 1982, p. 108.

the vaults of the Bank of England and became Britain's wartime gold reserves.

After the end of World War I, Britain, although militarily victorious over Germany, was economically devastated. The Americans, on the other hand, sat on the sidelines and watched as the massive influx of gold from Europe into the United States hedged its bets, leading to a surge in the strength of American industry and finance. At this point, the dollar has significantly outweighed the pound.

The war was over, but Britain, which had to print a lot of money during the war, while not experiencing vicious inflation, was in huge dollar debt, reduced from a pre-war creditor nation to a post-war debtor nation to the United States. London's status as an international financial centre has been snatched by New York, and the hegemony of the world currency of sterling has been overwhelmed by the dollar. The British financial system has been badly wounded, leading to a delay in the return of the pound to the gold standard and a serious disruption of the order of international trade and the division of labour in the world, which the United Kingdom has struggled to operate for centuries.

In 1913, the four major economic powers before the war, the United States, Britain, Germany and France, a total of $5 billion in gold reserves, of which the United States up to 2 billion, Britain 800 million, Germany 1 billion, France 1.2 billion. And after the war, in the four major powers of $6 billion in total gold reserves, the United States has sat on $4.5 billion, more than five times the United Kingdom, with an absolute advantage. But the British Empire was clearly unable to adjust to the hegemon mentality in time, and the Bank of England insisted on pricing gold in pounds only, while the pound was significantly depreciating against the dollar.

In this way, gold-producing countries such as South Africa would be out of the picture. The Bank of England was collecting their gold at a fixed price in a wartime state, and the price of gold was clearly rising, and if it continued at a fixed price it was clearly losing a lot. Of course Britain is sovereign and South Africa is reluctant to turn its back on New York, but they are desperate to find an outlet in London that truly reflects the price of the gold market.

Clearly, who can match the Rothschilds in London in terms of both financial power and prime position? Thus, the Rothschild family, under the common support of the gold-producing countries and gold brokers, gathered the five major London gold merchant families, on September 12, 1919 began the first "London gold pricing".

On this day, gold set a record for the first market quotation and the price of gold was fixed at: £4.18!

From then on, at 10:30 a.m. every working day, representatives of the four major London gold merchants came to the Rothschild family offices in the Financial City of London on time, and they were seated separately in a secret room, with the Rothschild representatives in total five people, and no one else was allowed inside. Each of them has a dedicated line to their own company's trading room, which in turn connects gold brokers large and small from around the world. Rothschild's pricing chamber is the nerve center of the world's gold trade, which closely integrates South Africa's seven major gold mines, gold exporters from the former Soviet Union, South America, Australia and the world's major gold suppliers, gold demanders from Hong Kong, the Middle East, India, Tokyo and other places, as well as speculators from various countries, into a network of world gold production and distribution channels. At the moment, the world is nervously awaiting the fixing price of gold that day.

In the secret room, five people were in the same position, and the chairman was naturally the representative of the Rothschild family. He will begin by announcing, "Gentlemen, we begin today with $498." (After 1968, London gold was priced in U.S. dollars, with reference to the New York closing price) Immediately afterwards, five people notified their respective firms' trading rooms of the initial price by telephone, and traders immediately began asking customers over the phone for buying and selling price ranges, while more customers were waiting on the line. Very soon, each trading room sorted out the orders of its own customers to buy and sell, calculated the rolling difference, and then quickly fed back to the Rothschild family secret room. Within seconds, five people announced whether they were buyers or sellers, or not interested in that price, based on the results of the rolling differential in their respective trading rooms. Generally, pricing comes into effect when the volume of sales and purchases announced by five people reaches several tons (a figure that has been kept secret) and the total volume of buyers and sellers is just about balanced. If the number of sales does not match, then the chairman must try another price and everyone is busy again until at that price, the total number of sales and purchases is balanced.[3]

When the five people finally settled on a satisfactory price, the London gold was "finalized". This fixing price was immediately announced to traders over the phone, and between lightning bolts, the pricing of London gold was quickly passed to all corners of the world, and the huge international gold market began to rumble.

When the price of gold is relatively stable, a single test is sufficient, but when the price of gold fluctuates sharply, it may have to be tried 20 or 30 times, and one time in October 1979 took 1 hour 39 minutes! The longest occurred on March 23, 1990, when a Middle Eastern bank asked to sell at least 14 tons of gold, extending the time to 2 hours and 26 minutes, and the price dropped $20 during the fixing process. The largest order fixing transaction occurred in March 1968, when the US lost the Vietnam War and the pound depreciated sharply, speculators flocked to buy gold, and the Gold Pool, formed by Western central banks, was squeezed to over 2,000 tons of gold. In response, the London gold market was closed for a full two weeks. With the reopening of the gold market, gold is no longer priced in pounds, but in dollars.

The Rothschild family dominated London gold pricing until 2004. That year, the Rothschild family announced that they had voluntarily relinquished their gold pricing rights, citing a lack of profitability. Be aware that gold is traded in the thousands of tons per day, nearly a million tons per year, for a total transaction value of no less than $20 trillion! Pricing power is prophetic power, the stock market high frequency traders to know the market 1 millisecond, can pay hundreds of millions of dollars in investment price, the Rothschild family in the gold price "prophetic" time is more than 1 millisecond? With such a huge power, no one else could fight for it, but the Rothschild family was able to voluntarily give it up, and it seemed that the Rothschild family's water depth had reached an unbelievable level.

Swiss gold: the heart of a lady, the life of a maid

---

[3] Ibid. p. 121.

The outbreak of "World War II" interrupted the good old days of London's monopoly of the world gold market. From 1939 to 1954, the London gold market was forced to close in the beacons of war and post-war chaos. If the British Empire could barely maintain its status as a world financial centre after the First World War, then the unprecedented loss of Britain in the Second World War, especially after the forcible dismemberment of its colonial empire by the United States, would forever deprive London of the opportunity to regain financial supremacy. In the gold market, another formidable rival has quietly risen to prominence, and that is Switzerland.

Switzerland was deliberately "protected" by Hitler as a "neutral country" during the Second World War as a hub for secret commercial transactions between Nazi Germany and the Allies. Swiss banks' general ledgers filed with the Swiss Treasury show that Swiss gold jumped from $332 million in 1941 to $846 million in 1945, at least $500 million of which came from Nazi Germany, a figure that coincides with a Clinton-era congressional inquiry. The report states that Switzerland received $440 million worth of Nazi gold during the Second World War, of which $316 million were looted by the Nazis from other countries.

Between 1945 and 1954, while the British gold market was still closed, Swiss banks began to move around, consolidating gold supply and distribution channels around the world in an attempt to establish a global gold market with Switzerland at the centre. In terms of supply channels, the Swiss had no ideological scruples, forging strong business partnerships with the former Soviet Union and the socialist camps in Eastern Europe, on the one hand, and even going to South Africa to dig up the British wall foot. In terms of sales channels, the Swiss' most successful expansion has been the discovery of the strong demand for gold in the Asian market, especially in China, where they made a fortune.

In 1949, China's Kuomintang regime was on the verge of final collapse, Beijing, Shanghai's gold prices soared to $50 ~ $55, while the European market gold prices were only $38. The rich and wealthy of the Minzu government went on a gold rush at prices far higher than those in Europe and ended up depositing this gold in Swiss banks. In and out, the huge profits were made by the Swiss. At the same time, the credit of Swiss banks is deeply entrenched in China, and even after the founding of New China, the main international gold business is conducted through Switzerland.

The rapid expansion of the Swiss gold market soon brought large and small gold dealers from all over the world into its own account, together with the Swiss gold refining technology, Swiss gold bars gradually became the most popular standard product in the world. By the early 1970s, 80% of South African gold was flowing into Switzerland rather than the UK. From 1972 to 1980, the former Soviet Union exported 2,000 tons of gold were pooled in Switzerland. In the mid-70s, the United States and the IMF in order to completely "demonetize" gold, a large scale in the market to sell gold bars, the smart Swiss quietly ate into one third of them. The Swiss also export 500 tons of gold to Italy and the Middle East jewelry industry every year, from Rome to Tehran, from Istanbul to Riyadh, from Singapore to Hong Kong, everywhere is the Swiss refined gold bars.

The huge gold market provides Switzerland with ample gold reserves, with the Swiss central bank storing 13.2 ounces (411 grams) of gold for every Swiss, a full 11 times more than the per capita holdings of the United States, the largest gold reserve country![4] The Swiss franc has become the strongest currency in the entire Western world, backed by bars of gold up to 1.1 times larger than any other Swiss franc note in circulation.

In the face of a formidable challenge from Switzerland, Britain finally lost its throne as the world's gold hub for 300 years and gradually evolved into a pure trading centre.

However, London's advantage in gold pricing has not been diminished. The British have seen a general trend, due to the global dollar's long-term over-haul, financial institutions and market speculators in the gold market to grasp the huge amount of money, has been in the financial strength of the final demanders of physical gold greatly exceeded, Britain as long as the financial capital firmly grasp the investment needs, it is far more profitable than control gold supply and marketing channels. Rather than being a world mover of physical gold, it's better to be a pricer of international gold prices.

Bottom line: let the Swiss do the manual work and be the boss themselves.

---

[4] Ibid. p. 125.

If the combination of London and Switzerland is seen as a "front shop, back factory" model, London is business, and Switzerland is production. London used its advantageous position as a European financial center, turned into a gold pricing center, transport, warehousing, testing, refining and other hard work outsourced to Switzerland, London will mainly focus on the expansion of gold investors channels, as well as for them to tailor a variety of products, the gold market clearing books firmly in their hands, will pick up and deliver such trivial matters to Switzerland to deal with.

Switzerland has the heart of a lady, but in the end it's the maid's life.

January 2, 1975, was a landmark day in the history of gold. After more than 40 long years, the U.S. government finally announced the unbanning of gold, and Americans can legally hold gold from now on.

The world knows that the dollar is also known as the "U.S. dollar" because the dollar is backed by gold and the United States is free to hold as many guns as it wants, so how can Americans be prohibited from holding gold? Is gold more dangerous than guns?

For the US government, guns can take lives, gold can take hearts, and hearts are harder to control than lives.

The British Empire was the first to introduce the gold standard in the early 19th century, followed by European countries. At that time, the United States was still seen by Europeans as the "foreign land" of financial civilization, with no modern central bank and no stable monetary system. Since the colonial era, there have been many different types of currencies. With colonial banknotes, gold and silver twin-track systems, Lincoln Greenbacks, and even the ability for every bank to issue its own legal tender, the 19th century can be described as 100 years of great controversy, chaos, and experimentation in the American monetary system. It's interesting to note that while America's currency is in disarray, economic growth has skyrocketed. It was also during these 100 years that the United States went from being a weak former colonial state to overtaking all the developed countries in Europe to becoming the world's number one power in one fell swoop.

Just as the first rich people got rich before they began to practice aristocratic manners, the United States became an economic power before it found its cluttered monetary system somewhat unseemly, although wealth and power were being concentrated while the monetary system remained chaotically dispersed. Eventually, the United States introduced the gold standard in 1900, with the law stating that 1 ounce of gold = $20.67.

World War I turned the United States into a frenzy, with large amounts of European gold pouring into the United States, thus stimulating the great economic boom and the great bubble that followed in the 1920s. The U.S. stock market crashed in 1929, and U.S. banks began a massive bankruptcy in 1931. Terrified savers flocked to the banks, using dollar bills to run out of gold, resulting in the collapse of thousands of banks. March 3, 1933, the day before Roosevelt was sworn in as President, the international and domestic run on the Federal Reserve Bank of New York's gold reserves were ransacked.[5] If Roosevelt doesn't act decisively on March 4, then the US central banking system will go bankrupt! This is bankruptcy in the true sense because the Federal Reserve Bank of New York is a private company, not a government department.

One of the first things Roosevelt did when he took office on March 4, 1933, was to immediately shut down the nation's banking system and take a 10-day vacation. On 11 March, Roosevelt issued an executive order halting the exchange of gold by banks in the name of stabilizing the economy, and on 5 April, he ordered American citizens to turn over all their gold, which the government compulsorily purchased for $20.67. In addition to rare gold coins and gold jewelry, any American who kept gold in private was subject to a heavy 10-year prison sentence and a $250,000 fine, and the Gold Reserve Act was passed again in January 1934, with the dollar depreciating dramatically to $35 for an ounce of gold, but American citizens had no right to exchange it. Americans just surrendered gold a few months ago, and the dollar bills in their hands depreciated by half before they even got hot.

Roosevelt's gold ban, which came to the rescue that year, actually lasted over 40 years! This situation became even more inconceivable after the war, when the United States, with 2/3 of the world's gold reserves and half of the world's GDP at one point, banned its citizens from holding gold for such a long period of time, with apparently no justification. This amply demonstrates that isolating gold from the daily

---

[5] Liaquat Ahamed, *Lords of Finance*, The Penguin Press, New York, 2009, p. 448.

lives of Americans is the key to this policy. In fact, the United States has long been determined to "usurp the gold and stand on its own", and to use the dollar to dominate the world.

The policy of long-term isolation has indeed been very effective. After the legalization of gold in 1975, ordinary Americans didn't go on a massive gold rush, because they did have "amnesia" about gold. Compared to the history of China, the history of the United States is but one dynasty in time. For the Chinese, "hiding gold in a troubled world" is the ultimate experience that has been repeatedly validated through the bitter lessons of thousands of years of history, while for the Americans, who have not experienced the rise and fall of a complete great power, they do not believe that the United States will decline and history will revert. There is no empirical counterpart in the American mind for such a way of thinking. Since the American system is the end of history, and if American hegemony can be perpetuated, then the dollar is naturally the ultimate form of human currency, can gold have any value at all?

In the gold market, which had just opened up in the United States in 1975, there was a general lack of understanding and bullishness about gold investment. Gold futures go virtually unasked for on the commodity exchanges, and gold traders are the least in the fringes. During their time in the gold trade, they are often bored and even pass the time by playing chess.

Of course, the temporary stability of the dollar is an illusion.

When the dollar was decoupled from gold in 1971, the price of gold gradually rose from $35 to $42.22 and inflation in the United States kicked in. But the average American thinks it was the result of the 1973 oil crisis and that prices would soon return to normal. After all, U.S. prices prior to 1971 had a long record of 170 years of price stability, and while World Wars can cause price volatility, prices under the gold standard have largely maintained a long historical trend of declining prices, and Americans are all too familiar with inflation. However, after the oil crisis, instead of showing signs of coming down, inflation in the United States has intensified and people are gradually getting nervous.

The dollar began to collapse on the international foreign exchange market in 1977, and by 1978 inflation in the US had soared from 4% around 1971 to 10%, reaching a staggering 14% in 1979! At this point the American psyche could no longer be calmed, and they went from nervousness to fear, with a sudden burst of enthusiasm for gold. Newspapers, radio, and television reacted quickly, and gold prices, which had otherwise gone unnoticed, quickly became front-page news. The Iranian hostage crisis and the Soviet invasion of Afghanistan have added fuel to the sizzling gold market.

The original obscure gold trader, immediately became the darling of the futures market, multiplying his value. In just one month in December 1978, the U.S. gold futures market surpassed a staggering 1 million contracts traded, compared to an average of just 800,000 contracts in all of 1975 and 1976.[6]

In three years, gold futures trading volume exploded at a 10-fold rate, spawning a futures revolution in the U.S. gold market. The dreary physical gold trade in Switzerland simply suffocates the wealthy American investor; and the conservative old business model of London cannot satisfy the huge appetite of American speculators. Americans are naturally adventurous and innovative and have an innate gambler's temperament.

Since you want to open up the gold market, you have to play big.

The New York Commodities Exchange (COMEX) has pioneered a revolutionary gold futures product with 100 ounces of standard gold bars containing 99.5% gold per COMEX contract, which is smaller than London's 400-ounce standard gold bars. The base customer base has been greatly expanded due to the lower prices. More importantly, the futures contract uses a margin model, with only about 5% margin required to purchase each contract. If the gold price is $1,000, then the total price per contract is $100,000, a price that is clearly too high to be conducive to retail participation. If only a 5% margin, or $5,000, is posted, then the client will be able to buy and sell $100,000 worth of gold for a mere $5,000. 20 times the leverage is just too much for the gambler!

COMEX is available in 1/4 of London bullion, supplemented by 20x leverage, which equates to an 80x reduction in the threshold for investing in gold! In those days, the Swiss painstakingly lobbied gold

---

[6] Timothy Green, *The New World of Gold*, George Weidenfeld and Nicolson, London, 1982, p. 136.

miners and jewelers around the world, then painstakingly built storage, refining, and transportation facilities in an attempt to make Switzerland the gold center of the world, and then worked hard for decades to be played for gold by the London financiers. And the Americans saw through the gold market investment leading trend, boldly lowered the threshold of investment in gold, fully stimulated and satisfied the greed and gambling in human nature, easily snatched the London gold market a large number of international customers.

The cowboy spirit of New York contrasts sharply with the aristocratic doings of London, where the bigwigs see gold investment as a highly private business where clients and traders can bargain in an atmosphere of relative informality and lack of regulation, and where the oppressive feeling of tight regulation and intense trading in the futures market is too strong. Simply put, London sees gold trading as an identity and privacy transaction, and the truly wealthy need a more comfortable and attentive service experience like London's. The London market believes that those who speculate in gold are just rich people, and those who hide gold are the world's richest.

Cowboys in New York don't care about the big and the small, it's hard to make money.

The opening of the COMEX public bidding market and the London gold pricing process is very different, without the London aristocratic style and private, as soon as the opening is in an extremely tense and exuberant atmosphere. Buying and selling information from around the world is gathered into a torrent of choppy orders through traders such as Merrill Lynch and Goldman Sachs, and orders are instantly sent down the phone to a telephone booth on the trading floor. The operators, who each had to deal with 15 dedicated telephone lines, had to sketch and time stamp the orders on the transaction slips as they answered the phone for customer inquiries. At this moment, the communicators (Runner) had long been waiting by the side, waiting for the trading ticket to just land on the table, they immediately grabbed it as soon as they could, and then sprinted straight at the traders in the hall with a hundred-meter sprint. Trading madness, hundreds of phone lines intertwined into a dense spider web, from the phone booths all the way to the closest place to the trader, the correspondent flew in layers of "tripwire" in the middle, surprisingly no one has ever fallen, is simply a miracle!

High-intensity, fast-paced, high-volume, low-cost New York gold futures market has been an unprecedented success, and the COMEX market has been a magnet for gold investors around the world, whose working hours are completely disrupted by New York trading hours. Europeans have to stay up late in their offices; Middle Easterners have a hard time getting dinner before midnight; and the worst off are investors in Hong Kong and Asia, who go to bed basically after 3 a.m.

In the early 1980s, New York's futures gold market increasingly outperformed London's physical gold market in both size and liquidity. Over the last decade, the power of pricing in New York has become increasingly dominant. In the gold futures market, the vast majority of investors are actually speculators, playing a heartbeat in this tense, exciting, down-and-out market. Futures markets often deliver less than 1% of their volume, and it's a pretty faceless thing for participating gamblers to end up having to withdraw their spot.

For any given commodity, the greater the trading volume of the market the greater the influence on price, the reason being that commodities are most liquid, most easily liquidated and most accurately price found in the market with the largest trading volume. The gold market is no exception. However, when the trading volume of futures, options and so on "paper gold" exceeds the volume of physical gold trading 100 times, this market is no longer a gold futures market, but a futures market named gold. More precisely, a casino that bets on the price of gold.

That's why the "Chinese big mama" and the world's physical gold investors buy gold in large numbers, but can't shake the price of gold.

As the casino gets bigger and bigger and the stakes get higher, but the gold chips become increasingly scarce, a risk arises: if the chips run out, the casino may be forced to close.

This potential risk was gathering in late 2012 and early 2013 and eventually set off a monstrous wave in the gold market.

U.S. QE3: One Stone Stirs a Thousand Waves, Dollar Confidence Shakes

QE3 will inflate the Fed's balance sheet to $4 trillion by the end of 2013. On September 14, 2012, the U.S. announced that the third round of quantitative easing (QE3) was about to begin, with the Federal

Reserve continuing to print money to buy $40 billion of mortgage-backed bonds (MBS) and $45 billion of Treasuries each month, for a total of $85 billion per month. Even more alarming is the Fed's claim that QE3 will continue until the job market improves, while hinting that the inflation floor can be tolerated to be breached. In this way, QE3 has become a "three-nothing policy" with no time limit, no limit and no bottom line! With a net increase of $1 trillion in base currency in 2013 alone, the Fed's balance sheet will be $4 trillion in size by the end of 2013, which will be four times the size it was before the 2008 financial crisis!

Although QE1 and QE2 did not bring about the most feared soaring prices, but QE3's "three no policy", whether the final will awaken the sleeping inflation demon, no one knows in the market. The main reason why the currency overhaul did not bring about immediate inflation was that the new currency was temporarily plunged into the swamp of the financial system, with an inefficient idling process. But this situation is not permanently stable, and the $85 billion monthly monetary infusion will increase the difficulty of maintaining fragile stability, and inflation is an inescapable doubt whether the end result will be a miraculous economic recovery or a tragic collapse. A proliferation of base currencies of this magnitude has created a massive monetary lake of daunting proportions.

Peter Schiff, CEO of Europacific Capital, put the dangers of QE3 to the world in a speech in which he simulated a future televised speech by the President of the United States:

> *"My fellow citizens, we will cut public spending sharply, raise taxes, eliminate basic health care, reduce pensions, and do so because the Chinese want us to pay them back. Do you think that's going to happen? Never! The American people will say, you abominable Chinese who insist on lending us money knowing we can't pay it back, you are usury vampires! We'll never pay it back!"*

Peter Schiff pointed out pointedly,

> *"The Chinese seem to be all ostriches when someone tells him that the Americans were never going to pay you back because they haven't been able to do so for several lifetimes. The Chinese reaction to hearing this was surprisingly to bury their heads in the sand and tell themselves, 'It won't, it won't, US Treasuries are the safest investment in the world.' Then, as always, China's resources were sent to the United States in exchange for pieces*

of green paper, and then to buy US Treasuries. And with 100 million more poor people in China, the lives of these compatriots seem completely less important than the U.S. national debt, it turns out that the most discriminatory people in the world are the Chinese themselves!"

In fact, all countries in the world understand that QE3 is a trick of the United States to draw the scourge to other countries and transfer the crisis, but each country's reaction is different. This is like a mob boss who is short of money, carrying a shiny machete, gets on a coach and demands protection money from the passengers one by one, and the passengers dare not say anything and honestly hand over their treasures. When the black boss got off the bus, the passengers immediately blew up their nests, vowing never to suffer such humiliation again. That's why countries have been doing currency swaps and local currency settlements, and people have had enough of blackmail from the mob.

The QE3 has undoubtedly turned national discontent with the dollar from quietly breeding and spreading, rapidly escalating into public outcry and anger.

The Fed is certainly aware of the consequences of announcing QE3, but without it, the mirage of economic recovery will be immediately beaten back into place.

In order to control the dollar exchange rate without a major crisis, or for other countries to make a new effort to get rid of the dollar, the United States will strike a three-dimensional combination of monetary, economic, market, media and geopolitical conflicts, both to indiscriminately distribute the dollar and for everyone to grab it, which is an absolute acrobatic feat of great difficulty.

Since everyone sees that the dollar will rot, the US will let other currencies rot even more, and since the emerging countries want to start another effort to get rid of the dollar, let the economies of those regions mess up first.

Echoing each other: developed countries come together, devaluation war drums heard

In the past, the United States was most annoyed by the devaluation of other countries' currencies and was always accusing and threatening by "manipulating the exchange rate", as the saying goes, only state officials are allowed to set fires and people are not allowed to light lamps. Especially for China and Japan, the two largest trading partners and the largest debtors, the United States is even more bullying and enticing, only hating the appreciation of the yuan and the yen is not enough.

On 22 January 2013, the Government of Japan and the Bank of Japan issued a joint statement on "Sustainable economic growth free from deflation", striving to achieve the 2 per cent price increase target. The means is the "most drastic" devaluation of the yen in 50 years, increasing the base currency by 60 trillion to 70 trillion yen per year (about 600 billion to 700 billion U.S. dollars), the goal is to double the total base currency within two years!

For Japan's super version of QE, the Germans are angry, the Brazilians are cursing, the IMF is yelling, the Russians are annoyed, the Koreans are scared, the Chinese are blinded, and the Americans are? Wash up and go to sleep!

In the final analysis, without the support or even secret connivance of the United States, how could Abe easily devalue the yen at the expense of the Americans? For the United States, trade losses are small and the dollar's position is large, the lesser of two evils. The dollar looks a lot brighter in the face of a sharp yen depreciation.

The core of Abe's economics is to create inflationary expectations, reverse Japan's 20-year-long deflation, and force Japanese consumers to accelerate their spending to boost the momentum of economic growth.

This line of thinking is a complete logical mess!

Deflation in Japan is the result, not the cause, of economic woes. The root cause of weak prices in Japan is sluggish consumption, and the cause of sluggish consumption is the sluggish desire of the population to consume due to deep aging. Can the problem be alleviated by the fact that the retirement of the elderly is extremely dependent on their previous savings, and that the over-issuance of money will only further deprive the elderly of their purchasing power, and that even rising prices will only lead to more severe consumption weakness? The essence of Abe's economics is wealth redistribution, transferring the wealth of the aging population to the younger population in an attempt to stimulate the economy with the spending power of the younger population. But in heavily aging Japan, can the growth in consumption of the young fully offset the shrinking consumption of the aging population?

Japan's strategy of devaluing its currency will inevitably be met with retaliation or even siege from other countries.

The elderly need moderation, but Abe insists on taking large doses of Viagra, which will only make the body weaken more.

In addition to the economic hand, the United States has also prepared a political hand. Just before the Fed announced QE3 on September 14, 2012, the Japanese Diet decided on September 10 to "nationalize" the Diaoyu Islands with 2.05 billion yen, which directly led to the escalation of the conflict between China and Japan.

There are no pure "coincidences" in this world!

The escalation of the conflict between China and Japan over the Diaoyu Islands has intensified tensions in the Asia-Pacific region, with China-Japan confrontation, North Korea tensions and South China Sea frictions, strengthening the dollar's hedging function. More importantly, with such sharp confrontational sentiment, who has the heart to start another currency stove in the Asia-Pacific region and get rid of the US dollar's grip?

The U.S. monetary strategy in the Asia-Pacific region is to take offensive action against the yuan and defensive action against the yen to stimulate East Asian contradictions and strengthen the position of the U.S. dollar to protect the launch of the QE3!

In addition to mobilizing the yen to depreciate, the participation of the euro is also important.

Devaluing currencies has a natural temptation for Governments, especially for highly indebted countries. In the short term, currency devaluation would not only alleviate the crisis and disguise debt, but would also stimulate exports, improve employment and demonstrate political performance. It's just that it's usually too obvious to do it alone, and it's easy to attract criticism and even trade reprisals, but if the United States and Japan dare to take the lead, the EU, which has been tortured to death by the European debt crisis, does not take the opportunity of the currency release, it would be too inopportune.

On 6 December 2012, the ECB let the wind out that it was discussing the idea of cutting interest rates on deposits to negative rates, supposedly with the aim of prompting banks to use their funds elsewhere. On the issue of negative interest rates, European Central Bank President Mario Draghi said: the European Central Bank Committee discussed for the first time the possibility of reducing the overnight savings rate to negative, and if necessary, "operationally ready".[7]

After all, the euro is known to be strong, and the Germans who dominate the ECB in particular have a pathological level of sensitivity to inflation, which I am afraid is related to the bitter lesson that the Germans have suffered three currency crashes in the last 100 years. No devaluation of the euro makes for a bad day, and a devaluation discredits it.

Whether lives matter or faces matter, the Germans are still painfully torn.

For the U.S., the Euro's statement of openness to negative interest rates was enough to turn the tide on the dollar.

However, a greater danger against the dollar is looming.

In China's history, whenever the power of centralized power has declined, it has inevitably given rise to local domination and warlord chaos. The same is true in the international currency hegemony. In the 1950s, the rouble was used against the dollar, in the 1960s, the franc challenged the dollar, in the 1970s, the gold rose, in the 1980s, the yen was aggressive, in the 1990s it was relatively calm, and then the euro split the border.

The success of the "currency uprising" in the euro was a huge stimulus for small countries to try to stand on their own feet by abolishing the dollar, which was ruthlessly suppressed.

In November 2000, the Central Bank of Iraq released the wind that it was going to replace the US dollar with the euro as the oil settlement currency and adjust its $10 billion foreign exchange reserves to the euro. Europeans are overjoyed and the Eurozone opens up. In December, Iraqi Deputy Prime Minister and Finance Minister Al-Azawi announced that, in view of the hostile stance of the United States

---

[7] Ambrose Evans-Pritchard, ECB mulls negative ates as Europe's economic crisis deepens, The Telegraph, 2012-12-6.

towards Iraq, Iraq had decided to formally replace the United States dollar with the euro as the currency of trade settlement beginning in early 2002. In order to ensure implementation, the Government of Iraq also required State and private enterprises to comply with the rules on the use of the euro for trade settlement, and in the summer of 2001, the euro continued to appreciate against the United States dollar, from which Saddam's euro settlement policy allowed Iraq to profit handsomely. Subsequently, many OPEC countries have also responded, ready to sell oil to the EU in exchange for a stronger euro, while turning away from the weak dollar.

The United States is now out of its rage. If the oil exporting countries of the Middle East follow Saddam's example, the dollar hegemony will have collapsed in half, and if the dollar cannot buy oil, who will still be willing to hold the ever-depreciating dollar?

He saw the door to the hegemony of the dollar and was ready to strike, but he didn't know how to fight for his life. Weak Iraq can only reap the benefits of a fierce struggle or even a war between the big powers. The EU and Russia, used as an umbrella by Saddam, have neither the will nor the strength to break out into conflict with the US. Saddam, who is very unpopular in the Middle East, is equally unlikely to get much help from the OPEC countries. To challenge the fate of the United States so alone is bound to be met with deadly retaliation.

In March 2003, just over a year after opening its doors, Iraq's euro business suffered the scourge of national annihilation.

Another person who died trying to challenge the hegemony of the dollar was Libya's Gaddafi.

Gaddafi had a dream in the 1970s that both the Middle East and Africa were on the fringes of the world system, rich in oil, with large populations, and vast markets, and that if the Middle East and Africa could be integrated from faith to market and the European and American powers pushed out of the continent, it would change the region's marginalized status. Later, due to the establishment of the petrodollar system, the Middle Eastern countries gradually turned away from his dream. Gaddafi left the Arab League in a fit of rage. Since then, he has been working to build the African Union.

To realize his dream of Africa, it is impossible to do so without funding. Gaddafi is keen to lock in his focus on passing through Africa on the currency. He is actively plotting a new monetary system, trying to join forces with Malaysian Prime Minister Mahathir and other Islamic countries to introduce a new Islamic currency – the golden dinar.

The golden dinar dates back to 632 and remained the currency of trade settlement in the Islamic world until the demise of the Turkish Empire in 1922. Under Islamic law, one dinar is equivalent to 4.22 grams (0.135 ounces) of pure gold. Gaddafi's Golden Dinar project clearly has a certain sense of mission and a strong realistic need for a return to history in the Islamic world.

In 2003, the gold dinar officially appeared, it did not cause a storm of monetary change, but the United States and the IMF has been shocked by this idea, gold monetization is not only a fierce conflict with the provisions of the IMF, but also in order to completely bypass the IMF and start another fire. In particular, the concept of the golden dinar has both a universal appeal and a strong ideological overtone, enough to resonate widely in the Arab world.

While promoting the new currency, Gaddafi is also actively planning to establish three major financial institutions, namely the African Central Bank, the African Monetary Fund and the African Investment Bank, in preparation for the issuance of a unified African currency based on the value of the golden dinar, which would bring Africa and the Arab world into monetary union.

Gaddafi wants the golden dinar to serve as the standard settlement currency when oil and other resources are sold in the Middle East and Africa, thus completely freeing the dollar from its grip on the euro. Arguably, Gaddafi's monetary ambitions were higher than Saddam's, and he considered not only striking the dollar and the euro, but also attempting to establish an independent monetary system for Africa and the Arab world.

However, Gaddafi's plans challenged both the dollar and the euro, and without the strong protection of the great powers behind him, Gaddafi's ambitions eventually fell to pieces in the face of the combined strangulation of the two powers.

The dollar, the most important cornerstone of U.S. hegemony, no matter who wants to shake the dollar's position, must be backed by a strong international alliance, as well as a credible war deterrent, otherwise it is nothing more than a showman's rebellion, a decade is hard to achieve.

On March 27, 2013, China, India, Russia, Brazil and South Africa, known as the "BRICS" countries, came together in a common need to protect their own interests and resolved to establish a BRICS Development Bank, ready to use the local currency for mutual settlement and lending among the BRICS countries, thereby reducing their dependence on the US dollar and euro.

The BRICS countries have finally embarked on a path of "currency uprising".

In addition to the BRICS countries, the 12 countries of South America, the Union of South American Nations, also dissatisfied with the "tyranny of the dollar", has announced on November 25, 2011, "currency uprising", the establishment of the Bank of the South, to promote regional trade local currency settlement system, gradually 120 billion dollars a year of intraregional trade "non-dollarization".

Never forget what you have done before, and never forget what you have done afterwards. Whether it is the BRICS, or the Union of South American Nations, the Shanghai Cooperation Organization, or the Cooperation Council for the Arab States of the Gulf, the only way to achieve true monetary independence is to be united in the hope of success. If these regions end up off the dollar's map, it will be the end of dollar hegemony and the hegemony of the United States.

That's what's at stake for the dollar. When the dollar was in peril, the Germans started messing around again. The Germans made a world-shocking announcement on January 16, 2013 that Germany would ship back home 300 tons of gold stored at the Federal Reserve Bank of New York and 374 tons of gold at the French Central Bank.

US magazine *Forbes* exclaimed,

> "The shocking news that Germans are preparing to ship gold reserves home from the US and France has precious metals speculators fearing that this is the first major signal that trust between central banks around the world may be deteriorating... The crisis of trust in the value of paper money has made owning physical gold an instinctive reaction."[8]

---

[8] Robert Lenzner, The Germans Want Their Gold Reserves Back In Germany, Forbes, 2013-01-19.

A spokesman for the German central bank told Forbes that Germany's gold shipments are not intended to be sold, but rather to preempt a future "currency crisis". A few months ago, the German central bank claimed to have shipped back a small amount of gold from the Federal Reserve for melting, to test the purity and weight, but the final announcement of the return of a much larger amount, which could not help but cause strong doubts in the market.

Britain's Daily Telegraph exclaimed on January 15: "This action means that trust among Western central banks has collapsed." Bill Gross, chief investment officer of Pacific Investment Management Corporation (Pimco), the world's largest bond fund, also tweeted: "Reports that Germany will ship gold from New York and Paris back home, do central banks no longer trust each other?"

In November 2012, the German weekly Der Spiegel reported that the United States had rejected Germany's request to "take a look" at its own gold reserves, citing "possible security risks and procedural problems to the vault", which has led to increasing calls for a recall of Germany's gold reserves.

During the Cold War, the Soviet army, with millions of troops, was watching out for the vault of the German Central Bank, and the Germans could not help but feel that their gold was under the noses of the Soviet army. So Germany kept some of its gold reserves in the United States, France and the United Kingdom, so that the family's money would not be wiped out in one pot. With the end of the Cold War, the Germans can't help but think about the wealth deposited with others, even if not shipped back, can look at the heart will feel more solid. Yet such a reasonable request is repeatedly rejected by the United States for clearly unconvincing reasons.

The Germans were beginning to wonder if something could have gone wrong with their own gold. As early as 2011, the Germans were worried about their own gold reserves, and in 2012 this sentiment was unstoppable. According to the German weekly *Der Spiegel*,

> "The Bundesbank (German Central Bank) has rejected the request (for the German Audit Office to verify overseas gold reserves), claiming that central banks do not normally verify each other's reserve assets, that the Audit Office's approach is not in line with the practice among central banks, and that there

> is no doubt about the honesty and credibility of overseas custodians."⁹

It is clear that the Bundesbank is reluctant to fall out with the Fed and that there is some sort of unspoken deep relationship between Western central banks. But the Reichstag quit, and a member of Parliament personally ran to the Federal Reserve Bank of New York to demand an inspection of Germany's gold reserves, and the receptionist was unable or unwilling to tell the German MP where the gold bars were. Soon, other European central banks were forced to disclose the news that gold reserves had been leased out in large numbers, and more and more Germans began to strongly question their own gold reserves had been "lost" by the Americans.

The German central bank is still arguing the benefits of gold staying in the U.S., especially if there is a crisis in Germany, where gold can be used immediately to finance a rescue. The German parliamentarians contradicted each other that since there is so much trust between the two central banks, there is no difference between gold in Germany and in the United States, financing relief is available everywhere.

The German central bank in the German parliament, the general public, all walks of life under the strong pressure of the coalition of prominent people, finally had to agree to recall gold reserves.

The fears of the Germans were not unjustified; in fact, even the Americans themselves had the same doubts. It has been more than half a century since Eisenhower was president in the 1950s and the Fed's gold inventory has never been audited again. U.S. members of Congress, represented by Ron Paul, have been trying to audit the Fed's gold reserves, but the proposal never passed.

On January 9, 2013, the American public sent out a petition on the White House's website, which read: "On December 31, 2012, the U.S. Treasury Department announced that it held 261 million ounces of gold, stored at Denver, Fort Knox, West Point and the Federal Reserve Bank of New York. The last full audit of these golds goes back as far as

---

[9] Checking the Vaults: Germans Fret about Their Foreign Gold Reserves, Der Spiegel, 2012-05-14.

1953." The American public believes that a public audit of this gold needs to be done now. Once the results of the quiz are available, they need to be verified in writing in order to confirm who is the true owner of the gold. For example, how much gold is leased to gold dealers or financial institutions and how much is sold or exchanged to non-Ministry of Finance entities (including foreign governments). The petition also requires the identity of the auditors, arguing that this time the auditors "must be professional auditors outside the United States Mint, the Department of the Treasury, the United States Comptroller General, the Attorney General and the Federal Reserve System".

As the saying goes, not long ago, the Belgian central bank had publicly admitted that 41% of its gold reserves had been leased out at an ultra-low interest rate of 0.3%, news that shocked both parties. Curious researchers have found that the gold reserves of Western central banks are not listed under physical gold, but gold and "gold receivables" (Gold Receivables), but it does not indicate how much "gold receivables". Anyone who has studied accounting knows that cash and accounts receivable have different meanings. Obviously, gold and gold receivables are not the same thing either.

The Belgian central bank's gold leasing behavior is not a special case, the Federal Reserve and the German central bank has long carried out similar operations, they will gold with ultra-low interest leasing to gold merchants, gold merchants will sell these gold in the market, the cash reinvested in U.S. Treasury bonds, both suppressed the gold price, but also a steady profit between Treasury bonds and gold leasing spread. The borrowed central bank gold has long disappeared in the market, gold merchants can keep "rolling" the loan, while the central bank's balance sheet, is always the "receivable gold", and the real gold can never be recovered.

If the people insist on audits, there will be trouble, and I'm afraid half the gold reserves of Western central banks will be long gone. The American public is clamoring to audit the gold reserves, the German parliament is clamoring to recall the gold reserves, the Swiss referendum demanded that central banks must not sell gold reserves, the Netherlands, Poland, Sweden and other countries are also dumbfounded. The Federal Reserve and the German central bank are shocked out of a cold sweat, if the real audit, inevitably the east window, we can not eat.

So, the Federal Reserve and the German central bank began to bargain, the media euphemistically called "the central bank began to distrust each other", the Federal Reserve can not openly reject the German central bank's request, but the terms can still be negotiated, just 40 tons a year, and if more, we all die together!

As a result, the Bundesbank announced the repatriation of 300 tons of gold over seven years.

Seven years?

In September 2011, Venezuelan President Chávez announced that 211 tons of gold stored in the United States and Europe would be shipped back to the country, and the shipment was launched in 2012 for a total of just four months.

Germany's shipment of gold home is making international noise, and another central bank is terrified, and that is the Bank of England.

Chain Reaction: Her Majesty the Queen as a prop, the Bank of England as a showstopper

Just as the Germans and Americans were closely negotiating the terms of the gold recall, the British sulked. After all Germany also has 440 tons of gold in the Bank of England's vaults, so wouldn't the German public be suspicious of the Bank of England when they don't trust the Fed anymore?

The more the Englishman thought about it, the more he felt guilty: "Then why did the Zhao family dog look at me twice? I was justifiably afraid".

On December 13, 2012, the German central bank is still in negotiations with the Federal Reserve, the British BBC suddenly high-profile report on the Queen's inspection of the Bank of England vault news.

On 13 December 2012, the Queen visited the Bank of England and toured the vault. The Queen of England usually asks very little about politics, let alone monetary policy and gold reserves. It was the first time in 15 years that the Queen had inspected the Bank of England and also made a point of visiting the vault. The Queen, who has not been to the Bank of England for 15 years, was not in the mood to visit the vault in December 2012, when no major event occurred. What is strange must have a strange cause.

The British press covered the Queen's inspection at length, focusing in particular on the dense piles of gold bricks in the Bank of England vaults, only to see the old lady caressing the piles, lamenting, "Unfortunately, not all the gold here is ours."[10] The Queen's words convey two meanings: first, that gold is a good thing; and second, that Britain is faithfully guarding the gold reserves deposited with it by other nations.

There is no such thing as "coincidence" in this world!

The logical corollary is that the Queen herself did not think of visiting the Bank of England vaults at all, but that it was a deliberate arrangement by the Bank of England, and asked the media to cooperate in making a big deal out of it, by exposing the Queen's inspection in high profile through pictures and words, implicitly displaying the huge gold stocks in the vaults, and indirectly dispelling any suspicion of the Bank of England gold reserves. This time, the Queen of England is the prop to showcase Britain's gold reserves!

As the saying goes, "Do not do a bad deed, and be not afraid of a knock at the door. Those who have strength do not show it deliberately; those who show it deliberately must lack it!"

It seems that Germany's move to bring back gold reserves from New York struck a sensitive nerve in the British.

Fears escalate: EU robberies busy, Cypriot depositors panic

On March 16, 2013, Cyprus blew up! The Eurogroup has issued an ultimatum to Cyprus that the condition for bailing out its banking system is that the savers have to be cut off with an unheard of savings tax!

Britain's *Daily Mail* exclaims, "This is a great EU bank robbery."

It is well known that bank savings are not bonds, not stocks, nor any form of investment, but the most basic form of existence of private

---

[10] Queen Questioned Financial Crisis, BBC News, 2013-12-12.

property of citizens. The essence of savings is a deposit of wealth, and the saver does not authorize anyone to use the money for risky investment activities in any name, which is why banks must unconditionally satisfy savers to withdraw their deposits at any time. The failure of bank investments has nothing to do with savers, and there is no reason for all losses to be shared by savers. Although banking risks are inevitable in real society, the deposit insurance system in place in Europe and the United States is designed to ensure that depositors' interests are protected from unlawful infringement, which is a minimum moral bottom line.

The principle of the sanctity of private property has long been the value basis of Western society. Without the consent of the savers, without a fair discussion in society, without a just judicial process, the "troika" of the Eurogroup, the ECB and the IMF, by means of coercion and inducements, have forced the Government of Cyprus to accept an "undercity alliance" with total disregard for the bottom line of justice, which is worse than an overt act of robbery, since it has flagrantly subverted the moral foundations of society.

The news came that the Cypriot people were so terrified that they ran to the bank to withdraw money, only to find that their accounts had been frozen. The angry crowd began to riot and some even drove bulldozers into the doors of the bank.

Even though the bank savings tax was not ultimately implemented, the huge losses to high savers turned into a financial nightmare. The EU move is seen as a model for future banking crisis rescue programmes in other member states, and Europe's wealthy are in a serious panic.

If wealth isn't even safe in a bank, let alone a volatile stock market, a highly bubbly bond market and a fickle foreign exchange market.

Wealth, at least some of it, desperately needs a safe haven away from the financial system. At the end of 2012 and early 2013, the United States QE3 provoked the currency panic, by the yen super depreciation and the euro negative interest rate expectations, has been multiplied, the BRICS countries are ready to start a new fire to strengthen the situation of the dollar turmoil, coupled with the Germans to transport gold suspicion, the British here and there is no silver 300 taels of performance, as well as the Cyprus savings crisis escalated, finally induced the market to the global currencies of the extreme unrest, the rich hoarding gold dark tide began to surge.

COMEX gold inventory pulls a red alert

Although the New York gold futures market can create "out of thin air" any amount of paper gold trading volume, but everything has an advantage and a disadvantage, 100 bottles with only one cap juggling sooner or later will go wrong.

Futures contracts are allowed to be physically delivered, although under normal circumstances, 99% of contract holders do not demand physical delivery (they only care about the profit generated by the spread). But in a given situation, it is possible for the holder of a futures contract to suddenly concentrate on demanding physical delivery, which creates a potential crisis of physical gold runs. Moreover, it turns out that the customers who only deposit their gold in the COMEX vaults are strongly stimulated by the Cyprus incident, if the depositors' savings in the banks can be deprived at any time, what makes them believe that the gold deposited in the futures exchange vaults will not be seized?

Under normal circumstances, people are willing to keep their cash in the bank, but when a crisis strikes, people will rush to the bank to run out of deposits, and the futures markets are doing the same in a panic.

New York COMEX's gold inventory can be divided into two main categories: "Eligible" and "Regulated". The term "qualifying gold" refers to gold bars that meet the purity and weight requirements of the COMEX, which can belong to anyone, are deposited and held in the vault of the COMEX, and which cannot be used for futures delivery. "Delivery gold" must first be qualifying gold, which is a registered bullion that can be used for the delivery of futures.

To be precise, COMEX does not have its own physical vault, its vault is made up of the vaults of the five major gold merchants together. The five largest gold dealers include JPMorgan Chase, HSBC, Scotiabank Canada (SCOTIA MOCATTA), BRINK'S (INC) and MANFRA. The five largest gold dealers submit daily inventory information to COMEX and COMEX publishes a daily inventory report based on this aggregation.

Note that COMEX only aggregates the inventory information provided by the top five goldsmiths and does not verify the veracity of this information.

Since 2010, gold inventories at the New York COMEX have been essentially stable at 11 million ounces (about 354 tons), and the gold supercasino appears to be operating as normal. However, the situation took a sharp turn for the worse in late 2012 when the COMEX gold stocks began to avalanche.

From December 2012 onwards, the US gold futures market began to see a dramatic shift in physical gold, with COMEX gold stocks dropping sharply from more than 11 million ounces to 8 million ounces (257 tons) in early April, and nearly 100 tons of gold being withdrawn by customers. (Note: The 400 tons of gold thrown off at the opening on April 12 is significantly more than the entire COMEX inventory! In less than 4 months, COMEX has lost a whopping 27% of its gold! At this rate of deterioration, the entire COMEX gold inventory will be difficult to support until the end of the year.

What happens if there is no gold in the COMEX vault? Quite simply, a massive delivery default occurs in the futures market. What about a breach of contract? The answer is that individual defaults are called accidents and large defaults are called crises. Financial markets play on confidence, without which they collapse.

In fact, the default had already occurred, and in early April, ABN AMRO, the largest bank in the Netherlands, was no longer able to deliver physical gold. In a letter of apology to customers, the bank said it was unable to submit physical gold to customers and was willing to make deliveries in cash. In a normal market, ABN should be able to easily buy physical gold in the market and deliver it to customers if the gold price falls, meaning there is an oversupply of gold. Obviously, at this point they were already having a hard time finding physical gold.

If the COMEX changes the futures delivery rules to cash instead of physical delivery, will the problem be solved? If physical delivery is eliminated entirely, it becomes a pure casino, which no longer has anything to do with gold. Then all the customers who have a demand for gold will be lost and the remaining gamblers can run straight to the casinos in Las Vegas where the gambling will be even better.

If the COMEX gold futures market runs out of spot, the U.S. will lose pricing power over gold prices, threatening pricing power over the exchange rate market and ultimately the shaking of the dollar's dominance.

Some argue that gold is nothing more than a common commodity, and has nothing to do with a penny of currency. Yes, legally speaking, indeed, gold was compulsorily "demonetized" by the IMF in the early 1970s. However, laws must be responsive to public opinion, and laws that are not supported by public opinion are nothing more than a piece of paper. It is this truth that the law does not rule the people. Gold is not money in law, but it still has the status of money in the minds of the world, which is beyond the reach of law. Central banks in all countries have gold reserves, but not steel or diamond reserves. This is not the so-called "relic of barbarity", but the eternal recognition of gold as the ultimate representative of wealth.

People can't help but take a few more looks when they see a beautiful woman walking down the street. If medicine can provide sophisticated instruments for testing, it will reveal the wonderful changes in the various hormones in a person's body when they see a beautiful woman. By the same token, if gold is placed in people's hands, that golden, brilliant, soft, noble, smooth and heavy feeling will also stimulate the changes in human hormone secretion, making people look away.

If a thought experiment is conducted, a kilo of gold bars and a kilo of pitch-black iron blocks are placed side by side on a busy street, and the reaction of pedestrians is observed, the situation will inevitably be that people will go to grab the gold bars by accident, and the iron blocks will be either kicked away or ignored. One does not need any economic theory or advanced knowledge to instinctively react in the same way. What everyone is clamoring to have, for exchange, no one will refuse, and that is inflation. True currency does not require a law; it arises naturally, evolves spontaneously, and circulates automatically, which is the currency to which the hearts of all people aspire. Therefore, the natural monetary properties of gold cannot be stripped away by any power, but on the contrary, all powers must fake their hands on gold in order to win the hearts and minds of the people.

Gold has historically been the natural enemy of all legal tender, and by virtue of the violence of French money, gold depends on the hearts and minds of people. When French coins go backwards and forwards, hearts will automatically turn to gold. The justice of the world is in the heart, the justice of the currency is in the gold.

The U.S. QE policy is really a monetary evil, called the rescue of the economy, is really a plunder of wealth, and the indiscriminate issuance of currency will inevitably lead to the departure of the people. While the United States may be able to suppress the price of gold through gold futures, it can't stop the public from snapping up physical gold in a big way.

From December 2012 to early April 2013, the COMEX's vaults have been in frequent decline. In particular, JPMorgan Chase's inventories were in desperate straits, with a sharp drop from 2.8 million ounces (90 tons) to less than 1 million ounces (about 30 tons), a drop of nearly 70%!

This is no longer a normal futures delivery, this is a serious gold run!

JPMorgan Chase is not only the biggest player in the gold market, but also in interest rates, exchange rates and almost all other financial markets. in January and February 2013, JPMorgan Chase alone accounted for 67% and 60% of COMEX's net physical gold deliveries, and 95% and 83% in March and April!

It is no exaggeration to say that JPMorgan Chase completely dominates the fate of the COMEX gold futures market.

If JPMorgan Chase's vault continues to lose gold at this rate, then it will struggle to support itself for even two months, meaning that the Optimus Prime of the COMEX will collapse and a massive default will be inevitable. The United States priced the situation of gold will change, and once the dollar lost the strong dollar weak gold cover, will immediately become the "emperor without new clothes".

Since December 2012, JPMorgan Chase's gold inventory has fallen from 2.8 million ounces to less than 1 million ounces in early April

The only way to save the scene is to create a gold super plunge of the "white terror", to thunderous gold futures sell-off, destroy all resistance will, fly straight down the gold price will completely shake the market, the gold in kind from investors trembling hands to shake out, on the one hand, let the Wall Street bigwigs in short trading to make a fortune, on the other hand, it is convenient for J.P. Morgan Chase in the lower price cheap sweep, rebuild the near-depleted gold inventory. At the same time, all gold buyers who jumped at the chance to buy gold in the face of a collapse will be scared out of their minds and run away, thus blocking any subsequent squeeze.

That's a great plan to kill three birds with one stone!

This is the fundamental reason why the United States launched the "4-1-2" coup d'état to suppress gold!

Such a plan perfectly integrates the multiple interests of a White House desperate to strengthen its dollar position, a Fed desperate to defuse serious public doubts about QE3, a Treasury Department deliberately avoiding gold reserve checks, and anxious Wall Street bigwigs.

Thus, the world witnessed a series of "coincidences" that were seamlessly intertwined.

At the beginning of April, the Wall Street media collectively turned, the sound of the gold bubble was incessant, gold from the highly regarded "darling" suddenly fell into the cursed "disaster star".

On 10 April, Obama convened 14 global financial giants to meet in secret to discuss their plans.

April 10, Goldman Sachs released a bearish gold report (previously has been more than bearish), blew the short gold "rallying cry", for a time, the mountain rain is about to come wind full floor.

On 11 April, rumours abounded in the market that Cyprus was planning to sell 13.9 tons of gold, followed by rumours that Portugal (382 tons) and Italy (2451 tons) might follow suit and that the gold market was on edge.

April 11, the Federal Reserve meeting minutes "accidentally" leaked ahead of time, the minutes reflect the Fed's internal proposal to end QE3 early. news came out, the bearish gold pessimism pervades the market.

All of this made for adequate psychological preparation for the "Golden Massacre" of 12 April.

Inventory cloud

Wall Street bigwigs are quite expert in technical analysis of the futures market, they can accurately predict the possible shocking effect of the 400-ton gold sell-off at the opening of the "4-1-2", but cannot judge the impact of the plunge in gold prices on physical gold buyers.

Just in the Wall Street big brother in the paper gold market to the gold many head killed in the armor, fleeing in disarray, "China big mother" and the world's physical gold buyers suddenly swarmed out, hit the Wall Street big brothers a surprise, they have not had time to collect the physical gold trophy, was "big mother" sweep clean. This is something that the Wall Street bigwigs did not expect, a phenomenon that completely contradicts the rule that physical gold sales will be effectively suppressed after every gold price crash since 2000.

Not only do ordinary investors around the world have to buy gold while it is low, but central banks are also quietly increasing their gold reserves against the market. Global central bank gold purchases reached a 48-year high in the fourth quarter of 2012 and continued to increase significantly in the first quarter of 2013 and after the "4-1/2" crash. Central banks in emerging market countries, in particular, have accelerated the pace of eating into long-neglected gold reserves at low prices. The central banks of Russia, Turkey, South Korea, Kazakhstan, Azerbaijan, Belarus, Kyrgyzstan, Mongolia and Ukraine have seen unprecedented interest in gold reserves.

The hot sale of physical gold has surprised Wall Street bigwigs, and even Terrence Duffy (CEO of CME), the owner of the gold futures market, had to admit in an interview on April 29, 2013:

> *"An interesting phenomenon about gold is that the plunge two weeks ago led to a significant drop in the volume of gold trading in all types of (paper) products, but the opposite is true for gold coins and physical gold. It shows that people don't want gold certificates, or anything else (paper gold), they just want physical gold."*[11]

In this way, while the Wall Street bigwigs are making a lot of money on the shorting of gold futures, their most important strategic objective is to rebuild COMEX inventories, and this plan has gone down the drain. Not only that, but COMEX stockpiles have been lost faster than before "April 1–2", and on April 25 alone, COMEX lost 7% of its stockpiles, while JPMorgan Chase's "Qualified Gold" stockpiles dropped by a whopping 65% on the same day!

---

[11] Terrence Duffy, President and Executive Chairman of CME Group Inc., on Bloomberg TV.

By May 7, JP Morgan's "delivery gold" had fallen to a record low of 137,000 ounces (about 4.3 tons), and on May 7 alone, 54,000 ounces, or 28.5% of its total, were withdrawn!

By June 10, JPMorgan Chase's gold inventory was even more dangerous. "Delivery gold" continued to decline to 136,000 ounces, with "qualifying gold" falling even faster. Its total gold inventory is just under 550,000 ounces (17.7 tons) remaining.

On June 12, 2013, JPMorgan Chase had just under 550,000 ounces (17.7 tons) of gold left in its inventory

With just over 4 tons of "delivery gold" in stock, it is already at risk, and even with the temporary convertible "qualifying gold", 17 tons of stock is a drop in the bucket to deal with the world's physical run on gold.

At this point, the biggest fear is a larger "delivery notice"!

As a result, whatever comes with fear!

June 10, COMEX surprised a huge scale of the "delivery notice", customers asked JPMorgan Chase in June to deliver 6208 contracts of physical gold, the total amount of 620,000 ounces (about 20 tons), nine times the normal month (January and February) delivery volume!

That's more than JPMorgan Chase's entire inventory of 550,000 ounces!

Simply put, JPMorgan Chase must urgently find gold from other sources or it will default. If the boss of the world's gold futures market defaults, all will be up in the air.

On June 10, 2013, JPMorgan Chase faced 620,000 ounces (20 tons) of gold "run" over its entire COMEX inventory. JPMorgan Chase's inventories are insufficient for June futures delivery, which means that the inventory reports of the Big 5 bullion dealers, such as JPMorgan Chase, may be seriously inflated. In fact, some customers have long suspected that the inventory of the five major gold dealers has a fishy, such as misappropriation of customer gold, private gold leasing and swaps (SWAP). The questioning of the Fed's vaults is likely to be even more prevalent and reckless among the top 5 goldman inventories. That's why the announcement of Germany's move to ship gold home in January 2013 caused panic among many customers who had stored their gold in COMEX vaults, and they were moving their gold out of COMEX vaults and simply storing it themselves. However, questioning is merely questioning when there is still stock in the inventory. But if JPMorgan Chase has reached the point where it can't deliver gold, it's no longer in question, but rather there is clearly fraud.

So, the very "coincidental" thing happened again.

On June 3, in the COMEX Daily Gold Inventory Report, a shocking statement appeared out of nowhere: "The information in this report comes from trusted sources, but we do not accept any responsibility for the accuracy or completeness of that information. This report is provided for information purposes only."

Why such a sudden statement? Why at this moment? If the accuracy of a goldman's inventory is all that matters, what is the point of COMEX regulation? Don't financial institutions ever lie? If they were all honest, where would there have been a financial tsunami in 2008?

J.P. Morgan's inventory is bottoming out and futures delivery is on the verge of default, which should have been good news for gold. However, June futures gold has continued to fall and is trending closer to the $1,000 price.

This suggests that JPMorgan Chase must have other avenues for obtaining gold, and the Gold ETF is one of them.

Gold ETF, Wall Street's "little vault"

One day in 1910, the German meteorologist Wegener was convalescing in hospital, bored and staring at the world map on the wall. He suddenly found that the outlines of the European and African continents were strikingly similar to those of North and South America, and that if the map was cut out and the two continents were put together, it could be almost seamless. Based on years of meteorological and geological research, he boldly proposed the "Continental Drift Doctrine". In this way, a meteorologist has inadvertently become the father of the plate doctrine of modern geology.

If one looks at the Gold ETF (GLD) gold outflow curve along the same lines as the COMEX inventory loss curve, one finds that the two are unusually similar in shape.

Left is Wegener's continental drift puzzle, right is gold ETF, COMEX inventory puzzle

If JPMorgan Chase's inventory isn't enough for futures delivery, is it likely to be replenished from the gold ETF's inventory?

The answer is very likely.

The recent 12-year gold bull market has spurred the desire for global investors to hold gold, and the mentality of investors is completely different from that of gold consumers, who hold gold not because they want to own it, but because they desire to make money through it. To them, making money is the end, gold is just the means. But owning gold is more troublesome, buying, inspecting, transporting, storing, and selling the goods all require costs. Although gold futures can also make money without the need to own physical goods, the futures market is volatile and risky, not fun for the heart. The market needs a gold product, it seems to have a physical gold, but without any trouble and expense, and can be bought and sold at any time, this is the reason why gold ETF funds shine.

The principle of gold ETF is: gold producers to gold ETF fund consignment gold physical, ETF fund to these gold as collateral in the exchange issued "warehouse receipts", the minimum unit is 1/10 ounce, in order to reduce the investor's entry threshold, these "warehouse receipts" (fund share) can be freely traded, management fees are also very low. 2003 gold ETF once launched, quickly fire all over the world, the current gold ETF fund giant is listed in the New York Stock Exchange GLD. 2004 listing, its scale rapidly expanded, in December 2012 had held 1,350 tons of gold, can be called countries outside the gold reserves of the largest gold holders. in September 2012, the world's all gold ETF fund has a total of about 2330 tons of gold. However, some gold ETFs hold gold that is actually futures contracts or exists in the form of other paper gold.

When the Wall Street media sings about the gold move, the most frequently cited reason is that the GLD's gold holdings are dwindling, indicating that investors are abandoning gold and money is flowing out of the gold market.

When the money comes in, the GLD fund uses the money to buy physical gold and hand over the "warehouse receipts" to the investors, a process that is easy to understand. So what happens when money flows out?

That's where the cat hides!

The holder of a "warehouse receipt" can transfer the warehouse receipt at any time and can also claim the gold in kind from the GLD. If it is a transfer, then GLD's gold holdings will remain unchanged, but claiming gold in kind will be different, this is called "redemption", GLD must hand over the gold and destroy the warehouse receipts, the two are not in arrears, the accounts will be written off, at this time GLD's gold holdings will decline.

The Wall Street bigwigs had a hand in designing the GLD, and only 15 major banks were able to deal with the Trustee of the GLD, the Bank of New York Mellon, and the Custodian, HSBC, who were supposed to be part of the group. The big boys hold at least 100,000 "warehouse receipts" before they can "redeem" the physical gold.

This arrangement will completely exclude all the retail investors in GLD from the threshold of "redemption" physical gold, their only way out is in the horror of the gold plunge, will "warehouse receipt" at the jump price transfer to 15 Wall Street big brothers, big brothers laughingly lick the blood of the retail investors on the "warehouse receipt", then find the client of the accomplice to eliminate the accounts of GLD, then get the bill of lading, then go to knock another accomplice HSBC bank's treasury door, HSBC identified and shipped, big brothers celebrate, each other congratulate and get rich. In the end, the big guys deliver the gold that originally belonged to the GLD retail investors to the COMEX futures clients. Both shuffling the GLD's retail investors and not defaulting on the delivery of COMEX futures.

Where is the gold of GLD hidden? They are held in escrow at HSBC in London, physically in the vault of UBS in Zurich, Switzerland, and the gold is completely invisible on COMEX's inventory radar.

What do you mean by "unscrupulous"? Wall Street bigwigs are the freshest specimen of this!

What is fraud, and the GLD rules are the most graphic case in point!

What does it mean to be miserable? Retail investors in GLD are the most readily available losers!

After Germany announced it was shipping gold home, the COMEX and Gold ETF there was a simultaneous decline in total inventories (Source: Bloomberg).

The beauty of GLD is that it's using retail investors' money to pit themselves. The skills of the big guys in shearing wool are really up to date and innovative, and it's fascinating to watch. If the retail investors own the gold directly, then it is not easy for the big guys to get the gold from the scattered corners of the world, but the GLD uses the method of stimulating human greed to concentrate the money and gold of the retail investors in the hands of the big guys, take it and feast on it.

In June 2013, JPMorgan Chase actually encountered a gold run, in the COMEX system has been unable to cope with futures delivery, GLD has become a convenient and convenient gold "withdrawal machine" of JPMorgan Chase. If the gold price rises or remains unchanged, then the GLD's retail investors will not honestly hand over their "positions", and only a plunge in the gold price can shake out the "positions" of the frightened retail investors. This is the root cause of another plunge in the gold price at the end of June.

If you look at the gold stocks of the gold ETF and COMEX together in a single chart, the problem is clear: in January 2013, when Germany announced that it was shipping gold home, the price of gold began to reverse, while the stocks of the COMEX and the gold ETF fell in a very "coincidental" synchronized and proportional way. To put it another way, COMEX's gold inventory losses may be partially replenished by gold ETF inventories.

In the long run, the ETF gold outflow is by no means a bad thing, and the interpretation of the Wall Street media is completely opposite, the gold ETF "blood loss", illustrates the COMEX physical gold shortage is serious, the ETF gold from the centralized control of the big guys regained the freedom, they again scattered around the world, and eventually into the pockets of Asian and emerging market countries "big mothers", they will cling to the really valuable treasure, the Wall Street big guys want to lure out these gold, close to a dream.

Insider disclosure

Some may ask, there is no impermeable wall in the world, and the "beheading operation" of gold since April, has not been leaked at all?

The answer is: of course there is.

A long article, "The Assault On Gold", published on the website on 4 April (eight days before the gold beheading), accurately "predicted" the upcoming "April Fool's Day Offensive" against gold by the United States.

This person is Paul Craig Roberts, a former Assistant Secretary of the US Treasury.

Roberts served as assistant secretary of the Treasury for U.S. economic policy in the Reagan administration and is credited as one of the founders of Reagan economics.

In his article, Roberts points out that the gold spike of $500 in 2011 strongly shook the Federal Reserve and the U.S. Treasury, and that in order to defend the hegemony of the dollar gold must be suppressed, the U.S. government is the dominant force in the gold and silver plunge.

> "For Americans, a financial and economic disaster may be close at hand. The Fed and the financial institutions it relies on have joined forces to crack down on gold and silver prices to deter investors, as evidenced by this."

I featured Roberts's Gold Alert in my April 7, 2013 Sina Weibo post (600,000 readers) This happened 5 days before the "4-1-2" gold price plunge

> "The Fed's 'April Fool's Offensive' on gold began by sending a message to gold traders (referring to JPMorgan Chase, among others) who quickly communicated (the Fed's) intentions to their clients and informed them that hedge funds and other large investment institutions were about to sell their gold positions and that clients should quickly exit the precious metals market before then. Because this inside information belongs to the government's own strategy, investors will not be able to prosecute such actions.
>
> "The Fed's crackdown on precious metals was a reckless act, as the policy is doomed to fail once it becomes widely known, As I explained earlier, the joint crackdown on gold and silver was designed precisely to protect the exchange rate of the dollar. If gold and silver didn't threaten (the dollar), the government wouldn't be cracking down on them.
>
> "The Fed is making a trillion dollars a year in new currency, but the world is moving away from dollars in international trade settlements, and dollar reserves, and the result is an increase in (dollar) supply and a decrease in demand. This means that the dollar will fall and domestic inflation will worsen due to higher import prices, which will lead to higher interest rates and the collapse of bonds, stocks, real estate.

> *"The Fed's combined strike on gold and silver is unlikely to be ultimately successful, and its purpose is simply to buy more time for the Fed to continue printing money to pay for the federal deficit while keeping interest rates low and securing bond prices to shore up banks' balance sheets."*[12]

The US government is smart in that they use the market's tools, the media's influence and Wall Street's enormous energy to manipulate market psychology to change expectations for gold and silver, thus accomplishing their policy objectives without showing any signs. This is far more effective than the use of administrative means such as purchase restrictions and number restrictions.

The influence of the United States Government on gold price expectations can be found in a number of "coincidences" in the successive gold rises and falls.

In March 2008, the price of gold topped $1,000 for the first time in history, reaching $1,011, and in April, the IMF began discussing the sale of gold financing, supposedly to better help poor countries. Such lame reasoning is, of course, designed to influence gold price expectations. And sure enough, gold plunged as much as 27% to $740 in September on the news.

In February 2009, the gold price reached $984, again approaching the $1,000 mark, and in March, at the G20 summit arranged to discuss the IMF's gold sale plan, the scale far exceeded expectations, as high as 403 tons. Unsurprisingly, the April gold price fell 12 percent to $870 on the news.

In November 2009, the price of gold topped $1175, another record high. In the same month, the IMF, out of "urgency", announced the sale of 200 tons of gold to India, as a result of which the gold price fell to $1,058 three months later, down 10%.

In June 2010, the price of gold reached an all-time high of $1261, and on July 7, the Wall Street Journal suddenly revealed that the Bank for International Settlements (BIS) had entered into a gold swap (SWAP) transaction with commercial banks: "If the loans (commercial banks) have secured gold from BIS, which for some reason cannot be

---

[12] Paul Craig Roberts, *The Assault on Gold*, PaulCraigRoberts.org, 2013-04-04.

repaid, then BIS may choose to sell this gold in the market, and a gold sell-off of this magnitude would greatly increase the supply in the market." As a result, the gold price fell to $1157 at the end of July, down 8.2%.

On September 5, 2011, gold hit an all-time high of $1920. From $1,328 in February of that year, it soared nearly $600 in 7 months! September 21, the United States launched a $400 billion distortion operation, the original market thought that gold would rise, but not expected similar to the "four – one two" tragedy occurred, the crazy futures sell-off on the 22nd and 23rd will be the gold price successively smashed through 1,800 dollars and 1,700 dollars of the barrier. Particularly on September 23, after the gold plunge, COMEX came to a "cauldron of pay", suddenly announced a substantial increase in gold trading margin of 21%, silver 16%. It "happened" to be another Friday, and the next day was the weekend, and the gold long collapsed exactly as it did on "4-1-2". As a result, gold prices fell 9.7% for the week.

So many "coincidences" and very small probability of events occur frequently in the gold market, this market is really "haunted", I'm afraid.

In addition to Roberts, another found that the gold market is "haunted" is the former senior U.S. government official Pippa Malmgren (Pippa Malmgren).

Bipa-Maglen, formerly Special Assistant to President George W. Bush Jr. for Economic Policy, reports to the President on financial market movements and serves as the White House's general coordinator with financial regulators such as the Federal Reserve, the U.S. Futures Trading Commission (CFTC), and the U.S. Securities and Exchange Commission (SEC).

On June 7, 2013, Bipa Magalhaes revealed a lot of gold inside during an interview.

The reporter asked,

> "What to make of the April 12 gold plunge?"

Bipa-Maglen replied frankly:

> "(The U.S.) government abhors the skyrocketing price of gold, and that is indeed true, especially as they conduct the largest currency devaluation policy in history... We have never seen so many developed industrial countries adopt this (currency

> *devaluation) strategy simultaneously. So it's natural for governments to feel nervous. Some of the biggest banks maliciously shorted (gold) and declared to the market, 'It (gold) will definitely plummet.' I'm not sure this behavior counts as surprising. What happened next was a very, very large (sell-off gold) volume, a historically rare trade size that happened in just a half hour on Friday (April 12)."*

The reporter asked,

> *"It's a clear act of manipulation, isn't it?"*

Bipa Margren replied,

> *"I see what you mean. It's interesting that all the people are calling for the government to investigate this incident, and it looks like it's not going to end well. So, ultimately it's that we will never know (the truth)."*

The reporter asked,

> *"If the CFTC is allowed to open an investigation in the name of the U.S. government and finally report to the government: 'We found a crime, but the suspects are the government and the Federal Reserve.' What about this?"*

Bipa Margren (laughs):

> *"Yes, you must arrest yourself immediately."*

The reporter asked,

> *"So it's actually impossible for you to investigate this type of event, is it?"*

Bipa Margren replied,

> *"No, you can't (investigate). I think that's why a lot of the institutions I advise are very concerned about gold investing because they do feel that it (the gold market) is being manipulated. The volatility of (gold) prices like this is too much for them to bear."*[13]

There is no doubt that either Paul Roberts, or Bipa Magalhaes, have seen the gold market from the perspective of the US government.

---

[13] Eric King Interviewed with Dr. Philippa "Pippa" Malmgren, King World News, 2013-06-07.

As Special Assistant to the President, she must have a clear understanding of the anomalies of the financial markets in case the President asks her. There should be no doubt about the US government's heavy focus on the gold market, which is naturally tied to the status of the dollar.

Interestingly, Bipa-Maglen revealed her views on the internationalization of the yuan in another interview:

> "They (China) want the yuan to be a strong, gold-backed currency in the world, while other countries are opting for inflation and devaluation of the currency. Recent (China's) bilateral currency agreements with Australia, France, Russia, Singapore and many other countries reflect a willingness to replace (the yuan) as the world's reserve currency."

How long will the red flag fight? Is there a future for gold and silver?

The 12 April strike on gold has been described as a classic example of "psychological operation", which aims to influence the value systems, belief systems, emotions, motivations, logic and behaviour of the target group, and in particular the impact on behaviour that will directly induce price fluctuations.

The dramatic fall in gold prices has successfully produced the expected effect of "psychological warfare", people began to doubt whether the concept of "hiding gold in a troubled world" is still valid, the confidence in the investment value of gold and silver has been seriously shaken, pessimism is widespread, the sound of singing and decrying is widespread, and even the basic logic of the over-issued currency will eventually lead to inflation has also become ambiguous. Market sentiment has become disconnected from calm reason, price signals are misaligned with wealth intuition, and, so to speak, perceptions of gold are in an unprecedented state of disarray.

To this end, a comprehensive and critical analysis is necessary.

In terms of need, people will always want to own gold, as has been validated by 5,000 years of human civilization, and the key is at what price point that impulse will be translated into action. From a supply perspective, it depends on what kind of gold price gold producers are willing to continue to provide.

This relates to the cost of producing gold.

With regard to the cost of production of gold, there are currently two statistical methods: one called "Cash Costs" (Cash Costs), the other is the "Total Costs" (Total Costs). The former calculates only the most basic costs of maintaining the normal operation of a gold mine, such as mining, processing, refining, etc., and finally the cost per ounce of gold mined by dividing the total production of the mine by the above costs. However, the method clearly underestimates the combined cost of gold. In order to maintain a company's profitability, any gold producer must continually drill for new gold resources and dig deep into existing gold reserves, the costs of which are enormous and must be incurred. In addition, the financial costs of enterprises (debt interest, etc.), tax costs should also be calculated in the gold production costs, and finally need to remove derivatives hedges, asset write-downs, other investment gains and losses (not related to gold production), such an analysis in order to truly and comprehensively reflect the financial situation of production enterprises. Although these costs are not directly related to the production of existing gold mines, they are real costs incurred by gold companies, without which the necessary overhead would not be sustainable. When these costs are considered together, they are the "full cost method" of gold.

Based on the cash cost method, some believe that gold costs $600-$800 per ounce, while others have reported it to be $1000-$1100, depending on the different gold mines.

Hebba Alternative Investments has conducted a systematic study of all listed gold companies in the world using the "full cost method". These companies are sufficiently representative, with a total gold production of 800 tonnes in 2012, or about 1/3 of the total global gold mined in 2012 (2,700 tonnes).

The average "full cost" of a listed gold enterprise is calculated to be.

In 2011, $1168/oz.

In 2012, $1287 per ounce.

Among other things, the cost of gold has risen to $1,399/oz in the fourth quarter of 2012!

Mining costs have skyrocketed due to the increasing technical difficulty of discovering new mines versus excavating existing mines, such as those in South Africa, which have reached a depth of 3,200 metres. In addition to mining costs, there have been significant spikes in labor costs, energy costs, equipment costs, transportation costs, and channel costs due to severe currency overruns since 2009. Also often overlooked are the hidden costs of environmental, legal and policy For example, Barrick, the world's largest gold miner, had its gold project in Pascua Lama, South America, halted by the Chilean government in April 2013, citing environmental protection reasons, as the mine straddled Chile and Argentina, and the huge sums of money Barrick had invested in the previous years were suddenly lost. The huge hidden costs experienced by such gold enterprises are not accounted for in the traditional "cash cost method", but are real.

In addition, Herba Investments also conducted a full cost measurement of silver and found that the average full cost of all listed silver companies worldwide (70 million ounces, or about 10% of global production) was $23.04 in the fourth quarter of 2012, compared to $20.80 in the same period in 2011, representing a 10.8% year-over-year cost increase.

If at the end of 2012, the full cost of gold had reached nearly $1,400, by June 2013, the price of gold had fallen to around $1,250, meaning that the world's gold producers will generally be in the red.

In fact, this has already happened.

On June 21, 2013, U.S. gold-listed Golden Minerals Company (AUMN) announced the closure of 470 production sites at its Velardena mine in Mexico. In May of that year, the company projected negative cash flow of $5 million for the next three quarters of the year at $1,500 for gold and $25 for silver. And the price of gold and silver has been well below its full cost in June, forcing companies to lay off workers and cut production.

On June 22, Barrick, the world's largest gold company, announced that it would lay off workers at 55 mines in Nevada and Utah on a massive scale because gold prices have made it difficult for Barrick to maintain production. Almost simultaneously, another world-renowned gold company, Newmont Mining Corporation, will make another layoff at its Nevada gold mine after laying off 33 percent of its employees at the Colorado gold mine. The company said soaring costs and falling gold prices have forced it to cut production.

On June 24, Newcrest Mining Ltd, which ranks among the top 5 gold companies in the world, announced an asset write-down of up to $5.5 billion, the largest in world gold history. There is no doubt that if the price of gold falls below the full cost of gold for a long time, then gold production will fall.

Since 2001, the price of gold has risen about fivefold, and according to common sense of supply and demand, the increase in profits should be accompanied by an increase in production, but the reality is that mineral gold production has barely changed significantly in 12 years, from 2,560 tons in 2001 to 2,700 tons in 2012.

The number of mega-gold mines currently being mined globally is pitifully small, with only 156 of the 400 mines producing more than 100,000 ounces (about 3+ tons) per year; of these, only 21 mines are producing more than 500,000 ounces (about 16 tons) per year; and no more than 6 mega-gold mines producing 1 million ounces (32 tons) per year. Since gold mining has been going on for thousands of years, all the easy gold mines on the planet have been excavated. While some large gold mines have also been discovered in the last 10 years, none of the mega-gold mines with total reserves of more than 20 million ounces (about 643 tons) of gold have been found.

It is argued that the cost of gold production does not matter because the vast majority of gold mined will not be consumed, the stock is much larger than the incremental amount, and the price of gold will be determined by the stock of gold. In fact, it's the same thing with new and used homes, if there's a shortage of new homes, the owners of used homes will scruple to sell and the overall price of the property will go up. Likewise, if new gold additions do not meet market demand, then that demand will have to resort to existing gold holders, and if the price is too low, no one will want to sell. Of course, countries' gold reserve selling can significantly change the supply and demand relationship, but in the current situation where global central banks have become net buyers of gold, especially in the light of the impact of the German central bank shipping gold home to other central banks, it is not easy to convince countries to sell gold reserves.

After the gold plunge in April 2013, China's Shanghai Gold Exchange's out-of-stock volume shows that China has eaten the vast majority of the world's gold mineral gold over the same period, while India's gold consumption is not on par with China's, China and India alone could eat more than 2,000 tons of gold in 2013, the Middle East and global central banks will buy at least 1,000 tons, and the rest of the world's physical gold fever is rapidly heating up, stimulated by lower gold prices.

It is important to note that the price of gold is already below the cost of production for gold companies, and that this cost is climbing rapidly at a rate of nearly 10 percent per year, and more and more gold producers will be forced to cut production or close mines, and the supply of gold will shrink rapidly. This raises the question of the inevitable tendency to reallocate the gold stock if new gold additions are not sufficient to meet rapidly growing demand.

In fact, this trend has persisted for the past 40 years or so, namely, that since the decoupling of the dollar from gold in 1971, the direction of the flow of the world's gold stock has been shifting from the West to the East, from the older developed countries to the emerging market countries, which is entirely consistent with what has happened in human history at the turn of civilizations: the direction of the movement of gold shows a shift in wealth creativity, a shift in prosperity and confidence, and ultimately marks a shift in global power.

Gold flows forever to places that respect wealth creation!

Expound

The darkness before dawn is the most desperate, but in the darkness breeds the dawn.

In 2013, the US government and Wall Street bigwigs pounded the gold market with a ferocity unseen in 30 years. This, in turn, illustrates another problem, such madness and such drastic behavior means that the dollar's fear of gold is also unprecedented in 30 years.

Weak confidence in the dollar is exactly what is hitting gold!

As Roberts says, the Fed's blow to gold and silver is unlikely to be ultimately successful. Its purpose is simply to buy more time for the Fed to continue printing money to pay for the federal deficit while keeping interest rates low and securing bond prices to shore up banks' balance sheets.

Compared to 2008, the U.S. financial system in 2013 was not more robust, but more fragile. It has been seen that the Fed's quantitative monetary easing has come to an end, and ahead of that end is another cliff with no bottom in sight, and for five years, the super-inflation of the dollar has brought not a real economic boom, but a much larger bubble on a global scale. Sustaining asset bubbles must rely on more accommodative monetary policy, which is destined to burst even larger bubbles.

What is still in question is not whether the crisis will erupt, but when and where it will start. If the 2008 financial crisis was a crisis of the financial institutions, and the government can transfer the rotten debts of the financial system to itself with a flood of money, then the next crisis will be a crisis of the money itself.

The United States has clearly realized that there can be no "good end" to QE policy, a currency crisis will be inevitable, and if the dollar must be guaranteed to stand in ruins after the crisis, the only exit strategy is to detonate the crisis in other countries first.

Any currency option that has the potential to replace the dollar, whether they are the euro, the yen, the renminbi, gold, or bitcoin, is something that the US will never tolerate. The U.S. has succeeded in letting the yen rot, leaving the euro to its own devices, leaving gold to its own devices, and bitcoin to its own devices, only to have the U.S. adopt the strategy of "surrounding the three queues and one" against the yuan and continue to force the yuan to appreciate.

At the root of the global currency wars to come is the decline of the dollar, which began with the decoupling from gold in 1971. From then on, free from any rigid constraints and without any checks and balances, the hegemony of the dollar became the dictatorship of the dollar. Absolute power leads to absolute corruption, as does monetary power.

All fruit falls to the ground, because of the gravitational pull of all; all money depreciates, because of human greed. In the end, gold still shines in the ruins of monetary desire.

CHAPTER II

The Truth Tunnel, Through the Space of the Bubble

Among the reasons for the "4-1-2" gold plunge, the Wall Street media is most enthusiastic about the extreme prosperity of the US stock market. Corporate profits have risen sharply and stock indices have hit record highs, signaling a brighter outlook for the U.S. economic recovery and a stronger dollar is inevitable. The purpose of holding gold is nothing more than to hedge the risk of a recession in the United States and the depreciation of the dollar, since the stock market has performed brilliantly, the value of gold is bound to dim.

In fact, optimistic expectations for the US economic recovery are nothing new. The Wall Street media had predicted that the United States economy would recover strongly in the second half of 2009, but the result was a lack of momentum, and the following year changed the narrative to say that the economy was bound to grow substantially in 2010, but what followed was a lack of growth, and then 2011, 2012, 2013, the year after year of optimism and expectations, year after year of poor performance. five years down the road, $3 trillion of quantitative easing, nearly $5 trillion of fiscal deficit, the United States has never been so crazy to print and spend money, in return for an immortal economy, high unemployment rate, monetary instruments and fiscal policy of the poor effect, is unprecedented. By 2013, the U.S. economy wears the QE "breathing machine" has been breathing for five years, but still do not dare to take it off.

Between record highs in the stock market and a sluggish economic recovery, which is reality and which is an illusion? This chapter will guide you through the tunnel of truth and through the space of bubbles!

The black vulture in the stock market

One day in December 2009, Ham Bodek came to New York to attend a party hosted by an electronic trader, where he discovered a major secret that had been haunting him for months.

A former stock trader at Goldman Sachs and UBS, Hamm founded a high-frequency trading firm in 2007. The so-called high-frequency trading is to replace the human brain's reaction with the speed of a computer, to convert positions in milliseconds and take profits. At first, the company's profits were good, but then business got tougher and tougher, and their stock orders were always out of reach and their profits were eaten up by trading fees.

Initially, he suspected that there was something wrong with the company's trading code, and after months of checking, he still couldn't find the problem. I came to the party on this day to find out from the sales representatives of this electronic trading platform to see what the problem was.

Finally, Ham stopped a sales manager by the bar, and after some more questioning, the sales manager had to get serious. He asked Ham's company what type of trading order it uses, and Ham replied: a Limit Order (Limit Order). The sales manager laughed and said: you can't use a limit order. Ham was puzzled, isn't a limit order the most common way to order? It's used by almost everyone from fund managers to the average retail investor. Simply put, if you have your eye on a stock that is priced at $10, that limit order will help you complete the trade under $10.

However, the problem lies in the matchmaking system of electronic trading platforms, where the most common trading orders are buried with "Trojan horses".

The sales manager's explanation made Ham woke up in a dream, it turns out that the computer program of the matching system, all purchase orders to be sorted, originally the highest price should be at the top of the order queue, the exact same price should be arranged in accordance with the order of first come first served, that is, the principle of price priority and time priority, but many trading platforms have left a "back door" in the order sorting, high-frequency trading special orders will be "hidden" at the top of the purchase order queue, while the ordinary limit orders are squeezed backwards. At the time of trading, special orders are always the first to be filled at the best price, and regardless of price movements, special orders always have a higher priority than limit orders. When prices rise, high-frequency trading special orders turn around and are at the top of the queue to sell orders to sell first at the best price, thus achieving the dream of "every single only earn no loss".[14]

If the market suddenly changes and the original order is looking in the wrong direction, will the special order for high frequency trading lose money? The answer is: no!

The algorithm for high-frequency trading will judge the strength of the sell order queue within milliseconds, confirm that the price trend is about to reverse, and before the price has time to change, the special order sells the stock at the original price to the buy order in the queue behind it, and the withdrawal is completed in a flash.

Ham's business is high-frequency trading, but he never dreamed that there was still something hidden in the collocation mechanism within the trading system. The sales manager advised Hamm not to tell this secret to anyone else; limit orders are the lowest prey in the food chain of stock trading, and they are exclusively for the high-frequency traders at the top.

Although not every exchange has such a "loophole", but it reflects the core concept of high-frequency trading is "rush to run", after the trigger is pulled, the bullet is not yet fired, the gun is not yet heard, all players are still waiting, rush to run people have already rushed to everyone in front.

In order to achieve the "rush to run", high frequency traders can be said to spare no expense.

The two financial centers of New York and Chicago are 700 miles apart, and in fiber optic cable, the data transfer speed is only 7 milliseconds, but 7 milliseconds is too long for a high-frequency trader. A high-frequency trading company spent $300 million to build a tunnel of fiber optic cables across the Appalachian Mountains, which are shorter in distance and can reduce data transmission time to 6

---

[14] Scott Patterson, Dark Pools: The Rise of the Machine Trades and the Rigging of the US Stock Market, Crown Business, 2012-06.

milliseconds. In the world of high-frequency trading, one millisecond is worth more than $300 million.

Once upon a time, U.S. stock exchanges were membership-based, non-profit institutions whose primary responsibility was to maintain fair, equitable and open markets. However, since its conversion into a for-profit organization, making money has become the number one task of various exchanges, and the "three publics" have become a rent-seeking tactic of the exchanges. The closer the company's server is to the exchange's data center, the easier it will be for the company to run away. The exchange actually uses the location of its own data center as a way to make money, allowing high-frequency trading companies to place server clusters next to it. In return, high-frequency trading companies import their own massive order streams into the exchanges.

Since the birth of high-frequency trading, it has accounted for 30% to 50% of the total volume of U.S. stocks, no exchange dares to slow down these new customers with large orders in hand. To make new customers more satisfied, the exchange also offers greater bandwidth, allowing them to extend the advantages they already have with higher data transfer speeds. Some greedy trading platforms, in order to cater to the needs of high-frequency traders, even planted "Trojan horses" in their matchmaking systems, allowing them to run over ordinary order holders in the market.

Once the servers of the HF traders occupy the best position in the exchange's machine room, they actually occupy the upper reaches of the market trading data stream. In this way, they can not only run, but also "take the road".

At the height of the IT bubble in the 1990s, the exchange was processing 1,000 quotes per second, and in 2013 it has reached a dizzying 2 million quotes per second, with high-frequency trading accounting for 90% to 95% of all market quotes! The purpose of creating the "noise" of mass quotes is not mainly for the purpose of transaction, but to slow down the speed of data processing on the stock exchange, crowding out the channel of ordinary shareholders and delaying the time for the market to obtain real trading information, which is equivalent to the "blocking attack" of the Internet.

Either way, high-frequency trading creates a serious injustice, as it hovers over the market like a black vulture, ready to prey on the defenseless. When the market is stable, it exploits all shareholders, with the effect of a disguised tax, and when the market needs liquidity, it quickly disappears, leading to intense market turbulence.

High-frequency trading is just one detail of the stock market, but a glimpse into the whole picture. When greed prevails, it inevitably distorts the market and undermines fairness; and, spurred on by cheap money, the desire for greed begins to viciously inflate, and it not only distorts the entire economy, but creates even greater wealth injustice.

Bernanke's shock

On June 19, 2013, Federal Reserve Chairman Ben Bernanke put out the word that if the economy continues to improve, "a modest tapering of debt purchases in the second half of the year would be appropriate". What does it mean for the economy to improve? For the first time, Bernanke gave a clear definition of a drop in the unemployment rate to 7 percent, at which point the five-year-long quantitative easing (QE) of monetary policy would be phased out.

Perhaps Bernanke's heart is full of strong confidence in the economic recovery, or perhaps he is aware of the enormous risks to the continuation of QE, and is keen to prove to the world before he leaves office in early 2014 that his money printing policy has been a success and that the US economy can function even without the maintenance of QE. He would become the first hero in human economic history to successfully save the world with money.

Outstripping Bernanke's expectations, the exit from QE came as a big shock to the market, and at the same time, he was caught off guard. Immediately after Bernanke's words, global financial markets were in a panic, with the gold market down 5.4%. Not surprisingly, the QE retraction means Bernanke was right, the US economy has recovered and the gold hedge function has become redundant, so why hold gold? However, the stock market, which had been confident of an economic recovery, also plunged, with the U.S. S&P 500 stock index plunging 2.5%, its biggest single-day drop in 20 months. The stock markets in Europe and Japan are also in bad shape, even China's stock market is not spared, and other emerging markets are all falling to the ground.

That's odd, doesn't QE's exit indicate a recovery in the economy? The stock market should be more confident, how could there be a crash?

The Wall Street media cheerleader's explanation is that a premature exit from QE could lead to an aborted economic recovery, which in turn could hit stock market confidence. However, the QE policy has been going on for 5 years, so if it's too early to exit in 2013, is it not too early for the Year of the Monkey?

At the time of the 2008 financial crisis, the US financial system was like a critically ill patient, hanging on by a thread. Immediately after that, the Federal Reserve Organization rescue, Congress emergency mobilization, the Treasury Department to take treatment, taxpayers forced blood transfusion, interest rate morphine, deficit pacing, monetary electroshock, all kinds of therapeutic means at all costs, finally hanging the breath of Wall Street patients. After wearing the "breathing machine" of QE, Wall Street bigwigs gradually slowed down, the stock market rebounded, and a few years down the line, bigwigs again earn a lot of brain fat, big belly.

How about Wall Street always jumping up and down with a QE breathalyzer on, always looking indecent. Whenever it is rumored that the market QE respirator to pull the tube, Wall Street is all over the place, looking for death to live, and the world is worried about the heart. If the tubes are really pulled, will Wall Street continue to sleepwalk, or will it go back to the ICU?

In the virtual world created by the Wall Street media cheerleaders, people's lives are haunted by good news every day: unemployment is getting lower and lower, consumer confidence is getting higher and higher; property prices are rebounding strongly and bank profits are getting higher and higher; shale oil and gas is bright and manufacturing is flowing back one after the other; cheap money is being printed to the Federal Reserve, but inflation is so low that Bernanke is worried; corporate earnings are unprecedented and CEOs are scrambling to buy back shares; capital markets are at record highs and economic prosperity has arrived.

U.S. stock market record highs is the "ironclad evidence" of economic recovery? That being the case, what exactly is Bernanke's fear of quitting QE? Why the hell is Wall Street rolling around?

The U.S. stock market has repeatedly reached record highs and is widely regarded as the "ironclad evidence" of the U.S. economic recovery, if the ironclad evidence can be opened, we can see whether the U.S. economy is healthy in the gut.

Stock market boom, or stock market puffiness?

The Dow Jones is a barometer of the U.S. stock market if you will, but the S&P 500 is more broadly representative of the S&P 500, the 500 most representative companies in all sectors of the U.S. economy, with a combined market capitalization of $13.8 trillion as of the first quarter of 2013 and $5.14 trillion in total assets linked to the S&P 500.

The S&P 500 hit an all-time high of 1,569 points on March 28, 2013, and the 2008 financial crisis seems to be a memory, at least the stock market has shown the contours of a new bull market, which has soared 135% since March 2009, when it hit a low of 667 points.

The reason for the stock's rise looks very good, as the S&P500's earnings per share (EPS, Earnings Per Share) climbed sharply from $85 in 2007 to an estimated $110 in 2013, a 29.4% gain. If you consider all the companies in the S&P500 as one, then the company's earning power per share is increasing dramatically and the value of the entire company is naturally rising.

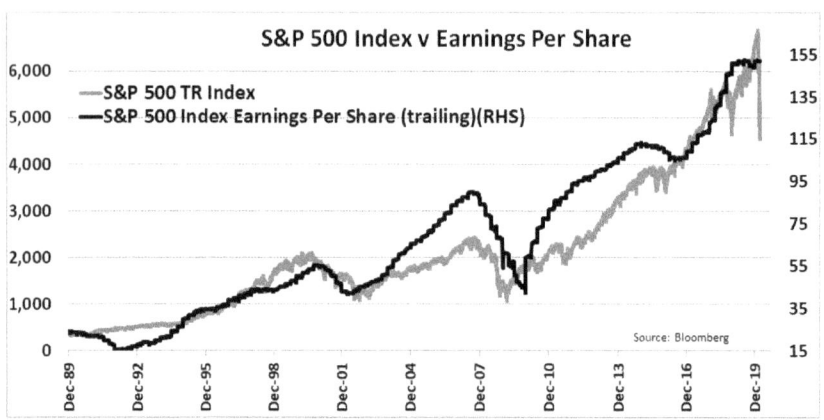

Annual change in earnings per share (EPS) for S&P500[15]

Earnings per share is what determines the value of a stock!

While the stock index has risen more than its earnings per share, the stock market's PE has fallen to 13.8 times from 15.2 times in

---

[15] Fact Set Earnings Insight Report, Bottomup EPS Estimates: Current & Historical, 2013-11-01.

October 2007. In other words, stocks in 2013 are cheaper than stocks in 2007. Shouldn't a good market like this go up big when you invest $100 in stocks that will return 7% of their value in 2013, far more than the interest on bank deposits and treasury bonds?

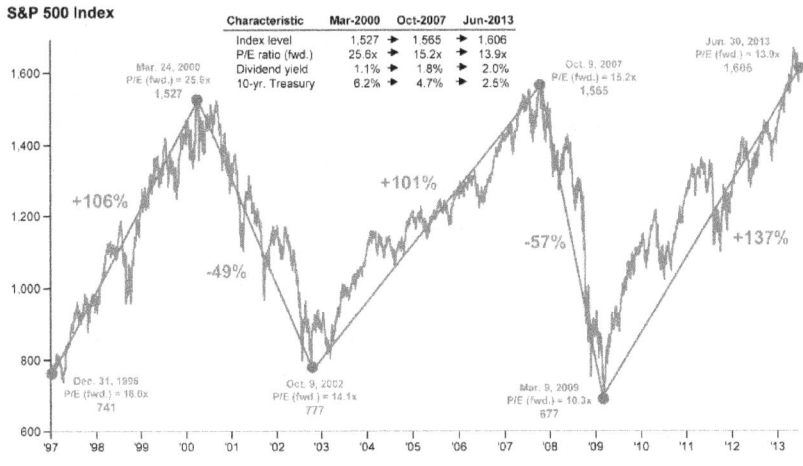

S&P500 Index 1997–2013

The mystery of it all lies in how exactly the increase in earnings per share is generated!

To run a good company, the most basic job is to open source and cut costs, open source is to increase sales revenue, cut costs is to compress internal expenses, two-pronged approach is more effective.

After a severe world economic downturn following the financial crisis in September 2008, corporate sales plummeted and by the third quarter of 2009, the S&P500's sales growth deteriorated to -15.81%. Faced with the rigors of survival, the first instinctive reaction of major companies was to lay off workers on a large scale, with one man doing the work of two, reducing operating costs and increasing productivity, which is why the U.S. unemployment rate has soared over the same period.

The Fed at this point launched the first round of $600 billion in quantitative easing (QE1), saving the soon-to-be-collapsed banking system and also giving the stock market a double boost of strong confidence and money. The Federal Reserve's operation to depress short-term interest rates to ultra-low levels of 0 to 0.25%, while massive purchases of Treasuries and MBS (mortgage-backed securities) depressed long-term interest rates, allowed the company's financial costs to fall significantly.

QE policy led to a significant depreciation of the dollar exchange rate, S&P500 companies are leading enterprises in various fields of the U.S. economy, their performance in 30% to 50% of sales revenue directly from overseas markets, the depreciation of the dollar makes them in a more advantageous position in international competition, directly stimulating the growth of overseas sales; in addition, when overseas income into dollars appear in the company's financial reports, but also to obtain "exchange rate dividends" of wealth increase effect. As a result, growth in overseas sales and the "exchange rate dividend" boosted the company's profit level.

As a result, the company's earnings per share have increased significantly since 2009 due to five factors: significant layoffs to compress operating costs, improved productivity, lower financial costs, overseas sales stimulated by the depreciation of the U.S. dollar, and higher book profits from currency dividends.

As a result of these factors, S&P500's earnings per share rose 39.4% from 2009 to 2010. Despite this, total sales of the S&P500 remained in negative territory through the first quarter of 2010, with negative growth of -8.35%.

The limit is not open source, the limit is throttling!

Once QE1 was terminated, US economic data quickly deteriorated again and the stock market plunged after a sharp rally.

That was the backdrop for the Fed having to launch QE2 in November 2010. Spurred by a new round of $600 billion in money printing, S&P500 sales growth finally began to turn negative, climbing from 3% to 6% at the end of QE2, and earnings per share rose 14% from 2010 to 2011. U.S. S&P 500 sales growth rate (S&P)[16]

In September 2011, the European debt crisis escalated again as the Greek default scare intensified. At this moment, it is the important inflection point of the United States economy, QE1 and QE2 can play the "positive energy" has been exhausted.

---

[16] Standard & Poor's, Current S&P 500 Real Sales Growth.

S&P500's sales growth is at an all-time high, and the company's potential for cost savings is at its limit. The productivity spike from layoffs peaked at 5.8% in the fourth quarter of 2009, then fell straight back to 0.6% in 2013. This is exactly what has happened in successive recessions where the oil has been squeezed out of the employees in the absence of a major technological revolution. At the same time, the impact of the monetary stimulus on open source has reached its peak, and the positive effects of the dollar flood on U.S. companies are being offset by a strategic shift in the world's attempts at local currency settlement.

After 2010, productivity in the United States declined sharply and the potential for efficiency gains from layoffs was exhausted.[17] Not surprisingly, when QE2 ended on June 30, 2011, the stock market plunged again.

If the strong rally in the US stock market prior to September 2011 basically reflected the real state of the US economy bottoming out under the stimulus of the first two rounds of QE, then the stock market since then has been divorced from economic reality and has flown into the space of illusion.

From the third quarter of 2011 onwards, the main drivers of earnings per share growth have changed fundamentally. A new factor is emerging as a dominant force, and that is the stock buyback behavior of public companies.

What is a share buyback like?

In the minds of Chinese stockholders, the main purpose of a company's listing is to make money, so companies can do whatever they can to falsify data, embellish statements, exaggerate projects, smooth relations, create public opinion, in short, everything for the listing, everything for the money. After being listed on the stock exchange, I have to pay the money to buy back the shares. Who would do such a stupid thing?

---

[17] Sam Ro, How Labor Productivity Evolves During Economic Recoveries, Business Insider, 2013-08-09.

The CEOs of the US S&P500 are definitely not stupid, they are usually not entrepreneurs, but professional managers who are motivated to buy back our company's stock precisely to line their pockets with more money!

Since the 1990s, the U.S. IT industry has pioneered a trend to stimulate employees with stock options, IT is a new high-growth industry, every dollar invested in the business can earn more returns in the future, so as to minimize the cost of cash wages, and the company's future expectations to attract and retain talent has become a popular means of the industry, stock options is the most attractive approach. The essence of a stock option is a benefit right that promises employees the right to choose to receive a certain amount of company stock at an agreed price for a certain period of time in the future. If the stock price is higher than the agreed price at that point, the employee can either cash out the spread gain directly or buy the stock at the agreed price and hold it for the long term. If the stock price is lower than the agreed price, the employee may choose to waive the option to exercise the option. Stock options use the current price of a company's stock as a fulcrum and future prices as leverage to pry the hard-working potential of employees, closely linking company growth to personal gain. Stock options are available to everyone from the CEO of the company down to the core employees.

For CEOs of large S&P500 companies, salaries are just pocket change, and stock options are the heavy hitters of revenue. The board thought it through, spending hundreds of millions of dollars a year to hire a CEO is very uneconomical, but it can provide considerable value in stock options, the stock goes up when the CEO does well, and the sky-high incentive bonuses come mainly from the stock market and don't require the company to break the cash. Thus, stock options became the carrot that the board of directors dangled in front of the CEO's eyes, and to eat it, one had to get the stock price up.

When companies report earnings each quarter, the CEOs of Wall Street and public companies kick off a big game of raffle-baiting about performance, with earnings per share being a classic item in the Big Sweepstakes.

Since September 2011, CEOs have had a hard time making a significant breakthrough by digging inside the company, and the expansion of external sales has been rigidly constrained by the global economic downturn. As we watch the betting date approach, the consequence of not meeting Wall Street's expectations is mental stress multiplied by economic pain and will continue to be multiplied by a time factor in the next quarter. The most effective way to increase earnings per share in the short term is to buy back your own company's stock, which is the company's money anyway, without paying for it yourself. A share buyback would result in a reduction in the number of shares outstanding, making the Company's stock more scarce. The huge cash buybacks, coupled with the reduction in shares outstanding, have certainly resulted in a rise in share prices. This was the first impetus to accelerate the stock rally.

Whenever the company announced the news of the buyback, the media cheerleaders often explain that the company believes its stock is too cheap, willing to buy back the stock out of pocket, which means that the company believes its stock will certainly rise in the future, after all, the company is more internal understanding of the operation of the enterprise, the CEOs are so confident, that investors do not have to follow the reason? This is the second impetus for the share price rise caused by the buyback.

After the share buyback, the reduction in shares outstanding, with the company's total earnings unchanged, will increase the level of earnings per share after flattening, in other words, earnings per share can be made! Wall Street took a look at the big rise in earnings per share, with positive reviews as expectations hit the mark. With the already strong temptation for the share price to rise, more investors have followed, forming a third impetus for the stock price to rise.

With the combined forces of these three, the strategy of stock buybacks to boost share prices has been a huge success. Boards of directors and shareholders were overjoyed by the increased value of their companies, CEOs were overjoyed by their huge bonuses, and Wall Street was overflowing with money as the stock market boomed and asset values rose, adding financing, buybacks, mergers, new stock offerings, and many other new businesses.

If we take out the buyback factor and let the truth come out, what we see is that the S&P500's corporate earnings have basically stagnated since September 2011, and that the stock market rally is not based on an increase in the true level of corporate earnings, but is a product of the "accounting technology revolution"!

S&P500's quarterly earnings after excluding stock buybacks Has been largely stagnant since September 2011. From the third quarter of

2011 through the first quarter of 2013, the S&P500's earnings per share increased by $3.7, with share repurchases "contributing" $2.2, or nearly 60 percent, and the "organic growth" portion of the company's efforts relying on its own was only $1.5.

Nearly 60% of S&P's incremental earnings per share were derived from Share buybacks (JPMorgan Chase). In the accounting revolution of high earnings per share, the practice is not only overestimating earnings, but also underestimating expenses.

Just as the S&P500 hit an all-time high, these companies are also experiencing record shortfalls in their pension accounts. Of that, the 2012 shortfall reached $451.7 billion, a 27% jump from 2011! The reason for this is that the ultra-low interest rate environment created by QE has squeezed the bond yields that pension accounts rely on. Despite the company's strong push in recent years for 401K retirement programs, where employees set aside future pension money from their paychecks and the company matches the money accordingly, the burden on the company is significantly reduced compared to traditional pension plans. However, traditional pension plans still cover 91 million people in employment, far more than the number of 401K participants.

Topping up pension accounts is a normal company expense, but it is deliberately ignored by many companies in order to artificially inflate earnings per share. Keep in mind that Ford's 2012 pension expense was a whopping $5 billion, almost equal to capital expenditures. When the "shackles" of pension payments are put on, the dance of earnings per share becomes a stumbling block.

It should be said that unlucky retired seniors are quietly laying the bill for the QE-fueled capital bonanza.

In the first quarter of 2013, as many as 328 of the 500 S&P 500 companies announced stock buybacks, a whopping 66%, with a total of $208 billion in planned buybacks, a record amount for the first quarter since 1985. Its proportions, amounts, and scope are only comparable to those of 2007, when the stock market bubble was about to burst. Of these, 212 buybacks resulted in a decrease in shares outstanding, and even if these companies did not grow at all, their earnings per share would automatically rise.

The comparison shows that the most pronounced pull-up in share prices was in 2007, when the buyback was at the height of the stock market bubble, the phenomenon came to the fore again in 2013.

At the rate and size of the repurchases announced in 2013, it is estimated that the total annual repurchase program will reach $833 billion, well above the $477 billion in 2012 and only slightly below 2007. It's no wonder Wall Street is confident that 2013 earnings per share will reach above $110, and if the PE can approach a relatively modest 18 times, the S&P 500 will be in the neighborhood of 2,000 points, meaning nearly 18% upside for the year.

Warren Buffett's Berkshire Company is one of the "oddballs" in a wave of stock buybacks. Buffett himself has consistently opposed stock buybacks as a manipulative tactic to artificially inflate share prices, and has vowed to never consider buying back his own shares unless Berkshire's share price falls below 110% of book value. However, on December 12, 2012, Buffett suddenly announced that he was buying back Berkshire's stock for $1.2 billion at 120% of book value. The paradox is that Buffett's buyback action was only directed at an "anonymous" investor, simply put, Buffett was directing $1.2 billion in benefits to a particular shareholder. Who knows exactly where this person came from, allegedly a long-time investor in Buffett.

Interestingly, the timing of Buffett's stock buyback is striking, which is the key moment when the U.S. is hitting the ground running to resolve the "fiscal cliff." Estate tax and capital gains tax are the mainstay of the bargain, and the tax burden is bound to rise sharply in 2013. Buffett is now buying back shares from the "mystery man" at a high price, which is suspected by many to be for profit and to avoid taxes for his rich friends. The funny thing is that just the day before, Warren Buffett had issued an open letter, screaming that "the rich should pay more taxes" and that "estate taxes should be raised substantially, not only because it's ethical, but also because it makes economic sense". With the ink still on the open letter and Buffett's words still ringing in his ears, it's no wonder that the next day he helped his rich friends save hundreds of millions of dollars in taxes, and people are exclaiming that "hypocrisy" needs a new definition.

Since 2009, the S&P500 has put nearly $2 trillion into stock buybacks and planned buybacks in 2013, representing 14.5% of the total market value of the stock!

Few people realize that publicly traded companies have become the number one buyer of the U.S. stock market and a major driver of stock indexes' rises, building an iron price floor for the stock market and then entering the market in a big way once it falls, pushing up share prices. Just as the Federal Reserve is the largest buyer of the U.S. Treasury bond market, this monopolistic power has reached the point where it can manipulate market prices. As long as the availability of capital is not a problem, a stock market rally is a given.

But where does the huge amount of cash repurchased by listed companies come from if not from market sales?

Buy stocks by borrowing, God knows what

In April 2013, Apple, sitting on $144 billion in cash, announced the largest stock buyback program in history at $60 billion! Meanwhile, Apple announced it was raising $17 billion in debt to help complete a stock buyback. It's odd that Apple has so much cash that it has nowhere to spend it, so why raise debt for a buyback? It turns out that 70 percent of Apple's cash ($102.3 billion) is overseas and just $42.4 billion at home in the U.S. is not enough to complete the buyback program. So why isn't Apple moving overseas cash back home? That's because 35 percent of the federal income tax on income in the U.S. is waiting with a bloody jaws open for the return of that taxable income. Make Apple pay $35 billion in income taxes to the government, unless Apple's head is in the clouds.

It is naive to suggest that the economic recovery of the United States could be imminent if only the United States were to introduce a "tax holiday for overseas earnings repatriation", which would bring back the earnings of United States companies sticking around overseas, but studies show that the money was not used to create jobs, but rather was invested mainly in stock buybacks and dividends.

Apple's sales revenue in overseas markets has been growing rapidly, but domestic sales in the U.S. have been stagnant for the last two years and even began to shrink in the first quarter of 2013.S&P500's overall sales have been decelerating quarter-by-quarter since September 2011 and, if inflation is excluded, have fallen into negative territory in June 2013. Money is always profit-seeking, the real economy at home in the U.S. is in pretty bad shape, so why should money come back from overseas? Even if it comes back, it is used to speculate assets to make a quick buck without going into an industry with a bleak future.

The beauty of corporate debt is not only that it can be used for buybacks to quickly drive up stock prices, but also that it can pay dividends and enjoy the "arbitrage" benefits between dividends and debt interest. Chinese listed companies rarely pay cash dividends, but 80% of U.S. S&P 500 companies pay cash dividends, and dividends are one of the main drivers for investors to warm up to a company.

Intel had $25 billion in cash on its books in 2011 and virtually no debt. Tempted by the ultra-low interest rates brought about by QE, Intel raised $6 billion in debt in 2012 for stock buybacks and dividends, which could be significantly higher in the future without better investment opportunities. Intel's logic is simple, the cost of paying dividends is about 4%, while the cost of raising debt is only 1.55%. In other words, borrowing to pay dividends can "arbitrage" 2.45%! In this case, whoever doesn't go into debt is a fool!

Thus, dividends and buybacks have formed two major channels for listed companies to send benefits to shareholders; and, in the ultra-low interest rate environment formed by the QE policy, borrowing money and dividends and debt buybacks have become a trend of listed companies. Of the two options, dividends and buybacks have a higher financial cost, while buybacks are significantly lower.

The U.S. tax code has a clear preference for debt, with interest on debt being deductible against taxable income and dividends being double taxed. If a company's income is $100, federal taxes take away $35 first, leaving the business with $65 to distribute, which is subject to a 20% profits tax, leaving shareholders with only $52 in their hands. By comparison, it's much more wonderful to be in debt. The interest on the company's liabilities is deductible against future taxable income, and the $65 after federal taxes is funneled to creditors by way of bond interest, who end up with $65 in their pocket.

Corporate debt financing is highly correlated with stock repurchases. In an artificially low interest rate environment created by QE, listed companies are incentivized to increase the size of their liabilities, whether they are repurchasing or paying dividends. The size of U.S. corporate debt raising is highly positively correlated with stock repurchase activity, in short, companies are highly leveraged for repurchases and dividend payments.

The deteriorating trend in the real economy in recent years can also be seen in the changes in the balance sheet of the US banking system, where the rate of credit creation has begun to decline since 2012, a clear sign of a cooling economy. It is important to note that the huge credit creation stimulated by stock buybacks is already included in the cooling curve of the economy, and the rate of credit shrinkage in the real real economy would be even worse if these speculative debt inflates were excluded.

The widespread stock repurchases, whether through bank loans or bond financing, have significantly increased S&P's overall debt levels. Stock prices are variable, while liabilities are rigid. On the hotbed of low interest rates created by QE, the virus of speculation and greed is rapidly festering and stock market prices have parted ways with the real economy.

"Ageing" of corporate assets

Why are listed companies sitting on huge amounts of cash and borrowing heavily? Why is the cash from debt not used to increase employees, expand capital expenditures and strengthen competitiveness?

Because money is always profit-seeking, and more accurately, the humanity behind it is always profit-seeking!

S&P500 executives borrowed money in droves, distributed dividends generously and bought back happily for the sole purpose of keeping shareholders happy, satisfying the board of directors, and finally pocketing the money from stock option encashments in good faith. As for future company growth and debt repayment, that's for the next executives to worry about.

This creates a serious problem, with a serious lack of "capital expenditures" and productive investment in general at the company level! A company's profitability depends on its core assets, which are stable, growing and generating cash flow, like a hen that lays a golden egg and needs careful care and attention. Even so, hens have a certain lifespan, and it's important to extend it as long as possible and ensure its health so that hens can lay more golden eggs. By the same token, any company's good assets have a life cycle, and companies must continuously invest in maintaining, improving, optimizing and extending the life of their assets in order to maximize returns, which is where "capital expenditure" comes in.

In the age of agriculture, where land was the core asset with a near-infinite life span, capital expenditure was spent on expanding arable land, improving soil, maintaining fertility, constructing irrigation, selecting good seeds, improving farming tools, deep ploughing, etc., with the aim of maximizing agricultural output from the land. In the industrial age, factories and production lines were core assets, and measures such as building new plants, running equipment, maintaining machines, optimizing processes, revamping technology, and upgrading skills were taken to increase capacity and expand sales to maximize profits. In the era of knowledge economy, patents, trademark rights, copyrights and creative ideas have become core assets, and the life of such intellectual property rights is protected by law on the one hand, but on the other hand, they have been eroded by piracy frenzy. For example, a film consumes a huge amount of money from filming to promotion to screening, and if it succeeds it will be profitable and if it fails it will be grainy. A new drug, from research and development to pilot testing, from audit and production, can take years or even a dozen years, costing hundreds of millions of dollars, if successful, is a super hen that lays the golden egg, becoming an excellent asset to feed a pharmaceutical group for several years or a dozen years.

Regardless of the era, and regardless of the industry, capital expenditures determine the life and effectiveness of an asset!

Capital follows the principle of profit-seeking, where returns are high, it flows. Historically, major technological revolutions have always led to increases in productivity, which in turn has meant increases in profitability, and in the lure of high profitability, capital has automatically flowed to the areas of production creation, further stimulating innovation and production and allowing for greater growth in social wealth. At this time, economic development is strong, people are fully employed, the country has a fiscal surplus, political stability is clear, and the currency is strong and inflation-free. However, in the "dry period" of technological innovation, the progress of productivity will stagnate, the high profitability of industry will be difficult to find a trace, and the return on capital expenditure will certainly deteriorate. At this point, capital will turn to asset mergers for higher returns in a way that redistributes social wealth.

The IT revolution of the 1990s, which led to significant productivity gains, is fundamentally different from the 2009–2011 productivity improvements in the U.S., which were triggered by technological innovation and resulted from layoffs; capital expenditures and productivity gains can be mutually stimulated and continue to cycle, while the latter can lead to a contraction of capital expenditures after the potential for layoffs is exhausted.

By September 2011, the spontaneous recovery of the U.S. economy had reached its limits, and significant productivity gains of the level of the IT revolution were still elusive, at which point no amount of cash in listed companies and sufficient liquidity in the financial markets would automatically flow to capital expenditures. Government monetary policy and fiscal stimulus can never counter the profit-seeking nature of capital.

Assets are depreciated, with diminishing benefits over time. The best option for capital expenditures is to keep creating new good assets, the younger the assets, the more capable they are of creating wealth, and secondly, to invest in maintaining ageing assets to slow down the rate of diminishing returns. If capital expenditures are stopped, or if they are severely underspent, the result is that new assets are undercreating, and depreciation losses on older assets continue to approach or even exceed the benefits they bring, then the eventual demise of corporate profits is a logical necessity.

U.S. capital expenditures fall quarter-on-quarter after September 2011 (*Wall Street Journal*). This is exactly what has been happening to the S&P 500 since September 2011, and whether you look at the total amount of corporate capital expenditures or the breakdown of equipment, software, construction, etc., September 2011 was the inflection point for a significant contraction in capital expenditures, and 2012 was even worse, as neither the Fed's distorted operations nor the QE3 of September 2012 have made it difficult to reverse the collapse of major corporate capital expenditures.

The lack of capital expenditure will lead to the problem of "aging" of company assets, which is an important reason for the deep mire of the European and Japanese economies. Of the countries with ageing assets, Japan has the most serious problem, with an average age of 14 years. After the financial crisis, the average profit margin of Japanese companies was only 1% to 2.5%, far below the world average. The average age of assets is slightly more than 10 years in Europe, slightly more than 8 years in the United States and the youngest in Asian countries, with an average of 7 years.

Since 2001, Japan, Europe, the United States and parts of Asia have had problems with ageing assets, and after 2010 there has been an accelerating trend of deterioration, with Asian countries approaching the United States in terms of asset age.

There are many reasons for the sluggish global economic recovery, ageing assets being one of them, the increasing scale of debt weighing heavily on the yield of increasingly aging assets, and the bullishness of the stock market ignoring the harsh realities of the economy altogether.

People will eventually pay the price for their own short-sightedness.

Comparison of asset age in Europe, America, Japan and Asia: Japan is the longest, followed by Europe. The United States is third and some Asian countries are the shortest.

Can the stock market still bounce after unplugging the QE ventilator?

How has the US stock market changed in the 5 years since the financial crisis whenever the Fed stopped its QE operations?

Data released by the U.S. Treasury Department visually demonstrates the impact of the size of QE's debt purchases on the stock market. The consequence of the Fed's bond purchases has been a significant climb in the Fed's balance sheet, where the size of bond holdings with maturities of more than five years is highly correlated with the movement of the US stock market.

While correlation does not imply causality, QE's bond purchases have a strong impact on equity markets, with the S&P500 issuing corporate bonds, mainly medium and long term bonds over 5 years old, which are financed primarily for equity buybacks, and when the Fed implements QE, it will be printing money in a big way to concentrate its purchases of medium and long term Treasuries and MBS bonds in the bond market, especially two rounds of distortion operations (OT) and QE3. Bond investors sell their medium – and long-term Treasuries and MBS to the central bank, getting a large amount of cash on the one hand, and having to invest their cash in the medium and long term on the other hand, medium – and long-term corporate bonds are bound to become an obvious substitute in a limited supply of Treasuries.

It is because of this asset conversion act of replacing treasury bonds with corporate bonds, the Fed's money printing machine and the stock market connection pipeline is completely opened, the new money created by QE, to be able to pour into the stock market, stimulating the stock market soaring.

In the U.S. Treasury Department's analysis, the size of the Fed's debt purchases has an impact on the stock market that can be accurate even to a single week. From January 2009 to April 2013, in 159 weeks when the Fed's weekly debt purchases were greater than $5 billion, the S&P 500 Index jumped 540 points, or 54%; in 62 weeks when it was less than $5 billion, the stock market rose 141 points, or only 15%; and in 29 weeks when the Fed stopped buying debt, the stock market fell 51 points, or 2%.

After the 2008 financial crisis, the United States stock market rally was broadly divided into two phases: the first phase, from early 2009 to September 2011, can be described as a "reflexive recovery" under monetary stimulus. During this period, S&P500 immediately laid off staff out of reflex, instinctively seized the lifebuoy of low interest rates and low exchange rates, held its ground amidst the financial crisis, lowered costs, improved production efficiency, took full advantage of the dollar exchange rate dividend, strengthened its profit base, and the stock market rebounded strongly.

From September 2011 onwards, the stock market rally entered its second phase, and in the continuing loose monetary environment, there was an "exuberant rally" in the stock market, where stock price performance began to be disconnected from economic realities, and gradually moved away, driven not by real growth in corporate performance, but by the "accounting revolution" of stock buybacks.

The stock market thrives on monetary stimulus.

Due to the nature of capital for profit, the huge amount of cash on the books of listed companies has not been invested in the consolidation of the long-term development potential of the company's capital expenditure, but rather wasted to meet the short-sighted interests of shareholders to pay dividends and buybacks, the vast majority of companies for this reason, at the expense of carrying huge amounts of debt. This not only exacerbates the worsening trend of aging assets and undermines future profitability, but also exposes companies to the twin risks of huge debt and sudden interest rate changes.

A large percentage of the money for stock buybacks came from the banking system and the bond market, which was flooded with extremely cheap money during the operation of the QE policy. The S&P500's high-quality bonds, naturally a must-have in the eyes of yield-crazed fund managers, have driven the cost of financing stock buybacks to unprecedented levels.

In an "exuberantly rising" stock market, whether the "exuberance" can be sustained depends not on the company's own performance growth, but on whether the funding chain for continued share buybacks will break.

QE's cheap monetary policy has made the stock market accustomed to an abundant supply of capital, and the ultra-low interest rate environment has paralyzed the pricing of risk in the bond market, which has become a far more bubbly bet than the stock market.

If the Fed does start to fade out of QE, it is the bond market that is in danger of collapse in the first place. A re-examination of risk will require higher interest compensation, and if interest rates soar past a psychological floor, the risk is beyond the limits of what bond investors can endure, and a wave of sell-offs will cause the bond market to bleed out. If the bond market can't sustain cheap stock buyback funding, excessive financing costs will scare off the CEOs of stock buybacks, and the chain of funds supporting the stock market boom will eventually break. At that time, no matter how beautiful the earnings per share story was, and no matter whether PE had investment potential, a stock market that had broken the main capital chain was destined to become a slaughterhouse that people scrambled to escape.

A raucous bond market

In China, when people talk about capital markets, the word that comes up most often must be the stock market. Since China opened up its stock market in the early 1990s, hundreds of millions of Chinese stockholders have been able to deduce many myths of overnight riches during the 20 years of stock market turmoil, as well as encounter countless painful lessons of being held captive and cut. While winning and losing are important, the excitement, tension, pain and pleasure that come with a sharp rise and fall are the real temptations to resist. The bond market, by contrast, gives the average person a rather distant and unfamiliar impression of what they can do with their bonds. Waiting six months or a year to pay interest? If the amount invested is too small, retail investors won't feel the appreciation of their wealth at all. In addition, bond prices look far less volatile than stocks, and stockholders who have long been accustomed to the excitement will have a hard time tolerating the monotony and tedium.

In fact, the U.S. bond market is far larger, with more products and deeper play than the stock market, and almost all of the major financial innovations have originated in the bond market.

In 2012, the total size of the United States bond market was $3,814 trillion and the total market value of the stock market was $18.67 trillion

In terms of size, the U.S. bond market has a capacity of $38 trillion, roughly twice the market value of stocks. In terms of type, there are national bonds, institutional bonds, municipal bonds, corporate bonds, mortgage-backed securities, asset-backed securities, short-term bills, etc. In terms of the number of products, out of the $9 trillion in corporate bonds alone, more than 80,000 companies have issued bond products of varying maturities and interest rates, with more than 37,000, and at least 5,000 actively traded bonds. The bond market far outstrips the stock market in both volume and complexity. Also, bond trading is much larger in capital than stocks, with more active bonds generally trading at 70 times the amount of stocks.

In the stock market, investors want to inquire about the shares of thousands of listed companies is not a big effort, each stock no matter how much liquidity, after all, the same quality, all represent a certain percentage of the company's ownership, the stock price calculation is also relatively simple, trading centralized, transparent information, and completely electronic, investment in stocks is fast and cheap.

But it's a different story when it comes to trading bonds issued by tens of thousands of companies, tens of thousands of bond products with different maturities and different interest rates, with prices that are far more complicated to calculate than stocks amidst constant changes in credit ratings, retention times, interest rate fluctuations, exchange rate movements, and other factors. The biggest headache is that the bond market does not have a centralized trading platform similar to a stock exchange, the main trading still relies on the traditional market maker approach, sales managers and traders are the soul of the market, and their relationships are the real channel for the bond market.

For example, when a pension fund manager was about to buy a $25 million 5-year U.S. Treasury bond, he first called the sales manager of a market maker, and although he knew a lot of marketing people, after years of screening, he finally locked down a few of the most reliable old relationships, who not only specialize in the 5-year Treasury bond market, but also have accumulated many years of large customer resources, and the most favorable price.

When the market maker's sales manager receives a call from the retirement fund manager, he immediately agrees to provide the best price, and he wants to make sure the deal is successful, because every bond sale means a big bonus at the end of the year for him.

The sales manager told the buyer to wait on the line for a moment, then ripped his voice out to ask the Company trader sitting nearby for a quote, "Five years and 25?" 25 is the abbreviation for $25 million, the trader is an old partner, more than 5 years of experience in treasury bonds trading, so even the word "treasury bonds" is omitted, time is money, every second has a cost! The trader yelled without thinking, "10!" which refers to 101-10, 101 being the nearest market price and 10 being short for 10/32 percent.

Traders start from a different point of view than sales managers, where sales are measured against total sales volume, whereas traders are measured against trading profits, and their instinct is to buy low and sell high to earn spreads. Although traders and sales managers are partners, money-losing deals are not done. For the sales manager, who knows the market and customer psychology well, he felt that the trader's quote was a little too high, and asked, "Can you do 9 and 3/4? It's an old client!" The sales manager wants the trader to yield another $1/128^{th}$ of a percentage point.

One of the basic training that the Jewish financial family gave their children from an early age was to memorize the fine spreads that corresponded to 1/8, 1/16, 1/32, 1/64, 1/128... Because in the financial business, the small spreads, the huge amounts of money, and the speed of response required are far beyond the imagination of ordinary people. The deal had to be finalized in the blink of an eye and there was no time to press the calculator. A little slow in the head, either the business is lost or the costs and benefits are miscalculated, and $1/128^{th}$ of a percentage point is $1,953,125 for a $25 million transaction!

Knowing the importance of the old client and the importance of the partner, the trader, after doing a quick math in his head, immediately replied, "Nine and three quarters is fine!" The sales manager immediately told the pension fund manager who had been waiting online, "I can give you 9 and 3/4 even though the market price is 10!" and the pension fund manager rejoiced with joy, "Deal!" The sales manager says "deal" into the phone! One side shouted to the trader,

"Sale 25, price 9 and 3/4, deal with the ×× fund!" The trader flew in to place the order and yelled, "Deal!" The sales manager finally confirms with the pension client and then hangs up the phone.

The entire transaction took only a few dozen seconds!

Retirement fund managers want to buy at the lowest price, while traders pursue selling at the highest price, and sales managers want the deal to close quickly, and if it drags on for more than a minute, then the buyer hangs up the phone to call the next market maker for a quote and business is lost. The sales manager must make a compromise offer on the fly, while the trader's brain must run at high speed when processing several sales managers' offers at the same time, ranking buyers in order of importance and then calculating spreads separately to assess the cost of buying and the risk of volatility. He had to make a decision in a second or two. A super trader's brain is no longer a matter of "software" processing speed, but rather "hardware" is born to grow differently.

Immediately after the order is confirmed, the "middle table" of the bond market maker takes over and their role is to control credit and risk. Since counterparties have different credit and vary in the amount and number of collaborations, they have customized different "credit lines" for each business partner and have the right to warn the company if the risk threshold is exceeded. At the same time, they must also have aggregate control over company-wide risk and monitor it in real time.

When the middle table is cleared, the order goes to the "back office". The back-office is responsible for taking care of logistical matters, such as accounting for the number and amount of purchases and sales, the time and manner of delivery and the means of payment, identifying possible discrepancies in orders, accounting for the company's profit and loss, and processing all remaining details on the same day. Finally, the accounting department accounts for the transactions and collates a schedule of bond interest income and amounts receivable.

The role of market makers is to promote liquidity in the bond market and reduce transaction costs between buyers and sellers. The largest of these 21 is the Treasury bond market, the first-level market maker, can directly deal with the Federal Reserve, the Fed's open market committee of interest rate policy, it is on these 21 first-level market makers to implement, their status is equivalent to the gold standard era of the Bank of England relied on the five major gold dealers. They are always ready to buy and sell bonds in the market and take a certain spread in them. Under normal conditions, the 5-year Treasury spread is only $1/128^{th}$ of a percentage point, or $1 million in trading volume, and market makers could theoretically earn $78,125. In practice, however, a good trader can only make about half the profit, or $39.06, by trading at the midpoint of the call-buy price and the call-offer price.

Also included in that meager $39.06 difference are financing costs, apportioned costs for front, middle and back office, as well as indirect payroll costs, sales bonuses, marketing, system support and more. After deducting direct and indirect costs, the net profit component is exposed to a number of market risks, the biggest variable being interest rate volatility, with international news, economic data, and unforeseen events all potentially causing significant interest rate shocks. During trading hours, changing interest rates often cause the price of 1% of Treasuries to fluctuate, i.e. the price of $1 million of Treasuries, which can go up or down by $10,000! A slight delay on the part of the trader and the $39 profit would be eaten to death by a $10,000 loss, which is the full result of 250 successful trades of $1 million Treasuries!

Market makers are licking blood on the tip of the knife, in the meager spread to make a living, you must rely on the huge trading scale to make money. 2012, in the 10 trillion dollars of circulation in the bond market, the total amount of daily trading up to $532 billion, second only to the foreign exchange market of $4 trillion a day trading volume. In addition to Treasuries, there is a total of $8 trillion in corporate debt, which trades at about $180 billion a day. Also, $20 trillion in other types of bonds are traded frequently in the market.

For a market maker to be able to absorb a bond transaction of this size, it must have a sizeable bond inventory and significant funding capacity to provide sufficient liquidity to the market. For the U.S. stock market, the impetus for the stock market's rally is increasingly dependent on stock buybacks, which in turn rely on bond financing from public companies. If the stock of corporate bonds of market makers falls to a certain extent, it will inevitably lead to a lack of liquidity in the bond market and rising transaction costs, which will eventually force listed companies' financing costs to rise sharply and weaken their stock repurchase capacity, thus leading to a weak stock market rise.

A market maker's inventory of corporate bonds becomes a weathervane for observing stock market changes.

Corporate bond inventory shrinks, market makers fail to adjust

It is well known that lakes play an important balancing role in the river system. When floods occur, the lakes can absorb the excess water to avoid floods caused by soaring river levels; when river flows are insufficient, the lakes can provide additional water to keep the rivers from drying up, thus playing a balancing role in regulating the flow of the water system.

Market maker's bond inventory is equivalent to the lake in the bond water system, if bond prices rise too high, the market maker will throw a large amount of inventory to make spread profits, suppress the momentum of the price surge; if bond prices are too low, the market maker will absorb low, expand inventory, waiting for the price to rebound to profit, thus pulling up the bond market price. Market makers therefore play an important function as price stabilizers in the bond market.

U.S. bond market maker's corporate bond inventory shrinks severely. However, since the 2008 financial crisis, market makers' regulatory functions in the bond market have failed so badly that the bond market has been "flooded" with absurdly low yields. Of these, the problem of corporate debt is most prominent.

In October 2007, US market makers' corporate bond inventories reached an all-time high of $235 billion, and extreme optimism in the stock market peaked, with market makers hoarding bond assets on a massive scale in the belief that they were a bargain. Ultimately, the collapse of the financial markets caused market makers to lose a lot of money.

Once bitten by a snake, ten years fear the well rope. Market makers' stocks of corporate debt have never recovered since the financial crisis, and as of February 2012, only $42.4 billion was left in corporate debt inventories, down 82% from their historical peak! As of March 2013, it was only about $56 billion.

Market maker's stock of corporate bonds serious shrinkage led to two consequences: first, the price of corporate bonds rose and lost the brakes, the appreciation effect is very obvious, thus attracting all sorts of funds into the bond market for gold, there is an obvious bubble phenomenon, this phenomenon is similar to the drying up of lakes, the rainy season river level soared; second, due to the lack of liquidity provided by the market maker, the result is that the purchase of corporate bonds is easy and difficult, which is like the dry season river break.

Market makers have sharply reduced inventories of corporate bonds, while at the same time massively increasing inventories of Treasuries. From May 2011 to the end of the year, treasury bond inventories nearly doubled to $74.7 billion, while corporate bond inventories fell by half to $61.1 billion, the first time that market makers' treasury bond inventories exceeded corporate bond inventories. In fact, the reason behind is simple, because the proceeds from holding Treasuries exceeded corporate bonds, which is naturally the credit of the Fed's quantitative easing, because the Fed only buys Treasuries and institutional MBS bonds during the QE operation, the price of Treasuries rose more significantly. From mid-2007 to the end of 2011, the total return on treasury bond holdings reached 38 per cent, more than 37 per cent of corporate bonds, and treasury bonds are safer and more in line with new financial regulatory principles.

Market makers have massively increased their treasury bond inventories while corporate bond inventories have plummeted. Here, one needs to figure out that bond prices and yields are the exact opposite. In the case of an investment house, for example, people will consider both the price and the rent when buying a house. If the home price is $1 million and the annual rental income is $50,000, the annual rate of return on an investment house is 5%. If home prices rise to $1.1 million and annual rental income remains the same, the return on investment falls to 4.5 percent; similarly, if home prices fall to $900,000 and rents remain the same, the return on investment rises to 5.6 percent. Housing prices are inversely proportional to the rate of return on investment. The rationale for bonds is similar to a house, where the price of a bond is equal to the price of a house, the interest income on a bond is equal to rent, and the yield on a bond is similar to the return on investment of a house. The more people who rush to buy bonds, the higher the bond price gets, but the lower its yield; when everyone sells, the bond price goes down and the yield goes up. In the process, the interest on the bond remains constant.

When the Fed launches QE, how does one eat a large amount of Treasuries and MBS bonds from the bond market each month? That is, printing money to exchange with 21 primary market makers. Of course, printing money is a figurative way of saying that the Fed doesn't need a money printer at all, it just taps a series of numbers on a computer screen, then presses the "enter" button and the money comes out, as much as it takes, without having to open a factory or struggle to operate one. The result of operating QE is that the market maker's bond inventory floods the Fed's balance sheet, and they are credited with a corresponding amount in the Fed's account. In this way, market makers hold a large amount of currency in their hands, and the total amount of money in the entire economy expands, which is how the Fed injects money into the financial markets through QE.

When the market makers have the money, they go to the Treasury to bid for new Treasuries, and as a result the government has the money to spend, which is the primary market. Then the market makers then distribute the bonds through their own channels, layer by layer, all over the world, and eventually everyone buys and sells bonds through market makers, which is the secondary market. The previous example of pension fund managers buying Treasuries occurred in the secondary market.

Market makers are also the largest investment banks, they help companies underwriting corporate bonds, often themselves first advance all the bonds to buy, so that the company got cash, change hands for stock buybacks, speculate high stock prices, and then CEOs laughingly share the bonus. Market makers can hold corporate bonds or resell them to bond investors such as pension funds, mutual funds, hedge funds, money funds, large corporations, foreign institutions, etc.

As there is too much money in the financial markets, fund managers are hot with the existence of large sums of cash on the books, the money does not hurry to invest out, stay in hand is idle. At this point, once a corporate bond is issued, everyone tends to rush to it. While bond prices have risen, yields have worsened. With the QE round of coding, the currency surplus has become a currency flood, and fund managers are like hungry wolves with green eyes at this point, who immediately pounce on bonds with slightly better yields when they see them.

Stimulated by QE, the size of corporate bond issuance grew by as much as 10% per year, and the cheap money obtained from bond financing turned into stock buybacks at the turn of the century, with the S&P500 growing by 16.7% amid strong expectations of stock appreciation.

Since 2008, corporate bonds have issued a staggering $5.7 trillion in total, while yields have plummeted all the way from 5.7% to 2.0%.

Yields plummeted by more than half, meaning bond prices soared. If market makers have large bond inventories, this is a good time to sell them for a big profit, and such selling will effectively dampen the bond price rise and thus achieve price regulation. However, due to the shortage of stocks, market makers were unable to effectively play the role of the lake's excess water intake, resulting in the bond market being flooded with money.

As bond investors gleefully snapped up exorbitantly expensive corporate bonds, they gradually realized that holding these bonds was a growing concern because when they wanted to sell them for cash, they had to find a market maker, who gave a very poor offer. And when other institutions wanted to buy corporate bonds, market makers were selling at equally disappointing prices. The gap between the buy and sell prices quoted by market makers is growing, and the anger of bond investors is growing. This is just like the new housing market is extremely hot, while the secondary housing market is very quiet, there are houses that want to sell to cash in, but people who want to buy a house can not start. The information of both buyers and sellers in the bond market is in the hands of market makers, who are reluctant to expand their bond inventories and provide financing. The market maker's attitude is, do you want to buy bonds? Sorry, I'm out of stock. Do you want to sell bonds? Sorry, I'm short of money.

The shortage of market makers' corporate bond inventory has created a serious bottleneck in the bond market.

The deterioration of the liquidity of the corporate bond market has finally angered bond investors, who have repeatedly communicated with market makers, but the market makers say they can't help. UBS, Goldman Sachs and BlackRock are all pioneers in building their own platforms. However, so far the effect has not been significant; in 2013, UBS' bond trading system had only 30 transactions per day, a sadly small number.

In fact, the market maker system has its reasonable points, the bond market is different from the stock, foreign exchange or gold market, in these markets price fluctuations are extremely normal, every day up and down 10% or even 20% have repeatedly appeared, for investors used to high risk, the fight is thrilling. But the nature of the bond market is completely different, and investors are in the mindset of seeking stability and safety. The role of the market maker "lake" throughput of water is by no means dispensable, but a basic property of the bond market. Where in the world would anyone dare invest in U.S. Treasuries if bond prices were plummeting and soaring every day? How can an investment institution with high security requirements such as pensions and insurance companies withstand such a toss? Electronic trading platforms that connect buyers and sellers directly to their needs can certainly reduce transaction costs, but it also inevitably creates a market resonance effect. When everyone is bullish on bonds together, there's a simultaneous mad rush; when everyone's pessimism is rapidly contagious, bond prices avalanche. It would be like filling in all the lakes, and there would be no impediment to the flow of water, but the rivers would flood uncontrollably during the rainy season and the riverbeds would dry up to the bottom during the dry season.

Difficulties in buying and selling corporate bonds due to declining inventories will eventually force buyers to demand compensation from issuing companies, which will be reflected in rising bond yields. The root cause of this problem is still the Federal Reserve's QE policy, without the Fed as the largest buyer of the bottom, the investment return on treasury bonds can not exceed corporate bonds, after all, should be high risk brings high returns, market makers will not reduce the inventory of corporate bonds to such a degree. the longer the implementation of QE policy, the bond market distortions will be more serious.

If the U.S. corporate bond market is seriously distorted, the junk in corporate debt can be described as extremely distorted.

Junk bonds, "subprime" in corporate bonds

Junk bonds, as the name implies, are junk in bonds, and are no different in nature from subprime. The "subprime" loans, which were hotly debated by the 2008 financial crisis, specifically refer to the U.S. mortgage loans "no job, no income, no assets" of the "three no-people" to apply for loans, these loans will be destined for a large-scale default when the price of the house falls. In the days of the real estate boom in the United States, banks desperately issued subprime loans to produce "virus pork"; investment banks boldly packaged into MBS bonds and CDOs, processed and packaged into standard "virus pork cans"; the rating company responsible for quality inspection turned a blind eye and arbitrarily affixed the AAA rating of high-quality products, resulting in the poisoning of the area of the world's investors.

The issuers of junk bonds are, of course, junk companies, which are the "three no-goods" in business. Most of them are "no fist products, no fixed customers, no steady cash flow". In the economic boom, consumers spend a lot of money, less concerned about the product brand and cost-performance ratio, and the junk company's products can also get a share of the pie; but in the recession, consumers tighten their purse strings, more sensitive to the cost-performance ratio, in the case of the same price, more valued quality. Garbage companies generally lack core technology, have weak product competitiveness, inadequate management level, low quality and high price, are often eliminated in the fierce market competition, cash flow is highly unstable, if excessive debt, the default rate will rise sharply.

In 2009, the U.S. junk bond issuance finally crossed the $100 billion threshold after the crisis; in 2010, it crossed the 200 billion mark for the first time; in 2012, it continued to perform the "junk legend", surpassing the 250 billion peak; in 2013, it is even more welcome to open the door, issuing 150 billion in early May, the whole year will easily surpass the record of 2012, setting a new "junk glory". The total size of junk bonds has ballooned to $1.1 trillion, and its share of the $9.2 trillion corporate bond market has reached 12%!

While history is surprisingly similar, markets are always forgetful.

Prior to the 2006 financial crisis, the total size of the U.S. mortgage-backed bond (MBS) market was about $10 trillion, of which $1.5 trillion, or 15 percent, was subordinated to MBS. 2013's junk bonds increasingly resemble 2006's subordinated bonds.

From 2009–2013, junk bond prices soared 21% annually and yields plummeted from 20% to an unprecedented 5%, and on May 8, 2013, junk bond yields fell below 5% for the first time since records began, hitting a record low of 4.97%! This is equivalent to the level of the 10-year U.S. Treasury bond in July 2007.

Treasuries are the most secure breed in the bond market as long as people don't worry about a US collapse. Among bonds of the same maturity, Treasuries have the highest prices and the lowest yields. In May 2013, junk companies successfully "upgraded" to the 2007 US National Credit!

If it is the other way around, it is that the U.S. national credit in 2007 has been reduced to "junk" by 2013.

History is repeating itself as mutual funds, pensions and insurance companies, which went on a buying spree for subprime mortgage-backed bonds, became big buyers of junk bonds in 2013, with mutual funds alone taking in 70 per cent of new junk bonds issued in the first half of 2013. Everyone knew junk bonds would become junk sooner or later, but with the Fed's QE program in place, no one believed the crisis would break out immediately. The biggest pain for investors now is that they can't buy, and the future is that they can't sell.

If U.S. home prices could rise indefinitely, subprime lenders would not be in massive default that year, and they would simply apply to the bank for a "value-added mortgage" for the portion of the house that appreciates each year and would be able to use the cash to pay off the mortgage. However, once house prices stop rising, the financial chain of the "three have-nots" will quickly break down, resulting in a massive default.

The price of junk bonds is like the price of housing, and as long as yields fall infinitely, then the price of junk bonds can rise infinitely. In this way, the junk companies can always borrow new money in the market, keep rolling in debt, and defaults don't happen. But can the hypothesis of an infinite decline in yields hold up?

Every time the Fed has created a hotbed of low interest rates since junk bonds became popular in the 1980s, the yield on junk bonds has fallen, but they are still more attractive than Treasuries and other normal bonds. With too much money in the hands of institutions, the instinct to pursue high yields drives money to "nice" junk bonds, which are easy for junk companies to borrow, so the default rate is not high. However, whenever a crisis strikes, such as in 1991, 2001 and 2008, junk bonds are always the first to experience a rise in yields, followed by a massive sell-off and a spike in default rates.

If you look at the default rate of junk bonds on a 10-year cycle, the historical trend is clear: BB-rated junk bonds are 19% defaulted, B-rated is over 30%, and CCC/C-rated is close to 60%! Clearly, junk bonds can never be held for long. So, the mentality of institutional investors is just short-term speculation, make money and run, and a consensus has long been formed that once the interest rate trend reverses, the price of junk bonds plummeted unusually sharply in the future.

When pestilence and disease set in, the elderly and children were often the first to fall ill. When a financial crisis strikes, it is always the weakest link in the debt chain that breaks first, and the precursor to a debt collapse is always the reversal of interest rate trends.

In early 2007, the subprime mortgage crisis began with an "interest rate reset" that triggered a break in the subprime lenders' funding chains and a tsunami of defaults that swept the globe in 2008, and by 2013, junk bond yields were absurdly low and the entire $38 trillion bond market was like a cauldron about to boil. Once the yield on junk bonds rises, institutional investors who suddenly realize that interest rate risk is grossly undervalued will wake up, junk companies will suddenly have a hard time borrowing money in the market, and CDS (credit default swaps), the wind vane of default risk, will skyrocket like a rocket.

While junk bonds are not the biggest bubble in the bond market, they are destined to be the first casualty.

Expound

Among the popular movie titles in the United States, there is a category of "zombie" blockbusters, where people are infected with some kind of virus and turn into zombies, and normal people are bitten by them and infected with the virus and turn into zombies, and then more zombies go crazy and bite people until entire cities and even countries are full of zombies.

That's what's happening in the bond market.

The Fed's bond purchase is actually spreading a kind of "virus" called madness, with the market in high quality bonds less and less, fund managers become "zombies", they fight for a piece of "yield" assets and bite each other, until the market in the sane normal people less and less, bond prices have been speculated up.

When there are no more normal assets in the US market, the "zombies" will rush to Asia, Europe and South America, spreading the "virus" to emerging markets and the world.

In an environment where the recovery of the real economy is weak, each economy is an "ageing" asset with slow cash flow growth, and when all the major countries of the world joined together in a monetary easing spree, the floods of money rushed to these unused assets, with no fundamental improvement in cash flow, but a severe overvaluation of the assets. The world calls this low-yield, low-risk situation the "new normal"!

Under the "new normal", as long as there is a central bank escort, as long as there is a continuous flow of loose money, the market risk will no longer exist. People seem to have invented the "economic perpetual motion" that printing money can bring about a perpetual asset price boom!

In fact, "loose money", "perpetual asset appreciation" and "economic perpetual motion" are logically impossible. If, as a thought experiment, we assume that the US bond market is in a completely closed state, with the central bank constantly printing money to buy bonds and forcing money into the market, what is its ultimate limit state? The Fed will gradually buy all the $38 trillion of bonds in the market, the bond market will be flooded with the same amount of cash, the central bank's own balance sheet also expanded to the same size, in this "ideal" state, bond fund managers will what? They will all starve to death because there are no longer any assets in the market that can generate cash flow and the bond market will cease to exist.

Thus, there is a theoretical limit to easy money, and central banks cannot eat into bonds indefinitely, so asset perpetual appreciation is a myth, and economic perpetual motion is even less likely to be invented. This is the fundamental reason why the Fed began winding down in May 2013 in preparation for its exit from QE.

When asset prices no longer rise, yields simultaneously reach their lowest limit point. Everyone wants asset prices to stabilize at a high level without having to fall, but history tells people that this never happens. Asset prices are like a jet plane, if it runs out of fuel, it can't glide through the high skies and will just go down headfirst, all that happens at the same time is the yields go sky high!

The fatal thing is that the central bank does not have a parachute for investors when asset prices fall from the heights.

One might ask, what if the economy did recover under the monetary stimulus? Growing cash flows will be able to support higher asset prices. Unfortunately, monetary movements have their own laws and do not transfer to the will of man. If money is compared to water, its laws of motion always flow along the "steepest" slope, and this "steepness" is the profit margin.

When the currency is overly loose for a long period of time, the margins generated by rising asset prices will be higher than the margins of the operating industry, and the wider this gap, the less money will flow into the industry and will only chase asset appreciation. In more extreme cases, it may even backfire on the industry's money and go on an asset frenzy. What if the government encouraged money to flow into industry, or forced money to change its flow? It's like building a dam to block water, as long as there's a big gap in the water level of profit margins, the flow of money will always bypass the barrier and continue to pour into high margin industries.

U.S. QE policy is bound to fail in the end, and the longer it lasts, the worse the failure. Likewise, monetary stimulus in Europe, Japan and other countries is unlikely to succeed, and is nothing more than a repetition of the disasters that have repeated themselves throughout history.

In the real world, in the midst of the bond price frenzy, there will always be a few sober and daring investors in the market, who are like extremely patient hunters, constantly building up their strength, preparing ammunition, and suddenly launching a short-selling attack when bond prices are at the end of a powerful surge. At this point, a small but determined amount of capital power is enough to rouse a large number of followers to turn against each other, resulting in a sudden reversal of market prices. The fall in bond prices will trigger an accelerated rise in yields, creating a strong expectation that bond holdings will shrink, leading more people to join the sell-off army, and the situation will become untenable under a vicious cycle. This is why asset prices are unlikely to stabilize at high levels once they top out.

Given the current state of the global real economy, where ultra-low interest rates have left both equity and bond markets severely overvalued, a reversal in yields would force a massive correction in asset prices, which, if it evolved into a price dive, would likely trigger a new financial crisis.

Naturally, the first to fall in the corporate bond market is junk bonds, which then ripple through the bond prices of normal companies, leading to a break in the chain of buy-backs of listed companies in the stock market, triggering the stock market collapse.

However, junk bonds are only the most dangerous bubble in the bond market, but by no means the worst. The plunge in asset prices in the corporate bond and equity markets is not the worst situation in the financial markets either. They only act as a fuse, and what triggers is a much larger financial derivatives market and a much more explosive sovereign credit market.

Monetary policy doesn't solve the problem, monetary policy itself is the problem!

CHAPTER III

The Money Scare, The Sleepwalking Shadow Party

It is impossible to understand the nature of twentieth-century finance without understanding the fractional reserve system, and it is impossible to see the financial markets of the twenty-first century without understanding that repo mortgages create money.

Current monetary and financial theory is still stuck in the traditional era of the 1980s, while the changes in the world financial markets today have rendered the intellectual content and analytical methods of the past largely invalid.

If in an article analyzing the world monetary and financial situation, you don't find the key words repo market, repo rates, collateral depreciation, asset swaps, sub-collateralization, shadow banking, shadow money, etc., you can basically just throw the article in the trash because it doesn't address the key parts of today's world financial markets at all, and it's impossible to get to the bottom of the problem!

In the US, the supply of shadow money is more than three times that of traditional M2, how can one understand asset prices in the financial markets without understanding the principles of shadow money creation? The importance of shadow banking lies not in the lack of regulation, but in the fact that it is the center of the creation of shadow money, which overrides all other problems with shadow banking.

Only by establishing a completely new knowledge system can people understand why such bizarre events as the "money shortage" can occur in the era of global monetary proliferation, and only then can they be deeply alerted to the fact that behind the money shortage lies the precursor of a more serious financial crisis.

Syria crisis, timely rain for Wall Street?

On 21 August 2013, the world was shocked by the news that Syrian opposition forces claimed that Syrian government forces had used chemical weapons and killed more than 1,300 people, and on 23 August, the United States Department of Defense began deploying military forces to the Middle East, and on 24 August, United States President Barack Obama said that the Syrian civil war had involved the "core national interests" of the United States, and on 27 August, the military said that the war was ready to begin only by presidential order. From the news of the chemical weapons to the completion of the U.S. deployment to the war, it took only seven days, and the war in Iraq and Afghanistan, the U.S. prepared for at least a year and a half.

Curiously, as recently as 18 August, the United Nations chemical weapons investigation team had just arrived in the Syrian capital, Damascus, at the request of the Syrian Government to investigate the use of chemical weapons by the opposition. The Syrian Government claims that in March, the opposition used chemical weapons to cause mass casualties, while the opposition denies this allegation and believes that the Government used chemical weapons. Because of the entanglement between the two sides, the United Nations investigation team was brought in by the Syrian Government to find out the truth. Right under the watchful eye of the United Nations investigation team, chemical weapons suddenly took a huge toll. The warring parties in Syria, whoever they are, would dare to use chemical weapons in such a situation, either with audacity or with utter stupidity.

However, regardless of the truth, the United States has struck out in a big way. This crisis of war has come at an extreme moment, has Obama been prepared to strike at Syria for a long time?

The age of big data might as well speak with big data. If you look up the global news headlines for "Obama, Syria" using Google's trending search tool, "Google Trend," you will find that Obama has rarely addressed Syria in the past five years. If Google's search technology is to be trusted, then as soon as Obama mentions Syria in public, all of these comments will quickly make their way into Google's search engine in today's online society.

However, the search results show that in the five years leading up to August 16, 2013, the set of keywords "Obama, Syria" appeared in news headlines worldwide with almost zero frequency!

It was only after August 16 that Obama began to talk heavily about Syria. Obviously, for Obama, the Syrian crisis came so suddenly that he didn't have much of a mind to prepare himself. If so, why make a hasty decision on whether or not to go to war in a matter of days? War is no child's play, after all! Russia questioned the evidence, China called for the truth, the UN argued, the EU objected, NATO refused to participate, Britain hesitated to back down, the American people were reluctant to go to war, and the people of the Middle East were even more reluctant to go to war. In the case of the Iraq war, the world had been ignored by the so-called evidence of "weapons of mass destruction" by the British and American intelligence agencies, and it was not easy to win the trust of others when the trust had been lost.

However, in the political atmosphere in Washington, the strong smell of gunpowder permeates everywhere, and the question of whether to fight or not seems to be no longer a question of evidence of chemical weapons, but rather a question of Obama and the United States Government cannot "lose faith in the world". Because Obama said he would fight, he had to fight. It's a strange and absurd logic. Even murder suspects must be guaranteed by law the right to plead their case, and the Syrian government has been convicted to death by the US with insufficient evidence of chemical weapons, and is ready to execute in 7 days!

The extreme perversity of the anxiety of the United States in such a hurry is less like preparing for a real war, and more like using the threat of war as a smokescreen.

In fact, just as the situation in Syria is rapidly deteriorating, Wall Street is experiencing a shockwave!

Bernanke exited QE in May, June again clear attitude, the international financial markets are in chaos. Even worse, the interest rate trend is starting to reverse and US Treasury yields are skyrocketing!

In early May, the 10-year Treasury yield was just 1.66%, and by August 16, it surprisingly soared to 2.83%! That's a magnitude not seen in 30 years!

The U.S. government is the borrower of national debt and the best credit in the market, and anyone can go bankrupt, but as long as the U.S. exists, the U.S. government can always print money to pay it back. So the yield on Treasuries is the lower bound in the bond market, and any other bond of the same type will yield more than Treasuries. If Treasury yields skyrocket 70%, other bonds will only go up more outrageously, and what about the junk in bonds? Of course it's miserable.

The spike in bond yields, the plunge in bond prices, means the bond market has suffered a terrible sell-off. One might ask, what's so scary about soaring interest rates with a yield of 2.83% still low?

Treasury yields, the pricing benchmark for financial asset prices across the U.S., have risen so dramatically that they will hit the pricing of the $38 trillion bond market and the valuation of the $19 trillion stock market hard! The reason why Wall Street financial assets are where they are now is that the 10-year Treasury yield is only around 1.66%, and when that yield gets to 2.83%, then the prices of all kinds of assets will be under heavy pressure for a downward correction, and in August, the U.S. stock market saw its biggest decline in a year and a half, and that's why.

So can the Fed continue to buy bonds in the market to ease the pressure of soaring interest rates? This is precisely the purpose of implementing the QE policy. But now that's a bad move!

Since the Fed has already said that it is ready to exit QE, then the future treasury bond market will lack one of the biggest buyers, the Fed ate 90% of the new treasury bonds, if it is absent, who in the market can afford the huge supply of treasury bonds? Chinese, Japanese and foreign investors will think this way, since you want to run, I can only run faster than you to avoid bigger losses in the future. As a result, everyone fled the national debt together, the price of the national debt naturally fell sharply, and the more the national debt was held, the more severe the depreciation of assets.

In June 2013, foreign capital fled US dollar assets to a greater extent than during the peak of the financial tsunami in 2008.

Just 3 months down the line, the Fed's balance sheet is in shock with a $300 billion floating loss! Central banks, which hold huge amounts of U.S. debt as foreign exchange reserves, are all frightened and scrambling for their lives. China and Japan, the two largest holders of U.S. Treasuries, reduced their holdings by a massive $42 billion in June, the highest single-month record for such a reduction! Throughout the month of June, foreign investors went on a frenzied sell-off of United States Treasuries, corporate bonds and stocks and all dollar assets, and the United States financial markets suffered an exodus of foreign capital even more violent than that which occurred in 2008 when Lehman Brothers collapsed and the financial tsunami broke out!

It is for this reason that yields on 10-year Treasuries have soared so violently that the Fed's approach to depressing interest rates through QE debt purchases is on the verge of spiraling out of control!

As asset prices fell dramatically, Wall Street fund managers in pursuit of risky returns snapped to find that their highly leveraged, already overinflated assets were instantly at risk of massive devaluations and liquidity depletion. To ease the pressure on funding, they were forced to sell off overseas assets on a large scale to recover dollars. Emerging market countries that have been hotly touted in the wave of dollar easing, especially those with more open capital markets, such as India, were immediately hit by the cold snap of the dollar.

In August, the global emerging markets were in dire straits. It is not that the dollar is flowing back because the US economy is improving, but that the interest rate reversal is forcing a dramatic asset price correction in the US financial markets, resulting in a severe shortage of dollar liquidity!

Bernanke never dreamed that the reversal of interest rate expectations would come so quickly and so violently. On the one hand, foreign investors are fleeing frantically from dollar assets, on the other hand, U.S. investors are pulling back from emerging markets to bail out Wall Street, currencies are running wild, and assets are on fire.

On August 16, just four days before the Syrian chemical weapons crisis broke out, the yield on the 10-year U.S. Treasury bond had soared to 2.83%! A number of Wall Street institutions report that once yields break 3%, the reversal in interest rates will be confirmed by the market with a break of 3.5% and both the stock and bond markets will turn bearish.

A grim interest rate defense battle is on the horizon!

On August 16, the yield on 10-year U.S. Treasury bonds surged to 2.83%.

On August 20, U.S. President Barack Obama urgently summoned the bigwigs of Wall Street and the heads of all financial sectors of the U.S. government to closely negotiate a response, including the heads of the Federal Reserve, the Treasury, the Securities and Exchange Commission (SEC), the Consumer Financial Protection Bureau

(CFPB), the Federal Housing Finance Agency (FHFA), the Commodity Futures Trading Commission (CFTC), the Federal Deposit Insurance Corporation (FDIC), the National Credit Administration (NCUA). Although the content of the meeting was not leaked, the state of emergency of soaring interest rates will hit all the above-mentioned institutions hard.

If national debt yields rise, then the cost of financing for society as a whole will rise. In February, interest on 30-year fixed-rate mortgages in the U.S. was just 3.6%, and in August it had soared to 4.8%! Financing costs in other industries are also rising sharply. The financial markets can't stand it, as can the real economy.

On August 22, the yield on the 10-year Treasury bond soared to 2.9%! The situation is becoming more and more urgent.

Hedge funds, mutual funds, pension funds, and insurance companies, like China and Japan, are large holders of U.S. Treasuries and other bonds, and have seen their yields skyrocket while bond prices have jumped, with equally heavy losses on their books. To avoid greater losses, they have only shorted Treasuries to hedge their risk, which in turn has exacerbated the decline.

The massive spike in interest rate markets from May to August has cost the global financial markets $3 trillion in market value! If the sharp rise in interest rates is not reversed quickly, it is bound to trigger a series of more serious financial market implosions.

For Wall Street, the Syrian crisis came at the right time!

When Obama announced that the United States was ready to use force, nerves in the Middle East and the world immediately tightened. Global funds instinctively flowed again into United States Treasuries to hedge against the risk of war, and the yield on 10-year United States Treasuries plunged from 2.9 per cent to 2.75 per cent.

The nearly out-of-control spike in interest rates since May has been greatly mitigated! The Federal Reserve in 4 months in a row of $340 billion QE debt purchases total, have not been able to suppress the interest rate crisis, surprisingly by the armed parade of several U.S. warships easily defused.

In the future, in the process of the Fed's withdrawal from QE, local wars, social unrest, geopolitical conflicts and other major international crises are likely to become the most effective means of "shock absorption" of soaring interest rates.

Either crisis, however, will only temporarily ease the rate of interest rate hikes, but will not change their trend. The repo market is one of the most critical points of gravity as the pressure for greater implosion in the financial system continues to rise.

A buyback is a pawn on a bond

If an ordinary person buys a treasury bond, there is nothing he can do during the time he holds the bond but wait, and his funds are locked up until the bond matures or he decides to sell it. However, the situation is different if a financial institution holds national debt, and they can turn "dead national debt" into "living cash".

That's the beauty of the Repo (Repurchase Agreement).

Financial institutions can borrow money from other people who have free money, using the bonds as collateral, and promise to redeem the bonds at a higher price after a certain period of time, the difference is the repurchase rate, the investor earns the spread, and the borrower signs the pledge of the money is the repurchase agreement. Because of the national credit, so in the market is very easy to liquidate, there is a national bond collateral, the borrowing time is not long, the shortest night, the longest is not more than a few dozen days, so many financial institutions and individuals with free money, they do not want to be bank time deposit by the dead, also do not want to be exploited by the demand interest rate; they both want the flexibility of the funds available at any time, but also want a higher yield, but also investment security, can also meet the above requirements is the repo market.

Buybacks are like pawns, people who are short of money come to the pawn shop with their family's antiques to borrow money, and the antiques are the equivalent of the collateralized treasury bonds that are bought back. Pawnbrokers tend to discount when valuing, which in a repurchase agreement is called a discounted amount (haircut); pawnbrokers usually ask for a few days to redeem the pawn, which is the repurchase time; the interest on the borrowed money is naturally the repurchase rate. If the person who owes money when due does not come to redeem the pawn, he is in default in the repurchase, and the pawnbroker has the right to dispose of it himself, either to sell it or to use it for himself. Likewise, if the repo defaults, then the collateralized treasury bonds belong to the lender.

The principle of the buyback is simple and the operation is not complicated, but its importance in the financial markets is seriously overlooked. Few outside the financial sector understand that repurchases have become the most central source of financing, the most critical means of liquidity provision, the most important center of money creation in modern financial markets, and it can be said to be the engine that drives the entire movement of the financial system!

In the U.S. bond market, the 21 primary market makers have been able to maintain hundreds of billions of dollars in bond inventories, relying primarily on the repo market for financing.

When the U.S. Treasury auctioned Treasuries, 21 primary dealers were eligible to bid directly on Treasuries, which constituted the primary market for Treasuries. They are also the primary market makers in the secondary market, and the Federal Reserve Bank of New York works closely with them in open market operations, buying and selling Treasuries and MBS bonds, expanding or contracting the Fed's balance sheet, QE, and any monetary policy that must be implemented by primary dealers.

In fact, the members of the Circle of First Traders are all bloodline branches of the 17 major financial families that originated in Europe in the 18th century, inheriting the global financial channels created by their ancestors over 300 years. They work with each other from generation to generation, and are connected by layers and layers of roots. The latter generation, at the beginning of the financial industry, are often stationed in each other's banks for internship and training, so as to familiarize themselves with the specific operational details of the industry, but also to establish mutual trust and friendship. They also compete with each other from time to time and even clash fiercely, but the underlying purpose is to reinforce an existing monopoly position. If there are black sheep who are grossly unruly and threaten the interests of the whole, or rotten people who are not well run, they will join forces to clear the door. Due to the hundreds of years of accumulation of customer resources and long-term fight on the front line of the market, their information is often more accurate and timely, practical experience is far more than the head of the Fed's academic origin. They are the real brain, heart, nerves, bones, muscles and arms and legs of the US financial markets, while Fed officials as far away as Washington are more of a mouthpiece for the media.

In the Ministry of Finance auction of treasury bonds in the bid, the size of each requisition is often hundreds of millions of dollars, and only the first-tier dealers have the strength to eat, and only they have enough channels to sell. The size of their holdings, often dozens of times their own funds, can be described as masterful and bold. When they got their hands on the bonds, primary dealers immediately collateralized the bonds in the repo market, and lenders flocked to them to scramble for the repo pie. These big players with free money mainly include: monetary funds, mutual funds, multinational corporations, insurance companies, state and local governments, sovereign wealth funds, foreign central banks and other heavyweight investors. Why don't the wealthy, big-time investors just buy Treasuries? Because overnight repurchases sometimes yield more than three-month Treasury bonds, other bond products with several months to maturity also pale in comparison to repurchases. At the same time, the repo time is ultra-short, the funds are highly flexible, the collateral is secure and the risk is almost negligible.

The first-tier dealers use treasury bonds as repo financing, and when the money comes in, they kill the repo market again, this time they do the lenders, also known as reverse repo, to lend back the exact same variety and amount of treasury bonds in the market. One might ask, isn't this a toss-up? It makes absolutely no sense to first press the coupons to borrow money and then press the coupons to borrow money. However, the primary traders hit the nail on the head, and holding hundreds of billions of dollars in bond inventory is a risky business, as interest rates are changing from moment to moment, sometimes dramatically. Once the interest rate changes, bond prices will change with it, and the turnover of such a large bond inventory takes a long time, if the throughput can not be completed in time, while interest rates have risen sharply, then the hard earned fees may be all gone, or even spit blood and lose money. The interest cost of the former can be fully hedged against the interest income of the latter. This is the "Matching Hedge" of the balance sheet (Matched Books). Without the interest rate risk, the primary underwriter can get his foot in the door and earn the spread between wholesale and retail bonds.

Of course, operating insurance in this way is insurance, but the profit between wholesale and retail treasury bonds is really a bit shabby, a million dollars just to make a few dozen dollars, a hundred million dollars to make a few thousand, even selling cabbage profit margin is much higher than it. Of course, Tier 1 traders go for volume, and the US adds trillions of dollars of national debt each year, and there is still some profit to be made.

Is there any way to earn more? Of course there is. If the primary traders "see" the interest rate will not soar, then you can reduce the latter pressure money to borrow the amount of securities, and use the excess money for the expansion of treasury bond inventory, increase the total amount of business on it. after 2011, the primary traders treasury bond inventory significantly exceeded the corporate bond inventory, is because they "bet" that the Federal Reserve will continue to expand the scale of QE, so, treasury bond yields are clearly a continuing trend of low, continue to engage in "matching hedge", it is clearly unnecessary. However, the greater the extent to which Treasury bond inventories are mismatched with hedges, the greater the risk of interest rate spikes.

Because primary traders have an invisible and critical influence on Fed policy, they often "bet" on the right thing.

You can't look wrong with the general direction of interest rates, and there are more ways to make a small tackle. Why are there so many scandals about interest rate manipulation at the London Interbank Offered Rate (Libor)? Because manipulating the interest rate market can expand the profit margins of primary traders! Many of these people are not only the titans of the US financial market, but also of the European market. The repo market is just a small case of interest rate manipulation benefiting, with larger profits in the interest rate swap and other financial derivatives markets.

Tier one dealers split the large orders of hundreds of millions of dollars of Treasuries they bid for into smaller, multi-million dollar orders, and the smaller dealers in the market rushed to buy them. Their practice and the big dealers are the same, financing with repo, hedging with reverse repo, the bold simply do not use risk hedging, directly "naked" hold treasury bonds, and then to the bond market on the phone to the new cronies old maniac, and soon the treasury bonds distributed to a finer market, eventually lying on the balance sheet of a thousand households.

The June Surprise of the Repo Market

In May, Bernanke said to exit QE with a bang, woke up all participants in the bond market chain, "naked" bond holders rush around to find "underwear", bond stocks too large and lack of matching hedge traders anxious to jump off the wall.

In June, China, Japan and other large U.S. treasury bonds began to "victory escape", treasury yields abruptly changed face, which in turn startled the repurchase market in many "securities borrowing money" hedge funds, treasury bond prices fell, collateral high platform dive. Lenders immediately quit and have issued ultimatums to borrowers to limit margin calls, while highly leveraged hedge funds have no cash reserves at all!

Hedge funds can only sell assets to hedge cash, a few of them can do it, but everyone sells at the same time and the market runs out of liquidity and asset prices plummet!

In late May and early July, the repo rate on 3 and 10 year treasury bonds turned negative! In June, when China and Japan dumped U.S. Treasuries, the repurchase rate of 10-year Treasuries reached -3%, which is an extremely rare spectacle!

A lender who originally had spare money to invest, actually caused the lender to put down 3% because the other party's collateral was a 10-year Treasury bond!

What the hell is going on here?

Reversal of negative 3-year and 10-year repo rates on United States Treasury bonds beginning May 2013

Still using the example of pawn shop to explain, you take the family heirloom antiques to pawn shop mortgage loan money, pawn shop guys picking their noses and eyes to say that only 5% off the loan, you immediately fire up claiming that less than 10% off is improper, the last depends on who consumes who, the result of the two sides compromise at 7% off, this is the normal situation.

Now the market has suddenly changed, the market rumors that this antique is being thrown wildly by several large collectors, increasingly worthless, which can scare the hands of other collectors who have inventory, they also have to sell to the market. In addition to collectors, the market is more speculators, specializing in the business of buying and selling short, they heard the news, immediately declared that they have goods, jumped off the building to sell, spitting blood to clear their positions. In fact, the speculators don't have the goods in their hands. There was always a sell and a buy in the market, so buyers flocked to short-selling speculators, paid cash and waited to pick up the goods. The speculators knew that the pawnbroker had the goods in his hands and ran to borrow them, and as the quantity increased, they were willing to pay a premium.

Why are speculators willing to risk a premium to borrow antiques? It turns out that speculators think that the price of antiques will also fall, first borrow the pawnshop antiques to deliver, when the price is lower in a few days, then buy back to return to the pawnshop owner, eat the difference in the middle of the price will be earned.

Originally, antiques plummeted, the market to sell more to buy less, antiques should be in excess of demand, but speculators involved in a large number of short selling, but led to delivery difficulties, they had to pay a premium to pawnbrokers to borrow goods to meet the delivery, as a result of the pawnbroker's antiques on the contrary expensive. At this point, those with antiques in their hands can earn a portion of the speculator's premium by mortgaging them to a pawnshop.

The same is true when the repo rate becomes negative. The sharp rise in yields as a result of the national debt sell-off has frightened banks, IMFs, insurance companies, multinational corporations and foreign investment institutions holding huge amounts of national debt assets, which have had to join the sell-off in order to reduce the significant losses from the depreciation of the national debt, which has exacerbated the horror of the national debt decline. As a professional short-seller, some hedge funds have seen the opportunity to kill. While the sell-offs in the bond market were large, the size of the short-selling was even more staggering.

Those who hold bonds in their hands simply sell their inventory, and there is no question of borrowing them, but those who sell them purely short must borrow them in order to complete delivery. If the size of the simultaneous short sale reaches a critical point, then the delivery of borrowed securities will inevitably be bottlenecked, resulting in many people being unable to borrow Treasuries to complete delivery. This is when the delivery default rate rises dramatically.

On June 5, 2013, the default rate on delivery of U.S. Treasury bonds reached $130 billion

And that's exactly what happened in reality, as on June 5, the default rate on the delivery of Treasuries reached a staggering $130 billion!

The short-selling of U.S. Treasuries was intense enough to dazzle Bernanke.

The reversal of negative repo rates and the continued rise in defaults on the delivery of treasury bonds indicate that the repo market is already in a state of extreme abnormality, which will seriously affect the liquidity supply and money creation function of the financial system, thus inducing a more violent implosion of the multi-billion derivatives market.

Traditional currency creation

By its very nature, the banking system is a service provider whose main function is to provide monetary services to economic activity. This is not fundamentally different from the telecommunications sector, which provides communications services, and the transport sector, which provides transportation services, where the banking system derives its revenue from the service fees paid by society for its monetary services.

Where does the money for the banking system come from? The answer is: bank money stems from the self-creation of the banking system.

The vast majority of people who use money on a daily basis are unaware of the mechanism by which it is generated and mistakenly believe that the bills printed by the government mint are the entire currency of society. In fact, in modern countries, banknotes make up only a tiny fraction of the currency, the vast majority of which is bank money created by banks.

How exactly do banks create money?

Looking first at the simplest bank balance sheet, if a bank in its initial state has neither assets nor liabilities nor ownership interest, its state can be simplified to.

Assets	Liabilities & equity
Cash: 0	Savings: 100

A bank's balance sheet is the state of the bank's operations at a certain point in time, which is like a snapshot, if you take a snapshot of every moment of the bank's operations and look at it continuously, you can tell the state of the bank's business development. Where the total assets on the left are always equal to the liabilities plus equity on the right, which is a constant equation.

Cash is an asset of a bank and savings is a liability because when people deposit cash in a bank, they may come to withdraw it at any time and the bank has to meet the depositor's request for withdrawal without any conditions, which is a duty and obligation of the bank.

At this point, a customer A comes to the bank and deposits $100 in cash, and if another snapshot is taken, the bank's balance sheet will become.

Assets	Liabilities & equity
Cash: 100	client A savings: 100

Quite simply, the assets on the left are still equal to the liabilities + equity on the right. The bank provides Customer A with a paper savings book, a plastic bank card, or a U shield for online transactions, either way, Customer A is given the right to withdraw cash from the bank at any time, and the essence of bank savings is the depositor's right to demand cash.

At this time came another customer B, he did not come to save money, but to take out a loan, the bank conducted a serious investigation of customer B, the loan needs also repeatedly reviewed, decided to take out a loan. But subject to central bank regulations, for example, out of a $100 deposit, only a maximum of $90 can be taken out for a loan, and the remaining $10 must be left with the bank for emergencies.

The general feeling is that the bank must be lending $90 of cash in assets to customer B, so the cash assets should be only $10, isn't it the role of the bank to lend money from depositors to people who need it? If the vast majority of people hold this view, it means that the vast majority of people don't get the mystery of making money in modern banking. In fact, instead of using $100 in cash, the bank created new savings "out of nothing", and if another snapshot were taken, the bank's balance sheet would become.

Assets	Liabilities & equity
Cash: 100	Client A savings: 100
Loan from Client B: 90	Savings from Client B: 90

Didn't get it? That's right.

Banks are really like magicians, they can actually create new savings "out of nothing"! It is difficult for the average person's mind to understand the rationality and logic of such bookkeeping. But in any case, since the financial families of Europe in the 19th century laid down such bookkeeping rules and gained recognition in the common law system, the fractional reserve system has now become the prevailing standard in the world, and whether it is reasonable or fair or not is irrelevant. It is important that ordinary people have a deep understanding of the injustices imposed on them by this system. Note that, with the exception of banks, which enjoy the privilege of keeping books "out of thin air", any other company that dares to do so is bound to be treated as a fraud and the legal person will be jailed. This illustrates an important point that the banking system has been granted a certain privilege in economic activity since the 19th century.

Why would Customer B's loan be considered an asset by the bank? Customer B's indebtedness is capable of generating interest income. For a bank, anything that brings in cash flow is an asset. The assets of the bank, therefore, are the debts owed to it by the rest of society. The total assets of the bank are now $190 and the total liabilities are also $190, and they are still equal. The debt on the right has increased by $90, a new savings account the bank has opened for Customer B, who can spend the money by transferring it by check, or withdrawing cash.

Note that when Customer B's savings account is activated, the total amount of money in the economy as a whole increases by $90.

No matter how Customer B spends the money, sooner or later the $90 will go into an account at another bank in the banking system. So this bank will add $90 in savings, while adding $90 in cash assets, of which it can also lend $81 and create new $81 in savings. This cycle can continue until the total amount of money in the entire banking system increases tenfold, and $100 of additional savings will eventually create a $1,000 money supply.

This is money creation by banks. Under normal circumstances, the new currency is not circulated in the market in the form of banknotes, but in the form of numbers on the books of the banking system, which are added to and subtracted from the books of the various banks, and the money flows quietly and without interest in the changes in the numbers on the books of the banks.

When customer B lends money to a bank, this demand is equivalent to the monetary demand generated by the growth of the real economy, the banking system creates money to meet this demand, and the interest income is the service charge that the bank charges society. When there is no new demand for money creation in the real economy, but the banking system is able to create new demand for money on its own, then the service fees paid by society to the banks become "management fees" that the banks forcefully assess on society.

Since the real economy is in the doldrums, it will be difficult for banks to issue loans, how to collect this "management fee"?

In today's financial markets, the ability of banks to create traditional savings money has atrophied and has been replaced by new mechanisms for shadow banking to create shadow money. Loans create savings liabilities that have given way to mortgages create repo liabilities. It is the repo market that is the most important center of money creation in the world today.

Money is evolving, and the thinking of the vast majority of people in society is not keeping up. Today's monetary and financial theories are still at the level of the 1980s, and this outdated knowledge, which is completely incapable of understanding the new phenomenon of money creation, has led to significant errors in many current interpretations of money, prices, exchange rates, interest rates and financial markets.

One cannot understand the essence of 20th century finance without understanding the fractional reserve system, and one cannot see the financial core of the 21st century without understanding that repo mortgages create money.

Shadow money: a new law of money creation

The easiest way to understand the finer points of money creation in today's financial markets is to look at how a hedge fund creates liabilities that resemble bank savings.

If, from the initial state, a fund raises $100 and then opens with a bang, the money cannot be idle, so the money manager first buys $100 in Treasuries, at which point the balance sheet is simple.

Assets	Liabilities & equity
Cash: 0	Liability: 0
National debt: 100	Benefits: 100

But the fund manager's purpose in buying Treasuries is not to passively hold and eat the interest, that's what Big Mom and Dad do, he buys Treasuries to further finance the expansion of asset size to make money. So, he secured $100 of Treasuries in the repo market and ended up with $90 in cash (just a simple concept note), and the balance sheet of the increased repo transaction began to change interestingly.

Assets	Liabilities & equity
National debt: 100	Repurchase liability: 90
Cash: 90	Benefits: 100

With the repo financing, the fund's total assets increased to $190, and the increased cash of $90 could be used for high-risk, high-yield adventures, hedging the spread between the interest cost of the repo and the high-yield return.

It is important to emphasize here that although the repurchase operation is "sell first, then buy back", which appears to be a "real sale", but is in fact a "real borrowing", since the borrower promised in the repurchase agreement to buy back the assets within a day or a few days, in fact, all the risk of interest rate or default still belongs to the secured borrower, therefore, the accounting rules require that the repurchased assets must remain on the balance sheet of the borrower, and not be transferred to the lender.

Lehman Brothers had done this by stealing the concept, leading to the famous "Repo 105" case.

On the eve of the financial crisis, the exposure of the subprime mortgage problem led to a severe asset depreciation at Lehman Brothers, which was deeply involved in that market, and in an extremely bad financial market, it was difficult for Lehman to sell that toxic junk in time to avoid a massive financial loss. In order to conceal its true financial predicament, Lehman engaged in a massive buy-back operation whenever its financial statements were issued, "selling" $105 worth of bond assets for $100 and using the cash from the "sales proceeds" to liquidate its liabilities, resulting in a significant reduction in both assets and liabilities on the financial statements and disguising its financial position. When the financial statements are released after 10 days, Lehman will refinance these assets and "buy them back" and restore the assets and liabilities to their original state. Lehman Brothers had used this tactic to "temporarily" move as much as $50 billion of assets out of its balance sheet by toxic trash, thereby seriously misleading investors' risk assessment of Lehman and constituting financial fraud.

In the normal state of the repo market, mortgaging $102 in bond assets would have yielded about $100 in loans, but Lehman mortgaged $105 worth of bonds in order to get $100 in loans, so why is that?

It turns out Lehman wanted to make "buy-back and borrow" look more like "real sales"! The fair value of the overcollateralization in the repo market is 2 per cent, and once this value is exceeded, the borrower is considered to have essentially lost actual control over the collateralized asset, thus moving closer to a "sale" of the asset and no longer a repo pledge, and accounting standards allow Lehman to move these "literally sold" bonds off the balance sheet. Lehman seized on precisely this loophole, preferring to take the higher discount rate as well as circumvent the risk of fraud from the letter of the law.

The 105% excess repo collateral has since become famous, and the "repo 105" will also go down in world financial history.

In the above example, a 10% discount rate was chosen for simplicity. If lenders do not want to take the risk, the 10% discount on treasury collateral lending is very safe, even if the hedge fund collapse, lenders can also sell the $100 treasury bonds in the market, can easily get back at least $90 loan, and even more.

The $90 that the hedge fund has raised through repurchase is equivalent to the cash deposit of Customer A in a traditional bank, the repurchase liability is equivalent to the savings liability, and it is also a duty and an obligation for the hedge fund to redeem the collateral asset at a slightly higher price within a set period of time. To put it another way, the lender holding the repurchase agreement has a right to claim its principal plus interest when the time comes.

If one looks closely at the balance sheets of hedge funds, one problem has bubbled up, and that is that Treasuries can be used almost as cash thanks to the repo market!

In traditional banking, money creation is the creation of savings liabilities through the issuance of loans based on reserves, the legal tender of the country, and in the context of the entire banking system, money creation is the amplification of the base currency of the central bank.

In the repo market, treasury bonds play the role of a base currency, which, in essence, is the "reserve" for the financial system to create "shadow money"!

A bank's savings liability is bank money, which has the function of paying for all market transactions. Whether people are withdrawing cash from savings accounts or paying bank checks, they are in essence mobilizing and transferring reserves on bank balance sheets. When a depositor writes a bank cheque, it is an instruction to transfer the reserves of the depository bank to another bank.

If the repo liability is equivalent to the bank's savings liability, does it have a paying function and is it able to mobilize and transfer the national debt on the balance sheet? The answer is yes.

This is the "rehypothecation" of the repo market!

In the figure below, it can be seen that the original treasury bond assets held by the hedge fund, the shadow currency "reserve", can be used repeatedly as collateral in the repo market, reused by all repo liabilities in a "collateral chain".

National debt is transferred from hedge fund assets to be reused in the collateral chain.[18]

The $100 treasury bond was supposed to be an asset held by the hedge fund, and when it was pledged to Goldman Sachs, the primary dealer in the repo market, Goldman Sachs may have made a "subcollateralization" request, meaning that the hedge fund's treasury bond would have had the right to pledge it again to someone else during the pledge period. The hedge funds would certainly have the right to say no, and Goldman Sachs would then charge a higher "repo rate", which would increase the cost of financing the hedge funds. The manager of the hedge fund turned his head and thought, who the hell is Goldman Sachs? It's the top man in the financial market, the national debt is definitely safe in Goldman Sachs, as long as Goldman Sachs does not collapse, the "sub-mortgage" is not too much risk to themselves, and the repurchase interest is lower, and people are convenient to their own convenience, why not do? And so agreed to Goldman Sachs' request.

Goldman Sachs changed hands and "paid" the Treasuries to Credit Suisse to liquidate its derivatives trading position with Credit Suisse. Note that the original "repo liability" on the hedge fund's balance sheet has now become an asset of Goldman Sachs, which is essentially the equivalent of a "savings account" opened by the hedge fund to Goldman Sachs to issue bank checks in the traditional banking business. Goldman Sachs' "payment" of a "check" to Credit Suisse was tantamount to an order to transfer the hedge fund's treasury assets to Credit Suisse, in the same way that a traditional bank's check transfers bank reserves. In the end, Credit Suisse "paid" the same bonds again to a monetary fund, which decided to hold the bonds temporarily, to be discussed later.

The energy created by the currency gradually decreases with each sub-collateralization due to the constant discounting of attrition. In such a chain of repo-collateralized money creation, Treasuries are the equivalent of high-energy money, the number of times the collateral is transferred is the length of the collateralized chain, which is the currency multiplier, and the discount rate (haircut) of the collateralized

---

[18] Manmohan Singh, Peter Stella, *The (other) deleveraging: What economist need to know about the modern money creation process*, 2012-07-02.

asset is the reserve rate. While traditional banks rely on a "fractional reserve" system to create money, shadow banks use "partially collateralized assets" to create shadow money.

Is repo liability money or not? It depends on who you ask, if it's a big mom or a big aunt, they certainly can't use the repo liability to buy food on the street; but if it's an institutional investment in the financial markets, it's perfectly fine, they can use the repo liability to buy any financial asset. The assets underlying the repo liability are treasury bonds, which are virtually cash, or "cash-like", receipts for which the repo liability is a "cash-like" receipt.

There is an American proverb: If there is an animal that looks like a duck, calls like a duck, and walks like a duck, then it is a duck. The repo liability has all the functions of a bank savings liability, the only difference between them being that the bank savings liability, or bank money, can be used in all areas of the economy to pay for goods and services, while the repo liability, or shadow money, is dedicated to the financial markets, buying and selling financial assets.

A sub-mortgage, a couple of bottles with a cap for acrobatics

Let's still take the example of a pawnshop, if you pledge your heirloom to a pawnshop in order to borrow money and agree to a three-day redemption period. In the meantime, the pawnshop owner demands that he has the right to mortgage your heirloom to someone else, and you'll probably be suspicious that it might not be in the pawnshop's hands three days later when you want to redeem it. In fact, the pawnshop owner did sub-mortgage your baby to the big Zhang family in town, who in turn sub-mortgaged it again to the Li family money bank. Under normal circumstances, the pawnbrokers, Zhang family bigholders and Li family money bankers are reputable and powerful bigholders with a family background, standing house lying on the ground, generally do not default. But if the economy goes south, their business will also be in a state of serial debt that will make it difficult to extricate themselves, and you may not get your heirloom back as soon as any of them go wrong.

With the extension of the collateralized chain, the risk of default will expand geometrically and the financial system will be as fragile as a cascade of wings, so much so that a butterfly can break the most vulnerable link in the chain with a flick of its wings, triggering a massive default and financial system implosion.

Whether the traditional bank's partial reserve system, or today's shadow bank's repo mortgage chain, its essence is to play a few bottles a cap game, the more financial acrobats play the more daring, next to watch the lively people under the stakes are also getting higher and higher, until the bottle is too much, the bottle cap unintentionally fell on the ground, everyone together for the birds and beasts.

This is exactly what happened in 2008.

U.S. financial regulators certainly understand the essence of financial acrobats and have therefore limited the size of subcollateralization for Tier 1 dealers to a maximum of 140% of their total customer liabilities, that is, to a 1.4x magnification multiplier for shadow money.

The British, however, are not so conservative. In order to win a greater share of the financial market, neither the UK nor the EU has legal limits on the number of sub-collateralizations for repurchases.

With Wall Street gamblers having trouble getting their hands dirty in the US, the UK has naturally become a haven for mega-bookies to repo and remortgage.

Fund managers flocked in droves to Wall Street's Tier 1 market makers for repo financing, with Lehman playing the most savage of the Tier 1 dealers. The Lehman's repo financing to the gamblers is the lowest cost, all of them are customers, the game is High. Lehman's explanation to the gamblers in advance, the bonds you bet on me, I am going to sub-mortgage to London, under English law, the ownership of your bonds need to be temporarily entrusted to me. London encourages all of you to gamble so that you can have the least cost and the most fun, and as long as you can trust me, Lehman Brothers, I guarantee that your bonds will be returned to their original owners, absolutely safe!

Who the hell is Lehman? It was one of Wall Street's biggest "pawnshops," a century-old shop with a reputation as a super-high level of acrobatics that could play thirty bottles a cap, and a financial magician who never missed a beat, and gamblers doubted anyone would ever suspect Lehman of collapsing. So gamblers rushed to bet their bond assets, which Lehman encapsulated and shipped in bulk to Lehman's London sub.

In 2008, Lehman actually went bankrupt!

This is something that no one could have thought of in advance. The gamblers got anxious, and the bond assets they had pledged to Lehman were all at once gone. In a bankruptcy discharge, it's not a simple matter of figuring out who exactly owns your assets. If the assets are held in escrow in the U.S., the issue is much simpler, and U.S. law is much clearer on the protection of the assets held in escrow, and getting them back is not an issue. However, Lehman has transferred the assets of its clients to the London branch of "Lehman Brothers International (Europe)" (LBIE), and the UK has very different fiduciary protection laws than the US.

The gamblers were so remorseful that in the first place, in order to buy back the interest could be cheaper, they trusted Lehman Brothers and voluntarily gave up their ownership of the assets after they were transferred overseas, and as a result, they lost the protection of US law. The London side believes that these gamblers have no legal relationship with their assets, the distribution of assets after bankruptcy is according to the asset-backed and non-asset-backed to prioritize creditors, they can now only be considered ordinary non-asset-backed creditors, after the Lehman London sub, the first to repay the asset-backed people, the last remaining rags by ordinary creditors to pick up, if there are still some tables, chairs and stools, that is already a lucky day. The gamblers immediately fell into a frenzy of shouting and screaming.

After the havoc, the gamblers learned the hard way that they could no longer believe the credibility of Tier 1 dealers. Who can say they're perfectly safe when Lehman can get down? They never cared about the details of repurchase agreements with primary dealers, only concerned about whether the repurchase interest is sufficiently favorable, while Wall Street and European repurchase agreements do not have a uniform template for the industry, the major dealers are each blowing their own trumpet, each singing their own tune, the agreement on the sub-collateralization is even less certain, the Lehman bankruptcy made everyone's heart ache. Gamblers began to wrestle word-for-word with dealers on terms such as placing restrictions on sub-collateral, requiring dealers to open special escrow accounts, etc.

Can a dedicated account keep my clients' assets safe? Financial magicians can't help but laugh, clients forget that the magician's profession is to "change" other people's money into their own pockets.

"Buyback expiry" deals: a new way for financial magicians to play

In November 2011, following the collapse of Lehman, another Tier 1 trader, MF Global, went bankrupt, with $1.2 billion mysteriously missing from clients' dedicated accounts.

MF Global is one of the smallest of the primary traders with only $1/30^{th}$ of the size of the other big guys, not to mention its small size, but not small courage, it aspires to become a mini version of Goldman Sachs, but ended up becoming a mini version of Lehman. The main reason for its failure was the investment of up to $6.2 billion in European sovereign debt, especially the national debt of the "Europig Five".

Naturally, MF Global's "Europig bonds" were also taken into the repo market for collateralized financing, where the cash was used to up the bets, which could then be collateralized for the cash, and so on until the black hand was put into the client's account.

MF Global's bond assets in Italy, Spain, Belgium, Ireland, Portugal, although the market is not bullish, but debt service is still normal, especially the interest return is quite attractive, in addition to the interest cost of repo financing, but also a considerable yield on the spread. MF Global feels like it has found a big gold mine. However, as the size of Eurobond holdings grows, so does the problem of insufficient own capital, with the Eurobond asset ratio reaching five times the company's net worth!

In order to meet the needs of financial regulation and beautify the financial statements, MF Global also needs to "trim" its balance sheet, especially after the onset of the European debt crisis, its asset prices have been deteriorating, "trimming" is not only "cosmetic", but more importantly to cover the exposure of the deterioration of assets, the most convenient tool is naturally the repo transaction. However, after Lehman's "buyback 105" global "gone", MF Global did not dare to play the "real sale" of assets anymore, and after some thoughtful thinking, it created a new trick of "Repo-To-Maturity"!

MF Global counts its "Europig bond" inventory, packages the bonds that are maturing at the same time, and takes them to the repo market to find a buyer for a mortgage, especially since in the transaction it explicitly requires the repurchase to be exactly the same time as the maturity of the bonds, which is called a "repo maturity" transaction. The lender felt odd, but didn't figure out the rationale behind it either, as long as there was collateral, the lending yield was good and the length of time was not an issue. As a result, MF Global has gradually converted a "Europig Bond" into a "repo maturity" type of financing transaction.

The accounting standard applicable to repurchase transactions in the United States is called FASB 140, which states that a so-called "true sale" must be a transfer of a financial asset, meaning that the original holder relinquishes control of the asset. The key word is "control", and Lehman has taken advantage of this by pricing 102% as control, while pricing 105% as loss of control. MF Global is also trying to exploit the same loophole, when it pledged the Europig bonds, these assets were still "alive", but when the repurchase deadline came, the pledged Europig bonds "died of natural causes", of course MF Global could not complete the repurchase.

On the face of the accounting rules, the "natural death" of the bonds during the repurchase period is clearly a loss of "control" by the holder. As a result, "repurchase maturity" transactions are allowed to be moved off the balance sheet by the accounting standards, and they are recorded underneath the financial statements in notes that are densely packed with notes that must be seen with a microscope and are completely devoid of detail. MF Global used this clever magic trick to "buy back" $16.5 billion in assets that were lost from the balance sheet.

How does the magic come apart?

It turns out that LCH. Clearnet, the European company responsible for clearing repo transactions, was unable to process bond repo transactions due on the same day, and as a result MF Global's repo time had to be advanced by two days. That's a lot of trouble, the obituary comes out two days early before the person dies, and the result is a total mess!

The repurchase occurred two days before the maturity date of the bonds, which meant that MF Global had not lost "control" of the assets, which were required to be brought back on the balance sheet, and the large Eurobond assets were exposed in the 31 July 2011 financial statement amendment. The sudden increase of $5 billion in assets and liabilities immediately caused MF Global's capital to fall seriously short of its requirements, and investors who shunned the "Europig assets" immediately sniffed out the big trouble.

MF Global's shortage of funds coincided with a major moment in the European debt crisis, when the price of Europig bonds plummeted and the value of the company's collateralized assets in the repo market shrank significantly. However, MF Global has stretched its leverage to the limit and its own funds are no longer able to cope with the lenders' pressures.

The Europig bonds are not in default, but the high leverage cost is so high that MF Global can't breathe, and the company's leverage ratio is now a staggering 40:1!

Like Lehman Brothers, MF Global has a large number of fund clients, and following the collapse of Lehman, funds have been alarmed by requests to open separate proprietary accounts to protect their assets. In fact, MF Global went so far as to pledge funds from its clients' proprietary accounts to the lenders when they were chased by repo lenders.

Eventually, when bankruptcy hit, the fund's clients' funds were frozen along with the repo lenders. As the old saying goes, if you're not afraid of a thief stealing, you're afraid of a thief remembering.

The "fantasy drift" of junk debt

In the repo-collateralized money creation mechanism, treasury bonds function as a base currency, equivalent to the reserves in traditional banks, and because of the existence of the repo market, treasury bonds are almost cash, or "cash-like". In addition to Treasuries, two-home MBS bonds, indirectly guaranteed by the U.S. government, can also be financed as repo collateral.

What if instead of national debt and two-room MBS, the holdings are junk debt? Can junk bonds act as "cash-like"? Of course, in the world of financial magic on Wall Street, there are only the unexpected and nothing that can't be done, this is the collateral transformation trick.

If a hedge fund holds junk bonds but wants to do repo financing, it has two options, the first is to go all over the world itself to find a counterparty willing to accept its junk bond collateral, of course the discount rate will be much higher, the interest rate is naturally not cheap. The biggest problem is that hedge funds have limited resources for clients, and also have to deal with their own asset delivery, inventory management, funds transfer, default prevention, risk control and a series of back-office work, hedge funds both lack of well-connected repo market sales managers, and no experienced traders, the back-office processing capacity is even more lackluster, their own direct repo counterparties are not cost-effective, which is the disadvantage of bilateral repo (Bilateral Repo).

Another option is the Tri-party Repo, where any spontaneously formed market will rule, and the repo market is no exception. Two of the biggest names in the Wall Street repo market are JPMorgan Chase and the Bank of New York Mellon, which have assumed the role of clearing house for repo transactions. Both buyers and sellers open accounts at clearing houses, funds and bonds are transferred through clearing houses, and the two big boys set the rules of the game for the repo market. Buy-back participants "outsource" all logistics other than the buying and selling itself to the clearing house, so that everyone needs to focus only on the buying and selling business itself.

The hedge fund thinks it is better to find a clearing house to carry out junk debt repurchase financing is more reliable, so find JPMorgan Chase to explain the intention, JPMorgan Chase people look at the collateral is junk debt, immediately send the manager of the hedge fund to leave. It turns out that the bigwigs also have their own strict standards, the tripartite repo market only accepts government bonds or government-guaranteed institutional bonds as collateral, not to mention junk bonds, and even good quality corporate bonds are not welcome.

Hedge fund managers out of the frown, just happened to come across a repo market on the ordinary traders, after learning of the situation, the traders laughed, this is nothing, to deal with this difficulty is easy. The trader proposed an arrangement whereby the hedge fund first made a bilateral repurchase with the trader and pledged the junk bonds to the trader, who was responsible for providing the bonds, and the hedge fund promised to return the bonds after a certain period of time and get back its own junk bonds, which is called a "collateral swap". Of course, hedge funds naturally have to pay quite a bit, and the amount of junk bonds collateralized has to be exceeded even more. The hedge fund manager did the math, and although it was not expensive, it was still more cost-effective than looking for bilateral buybacks, and finally agreed to come down.

However, the trader did not necessarily have excess Treasuries, but knew that a pension fund manager had the goods in his hands, so the trader found the pension fund manager and offered to do a "mirror swap" with the pension fund, that is, the hedge fund's junk bonds and the pension fund's Treasuries for the exact same collateral swap, and promised to return the Treasuries by then to get back the junk bonds, in return, the pension fund will receive a substantial fee. Of course, this is only a portion of the fees paid by the hedge fund to the dealer, with the remainder naturally going into the dealer's pocket. In the end, the pension fund manager readily agreed.

Don't pension fund managers know that junk bonds are far more risky than Treasuries? Isn't he afraid it's hard to account for the junk piled up on his balance sheet? What need did he have for such a high-risk operation? The pension fund manager was certainly aware of the risks, but he wasn't worried.

It turns out that retirement fund managers are having a hard time, too, as the monetary flood brought about by QE has caused the prices of safe bonds that can be invested in the market to be outrageously high, while yields are heartbreakingly low. Retirement funds must take on the major responsibility of paying retirees for their lives. The investment risk must not be high and the return must not be too low, otherwise the return will not catch up with inflation, retirees will not get enough money to support themselves, and once investors withdraw their investments, the fund will close down. The pressure on investment income has left fund managers deeply distressed.

The dealers are sending a good opportunity for high yields, retirement fund managers can't just go and buy junk bonds, policies and regulations don't allow it, but "mortgage replacement" is a different story. For the fund manager, he only needs to sign a paper contract to get an excess return. Since the "asset swap" model is similar to a repurchase, national debt remains on the balance sheet of the Fund. On the face of it, nothing is happening, and it's short, risky and rewarding. Is all this good just because the sky can still fall for just a few days of holding junk debt?

A "mortgage replacement" down, hedge funds cheerfully find JPMorgan Chase to do repurchase financing, retirement fund managers comfortably sit and enjoy the excess income, traders smile and go home to count money.

Who really owns the junk debt? That's a lot to say. The hedge fund has Treasuries in its hands, and has received real cash from JPMorgan Chase; junk bonds are certainly not in its hands; the trader is buying and selling them, and in fact has no junk bonds in his inventory; and legally, Treasuries remain untouched on the balance sheet of the pension fund.

But the junk debt is nowhere to be seen!

Financial Magic = Legal Loopholes + Accounting Revolution, Welcome to the financial magic space of Wall Street!

High-risk junk debt is the toxic junk of assets in the current financial markets, and after a "miraculous drift", it has not really disappeared, but has drifted from the books of hedge funds to the warehouses of pension funds, and no matter how the law is interpreted, the real risk has been transferred to the pension funds.

If the price of junk debt doesn't go wrong, the game can go on endlessly. But then, suddenly one day interest rates started to spike and trouble hit. If the price of junk bonds plummeted 30%, the pension fund manager would jump up and frantically hit the dealer and either return my treasury bonds immediately or add at least 50% of the collateral or I will dump your junk!

Geez, it really is rubbish! Staring at the computer screen, the pension fund manager is in a cold sweat and already speechless as junk bonds are being dumped by everyone in the market together.

The trader who was driven crazy by the retirement fund manager, at this time is also anxious, if he does not want to declare the collapse, he has a legal obligation to collect the junk debt and return the national debt, only desperately rush the hedge fund manager, hurry to return the national debt, pick up his junk back, there is another way is to immediately raise the margin. At this point, the hedge fund manager is also sitting on pins and needles, junk bonds are on his balance sheet, and a sharp drop in price will directly affect fund performance. National debt? Where there are treasury bonds, long ago mortgaged to JPMorgan Chase, this old boy and do not know how many times to turn mortgage, in whose hands only God knows. Additional deposit? The money from the buyback meltdown has long since bought more junk debt, and Indian stocks and bonds, where is the free money? Pure Indian stuff, want it? Traders noses are already pissed, junk debt in the market is junk, and Indian assets are more junk than junk. The hedge fund manager posed a pose of wanting no money, wanting life. Despite this, hedge funds have also begun to liquidate junk debt on a large scale in an attempt to protect themselves.

The spike in interest rates in May 2013 was only a prelude to a larger interest rate volcano in the future, and global financial markets have already lost $3 trillion since May, with emerging market countries, such as India, Brazil, South Africa and Indonesia, being the direct victims of this spike.

India's inward investment is different from China's, where direct investment (FDI) is the overwhelming predominance, and although there is no shortage of hot-money gamblers who are looking for the appreciation of the yuan, most of the industrial companies that want to expand their investment in China are looking at the long term, and they will not be affected much by the soaring interest rates. The Indian model, which has been touted by the Western media in recent years, has become an international star. As soon as India's mind gets hot, it opens the door to capital entry and exit, especially by allowing foreign capital to enter the Indian capital market directly. As a result, most of the foreign money invested in India belongs to the portfolio management type of financial hot money, in which hedge funds are the mainstay, betting on the appreciation of the Indian capital market, but have little interest in Indian industrial investment. Once the wind blows on Wall Street, they can run faster than a rabbit.

Those head over heels and Wall Street hedge fund managers, who don't even have their underwear on, have the audacity to plunge into India in a big way. Fortunately, China has not opened up its stock and bond markets, and if China were like India, it would be on the list of emerging market countries to die in June.

If one day in the future, the interest rate volcano suddenly erupted, the first thing to burn is 1.1 trillion junk bonds, the serious burn is not only the high-risk hedge funds, traders are also in danger, the liquidity of the bond market will be paralyzed by traders and market makers on the verge of drying up, as a result of the blockage of high-quality bond buying and selling, the cost of repurchase soared, triggering a wider range of yields soared, short selling self-insurance and short selling speculation spread throughout the market, the bond market began to implode violently. As the ultimate holder of junk debt, the national debt is gone, the junk debt has lost a lot of money, the audits have exposed the "mortgage replacement" scandal, investment institutions have been scolded for being deceived and have withdrawn their capital.

From another perspective, the junk bonds of hedge funds, through modern financial alchemy, were transformed into Treasuries, which then spread deep into the entire financial system through a chain of repo collateral, sowing toxic assets along the way that would continue to take root and grow savagely. The longer this mortgage chain is, the more violent the future liquidation will be.

One can only pray for the almighty rate, the climb is too much to bear, the spike is a dead end.

Shadow money and shadow banking

Shadow money is the money supply created by the shadow banking system, which circulates in the capital market, buys and sells financial assets, fictitiously creates the wealth effect, creates asset inflation, changes the distribution of wealth, affects the flow of funds in industry, and affects the allocation of resources of the whole society.

What is the shadow banking system again?

Simply put, a system that is free from the regulatory constraints of traditional banks, has the ability to create shadow currencies, and mutually accepts shadow currencies as a means of payment. Traditional banks must be regulated by the Central Bank, the law allows for the absorption of deposits from depositors, the privilege of creating bank money, and deposit insurance has features such as government guarantees. The shadow banking system does not have a unified global management mechanism, cannot directly absorb depositors' deposits, mainly relies on repo collateral financing, the creation of shadow money all depends on market acceptance, lacks legal norms, business failure without any government guarantee.

Why has shadow banking gone viral?

The root cause is the loss of effective checks and balances on currency creation following the abolition of the gold standard in the United States in 1971 and the intensification of the dollar, with asset prices rising much faster than the profitability of the real economy. The ecology of entrepreneurs is changing rapidly, and in order to survive and thrive, more and more manufacturing companies in the United States are moving to East and Southeast Asia to maintain higher profit margins at lower production costs. Under the influence of U.S. monetary policy, Europe and Japan have also started a wave of overseas investment, which is the industrial hollowing out of the cheap money expulsion industry.

With the unprecedented massive shift in the U.S. industrial economy over the past 40 years, and the consequent loss of quality assets capable of generating stable cash flows, assets that remain in the U.S. can only become increasingly dependent on real estate loans and consumer credit, and the profitability model of traditional banks is beginning to face significant challenges. When a bank lends money to a business, especially a high-margin, quality manufacturing business, the bank is not worried about the security of the loan because it knows the business can generate more cash flow to repay the loan. But when a bank lends money to a consumer to buy a house and a car, it has to carefully assess the consumer's income level and ability to repay the loan, because the loan is not for people to increase their ability to create wealth, but simply to satisfy an individual's desire to spend. At this point, funds are being consumed, not used to create. For banks, there is a fundamental difference between productive and consumer assets, in that while both generate income for the bank, the former creates cash flow for the economy, while the latter consumes cash flow. When consumption exceeds creation, the country will become increasingly dependent on the supply of funds from abroad to subsidize the "internal bleeding" of the economy, i.e. the return of the dollar to the subsidized economic model.

The asset quality of traditional banks has generally declined and earnings have been much weaker, while the threat of inflation from the dollar overdraft is eating away at their balance sheets. As a result, the banking system has been forced to react in a stressful way by reducing the size of its assets and liabilities and "downsizing" significantly. As a result, the banking system has developed a strong impulse to "dump" its assets and liabilities. This trend has coincided with the tidal wave of dollar repatriation, creating a new profitability model for the banking system, one that creates a large and complex financial market, with a new way of playing with bursting financial assets to obtain profits above loans. It is for this reason that asset securitization, repo financing and other financial innovations sprang up after the 1970s.

The huge demand for "dumping" assets and liabilities gave rise to a new set of markets and new services, and in the early 1970s, the United States made it illegal to pay interest on checking accounts in banks (where depositors could always make check transfers or cash withdrawals). After the abolition of the gold standard, the massive over-abundance of the dollar enabled banks to create huge new savings, which, under the threat of severe inflation, were desperate for an interest-bearing refuge and money market funds were created. Because IMF invests in the repo market and is therefore able to offer higher interest rates and is not subject to bank-like interest controls, it has "run away" from savings that would otherwise be in banks and has emerged as a major lender in the repo financing and commercial paper markets, currently sitting on a massive $2.6 trillion. The money fund appears to be safe because it only invests in ultra-short term products like repo mortgages, but in extreme cases, it instead becomes the most dangerous market.

On 18 September 2008, after Lehman declared bankruptcy, a number of money funds suffered severe losses as a result of their investments in Lehman, with a rare drop below the net value of $1. Americans, who usually think of monetary fund accounts as bank savings, did not expect monetary funds to lose money at all, and strong panic throughout society triggered a massive capital flight. At 11:00 a.m. that day, the Fed found a whopping $550 billion in monetary funds, which were "run down" by investors within an hour or two, and the Treasury urgently injected $105 billion, but was unable to stop the fleeing investors. The U.S. government immediately froze all accounts and, without drastic measures, the $3.5 trillion in the IMF was on the verge of being depleted by 2 p.m.

Since money funds are the main lenders in the repo market and commercial paper market, which are the most critical links in the chain of short-term financing for major U.S. companies, once the money dries up, the U.S. will experience massive corporate debt defaults and even direct corporate insolvency, and the collapse of thousands of banks and tens of thousands of companies in 1933 will be repeated.

The commercial paper market has not recovered after the "scare" of September 2008. At present, the repurchase market has become a "lifeline" for short-term capital replenishment for US financial institutions and major companies.

Sitting atop a $13 trillion mutual fund and an active player in the shadow banking market, it provides the repo market with a significant amount of bond and equity assets as collateral, as well as some of the money needed to finance repo.

They control about 2 trillion dollars of capital, repeatedly "press securities to borrow money" in the repo market, then "buy securities with money", expand the scale of assets, arbitrage, bet, buy and sell short all kinds of markets around the world, capture the war machine in the market volatility and key events, with high leverage to make huge gains.

The seemingly conservative pension funds are also uncomfortable with the $6 trillion in their hands, and instead of lying dumbfounded in bonds and other low-risk assets, they are secretly fiddling with new gadgets like "asset swaps" and are indirectly involved in repurchase transactions and other shadow banking operations.

In addition, trillion-dollar insurance companies, ETF funds, and foreign sovereign wealth funds are all integral players in shadow banking.

These "non-bank" but "bank-like" institutions together constitute the so-called shadow banking system. The shadow banking system runs roughly along two chains. The first chain is to help banks "sell" their assets "for real", which is the asset securitization chain; the other chain is to help banks pledge their assets on a large scale, which is the repo chain. Ultimately, the two chains are linked together, and the end products of asset securitization are MBS (mortgage-backed securities), ABS (asset-backed securities), CDOs (debt-collateralized notes), etc., which can be used as collateral for financing in the repo market, i.e., they become the base currency for shadow banking, and participate in a larger scale of shadow currency creation, together with treasury bonds, corporate bonds and even junk bonds.

Under the combined effect of the return of the dollar, traditional currencies and shadow currencies, the price of U.S. financial assets have been rising, the bank's profits have been rolling in, and the "class banks" are also making a fortune.

The fundamental purpose of these two industrial chains, "real sales" and "repurchase collateral", is to realize the assets of banks as quickly as possible, shorten the cycle of holding assets, accelerate the speed of capital turnover, avoid the risk of deteriorating asset quality and inflation, shift the focus of profit to financial asset trading, and embark on a path of development that is asset-light and transaction-heavy.

That was the impetus for Wall Street's rush to break the line between commercial and investment banking in the 1990s.

The Glass Steagall Act of 1934, after reflecting on the extreme greed that led to the Great Financial Crash of the 1930s, completely isolated commercial and investment banks and ensured the smooth functioning of the financial system for more than 60 years, and in 1999, President Clinton, with strong lobbying from Wall Street, signed the so-called Gramm Leach bliley Act, which abolished the boundaries between commercial banks, investment banks and insurance companies, and in just 10 years the world witnessed the first serious financial crisis of the "financial modernization" era, which was as big and as devastating as the Great Crash of the 1930s.

After the financial crisis, the asset securitization and repurchase market was once quite cold, but the Federal Reserve to create the miracle of "asset reflation", at the same time used the suppression of short-term benchmark interest rates to close to zero, suppression of medium-term interest rates by strong policy expectations, suppression of long-term interest rates by QE three kinds of unconventional means, as a result, the financial market is active again. However, the protagonist of shadow currency creation has changed from subordinated, corporate debt to national debt and two-room MBS, and financial risk is rapidly concentrating towards sovereign credit.

How much of the shadow currency was created by the repo mortgage?

In December 2012, the total amount of collateralized assets repurchased by the three parties was $1.96 trillion

In the US repo market, tri-party repo is the most common, and its collateralized assets are most likely to be "sub-collateralized". At the end of 2012, the total assets pledged in the tri-party repo market were $1.96 trillion, the base currency created by the shadow currency, which can also be called SM0 (to correspond to the M0 of traditional banks). On the basis of 1.96 trillion, the shadow currency is amplified by a currency multiplier, which is currently about 2.5 times,[19] i.e., the collateralized assets in the three-way repo market, which have been subcollateralized on average 2.5 times. At this rough estimate, the three-way repo market has created a shadow money supply of nearly $5 trillion.

---

[19] Ibid.

In the age of financial globalization, countless huge and invisible chains of collateral tighten the balance sheets of the world's financial institutions, as well as those of billions of people. The "Europig bonds" may have been initially held by German banks, then sub-mortgaged to British dealers, then after numerous sub-mortgages in the London market, they fell into the hands of MF Global or Lehman London, then through "asset swaps" to hedge funds, and finally "drifted" into the accounts of American pensions, when the crisis came, the losses were suffered by American pensioners. Likewise, junk bonds "made in the US" can flow into London through hedge funds, international cents of primary dealers, which are then sub-collateralized to financial institutions in Hong Kong and then held by Chinese QDII funds, thus lurking on the balance sheets of the Chinese people.

When the European debt crisis struck, the US banking system claimed to hold very small Eurobonds, but the Bank for International Settlements estimated that there was at least $181 billion in exposure. Despite Germany's confidence in having the strongest banking system on the continent, the Grant's Interest Rate Observer reveals that Deutsche Bank, with a leverage ratio of 43:1, is at the top of European financial magic.

A repo mortgage chain is like a rubber band, the longer it is pulled, the more bounce it has and the greater the risk of breakage. The end of this rubber band is linked to the wealth of hundreds of millions of families, and the starting point is in the hands of the central bank. Financial markets high proportion of tight leverage tension, will also be transmitted to the central bank, the German central bank's leverage since 2007 doubled, as high as 75:1, while the average leverage ratio of the world's central banks is dizzying 153:1!

If the rubber band breaks, the financial institutions will fail and the bailout will be the central bank, but what if the central bank is also insolvent? It is the wealth of the whole nation that will ultimately save it.

Why is there a money crisis in June?

If we look at the monetary theory in a narrow sense and compare the data in September 2013, China's M2 is 106 trillion RMB, while the U.S. M2 is 10.8 trillion USD (1 USD = 6.2 RMB), and the U.S. M2 is about 67 trillion RMB, so many people exclaim "China's M2 is much higher than the U.S."!

However, I'm afraid this perception needs to be corrected a bit once the realities of the US financial markets are understood.

The existence of shadow money, has made the traditional money banking on the basic concept of money creation completely obsolete. 2013, the U.S. Treasury Department's Office of Debt Management (Office of Debt Management) on the total amount of U.S. shadow money assessment, concluded that the total amount of U.S. shadow money is about $33 trillion (of which the repurchase and re-pledging contributed 5 trillion), more than three times the M2, the total effective money supply is about $45 trillion,[20] about 279 trillion yuan!

If shadow money is defined as SM2 (Shadow M2), it would include all bond assets that can be used for collateralized financing in the repo market. Simply put, bonds are money! If there is no collateralization, the multiplier of the shadow currency is one and the number of collateralizations is the multiplier of the shadow currency.

Therefore, the definition of the total effective supply of money in a country needs to be amended, namely.

Effective money supply = M2 + SM2

US effective money supply = shadow money + M2

Of course, there is also the problem of shadow banking and shadow money in China, the size of which has various estimates, roughly between 20 trillion and 36 trillion yuan, plus shadow money, China's effective money supply is estimated to be between 126 trillion and 142 trillion yuan, about half the size of the United States, and China's GDP in 2012 is also about half the size of the United States. Thus, the proportional relationship between China's money supply and economic development is roughly comparable to that of the United States.

The difference between China and the United States is that the scale of shadow currency creation in the United States is 5.7 times to 10.2 times that of China, while the scale of traditional Chinese currency

---

[20] Dept of Treasury, Office of Debt Management, 2013 fiscal year Q2 report.

creation is 1.6 times that of the United States. In terms of wealth expression, China's wealth has the highest gold content in real estate, while US wealth is concentrated in financial assets. Given that China's total currency is so large, how could there be a sudden money shortage in June 2013?

In fact, China's banking system has been cash-strapped since the end of May, and the problem became serious in June. In terms of timing, this roughly coincides with the Fed's announcement in May that it was preparing to exit QE, and in June, the US 10-year Treasury repo rate saw an extremely rare -3%, while the Chinese repo rate soared to 30%! The main reason for such a dichotomy is that U.S. Treasuries allow speculators to sell short on a large scale! Without the disruption of short selling, U.S. repo rates would also have soared in tandem with Treasury yields.

In fact, it's not just China that is in a money shortage, it's also the United States that is in a money shortage!

The United States financial market in May and June was the panic crisis of soaring interest rates, which led to the near paralysis of the repurchase market in key parts of currency creation, soaring yields meant that the value of the repurchased collateral jumped, forcing highly leveraged financial institutions to sell assets, resulting in a serious lack of dollar liquidity, Wall Street "dollar vacuum effect", the formation of a global cold wave of dollar repatriation, resulting in a series of crises in emerging market countries such as stock market crash, capital outflows, currency devaluation. China is no exception, and the sharp contraction in the foreign exchange account in May is a sign of that.

Note again that the dollar pullback is not due to a strong recovery in the US economy, but rather to a sharp increase in pressure from the implosion of the US repo market!

The real risk of shadow banking is its money creation function, which at its core is the repo market! Thanks to the repo market, $1 bonds are turned directly into $1 class cash, which immediately doubles the effective money supply! If "sub-collateralization" is allowed, the money supply will expand further. This, in turn, makes the importance of the repo market outweigh all other issues with shadow banking.

It is the currency of the repo that creates this feature, allowing numerous financial institutions to take advantage of the bond assets in their inventory, obtain new cash immediately, further expand the bond inventory, and then repeatedly repurchase to expand the size of the assets, thus easily hedging the spread between the interest cost of the repo and the bond interest yield. In the normal case of low repo rates, rolling money is not an issue, and this profit model is far safer, more flexible, and more attractive than investing in real estate, the stock market, and industry.

The widespread problem of "feeder bonds" in China's financial markets is exactly the same as the operating principle of Wall Street hedge funds with high leverage, except that Chinese financial institutions do not do any risk hedging at all, let alone "matching hedging", and once the financing costs of the repo market continue to rise, the consequences will be unimaginable. Because of this, during the June money shortage, all financial institutions are counting on the "central mother" to hurry "breastfeeding". There is no doubt that a systemic crisis in financial markets is bound to erupt if central banks refuse to provide liquidity.

Interestingly, it was the bond market that was the biggest victim of the June money shortage. High-yielding bonds, represented by municipal bonds, were sold off sharply and the bond market traded in a slump. The interbank bond market saw a cumulative 1.2 trillion yuan in spot transactions, down 81.1 percent year-on-year and a steep 49.0 percent year-on-year decline. In the same month, bonds were issued for a total of 534.2 billion yuan, down 34.6 percent year-on-year and 43.3 percent year-on-year. The stock market has also apparently suffered a ripple, and it cannot be ruled out that a portion of the shadow money has flowed into the stock market.

If financial institutions are investing primarily in long-term projects, such as real estate, then what gets sold off when liquidity is tight should be trusts, pooled finance or other similar real estate financing products, and real estate will also be under significant funding pressure. But in June, the land kings of the country's provinces rose in turn, just as the money was rampant in late June, Shanghai, Chongqing, Nanjing, Wuhan and other cities frequently hit a record high land prices.

China's repo market is expanding rapidly, and in repo transactions, there are problems with the conversion of corporate bonds and standard bonds, which is similar to the "fantasy drift" of U.S. junk bonds, except that even the "drift" is omitted. If corporate debt is sufficiently guaranteed in terms of quality and the discount rate is high enough, then the problem is not serious, but this discounting system leaves hidden dangers for the future that deserve the vigilance of financial regulators.

In addition, China's repo market does not have a "sub-collateral" provision, but it is not excluded that the future will be "innovative". Until a uniform legal framework for "subprime" emerges globally, subprime will be the biggest hotbed of the repo market crisis.

It should be borne in mind that the June money shortage is just a modest preview of a future interest rate volcano eruption.

Expound

What the bank provides to society is a monetary service, and its revenue is the service fee that society pays for that service. Society places various assets in trust with banks and then obtains receipts for the assets in trust, which are the currency in circulation. Monetary receipts correspond to claims on custodial assets, and people make payments in the market with monetary receipts, and when monetary receipts change hands, it means that the ownership of their counterpart bank custodial assets also changes hands.

Of the assets held in custody by banks, the one that is most widely accepted by society is the one with the best liquidity, and when you take that asset and trade it with anyone in the market, everyone readily accepts that the one with the best liquidity is the one that represents wealth, the real money. Thus, money is not money, but a receipt for money; nor is money wealth, but the right to claim it.

In the gold standard era, gold was the real money, banks were where the money was deposited, bank notes issued by banks were the receipt for the gold, and anyone holding bank notes could always ask the bank for the gold in trust. After the gold standard was abolished by the United States in 1971, national legal tender replaced gold, and monetary receipts corresponded to national legal tender. Monetary receipts exist in different forms, whether they are paper savings books, plastic bank cards, or numbers in an online bank account, they are all essentially the same, proof of claiming the national legal tender from the bank.

If gold is used as a benchmark for money, the ability of banks to create their own money will have to be matched by incremental gold growth, which is largely in sync with industrial growth. So what happens if some areas of industry are growing much more than gold, and the quality and quantity of their products and services do not have enough gold to warrant trading? Obviously, the prices of these products will come down. Does this create price deflation? It is possible, but it does not pose a harm to the economy. In the end, gold is just a "calculator" to help exchange commodities, and the size of the calculator does not affect the results, so the price relationship between commodities has nothing to do with the amount of gold. When the money supply is stable, the ultimate influence of money on the economy is "neutral".

This is exactly what has actually happened in the history of world economic development. The British system of price statistics was established in 1664, and if the price benchmark was set at 100, then 250 years later, in 1914, the British price index was only 91. Under the gold standard, prices were deflationary for a long time, but this did not affect the British Industrial Revolution, which increased productivity by thousands of times compared with the agricultural era, and the variety and quantity of goods was not at all an order of magnitude. In fact, the essence of economic prosperity is the increase in productivity and the sharp decline in the cost of production, which is matched by what would have been a steady decline in the prices of various commodities to reflect the increase in productivity.

This phenomenon is even more evident in today's Internet and electronic age, where the price of computers and mobile phones is always falling, but this has not caused everyone to wait with their money, but rather to update more frequently and buy more in larger quantities, and isn't this the result of increased productivity? Rather than stagnating because of "price deflation", these industries are moving forward more rapidly.

The United States is another example: in 1800 the US price index was 100, by 1939 it had fallen to 81, and during 139 years of "deflation" the United States was transformed from a marginal colony to the world's number one power, an economic leap that was also made under the gold standard. No wonder some Western thinkers believe that the gold standard era is the golden age of capitalism.

The monetary system is in fact a contract for the distribution of wealth in society, where monetary stability makes the world public and monetary chaos makes the world sick.

After working hard every day, people hold the fruits of their labour in the bank and receive a receipt, which they expect to use when they retire or are unable to work, to get back the fruits of their labour equivalent to the contribution they made to society in order to ensure that the quality of life is as close as before. But if receipts depreciate significantly, doesn't that amount to looting and fraud? In a society, people may not know each other, but because of the existence of a monetary contract, they can trust each other to create more wealth together. If the currency is devalued, it tramples on the principle of fairness in the distribution of wealth, creates deep-seated mistrust throughout society, which in turn destroys the social division of labour, discourages labour enthusiasm, encourages speculation, undermines the basis of integrity and leads to increased transaction costs.

How can a country that is not honest about its currency expect the population to be honest about the country? How can one expect there to be integrity among the people? The damage done to a country and a civilization by currency devaluation is profound, lasting and irreversible.

When Britain left the gold standard in 1914, the fate of the British Empire was already destined for decline; when the United States abolished the gold standard in 1971, she abandoned the foundation of the country of integrity, creativity, hard work and thrift, and indulged in the degenerate style of greed, speculation, pleasure and luxury.

The financial crisis of 2008 was only the prelude to a series of more serious economic and social crises. Sadly, the devaluation of currencies, represented by the United States dollar, is taking hold around the world, and it is this devaluation that has given rise to shadow banking and shadow money, whereas in the 300 years of industrialization prior to 1971, banks did not need the "shadow of the bank" to make profits, nor did society need the "shadow of the currency".

The inherent tension in the increasingly long collateral chain of shadow currencies is reaching its breaking point, and the worldwide money famine of June 2013 was merely a precursor to a much larger financial earthquake.

Financial globalization, which already binds countries together through chains of collateralized assets, means that future crises will inevitably become global crises.

CHAPTER IV

Interest rate volcano, the final day of reckoning

Of all the data on the economy and finance, I'm afraid none is more important than the yield on the 10-year US Treasury bond. It's the last beacon of escape before the interest rate volcano erupts, and by the time it starts flashing violently, your time is running out.

If you haven't heard of interest rate swaps, it's best to do a quick Google search, interest rate swaps are going to be as famous in the near future as credit default swaps were in 2008. The credit default swaps (CDS) that brought down the U.S. financial system back in the day were nothing more than the nearly $60 trillion derivatives market, while the interest rate swaps (IRS) will be more than seven times the size, if CDS is the power of an atomic bomb, then IRS is the equivalent of a hydrogen bomb.

Never before in the history of mankind have we seen countries hold interest rates down to such a low level and for such a long time. A rare hotbed of ultra-low interest rates breeds a rare monster of an asset bubble that grows deformed in distortion, constantly plundering the nourishment of industry, squeezing the balance of wealth and destroying the health of society.

Quantitative easing and asset bubbles are coming to the end of time and efforts by central banks to suppress interest rates will eventually fail.

When the new heads of the ECB and the Fed start talking about "negative interest rates" more and more frequently, you need to be alerted immediately, which means that even zero interest rates are no longer enough to support continued asset price increases. Negative interest rates are definitely a crazy idea, and it will show the world just how far crazy can go.

Ultimately, the eruption of the interest rate volcano is the judgment day for this round of bubbles!

Federal Reserve suddenly "impotence", Bernanke unexpectedly changed his mind

On September 18, 2013, the Federal Reserve announced that it would continue to keep the QE3 monthly debt purchase size unchanged at $85 billion. News came out, Wall Street is boiling again, the S&P500 and the Dow Jones Index both set new record highs, the United States 10-year Treasury yields fell sharply from 2.9% to 2.7% on the day, emerging market countries' stock markets, debt markets, foreign exchange rumors soared, gold, silver, oil rebounded strongly.

The Fed's decision was too much out of the market's expectation.

Since May, Bernanke repeatedly chanted "fade out" (Tapering) QE's tightening spell, the global financial markets overnight, the national debt yields bloody wind, the Syrian war on the strings, stock bonds, the financial system money shortage rampant, the dollar flow back to the high wind and waves, emerging markets full of chicken feathers.

Bernanke also scared a big jump, in his view, "fade out" does not mean that the currency tightened, but only printing money to slow down, overall is still monetary easing, the market should not be excessive "interpretation" ah, not to mention he also attached a series of "if" "hypothetical" and other preconditions. He has been playing the "expectation management" over the years, the sudden failure of this, especially the soaring Treasury yields almost out of control, which made Bernanke and the Federal Reserve are darkly alarmed.

In terms of the effectiveness of QE policy, there are increasingly sharp disagreements within the Federal Reserve, even among Europe, the International Monetary Fund (IMF) and the Bank for International Settlements (BIS), the so-called "central bank of banks". The monetary pigeons, naturally represented by Bernanke and the central bankers in power, believe that monetary easing has saved the financial system and the economies, and that with time, the miracle of economic recovery will happen; but the monetary hawks believe that in the five years since the financial crisis, central banks have wasted precious time, and that excessive monetary easing has fostered paralysis and laziness in the countries, and that economic imbalances have remained, fiscal deficits have worsened, employment recovery has been weak, and asset bubbles have spread, all similar to 2007, while financial risks have become even more serious.

BIS's approach to QE is quite negative, with its former chief economist, William White, issuing a stinging warning ahead of the September Fed meeting: "In my opinion, this is a rehash of 2007. All the economic imbalances that existed then are still unresolved, the ratio of total public and private debt to GDP in the developed world is 30% higher than it was then, and now we have a whole new conundrum of an emerging market bubble that is headed for a bursting cycle... The (ultra-low) interest rate levels in the US are the ultimate driver of (asset bubbles) around the world, and when interest rates start to rise, everyone will be hit." The BIS even insinuates that the European and American central banks' attempts to suppress long-term interest rates with mere rhetorical "expectation management" have "fundamentally failed" and that "the limits of good communication (of central bank policy) and control over the market have become very clear".[21]

The notion that ultra-low interest rates in the US are the ultimate driver of the global asset bubble can be said to be spot on!

Watching the bubble blowing bigger and bigger, the magic playing more and more evil, the acrobatics playing more and more dangerous, the BIS and IMF viewers who were watching with trepidation and cold sweat, they expected the strong monetary hawks to come to power to stop this crazy game, the former US Treasury Secretary Summers was their hope.

Bernanke went to the day is not much, in the Federal Reserve chairman of the contenders, the highest voice is Ben Summers, he abruptly announced his withdrawal, making the situation a bit clearer, the currency pigeon pie of the new leader Yellen is already crying out for. Yellen's extreme belief in loose money even makes Bernanke look more hawkish. She has supported easing, easing, and easing again in all of the Fed's monetary policy votes, without exception, and in 2010 she even called for the benchmark interest rate to be simply rounded to "negative"! This is the "courage of the bears" that even the

---

[21] Ambrose Evans-Pritchard, BIS veteran says global credit excess worse than pre-Lehman, The Telegraph, 2013-09-15.

pigeonheaded big brother Bernanke and the pigeonheaded predecessors of the Bank of Japan are willing to submit to, who says that women are inferior to men?

Bernanke is gone, Yellen is here, good, good, both of which are worth "celebrating". The Federal Reserve has held back for 3 months "fade out" passion, finally "impotence" and the end.

QE's Titanic, headlong into the repo iceberg

In May 2013, the Federal Reserve began to strongly hint at an imminent exit from QE, the global market could not help but be astonished, the sharp rise in U.S. Treasury yields shows the extent of the market shock. QE3 has been promoted for just over half a year, the U.S. stock market, debt market, real estate has appeared a booming scene, the results of asset re-inflation has just emerged, what is the reason why Bernanke is so anxiously preparing to exit QE?

There are indeed very few people looking out the door, mainly researchers at the Federal Reserve Bank of New York, BIS, IMF and a handful of academics discussing these topics in some studies and on the internet on a small scale, with little to no attention from the mainstream media. It wasn't until May 2013 that a handful of media outlets woke up as if in a dream and started talking about the repo market woes unheard of by the average American public.

The May 23 Wall Street Journal exclaimed, "The Fed's squeeze on shadow banks, central bank purchases of Treasuries, is causing a collateral shortage in the critical repo market." The article states, "The way money and credit are created has changed dramatically in the last 30 years, throw away your textbooks." Although the article misunderstands the concept of "collateralization", it correctly captures the paradoxical essence of QE policy:

> "The $1.8 trillion of treasury debt sitting idle in the Federal Reserve account is starving the repo market of safe collateral, which, given the (monetary) multiplier effect of 'collateralization', means that economies have created about $5 trillion less credit. This is the unintended consequence of the classic. Bernanke's Fed (by printing money) has been heavily criticized for enabling the US government to make huge deficit

overdrafts, and screwing with the blood of the US economy is even worse."[22]

The reasoning is simple, the repo market needs collateral and Treasuries are the most important collateral, QE's purchases have created a conflict between the Fed and the repo market for collateral, the longer the Fed executes QE, the weaker the ability of repo collateral to create shadow money.

In fact, there are $1.1 trillion of two-room MBS bonds "idle" in the Fed's accounts, which are considered to have government-grade credit and are also "safe" repo assets. If both Treasuries and two-room MBS bonds are used as the base currency for shadow money, then the shadow banking system may have a $7 trillion to $9 trillion shortfall in shadow money expansion due to QE policies.

How serious is the problem of repo collateral being squeezed by QE? You could say it's urgent!

In QE, when the Fed buys Treasuries in the market, it buys everything from short to long bonds, but it is mainly focused on medium and long term bonds. In this way, the Fed's "treasury bond inventory" becomes very complex, there are various maturities of treasury bonds, and the amount varies greatly. One of the methodologies of scientific research is to find simple proxy variables (Proxy) for complex systems and to understand the state of the whole system by studying the proxy variables. "10-Year Equivalents" are effective proxy variables for the Federal Reserve's "Treasury Bond Inventory", which replaces the interest rate risk associated with various maturities and different amounts of Treasury bonds with a certain number of 10-year Treasuries. In short, all of the Fed's treasury bond holdings can be represented by "class 10-year treasury bonds".

Using the "Class 10-year Treasuries" method, by August 2013, the Fed already held 30% of all outstanding Treasuries, and if we continue to follow the QE3 pace, it will reach 45% in 2014, 60% in 2015, 75% in 2016, and 90% in 2017, and by the end of 2018, all Treasuries in the

---

[22] Andy Kessler, *The Fed Squeezes the Shadow-Banking System*, Wall Street Journal, 2013-05-22.

market will be eaten by the Fed. Of course, long before that, the repo market had collapsed.

I'm afraid Bernanke really did not anticipate that QE would cause serious distress in the repo market, 7 trillion ~ 9 trillion shadow currency expansion is insufficient to offset the effect of the Fed QE money printing machine. The implosion pressure on the repo market will grow by the day if it continues to eat into Treasuries and two-room MBS bonds at a rate of $85 billion per month.

That's the real reason Bernanke is so desperate to end QE in 2014!

In the repo market, originally played is 10 bottles 3 caps of high difficulty acrobatics, if the Federal Reserve at the rate of 85 billion per month from the market to continuously recover "bottle caps", then a year will make the market reduce 1 trillion U.S. dollars of collateral, considering that the U.S. tripartite repo market of all mortgage assets size is only 2 trillion, such bottle cap loss rate can not be said not alarming. As the number of caps decreases, the acrobatics gradually becomes 10 bottles per cap, or even 20 bottles per cap, and the more technically difficult the acrobatics become, the greater the risk of misses.

Don't underestimate the trillions of collateral in the repo market, which acts similarly to the base currency of the traditional banking system and provides critical liquidity to the multi trillion dollar shadow banking system in the US. Despite being extremely large, the shadow banking system relies heavily on market confidence, with mortgage chains in a severely stretched state and extremely sensitive to any whim of counterparties. In addition, shadow banks are unable to absorb traditional savings and have to rely on ultra-short-term financing from financial institutions, with maturities as short as overnight. Whereas savings pooled the scattered funds of thousands of small savers, repo financing is a highly concentrated and huge amount of money in financial institutions, and when markets are volatile, institutions are better informed, take less time to make a decision to divest, and the funds escape faster.

In a calm repo market, overnight repo financing is not a problem, and in order to save on transaction costs, borrowers and lenders will always continue to roll contracts the next day. However, this is based on continued trust in each other, and if the financier suddenly hears rumours about the market for the borrower, the next day they may refuse to continue the rolling repurchase contract, and the borrower will immediately run the risk of the funding chain breaking. Of course the borrower can go to a new financier right away, but bad news on Wall Street always spreads faster than good news, and one institution's refusal to repurchase often means that everyone closes the door like a plague god. While Bear Stearns, Lehman Brothers, and MF Global's problems are rooted in holding a lot of asset toxic junk, the deadliest hits when the crisis hit all stemmed from the repo market.

Under normal repo market conditions in 2007, asset-backed bonds (ABS) and high-quality corporate bonds were discounted at only 3 to 5 per cent, while in the 2008 financial crisis, ABS and junk bonds were discounted at 40 per cent and high-quality corporate bonds at 30 per cent. Such a sharp jump in discount rates would force repo financiers to add huge amounts of assets at a time when their expansion is at its limit and they would either be forced to jump off buildings to sell their assets, or a break in the funding chain would lead to a default and liquidity in the repo market would be completely frozen in an instant.

The ultimate consequence of continued QE will be a gradual contraction of the repo market until a sudden freeze, followed by the crashing down of the multi trillion shadow banking system!

What about the stock market? The stock boom relies on stock buybacks, the funds for stock buybacks originate from the low interest rate of the bond market, the low interest rate of bonds rely on the liquidity support of market makers, the working capital of market makers rely on the buyback market, the buyback market hit the iceberg, the stock market capital chain will also break.

If in September 2012, Bernanke and the Federal Reserve excitedly engaged in QE3, has not yet realized the seriousness of the problem, then the latest May 2013, all connoisseurs have seen in QE this "Titanic" front, towering a huge repurchase iceberg!

In May, Captain Bernanke prepared for an emergency slowdown, helpless passengers were playing high, not the slightest perceived risk, angry players dropped pots and pans, fussed, long-term interest rates suddenly soared, the repo market crisis suddenly, Bernanke scared to hurry to change the word. in September, the QE maintained the original speed, direction remained unchanged, continued to hit the iceberg.

Bernanke is in a dilemma, continue QE, the front will hit the repurchase iceberg; exit QE, again will trigger a spike in interest rates.

Just in between hesitations, time was ticking away, and the distance to the iceberg was getting closer.

The repo market is the lifeblood of almost all European and American financial institutions short-term funds, and the market is completely without international uniform legal norms and accounting standards, because the repo collateral chain spans both sides of the Atlantic, as far as the Asia-Pacific and the world, therefore, the health of the repo market not only the Fed sleepless, even the United Kingdom, the European Union, the International Monetary Fund (IMF) and the Bank for International Settlements (BIS) are worried about this.

Collateral shortage worsens as regulatory chill hits

In the "Wall Street Journal" began to report that the repo market collateral shortage at the same time, the Bank for International Settlements (BIS) has long been investigated in May also published a high degree of concern about "quality collateral" (HQA, High-Quality Collateral) shortage of reports.[23]

The BIS has been expressing a rather dismissive attitude towards the monetary easing in Europe and the United States, and has already started to formulate new rules of the game, which is the Basel III Agreement.

What's the origin of this BIS? Why does it create agreements that financial institutions around the world must follow? How did you get this status as the world's "Banking Regulatory Commission"?

The origins of BIS are not simple, as Carlo Quigley, a famous historian at Georgetown University and a mentor of former US President Clinton, once said of BIS.

The forces of financial capital have an extremely long-term plan to create a financial system to control the world, a mechanism that is controlled by a few and can dominate the world political system and the world economic system.

---

[23] BIS Report, Asset encumbrance, financial reform and the demand for collateral assets, 2013-05.

The system was controlled in a feudal autocratic mode by central bankers who coordinated it through secret agreements made in frequent meetings.

At the heart of this system is the Bank for International Settlements in Basel, Switzerland, a private bank, and the central bank that controls it is also a private company.

Each central bank is committed to controlling its respective government by controlling fiscal lending, manipulating foreign exchange transactions, influencing the level of economic activity in the country, and providing rewards to politicians who remain cooperative in the business world.

The ultimate goal of BIS is, of course, to protect the interests of international bankers as a whole and to bring the world's banking system directly into its own orbit across sovereign states, to clamp down on governments with financial power and to run the world by monetary means. In order to achieve this "ambitious" goal, it is necessary to resolutely eliminate those short-sighted, greedy, fraudulent and irresponsible financial risks, and strict self-discipline is a prerequisite for international bankers to achieve their "great work", and the Basel III Agreement is a specific requirement for strict self-discipline.

An agreement that is not enforceable is a waste of paper. What would happen if a bank refused to accept the leadership of BIS and did not implement the requirements of Basel III? Quite simply, other banks around the world will refuse to do financial business with the "troublemakers". Want to send money to another bank? No bank dares to take it; want to buy back financing in the financial markets? No counterparty dares to lend; want to grant a loan to a customer? No one wants your check! Who would dare keep money in a bank like this? The "troublemakers" who are excluded from the financial system have no choice but to die.

What if a country refuses to implement the Basel III Agreement? The consequence would be that all the country's banks would be excluded from international financial markets, which would amount to financial sanctions, that the country's import and export trade would be forced to be interrupted because international disbursement and receipt of funds would not be possible, and that the country's investment abroad would be interrupted because overseas funds would not be accessible. Can a modern country last a few days without international trade and overseas investment? For small countries, it is like prison; for large countries, it is like financial exile.

That's where Basel III really comes in! The sovereign government of a country must be subservient to it. Professor Quigley saw all this half a century ago, that the very few who control BIS are the true masters of the world, without democratic election or any oversight; accountable neither to the voters nor to the governments, a special and absolute power that is extremely rare in the international community! This trend will continue to grow in the foreseeable future, which is the ultimate goal of financial globalization.

Absolute power does not mean that it is not accountable, but that it is accountable only to itself. If the few who wielded this power possessed a high degree of intelligence and ability, their management would produce even greater efficiency and better results, at least the BIS masters thought they did.

In terms of liquidity, Basel III imposes higher requirements on banks. All banks must maintain sufficient quality collateral, such as U.S. Treasuries, to ensure that they are able to liquidate their assets to keep their cash flow from drying up for 30 days in the event of an extreme situation. That alone would create a $2.3 trillion shortage of quality collateral. At the same time, the U.S. Dodd-Frank Act (Dodd-Frank Act) put forward higher requirements for margin on financial derivatives transactions, which in turn will cause a shortage of $1.6 trillion to $3.2 trillion in high-quality collateral. In addition, official demand for quality collateral is expected to grow significantly, as the foreign exchange available to countries through foreign exchange management and monetary policy has increased from $6.7 trillion at the end of 2007 to $10.5 trillion in 2012. Doing the math this way, the shortage of quality collateral will expand to $5.7 trillion over the next few years if the financial markets run smoothly.

This is in normal market conditions, so what if the market is under pressure? U.S. Treasury estimates: shortfall cap on quality collateral will surge to $11.2 trillion![24]

---

[24] Office of Debt Management, Fiscal year 2013 Q2 Report-US Treasury Department.

QE has already led to a shortage of high-quality collateral, the pressure on the highly leveraged shadow banking system is increasing, and the Basel III and Dodd-Frank Act jumped out to compete for high-quality assets, which will lead to greater pressure on the repo market.

Instead of melting, the iceberg is getting bigger!

How shadow banks can kill off the competition

The BIS, the Federal Reserve and the US Treasury, all of whom have seen the increasingly acute shortage of quality collateral in the shadow banking system, are again relatively optimistic in their conclusions because they believe the shortage can be alleviated by increasing supply.

The so-called quality collateral is those assets that are closest to the core in the three-dimensional risk of duration, liquidity and credit. Duration risk is easy to understand, someone puts you on a white note to borrow money and if he pays it back tomorrow it's less risky, whereas if he says he won't pay it back until 30 years later you'll lose sleep at night; liquidity risk is whether you can change hands very easily in the market if you don't want to keep holding the note, and the smaller the discount the better; credit risk of course looks at how likely the person borrowing the money is to get into money trouble in the future.

Quality collateral is the asset closest to the core in terms of duration, liquidity and credit 3D risk. In the three-dimensional risk, the part closest to the core is the cash itself, as long as the country still exists, the government has not collapsed, the cash is not afraid to hold for how long, take out anyone will grab, there is no default; 10-year treasury bonds in liquidity and credit risk is only slightly worse than cash, but the risk of holding too long is higher than cash; high-quality corporate bonds (IG, Investment Grade Bond) is higher risk than treasury bonds, ABS (asset-backed bonds) is a bit worse than corporate bonds.

In the U.S. Treasury definition, quality collateral includes: cash, treasury bonds, government agency bonds, and two-room MBS bonds. One might ask, does cash count as collateral? Of course, buying something in cash can be understood as a repurchase agreement "to borrow something back with cash as collateral, the repurchase period is unlimited, the repurchase rate is zero, and the discount rate is also zero". In this sense, QE is nothing more than a swap of cash, a premium collateral, with another premium collateral, treasury bonds. Cash can create money in traditional banks, while treasury bonds can create money in shadow banks. Thus, the essence of QE is to "replace" shadow currency creation with traditional currency creation, but with less than ideal results.

Theoretically, quality collateral can be greatly increased, but it is just a big fiscal deficit to increase the issuance of more national debt, but also can push up real estate prices to increase the supply of MBS, as long as sovereign credit can be unlimited overdraft, quality collateral can be unlimited growth. Therefore, BIS believes that there is no absolute shortage of quality collateral, only regional or local tensions.

The problem is that a quality asset in finance does not equal a quality asset in the real economy. National debt is a quality asset because it is collateralized by cash flows from universal taxation, which can only be generated by real economic activity itself, and in the final analysis, corporate operations and private consumption combine to create quality assets and stable cash flows. Thus, it is not the government that is the true creator of quality collateral in a country, but the quality assets formed by the private economic sector.

However, in an environment of ultra-low interest rates, companies do not invest cheaply acquired capital in activities that create good assets, but instead turn to quick-money financial activities, which is reflected in the shrinking of corporate capital expenditure and the "ageing of assets" of the economy as a whole. If one looks at the country as a company, what is happening is that this company is growing at a shrinking rate of cash flow, while the CEO of the company is going into debt to invest in assets that have no cash flow, such as Picasso or Van Gogh paintings, and then in the course of doing the accounting, he keeps raising the valuation of the paintings from 1 million to 10 million and then to 100 million. While on the books, total assets are appreciating rapidly and consistently outstripping total liabilities, the shrinking cash flow is being overwhelmed by an increasingly heavy mountain of liabilities, and the company must continually raise the valuation of oil paintings and package them into bonds, collateralizing financing from other companies to maintain normal working capital. Does a company like this with a higher total asset value indicate that it is getting better credit?

Sovereign credit is like a credit card, it has its own intrinsic credit limit, without the effective support of the real economy, the credit card will always be burst, "Eurobond" is the latest example.

The U.S. Treasury and BIS theory of unlimited supply of quality collateral actually assumes that U.S. Treasuries have unlimited overdrafts, a premise that is itself a fracture point in market logic.

By this logic, the U.S. government must run deficits, and they will continue to grow, because where is the national debt without deficits? Where is the quality collateral without the national debt? How can the shadow banking system's trillion-dollar heavy body be afforded without quality collateral?

How do shadow banks stand out in the face of QE and regulatory pressure? The simplest way is to "recycle" high-quality collateral, but the "environmental protection and green" sub-mortgage is stuck by the Basel III Agreement, the United States legal framework is not easy to break through, the road is full of thorns.

There is another way out of QE for the Fed to ease the pressure on the supply of quality collateral, but Bernanke is still dithering about the consequences of doing so, there is more collateral, but no one wants long term bonds, the Fed must be careful and cautious, although it must eventually abandon QE, but it is not due to the economy or employment, and the choice of timing is critical, it is better to achieve both an exit from QE and long term rates without getting out of hand. A combination of market "expectations management", economic data, monetary policy, geopolitics, military crises, etc. must be used, and such an opportunity requires patience.

The point is that others can wait, shadow banks that are being set on fire and roasted on a stove can't wait.

If the "Basel III" has forced the shadow banks, they can only take greater risks and carry out a large-scale "junk bond fantasy drift" to "replace" the "idle" United States treasury bonds on the books of pension funds, retirement funds, insurance companies and sovereign funds, and then "fill" back the junk bonds and other assets toxic junk, not only to meet the requirements of the "Basel III", but also to obtain high-quality collateral, the key is that there is no change in the books. Regulation will always be unresponsive compared to the strong desire for innovation of financial players in the market.

Under the double squeeze of markets and regulation, shadow banking will fission! More risky and more insidious "asset swaps" are likely to expand rapidly. This is a way out of shadow banking, but a way out of world financial stability!

Twisting interest rates, the Fed acts as both referee and goalkeeper

The sudden spike in interest rates in May 2013 left the Fed in a state of shock, how could the interest rate market, which has always had a firm grip, be on the verge of losing control?

The Fed has direct control over short-term interest rates, such as through Fed Fund rate setting and open market operations, which can "fix" short-term rates near policy targets. What are federal funds? It's actually the reserves that traditional banks have for creating money, which are either in their own vaults or in the accounts of the Federal Reserve. Many regional banks, having absorbed the deposits of depositors, were unable to find a sufficient number of sufficiently reliable lenders, so that the potential of money creation was not fully unleashed and the excess reserves were left idle in the accounts. However, other big banks have more access and more opportunities to lend, yet insufficient reserves constrain their ability to create money. To make up for the shortfall with the surplus, under the coordination of the Federal Reserve, each bank can "buy and sell" the excess reserves in the money market, when there is more money, the interest is low; when there is less money, the interest is high. After the Fed has set a short-term interest rate target, it releases or recovers money by continuously gobbling up treasury bonds in the money market, affecting the supply and demand of funds in the market until the interest rate is close to the set target, which is an "open market" operation.

In recent years, the Fed has fallen more and more strongly in love with the repo tool. If the market is tight, the Federal Reserve and the first level of dealers to do transactions, the Federal Reserve let dealers borrow money to bond as collateral, that is, "securities lending" to release money, to ease the pressure of the market shortage of funds; when there is an excess of funds, the Federal Reserve, in turn, "out of securities to collect money", their own bonds collateral, the dealers in the hands of the currency "lent back", thus achieving the purpose of contracting market funds.

The biggest advantage of a buyback is that it's super flexible and super short term, the voucher swap can be as short as just overnight, and after a day, the vouchers go back to their respective owners and everything goes back to normal. If the desired results are not satisfactory, the next day you can gradually add the code until satisfied. The repo operation provides the Fed with a powerful, precise, efficient, new-style weapon with fewer side effects and more flexible management of the money market.

Short-term interest rates are good, controlling long-term rates is more trouble. In the repo market, the longest repo would be no more than a year, and now that the world is changing so fast, who would pledge bonds for 30 years to finance? Moreover, the life of most bonds is unlikely to be that long.

So can the Fed just buy long-term bonds? This is the operation of QE, which is typical of price control and obviously violates the basic spirit of marketization of interest rates. Not to mention the fact that forced intervention in the long-term interest rate market is tantamount to putting the central bank in the position of a risk taker, rather than a risk manager. Even more explicitly, QE and "distortion operations" are more intrinsically designed not to simply print money, but to directly control long-term interest rate trends.

And what is Operation Twist? To "distort" the market price of interest rates, of course, in this case the yield curve.

In bond market trading, every moment is shaping the price of a bond, as well as the corresponding yield. Imagine if someone took a snapshot of the yields of various maturities of treasury bonds at a particular point in time with a camera and got a yield curve for all varieties of treasury bonds from 1 month to 30 years at that point in time.

In the course of QE and "Operation Twist" in the United States, the focus has been on buying medium – and long-term bonds, the main purpose of which is to depress the trend of long-term interest rates. The so-called "distortion operation", that is, the Fed will hold the short-term treasury bonds thrown out, and then exchange the operation of long-term treasury bonds, as reflected in the yield curve is the long-term interest rate is "distorted" downward.

In January 2007, financial markets remained oblivious to the impending crisis, with one-month ultra-short-term Treasuries yielding similar yields to 30-year Treasuries and seemingly unconcerned about inflation; yields on 10-year Treasuries declined slowly from six months to 10 years, as if unprepared for the danger of a future liquidity depletion.

The biggest difference between the yield curve in September 2013 and 2007 is that short-term yields are being pressed directly into the ground from mid-air, demonstrating the Fed's strong and direct control over short-term interest rates, while the longer the maturity of yields, the more difficult it is to control them. 10-year Treasury bonds have been depressed by 2 percentage points, while 30-year yields have fallen by only 1 percentage point, and the suppression of long-term interest rates by QE and distortion operations is still evident, but this is at the expense of the central bank's $3 trillion asset-liability expansion, side effects include asset prices bubbling again, the scale of liabilities continues to rise, the deficit problem is difficult to ease, the global economy resource mismatch, financial market imbalances, the real economy recovery is weak, the job market sluggish.

The Federal Reserve rolled up its sleeves and went into battle personally, regardless of the head into the long-term risk, where it is not easy to buy and sell long-term bonds are all eaten, as long as the long-term interest rate control in the ultra-low level, mortgage loans will be incredibly cheap, so that real estate will be able to come back to life, asset re-inflation dream can be achieved. 1990s, the United States normal 30-year mortgage interest rate of 8% ~ 9%, and 2013 was 3% ~ 4%!

The United now plays both referee and goalkeeper, and whenever the ball runs into the second half, it steps up to the plate, hands and knees, grabbing and kicking to get the ball back into the first half. In this way, the "big but not down" of the players came to the spirit, everyone brave, one by one, not risking nothing, fast money not fishing for nothing. Foul play has become the norm, and fraud is more commonplace, just a fine.

Thus, Libor scandal, repo fraud, European debt fraud, oil fraud, gold and silver manipulation, foreign exchange devil, "London whale" violations, interest rate swaps, in all areas that can be called the market, no one can not see the manipulation of the black hand, behind all the black hand, no is not "big but not down" figure.

Interest rate volcano, the ultimate killer of asset bubbles

If the QE going forward will hit the repo iceberg, then the QE going backwards will trigger the interest rate volcano!

The repo market is facing a deadly squeeze on QE, if QE does not exit in 2014, the market will be 45% taken away from Treasuries by the Fed, MBS will be squeezed even more than Treasuries, and the repo market will be depleted of collateral, so the Fed will have to end QE in the short term.

If QE exits altogether in 2014, Bernanke claims that the benchmark rate will stay put for the time being and that a hike may only begin in 2015, with a modest 2% to 2.5% expected for the end of 2016. Such low benchmark interest rates don't seem to have much of a negative effect on the economy.

That's just the surface of the problem.

While the Fed's debt purchases are primarily aimed at suppressing long-term interest rates, their impact on short-term rates should not be underestimated either. Despite market calculations, it is generally accepted that the size of the Fed's $800 billion annual debt purchases has an impact on GDP equivalent to a 1 percentage point reduction in the benchmark interest rate, while the total size of QE purchases through 2013 is equivalent to a 3.7 percentage point reduction in the benchmark rate. In other words, despite short-term interest rates of 0 to 0.25%, the real economic effect is equivalent to the Fed lowering its benchmark rate to -3.7%!

Imagine that when the U.S. real economy and financial markets face a process of short-term interest rate "reset" from -3.7% to 2% to 2.5% in the next few years, it will be as much as 600 basis points (100 basis points = 1 percentage point) of soaring!

There are two schools of thought on the effect of debt purchases on interest rates. One view is that when the Fed announces the size of debt purchases, interest rates have already been changed accordingly, and that future reductions in the size of debt purchases will not affect interest rates, and that the "size of static assets" held by the Fed determines the level of interest rates, i.e., "stock" determines interest rates; another view is that the "flow" of monthly debt purchases has a more important impact on interest rates, i.e., "flow" determines interest rates. In fact, if you observe the drastic changes in interest rates since

May, you will find that the Fed's "stock" and "flow" have not changed, but the change is the hearts and minds! More precisely, changes in "flow expectations" can also have a serious impact on interest rate levels!

In the medium and long-term interest rate trend, the Fed's withdrawal will cause a monthly shortage of $85 billion in medium and long-term bond buying funds, the Fed is the largest buyer of Treasuries and two-room MBS bonds, if it withdraws, how will other buyers in the market continue to "carry the sedan chair"? The Fed's influence on long-term interest rates would have been weaker, the market will be more alarmed by the Fed's exit after the "expectations", long-term interest rates are likely to soar much more than short-term rates.

Congress' annual debt ceiling brawl is as hilarious and funny as a circus show; dare the debt ceiling not be raised? Can the budget go without a deficit? The size of the United States debt has been far from the 1990s can be compared to the 60 trillion U.S. dollars of traditional debt + shadow debt, has been as high as 370 percent of GDP, interest rates rise by 1 percentage point, the economy's cash flow pressure will increase by at least 600 billion U.S. dollars, if the encounter is 600 basis points of interest rate "reset", cash flow will bear at least 3 trillion ~ 4 trillion U.S. dollars of pressure, close to 20 percent of GDP, far more than fiscal revenue! Forget about the economic recovery and get ready to save another financial crisis.

A policy of ultra-low interest rates that is not only in the interest of the United States, but a deadly core interest! Why does the US hate the rising price of gold? Because the price of gold represents the world's expectation of future inflation, a spike in the price of gold will change the market's assessment of the cost of funds, and lenders will demand higher interest rates to cover inflationary losses, so the price of gold directly affects expectations of interest rate trends. In turn, soaring interest rates can change market expectations of inflation, which in turn can change the valuation of the gold price.

The US certainly wants an environment where interest rates are always ultra-low so that asset bubbles can inflate indefinitely, just as people in 2008 were understandably in the mood for house prices to rise forever, but eventually one has to face reality. In any case, the Fed must exit QE as soon as possible, and the price will be soaring interest rates.

If poorly controlled, the spike in interest rates will turn into an interest rate volcano, which in turn will trigger an even bigger crisis.

Interest rate swaps, New Yorkers can't afford to be hurt

When you drive from New Jersey to the entrance to Manhattan, there's the 1.5-mile Lincoln Tunnel ahead of you, and you're shocked when you pay the toll: at the end of 2012, the toll suddenly went up to $13, a 50% increase over the past; when you get to Manhattan and jump on the subway with a grumble, you find that the one-way fare has become $2.50, a 60% increase over the pre-financial crisis fare; when you finally get into a hotel and unscrew the faucet to wash your face, only to find that the water stops in the morning, call the front desk and ask, and get the reply that the pipes are being serviced and they're short-handed.

Welcome to the largest city in America – New York!

New York's funding woes for municipal services are not the result of massive new infrastructure construction or widespread wage increases, but rather New York municipalities have fallen into the trap of the little-known Interest Rate Swap.

Under normal circumstances, state and local governments borrow primarily to maintain infrastructure such as roads, bridges, tunnels, schools, public buildings, etc., and then pay off the debt through local taxes. Due to the long time span and high cost of these projects, local governments often choose a 20 to 30 year term when issuing bonds. When issuing long-term bonds, the government has the option of either fixed or variable interest. The advantage of fixed-rate bonds is that the risk of interest rate fluctuations is manageable and the budget for costs is known; the disadvantage is that the interest rate issued is slightly higher than the market rate, so the total cost is larger. And while floating-rate bonds are issued at a lower cost, fluctuations in the interest rate market could cause future government interest payments to skyrocket unexpectedly.

At that point, the bank, sensitive to the needs of its customers, sold the Government a "best of both worlds" option that would allow the Government to enjoy a lower floating interest rate when issuing long-term bonds, while ensuring that future interest rate fluctuations were "locked in". The choices banks push sound like a free lunch, of course there is no such thing as a free lunch in the world, but the government takes it on faith.

Interest rates on long-term bonds issued by local governments remain variable, but banks are willing to enter into a separate agreement with the government in which the government commits to pay the bank a fixed interest rate on the total amount financed by the bonds and the bank commits to pay the government a variable interest rate. In jargon, it's the government exchanging a fixed cash flow for a floating cash flow from a bank, which is called an interest rate swap.

Interest rate swaps between governments and banks

The essence of interest rate swaps is actually a kind of interest rate insurance, the government's municipal bond term is as long as 20 years to 30 years, and the interest rate fluctuates every day, sometimes even violently, in such a long period of time, will cause great trouble and risk to the municipal debt interest payment, in order to avoid this risk, the bank to the government to sell a kind of interest rate insurance, if the interest rate within a certain level, such as 6.07%, this is the government is willing to bear the interest risk; below this value, the government to the bank to pay the difference of 6.07% market interest rate, as the interest rate insurance premium; and in excess of 6.07%, the bank's compensation will be charged. So, in December 2007, the New York City Department of Transportation (MTA) bought 6.07% interest rate insurance.

The government feels that it can sleep well from now on, under normal circumstances, the market interest rate for municipal debt should float around 5%, the government pays about 1% of the annual insurance premium, in return for 20 years of solid, if the interest rate goes up to 8%, it can also net nearly 2% of the annual bank compensation. In other words, it's the government betting that interest rates will go up and the banks betting that they will go down.

If the City of New York truly understands the Fed's thinking, it should never bet on interest rate hikes, because interest rates are the most important pricing basis for U.S. financial assets, and a big increase would mean a big bear market in the financial markets, which is never what the Fed wants. There is only one scenario in which a long-term interest rate spike will occur, and that is when the Fed loses its ability to control interest rates. The big banks have known this for a long time, and over the past 30 years, with the connivance of the Federal Reserve, interest rate levels have continued to fall and asset bubbles have gotten bigger and bigger.

Not only did the bank make a large bond underwriting fee in the first place, but it soon had a free lunch every day, while the nightmare of New York City government continued night after night.

In 2008, Wall Street's big banks created a financial crisis when the federal government lowered interest rates to near zero to bail them out, and as a result the City of New York was forced to continue paying a fixed 6.07% to the banks, while the banks paid less and less to the government; in 2007 the banks paid 3.36%, in 2008 it fell to 0.7%, and in 2009 it fell to 0.09%, resulting in a net gain of 6.06%. This is just one of dozens of interest rate swap contracts in the MTA. From 2000–2011, NYSDOT has paid out a cumulative $658 million to banks, and the losses continue.

Date	MTA's Fixed Rate	Bank's Variable Rate	MTA Payments to Bank	Bank Payments to MTA	Net Monthly Cost to MTA
Dec. 2007	6.070%	3.36%	$1,017.130	$563,024	$454,106
Dec. 2008	6.070%	0.70%	$954,002	$110,017	$843,985
Dec. 2009	6.070%	0.09%	$633,809	$9,398	$624,411

Interest Rates & Net Monthly Costs on MTA's 2000CD Swap Deal

For all bond issuers looking to lock in interest rate costs, not only does interest rate insurance result in huge losses, but the floating bond interest has to be paid as usual. The issuer, hoping for a win-win situation with the bank, ended up with a "lose-lose" situation for itself.

Don't forget that an interest rate swap is just another agreement in addition to the bond issue, and the original normal terms of payment of floating interest on the bond remain in effect. Very unfortunately, when the issuer misreads the interest rate trend, the issuer has to pay two interest rates, one is the normal floating interest on the bond, which is paid to the creditor, and the other is the expensive interest rate insurance fee paid to the bank.

The floating rate standard for interest rate swaps is based on the LIBOR (London Interbank Offered Rate) rate, while the floating rate for long-term bonds may be linked to other interest rates, such as the 30-year US Treasury yield. When the LIBOR rate fell to 0.1%, the floating rate on long-term bonds also fell, but was still much higher than

LIBOR, say 3.5%. If the issuer's interest rate swap with the bank was originally locked at 6.07%, the issuer now has to pay two fees: first a 5.97% (6.07%-0.1%) interest rate insurance premium paid to the bank, and then a 3.5% interest payment to the bond investor, turning the issuer's financing costs into 9.4%! The thought of having to endure a huge financing cost of 9.4% in an environment where the interest rate on long-term bonds is only 3.5% makes one spit blood.

The perpetrators of the financial crisis have not only received trillions of dollars in federal bailouts, but also continue to receive $236 million a year in interest subsidies from the City of New York, whose redemption price to get out of the "golden handcuffs" of interest rate swaps is a whopping $1.4 billion! New York City wanted to return the favor, and the bank replied, no way, that's all the cash flow in the contract for the next several years was worth.

Note that New York City has not only paid tens of millions of dollars to the banks for the underwritten bonds, but is now forced to pay back huge annual "payouts" to the banks, all of which are tax dollars for New York City residents who were sheared once in 2008 when Wall Street was bailed out, and are now being sheared a second time, and will continue to be sheared for many years. Now understand why New Yorkers are occupying Wall Street!

What's even more irritating is that if the banks on Wall Street fail, the City of New York will have to pay "funeral costs" to terminate the interest rate swap contract. Because interest rate swaps require a third party guarantee, even if New York City does not default, New York City still owes the bank money if something happens to the third party and the contract is terminated. For example, when Lehman Brothers collapsed in 2008, the New York City Department of Transportation was forced to pay $9.4 million to close two interest rate swap contracts.

New York State and New York City entered into 86 interest rate swaps with Wall Street, involving $10.6 billion, in addition to the transportation sector, and agencies such as the Public Library, Water Authority, and Industrial Development Authority, with contracts lasting an average of 17 years, some as long as 2036.

The money that the City of New York should be spending on infrastructure maintenance is flowing into Wall Street's pockets, and the wool is ultimately coming out of the sheep's pockets. So more than 1,800 people were laid off, the price of the Lincoln Tunnel went up, the subway went up, buses went down, the city budget shrank, hotels went down, and the quality of service throughout New York City deteriorated.

If the financial hardship caused by the interest rate swap to New York is unfortunate enough, the fate of Detroit is simply awful.

The interest rate swap hacks behind the Detroit bankruptcy case

On July 18, 2013, the city of Detroit, known as the "City of Cars" with more than $18 billion in debt, officially filed for bankruptcy protection, becoming the largest city in the United States to file for bankruptcy.

On July 18, 2013, Detroit, the automotive capital of the United States, declared bankruptcy. Cities can go bankrupt too? Yes, bankruptcy is also an option when the city's finances deteriorate and there is no way back.

Detroit is not without financial revenue, or a complete disruption of cash flow, but is unable to pay the principal and interest on the debt owed on time, while losing the possibility of paying the debt in the foreseeable future. If a city can still pay its bills on time, then a bankruptcy court judge will judge whether to grant the bankruptcy petition based on the sustainability of the city's current financial situation.

If Detroit goes bankrupt, who will pay off the $18 billion in debt? The answer is simple: no one is still. The creditor will sell the municipal assets and divide the remaining value. Who are the creditors again? Count everyone who the city of Detroit has promised to pay and hasn't, and its total is as many as 100,000 people, including 20,000 retirees whose pensions have been severely cut. In addition, banks, bondholders, bond guarantors, etc. are also creditors.

While all men are created equal, creditors are not. Creditors who have assets secured (e.g., construction, income security) can not only continue to enjoy Detroit's debt payments, but can also own or sell the pledged assets directly. Other creditors, except in special circumstances, can only wait for the bankruptcy court's decision, during which time they will not get a penny. While Detroit's municipal facilities may not be worth much, art museums contain $3 billion worth of paintings, works of art and curiosities that could be auctioned off if they drive creditors crazy.

How did a once proud automotive capital of the world, a great city that was once a symbol of American industry, fall into such disrepair as it is today?

Its roots are also the inevitable result of the expulsion of industry by bad currency since the abolition of the gold standard in the United States in 1971. As the tide of industrial hollowing sweeps across the east and west coasts of the United States, quality industrial assets that generate stable cash flows continue to move overseas, while new good assets cannot compensate for the economic harm caused by the loss, with the result that liabilities continue to accumulate and deteriorate. Detroit is a prominent example of America's rusty economic downturn belt.

The last and deadliest liability is the $1.4 billion in new debt that Detroit borrowed in 2005, which the government is trying to use to bail out two severely shrunken pension accounts, where municipal retirees' salaries have been severely cut, and where failure to address it will lead to serious consequences.

In 2009, Detroit's credit was downgraded, automatically triggering the termination of the interest rate swaps, and Detroit was forced to pay hundreds of millions of dollars in mandatory "redemption fees" to the banks.

Detroit, which is running out of money, can't get the big money and has to plead with Merrill Lynch and UBS. At this point, the banks were so profitable that they couldn't let such a big fish off the hook so easily that they offered to lend money to Detroit to "redeem itself" on the condition that Detroit pledged its fiscal taxes. The desperate Detroit had to dutifully agree to come down, and it got even worse as Detroit jumped from one fire pit into an even bigger one. As a result of this transaction, Merrill Lynch and UBS were upgraded from ordinary unsecured creditors to senior creditors secured by financial income, who not only enjoyed ongoing debt payments during the bankruptcy, but also had priority in the allocation of good assets.

Merrill Lynch and UBS played their hand so hard that Detroit's original debt was not reduced by a penny, but instead lost the mortgage on the fiscal tax.

By June 2013, when the math was done, and it scared everyone, the original $1.4 billion debt ballooned dramatically to $2.7 billion, almost doubling! Of that amount, $770 million was directly attributable to the "redemption fee" on the termination of the interest rate swaps, far exceeding the total interest expense of $500 million! And to pay off this new debt, plus necessary expenses such as pensions, these expenses have eaten up 65% of Detroit's revenue until 2017!

Detroit is finally backed into a corner.

Merrill Lynch and UBS, too, I'm afraid, feel they've done a poor job, with bank representatives involved in bankruptcy negotiations admitting,

> *"Nice, it's our money, but no one wants to be that bank because it's the one that forced a great American city into bankruptcy."*[25]

From interest rate swaps to interest rate "drop traps"

The victims of interest rate swaps are not only local governments, but also schools and hospitals.

The University of Maryland Medical System (UMMS), which derives 58% of its operating funds from local residents' taxes, is $180 million in debt, and unfortunately, those debts are also contracted with banks for interest rate swaps. Like the City of New York, the University of Maryland bet on the wrong direction of interest rate changes and fell into the trap of interest rate swaps.

The interest rate swaps became a huge liability for UMass because the interest rates on the swaps were so wrong that it exposed another big problem, the interest rate swaps on the swaps required collateralized assets, and when interest rates continued to fall, the value of UMass's swap contracts shrank rapidly and the collateralized assets were no longer sufficient. The bank, as counterparty to the bet, demanded immediate additional collateral assets, and as a result UMass Health System was forced to freeze $93 million in assets, a fatal blow to the institution, which has annual revenues of just $70 million. With

---

[25] Henny Sender and Stephen Foley, *Details of Detroit's troubles come to light*, Financial Times, 2013-07-25.

millions of dollars in interest lost each year, it is already a disaster, and the freezing of $93 million in assets will make it even worse, and the cash flow of the UMass health system will be in jeopardy. At this point, the rating agencies began to pay serious attention to the balance sheet of UMass Health System, which would have higher financing costs and more frozen assets once the credit was downgraded, which in turn would cause more serious cash flow deterioration.

UMass Health System, which operates 11 hospitals in Maryland and employs more than 5,000 people, has been forced to make significant cuts in medical staff and cut normal medical expenses under the pressure of an asset freeze and cash flow shortages. In a health care system that relies on residents' taxes for most of its funding, when patients need doctors, nurses, drugs and medical devices, those life-saving funds go to the banks' pockets. UMass Health System can also terminate the interest rate swaps if it wants, as long as it compensates the banks for $183 million in cash, which is nearly the entirety of the system's liabilities, and the health system can't escape the interest rate swaps except to declare bankruptcy.

It's not just the University of Maryland's health care system that has fallen prey to the trap, it's Johns Hopkins University's health care system, and more than 500 hospitals of all types.

The University of Maryland fell solidly into the pit of interest rate swaps, and Hopkins was financially strong and survived the loss, though worse than UMass. The most surprising was Harvard University, which nearly had its funding chain broken in 2009 by a huge loss on an interest rate swap bet.

Harvard University, a $30 billion university and arguably one of the richest in the world, suddenly found itself losing money on a betting interest rate swap in 2009, and the consequences would have been even more dire had it not been for the strongman's bold move to end the swap decisively with a $500 million call. In fact, the size of the total assets doesn't matter in a given situation, what matters is the cash flow, and as soon as that cash flow breaks, creditors can send you to bankruptcy court immediately. At the time, Harvard's CFO dreaded the thought of interest rate swaps:

> "As we entered the fall, we faced some serious liquidity management problems, and the freeze on collateralized assets from swaps was one of them."

It turns out that in 2005 Harvard University was ambitiously preparing to expand its campus by issuing billions of dollars in floating-rate bonds and, in order to lock in interest rate risk, entered into an interest rate swap contract with the bank for up to $3.7 billion on June 30, 2005. And it was Summers, then president of Harvard University, who was at one point the most vocal of the successors to Fed Chairman Ben Bernanke. More interestingly, when Summers was in charge of the U.S. Treasury Department in the 1990s, he was the leading advocate of repealing the Glass-Steagall Act, arguing that the line between commercial and investment banks was long gone, that financial derivatives did not need government regulation, and that all was well with market self-regulation.

The interest rate swap signed right under Summers' nose was also the culprit that nearly led to the break in Harvard's funding chain. Had Summers terminated this interest rate swap at the end of 2006, the year he left office, there would not have been a huge loss on the $500 million interest rate swap in 2009.

Summers' judgment of the financial markets can be seen in this.

The origin of Libor

Since the floating rate in an interest rate swap contract is usually tied to Libor, and the net profit a bank makes is the difference between the fixed interest it receives and the floating rate it pays, the lower the Libor rate for the banks, the more they net, which is the profit motive for the big banks to join forces to manipulate Libor.

Where exactly is this Libor? Why do financial institutions in the U.S. and around the world do business by reference to its interest rate, and does the Libor rate have more influence than the Fed's benchmark rate? To make sense of these questions, one must explore to understand where Libor is coming from.

Libor (London Interbank Offered Rate) is the London Interbank Offered Rate (LIBOR), whose earliest origins date back to the 1960s, when the rise of the European dollar was in full swing. After World War II, Europe gradually re-emerged from the ruins and had a growing surplus in trade with the United States, while the United States, due to the Korean War, the Vietnam War, the Soviet-American arms and space race, the maintenance of global military hegemony, and the great social program at home, led to excessive financial expenditures, which were eventually solved only by money printing.

By the 1960s, the huge dollar surpluses of European countries, the overseas dollar investments of U.S. multinationals, the dollar savings of the Soviet Union, Eastern European and Middle Eastern oil-exporting countries, and the dollar military expenditures of the U.S. military at overseas bases were all pooled in the European financial markets. With the total size of the overseas dollar surpassing the gold reserves of the United States for the first time, the dollar has gone from scarcity to surplus, and these "idle" so-called European dollars are desperate to find new investment opportunities.

Europe in the 1960s was in a sharp predicament, with a surplus of dollars on the one hand and fragmented financial markets on the other. Cross-border loans and investments are rare, foreign exchange and capital flows are impeded, and all financial operations of companies are usually handled by national banks. Why aren't European dollars flowing back to the US? Because of tighter financial controls in the US and London's ongoing efforts to regain its role as a financial centre, it has a laissez-faire attitude towards the European dollar. When Sigmund Warburg pioneered the concept of European dollar bonds in London, large amounts of European dollars began to pour into the highly financially free city of London from all sides, and dollar-denominated bonds of all kinds "grew wildly".

However, these U.S. dollar-denominated bonds have a disadvantage, that is, the scale of financing is not large, usually not more than 20 million U.S. dollars, while investment banks charge underwriting fees are often as high as 2.5%, the reason is that the continental European dollar to come to London across the sea is not easy, standardized bonds require very low capital mobilization costs in order to be large, apparently the fragmented financial markets and foreign exchange controls limit the large-scale cross-border U.S. dollar.

This dilemma has drawn the attention of another financial mastermind, Minos Zombanakis, known as the "father of Libor".

In the 1960s Minos worked at the Roman sub of Manufacturers Hanover, not a factory but a century-old New York banking shop, and in 1913 became one of the founding shareholders of the Federal Reserve Bank of New York, holding up to 7% of the stock. Hannover Manufacturing controlled 89 of the top 130 board seats in the United States in the 1970s. Later, Hannover Manufacturing was merged into

JP Morgan Chase. Minos has been impressed by the huge success of Eurodollar bonds, but has also discovered the gist of it – how can the constraints of small bond financing be broken?

Minos' plan is to create a new concept of "European Dollar Loans", similar to "Eurodollar Bonds", by creating large syndicates! He is convinced that large-scale dollar loans can better meet the financing needs of large corporations and sovereign governments. His main competitors were precisely the bold and innovative investment banks, and Minos convinced several banks and insurance companies, including the Rothschild Bank, and obtained the Bank of England's nod to embark on a landmark quest in 1969.

The first problem faced was the issue of loan duration, with those with large capital needs preferring loans of five years or more, when commercial banks were neither such long-term savers nor willing to consider such long-term loans.

The second difficulty was the size of the loan, when no bank was willing to take the risk of a large loan on its own. Therefore, Minos' plan is to establish a syndicate, with one bank leading the management and the other implementing it, and to standardize the terms of the loan internally and the promotion externally.

To solve the problem of long loan terms, Minos creatively had syndicate members commit to a type of continuous rolling short-term loan, such as three or six months, which could be matched by short-term savings for the same term, with interest rates adjusted at each end. So Minos developed an operational process where he had the syndicate's member banks report its current cost of financing to the executing bank two days before the short-term loan was due, and then weighted the average to exactly $1/8^{th}$ of a percentage point, and this rate, plus the bank's profit points, formed the rate for the next short-term loan.

That's where the Libor rate comes from.

Minos' innovation was a huge success, with hundreds of millions of dollars in European dollar loans launched within a few months and other banks following suit, and by the early 1970s the market for European dollar loans had reached billions of dollars a year, with hundreds of banks becoming active participants in this new market.

Minos' idea of short-term interest rate pricing spread widely, becoming Tibor in Tokyo, Euribor in Europe, Sibor in Singapore, and

Shibor in Shanghai, which the British Bankers' Association in London named Libor in the 1980s and has since become the standard for pricing interest rates on overseas dollars worldwide.

Libor's influence on dollar rates is even greater than that of the Federal Reserve, as 2/3 of the dollar's issuance goes overseas, reflecting more realistically the relationship between supply and demand for the dollar, and Libor's interest rate levels are generally slightly higher than the Fed's benchmark rate, making it a key window into global dollar movements. When Libor is significantly higher than the US benchmark interest rate, it is an indication that the level of distrust among banks is becoming greater, which is often a precursor to a crisis.

Libor has interest rate quotes for 15 maturities in 10 major currencies, the most important of which is the US dollar Libor quotes for 3 month maturities. 18 banks publish their willingness to lend at 11 am each day, and the average of the remaining 10 quotes is the Libor pricing for the day, after removing the 4 highest and lowest quotes.

Minos could never have dreamed that the interest rate standards he proposed to address the internal management of the syndicate would now extend long beyond interbank lending, with billions of dollars of mortgages, bonds of all kinds, commercial paper, credit cards, and even commodities such as oil, gold, and grain traded globally tied to Libor, and the multi-billion dollar interest rate swap market tied even more closely to Libor.

In Minos' day, there was no such thing as rigging Libor rates, not that the integrity of the day was more reliable than the modern day, but the lack of motivation to rig. At that time, Libor was used only to estimate the cost of interest rates within the syndicate that provided "European dollar loans" and did not address the issue of reference to its indicators in other financial areas. And the Libor rate, now estimated by *The Economist* UK, relates to the pricing of global financial assets worth up to $800 trillion in total.

Anyone who wants to tinker with this market, a 0.1 basis point swing would create a substantial profit of millions of dollars!

Libor itself is naturally fraught with obvious vulnerabilities. First, the 18 banks' quotes were based on their own "estimates" rather than on real transactions between them, which lost any "evidence" to pursue. Even London's gold pricing system is more reliable than Libor's, after all, gold prices are traded by the clients of the Big 5 gold dealers to each other. To be precise, Libor is not a real market price, but an "imaginary" price for 18 banks sitting together. Since it is a contest of imagination, each of the participating banks has a strong incentive to lie, since the results of the day's interest rate calculations will directly affect their own profit and loss, and even trigger rather lethal suspicions about their credit. the Libor mechanism gives the participating banks an incentive to cheat and creates the conditions for them to cheat.

The rest of the question is just how far they will go crazy.

Who's manipulating interest rates?

Rumors of Libor's manipulation are not uncommon in financial circles; what is uncommon is that the manipulators are caught with evidence that cannot be denied.

The earliest disclosure of Libor's manipulation was in the Wall Street Journal, where in several stories in April and May 2008, the author questioned the deliberate underestimation of their borrowing costs by some banks, resulting in a wall-to-wall war of opinion. The British Bankers Association strongly believes that Libor is a trusted market indicator, even in the midst of a financial crisis; the Bank for International Settlements (BIS) claims that "available data do not support the kind of assumption that banks manipulate interest rates and profit from them"; and the International Monetary Fund (IMF) found that

> "while some market participants and the financial media doubt the integrity of the dollar Libor pricing process, the facts suggest that dollar Libor pricing, remains an accurate measure of trustworthy bank lending of unsecured funds".

Thus began an official vs. official, media vs. media, academic vs. academic interest rate manipulation debate.

The engagement of academia has put the issue of interest rate manipulation in a much more rigorous and intense spotlight. Studies have shown that banks have large portfolios of Libor-linked assets and that interest rates are manipulated in order to make huge profits. For example, Citi's interest rate swaps in 2009 were worth a notional $14.2 trillion, Bank of America's $49.7 trillion, and JPMorgan Chase's $49.3 trillion. An interest rate swap contract of this magnitude, with a slightly larger exposure, can make a huge profit in Libor manipulation. In its first quarter 2009 report, Citi admitted that net interest income would generate a staggering $936 million profit if interest rate levels fell by 0.25 percentage points per quarter; a 1 percentage point reduction would result in a profit of $1.9 billion.

How did lowering interest rates allow banks to generate such amazing returns? Don't forget the thousands of states, counties, and city local governments, schools, hospitals, libraries, water utilities, and transportation authorities in the U.S. that have entered into interest rate swap contracts with banks where falling interest rates will force them to pay huge interest rate premiums to the banks.

In fact, it's no secret that the Crown is well aware of Libor's manipulation; in late 2008, the Governor of the Bank of England, Mervyn King, in describing Libor to the British Parliament, explicitly said,

> *"It (Libor) is in many ways the rate at which banks refuse to lend to each other, not the rate at which anyone would actually lend."*

The Federal Reserve Bank of New York has also taken an open-minded approach to Libor manipulation, with a 2008 Barclays employee filing with the Federal Reserve Bank of New York stating, "We know we're not making an honest Libor offer, but we're doing it because if we don't, we're instead attracting unnecessary attention." Geithner, then governor of the Federal Reserve Bank of New York, had written a memo to the Bank of England in 2008 alerting Marvin King to Libor's manipulation, but Geithner did nothing to force the Bank of England to conduct a substantive investigation. A few months after Geithner's memo, a Barclays employee told the Federal Reserve Bank of New York that Libor was still "absolute garbage".

The Wall Street Journal has been pursuing the Libor manipulation case, and in March 2011 and February 2012, it came out that the United States financial regulators and the United States Department of Justice had opened criminal investigations into Libor manipulation.

The question arises here, the Libor manipulation took place in London and US jurisdiction is limited to within the US, so on what basis can the US Department of Justice investigate and prosecute those involved in the case in the UK? Because Libor rates are also the pricing benchmark for financial products such as mortgages, credit cards, and student loans in the United States, manipulation of Libor rates violates U.S. domestic law, and the U.S. Department of Justice has authority to conduct international investigations and depositions.

The same applies to other countries, such as Kunming, Yunnan Province, where a person sued the Federal Reserve in Chinese court after suing the United States for depreciating the value of his dollar deposits as a result of its QE policy, as reported in the domestic media. This allegation is clearly beyond China's jurisdiction; however, if plaintiffs' counsel can find evidence that the depreciation of the U.S. dollar has indeed harmed plaintiffs' legitimate interests and is in clear violation of Chinese law, then such an allegation would also entitle the Chinese judiciary to conduct an international investigation. China clearly lacks international experience, and its economy has long been tied to the world, and when foreign actions infringe on China's domestic interests, China should also act to protect its own, or at least inspire a strong sense of self-preservation from the US international investigation of Libor.

Although China's financial markets are not open, many domestic investors have gone out into the world through QDII (Qualified Domestic Investor) funds, which, regardless of their asset allocation, will almost certainly involve Libor rates, and these investors are effectively entitled to make claims against the banks that are manipulating Libor.

As the Libor investigation progressed, more and more direct evidence was uncovered. A trader at RBS admitted that their bank's senior staff regularly asked the bank's Libor rate quoters to submit Libor rate quotes that were favourable to the bank, and from time to time satisfied Libor rate requests from some of their old relationships, which had become commonplace internally. Even more explosive evidence of interest rate manipulation is the content of the conversations provided by emails, cell phone texts and other means of communication between traders, which finally came to light.

Financial regulators in at least 10 countries around the world have opened investigations into Libor's interest rate manipulation, and 20 major global banks have been named for investigation.

The end result of the Libor manipulation case is likely to be criminal prosecution of a few traders and nothing more than a fine for the big banks. Don't the executives at the big banks know that traders are playing with interest rates? Aren't they involved? It's unthinkable, but hard to catch evidence of these people. Unlike the stupid and reckless traders who expose manipulation in text messages or record it on their calendars, they are more legally aware, more protective, and less exposed.

As the saying goes, the top beam is not the right beam and the bottom beam is not the right beam, traders dare to manipulate Libor recklessly, indicating the acquiescence of the bank executives; big banks dare to do whatever they want, because central banks such as the Federal Reserve are openly manipulating interest rates every day. The purpose of the loose monetary policies of the countries is to artificially suppress interest rates, and since the bosses in power are doing this, how can they be so good as to restrain their minions? The whole debacle was not triggered by central banks cleaning up their own doors, but by the intervention of other branches of government.

If the answer to the question of who is the biggest interest rate manipulator, it is clearly not traders, who are the scapegoats; nor the major banks, who are at best complicit; it is central banks that are the masterminds of the unprecedented interest rate manipulation in human history, and it is Governments that are the biggest complicit.

The United States Government is a major beneficiary of ultra-low interest rate policies, and the huge deficit urgently needs to reduce the cost of financing the national debt, which in 2008 cost the federal government an average of 4.5 per cent of its $10 trillion in 2008 and cost $451 billion in annual interest payments on the national debt. In 2012, the total U.S. national debt reached $16 trillion, while the federal government's interest payments on the national debt fell to $360 billion and the average interest rate on the national debt fell to 2.3 per cent, while the average yield on the iconic 10-year national debt was only 1.75 per cent, even below inflation. That's thanks to the Fed's interest rate manipulation.

If the yield on the 10-year Treasury bond had remained at the September 2013 level of 2.75 percent, the average interest rate on Treasuries would have been 3.6 percent, and the total interest expense would have exceeded $600 billion, which is roughly equivalent to the total U.S. defense and military budget. If the average interest cost of the national debt returns to the normal level of 4.5% in 2008, the national debt interest payments will soar to $765 billion, to know that the total tax revenue of the United States in 2012 is only 2.45 trillion, if the national debt interest payments alone accounted for nearly a third of the total tax revenue, then what will the creditors of the United States think? Is there any hope of paying such a debt? Even if the U.S. can print money to pay its debts, how much confidence will remain in the "gold content" of the dollar?

There is no doubt that the US government is a strong supporter of ultra-low interest rates.

Of course, it is not only the US government that actively embraces ultra-low interest rates, but also all developed countries that are panting with high debt that have a common interest. Governments were initially victims of the financial crisis, but then implemented huge deficit State policies that only cheapened the banking system and did not contribute to the recovery of the real economy, and eventually Governments were finally "held hostage" by the banking system, trapped in a debt trap that they could not extricate themselves from.

The U.S. government's desperate need to reduce the cost of deficits, the Fed's fetish for asset re-inflation, and the banking system's strong appetite for huge profits have perfectly formed the unbreakable deadlock of interest at ultra-low interest rates. They used each other, joined forces and looked out for each other. Against this backdrop, interest rate manipulation has risen to become a common platform, with central banks responsible for "expected intervention" and "policy suppression" of interest rate movements, banks responsible for "market intervention" and "trading suppression", and the United States government constantly creating geopolitical tensions, war crises and terrorist attacks, with one goal in mind: in an extremely "insecure" world, United States Treasuries are the only safe haven.

Libor manipulation is nothing more than a blip in the broader context, and a lower Libor is good for lowering the cost of financing Treasuries, pushing up the price of Treasuries, and for the larger picture of asset reflation. It's just that it's played out too explicitly to the point where "no investigation is enough to make civilians angry".

Ultra-low interest rates blow up the biggest financial bubble in history

It is widely believed that banks instinctively abhor inflation and prefer higher interest rate levels because they are lenders whose fundamental interest is in protecting interest income. In fact, the conclusion is just the opposite, low interest rates, super low interest rates, permanent super low interest rates are the biggest boon to the banking system.

Because low interest rates push up the prices of all financial assets, and banks are the biggest beneficiaries of this.

The fundamental purpose of monetary easing is to create asset re-inflation, and the gradual rebound in asset prices is like a rising tide of seawater, drowning out the reefs of bad debts hidden both on and off the bank's books, presenting a calm and blue sea before people. Ordinary swimmers can neither see the jagged and steep rocks beneath the surface, nor feel the fierce dark tide, nor spot the bloodthirsty man-eater sharks. Such an ecological environment is best suited for predators to thrive.

In a low interest rate environment, anything weird can happen. The yield on 10-year U.S. Treasuries, for example, is below inflation for a long time, which means that a sane investor who invests in 10-year Treasuries will have his principal slowly eaten away by inflation. At the same time, the share of national debt in GDP is increasing each year, which means that the risk of debt servicing is increasing. But he still did not hesitate to invest in U.S. Treasuries, because he knew that the Fed was constantly buying Treasuries, despite the fact that yields were getting lower and lower, but the price of Treasuries was getting higher and higher, and it was no longer interest income that he was after at this point, but price income.

Rather than seeking cash flow, do investors expect prices to keep rising? It sounds a bit like a real estate bubble. Back then, rental income was negligible, but home prices were forever rising, and there was always someone willing to offer a higher price to take the house. The stock bubble was very similar in that the investor had no sense of dividends but was absolutely convinced that the stock price would keep going up and up and another bunch of fools would scramble to overbid him to buy the stock out of his hands until he realized he was the last one.

Increases, not stocks, determine price trends.

Interest rates must be constantly shaken down to create volatility while maintaining the momentum for asset prices to continue to rise. The Fed's constant bullishness has created an up and down market, while interest rate swaps have perfectly ensured a downward trend in rates.

The banks bet on lower interest rates signed by the interest rate swaps, equivalent to shorting interest rates in the market, which is completely consistent with the principle of shorting paper gold in the gold market, the larger the scale of shorting gold, the greater the downward pressure on gold prices.

From 2007–2012, the nominal value of interest rate swaps doubled from $20 trillion to a staggering size of nearly $40 trillion, which amounts to adding another heavy piece of weight to the Fed's interest rate suppression QE leverage. In the five years after the crisis, the Federal Reserve, the European Central Bank, the Bank of England, the Bank of Japan and the Central Bank of China purchased a total of $10 trillion in treasury assets. $10 trillion in central bank debt and $400 trillion in interest rate derivatives were combined to create an unprecedented ecology of ultra-low interest rates, creating the worst asset bubble in human history.

From 2007 to the end of 2013, the Federal Reserve, the European Central Bank, the Bank of Japan and China's central bank's total debt purchases to reach $10 trillion

The two ways in which central banks purchase debt and swap interest rates to suppress interest rates can be graphically expressed as: central banks set the stage and swaps play.

According to a 2013 report released by the Office of the Comptroller of the Currency (OCC), financial derivatives trading in the United States is concentrated in the hands of a very small number of large banks, with the four largest banks having a monopoly on 93% of the total nominal value of financial derivatives: JPMorgan Chase, Citibank, Bank of America and Goldman Sachs. Interest rate swaps again account for an absolute share of financial derivatives, with a nominal value of $188 trillion or 81% of all derivatives.[26]

One can say how confident a handful of big banks are betting against the world on interest rate movements, with their own multi-million dollar exposures, that interest rates will not rise! Come to think of it, their confidence makes sense. These big banks have critical influence over Fed policy, and many of them are also the decision makers and enforcers of the Fed's open market operations, both as

---

[26] Quarterly Report on Bank Derivatives Activities, Office of the Comptroller of the Currency, 2013.

referees and as athletes. They have a right to participate in the policy discussions within the Fed, and even less in the implementation of the implementation plan, and they have unparalleled market foresight and even decision-making power. So they dare to bet big because they are the owners of the casino and they have the power to change the rules of the casino.

In addition to absolute market foresight, the big banks have another advantage, which is the "big but not down" absolute insurance factor. No matter how risky they are, the Fed will end up taking the risk, because their life or death will be linked to the survival of the entire U.S. financial market, directly affecting the security of the U.S. economy and the world economy. Whoever is in charge of the White House and the Federal Reserve has had to save, and dare not save, the "big ones".

Absolute market foresight + absolute insurance factor = absolute greed.

What other reason do these banks have to be afraid to gamble so boldly?

But what should happen always happens, and there are moments when the betting ends. When a global financial mega-bubble blown up by ultra-low interest rates bursts, the disaster will be violent and brutal.

As one hears the fuse for Treasury yields begin to sizzle, interest rates, this sleeping volcano is about to erupt!

To quit QE is to seek death, to continue QE is to wait for death

In May 2013, Bernanke conducted a dangerous experiment in which he attempted to test and assess the global market reaction to the Fed's exit from QE by shouting and the result was a disastrous spike in interest rates! Treasury yields are nearly out of control, bond values are shrinking sharply, stock indices are plunging, repo markets are under pressure, shadow currencies are in desperate shortage, and emerging markets are bleeding to death.

Bernanke finally understands that QE is far more dangerous than he previously thought to get out in one piece, and that the Fed is far from ready to deal with the dire consequences of soaring interest rates.

As a result, he had to pull back at the Fed meeting in September and continue QE with his head held high.

The biggest benefit of QE has been the creation of an ultra-low interest rate financial environment, with the banking system profiting from five years of asset re-inflation. However, everything that has an advantage has a disadvantage, and the consequence of artificially suppressing interest rates is that one must face a retaliatory rebound in interest rates after the release of the suppression, and the greater the force of the suppression, the more destructive the rebound will be.

From the economic effect, the overall level of interest rates distorted by at least 800 basis points than normal, including zero base rate policy distorted by at least 400 basis points, while the $3 trillion debt purchase scale "contributed" another 400 basis points. between May and September, 10-year Treasury yields rebounded only 100 basis points, the global financial markets are already in turmoil, 8 times the soaring interest rates will mean what?

Bernanke knows that the consequence of continuing to push QE is to eventually hit the buyback iceberg, so he has no choice but to exit QE sooner rather than later.

If a sandboxing exercise to simulate an exit from QE is done, then the Fed will have to weather the shockwaves of a three-round interest rate explosion.

The first shock wave will begin with the Fed reducing its purchases of long-term Treasuries and MBS, triggering the first spike in long-term interest rates.

In the case of negative or insignificant real yields of treasury bonds, treasury bonds are considered a safe haven, mainly because investors bet that treasury bond prices will rise infinitely, and the Federal Reserve, as the largest buyer in the market, in fact, for treasury bond prices cast a "diamond bottom". The Fed's reduction in the size of debt purchases will mean that there is no guarantee of a "diamond bottom", then investors will inevitably demand higher yields to compensate for the risk they take, and long-term interest rate levels will rise significantly.

This market reaction, in turn, will be interpreted by more investors to mean that rising interest rates are already the general trend, so more investors have to deal with the future change in advance, they either begin to sell bond assets, or to sell bonds short to speculate for profit.

At this point, even if the Fed keeps the benchmark interest rate unchanged to zero, but the rise in long bond yields will gradually get out of control, which will stimulate more investors to join the army of selling and short selling.

Long bond rates are out of control and yields on short and medium term bonds are contagious to market psychology, albeit to a lesser extent, but the bond market cannot avoid an overall interest rate panic. In this way, hedge funds, monetary funds, pension funds, and insurance companies that hold bond assets will face heavy pressure from asset losses caused by falling bond prices. Hedge funds operating at high levels of leverage would be in a state of extreme anxiety as their funds were almost entirely dependent on repo collateralized financing, but suddenly the value of these collateralized assets shrank dramatically, market makers or traders began to call hedge fund managers in a frenzy, urging margin calls or more on collateralized assets, and desperate hedge funds were forced to sell their risky holdings to cash in on the pressure. When such a situation prevails in the market, the financial market has caused a "money shortage".

When several of the most leveraged hedge funds announce that their funding chains have broken, the market will erupt into risk-taking phobia, and the already overstretched repo chains will be full of traps, rings that could break, London will be the center of the wind, Germany, the United States, Hong Kong, China, Singapore, South America, and everywhere the repo chains are strung together will become panic-stricken.

This is just the first shockwave that started with the runaway long-term interest rates. The second shockwave will be triggered by a spike in short-term interest rates.

The Federal Reserve, the Bank of England, the European Central Bank and the Bank of Japan, did not and do not dare to raise short-term interest rates, but Libor interest rates will not be controlled by the central bank "knee-jerk reaction". 2008 crisis, the British and American central bank's benchmark interest rate soon fell to zero, but Libor was once as high as 4% or more, and the central bank benchmark interest rate parted ways. Libor is a pure market interest rate, after all, to participate in the offer of the big banks themselves have suffered from asset shrinkage and insufficient funding, the financial market money shortage will naturally affect the Libor offer. In particular, the Libor market has just experienced a "severe beating", the likelihood of the bank "topping the wind" again greatly reduced, Libor rates will inevitably rise.

This is where the trouble escalates!

Of the $40 trillion in interest rate swaps, the floating rate is essentially locked in Libor, with the risk highly concentrated in a few of the biggest banks, the big ones that made a fortune in previous years now foolishly. After the financial crisis, interest rate swaps doubled, and the new $20 trillion contract was naturally a bet against the banks at ultra-low interest rates, and when the banks checked their books, they couldn't help but take a cold breath. The feng shui turns, unlucky to their own, and worse, the contract value becomes "negative", which will force the bank to "freeze" more assets, also "freeze" the already short cash flow. Terms that used to be used by banks to bully thousands of local governments, schools, and hospitals are now, in turn, a noose around their necks. Of course, if the big banks are sufficiently "cunning", such conditions could be "unequal treaties", directed only at others, without limiting themselves, i.e., unequal terms.

If interest rates continue to soar, the noose around the bank's neck will get tighter and tighter.

Wait a minute, isn't it true that banks still have $2 trillion in cash in the Fed's excess reserve account? The idle money has been lying there silently eating the 0.25% interest on the Fed's supply. Yes, $2 trillion does "exist" on the banks' balance sheets, but one would be wrong to think that the banks would be idling such a large sum just to eat a little handout-like interest. The "body" of the money is still there, but the "soul" has long since flown off the balance sheet of the bank.

This is also thanks to the accounting guidelines for repurchases, where cash is a quality collateralized asset along with bonds, and since there is a chain of collateralization for bonds, the same can be said for cash. The more than $6 billion that JPMorgan Chase failed miserably in the 2012 "London Whale" incident is in fact a prime example of the transfer of "excess savings" to London for gambling, where savings are still on the books, but actually lose all.

The collapsing state that emerged in the interest rate swap market will have another terrible effect. The nature of interest rate swaps is the equivalent of big banks shorting rates, and if this market disintegrates, then the biggest glacier pressed on top of rates will quickly melt and interest rates will see a retaliatory spike, which will evolve into an eruption of an interest rate volcano!

Look no further than the prices of bonds, they only give bond investors a sudden brain spill.

The second shock wave will detonate the "hydrogen bomb" of interest rate swaps! The epicenter of the 2008 financial crisis is the credit default swaps (CDS) market, which is only a $60 trillion "atomic bomb", and the size of interest rate swaps is nearly seven times the size of the CDS market, if the interest rate swaps collapse, the 2008 financial crisis is like a cold dish before the main meal, not enough to gag.

When the central banks tried to come to the rescue of the "big but not dead" again, they found that they had neither weapons nor ammunition. Can't the central bank print money again? Let us not forget that it was the printing of money that caused the hydrogen bomb to explode, and does anyone believe that further printing can save the crisis?

The most important weapon of the central bank is not the power to print money, but the confidence people have in it. The loss of this confidence, and the meaning of power, has been demonstrated in action by both the German Central Bank in 1923 and the Central Bank of the Republic of China in 1949.

A third shockwave is also feared to be pulling away from the precarious monetary confidence. Since there is such a horrible risk of exiting QE, what are the consequences of continuing QE?

That's the quality collateral in the repo market, drained step by step by step by the central bank. On the buy-back chain, there will be an increasingly thrilling "acrobatic show", with 5, 10 or 20 bottles needing to be covered by one lid. An overstretched rubber band of repurchase will build up a stronger pullback tension that will either snap or rebound to hurt. Liquidity will also dry up quickly when a panic over risk to home causes a sudden freeze in the repo market.

The main purpose of investors buying large amounts of Treasuries is to finance repurchases in order to increase the size of assets and generate higher yields. If the repo market is too risky, then demand for Treasuries will also fall rapidly, which is equivalent to the effect of the Fed's exit from QE, i.e. an oversupply of Treasuries, with the result that interest rates also rise. At the same time, market makers will not be able to maintain large bond inventories with the help of repo financing, which will lead to a decline in the liquidity of the bond market, as is already the case with the deteriorating corporate bond market. Bonds are good to buy and bad to sell, and frustrated investors are bound to demand higher yields to compensate for their losses, which, if translated, is still higher interest rates.

What's next? Please jump back to the first round of Blaster. Quantitative monetary easing is coming to the end of history, and there is no safe exit from QE! The world is facing either another round of more severe financial crises, or localized wars and social unrest, or worse, possibly both.

The cloud over the Syrian war is nothing more than a prelude to a global crisis, with the Middle East, South Asia, East and South-East Asia all at high risk of future geopolitical conflict. Historically, when economic and financial crises have reached the point where they cannot be mitigated, war has often been the ultimate solution.

Expound

In a well-policed city, there's no need for heavy-duty burglar doors and windows in every home. City managers who focus on burglary, rather than on eradicating poverty at the root and eradicating hotbeds of crime, will not be able to cope with the rampant theft with an expensive burglary system.

Interest rate fluctuations in the market have existed for at least five thousand years, and interest rate risk has always accompanied the evolution of civilization since the Mesopotamian civilization. The hedging of interest rate risk is not a problem unique to our times; the industrial revolution, the electric revolution, the aerospace revolution all had interest rate risk, but until the advent of the "European dollar", there was no need to worry too much about interest rate volatility. When the anchor of the value of money is highly stable, interest rate fluctuations do not make big waves.

When the gold standard was abolished in the United States, the anchor of the currency was lost, and the excessive dollar overdraft seriously disrupted monetary stability worldwide. Interest rates fluctuated dramatically, exchange rates fluctuated greatly, the financial world suddenly lost good security, as a result of which everyone was in danger, and every household engaged in risk hedging, which is the fundamental reason for the survival and expansion of derivatives such as interest rate swaps, currency swaps, credit default swaps, asset securitization. The monstrous expansion of financial derivative markets is not the cause of economic prosperity, but the result of monetary chaos!

The more dangerous the world is, the more insurance is needed. This is not a scene of peace and prosperity, but a sign of the end times.

Risk hedging is costly, and if everyone in society needed to be hedged, it would mean a geometrically higher cost for society as a whole. Installing burglar doors in every home will not increase the prosperity of society, but will only make the burglar door merchants happy. The burglar-proof door merchants are anxious for society to get as messy as possible, and city dwellers are certainly eager to live in peace and prosperity.

For a large country with its roots in the real economy, the larger the size of financial derivatives, the higher the cost of insurance for industrial expenditures, which is not helping the industrial economy, but exploiting the rest of the rest of the population. In such a fierce and harsh existence, the good people will also become wicked, and the industrious will be alienated into treachery.

Ironically, instead of reducing financial risk, risk hedging has created more destructive financial disasters.

CHAPTER V

Wall Street speculators in action

The rebound in housing prices is seen as another "ironclad proof" of the U.S. economic recovery, and the truth is once again obscured by disillusionment and fanaticism. The reason why prices can confuse the vast majority of people is that people tend to look only at the prices themselves and do not analyse the underlying reasons for their formation.

March 2012 was an inflection point in the reversal of US real estate prices, and the six-year-long real estate bear market finally took a turn for the worse. The key factor in achieving the house price reversal was the change in the supply and demand of bank foreclosed homes. On the one hand, the backlog of foreclosure cases in banks has slowed down the heavy pressure of foreclosure auctions on home prices; on the other hand, with the support of the U.S. government, Wall Street speculators began to enter the market in a big way, sweeping through the inventory of foreclosed homes in the five major real estate disasters on the east and west coasts of the United States, reversing the trend of real estate in one fell swoop within a few months.

Wall Street speculation in the tens of billions of dollars of funds, mobilized hundreds of billions of speculative army, pry billions of real estate market, its use of funds as little as the short time, the effectiveness of the great, can be called a classic case of financial means to change the trend of real estate war.

The problem is that financial manipulation can change market prices in the short term, but is powerless to maintain long-term trends. Determining the future of real estate is the younger generation of potential home buyers who are struggling on the brink of losing their dreams.

Under the threat of an interest rate volcano, Wall Street speculators have begun to prepare for a "triumphant escape", with one of their two retreat routes having failed and the other just beginning to try.

Remember, the success of the "rent-mortgage-backed securities" concept will determine the success of the Wall Street speculators in breaking through.

The Wounds of Bleeding Home Prices: Foreclosed Homes

In January 2012, just as China was struggling to keep house prices down, the United States was fretting over the fact that it couldn't keep them down. The Chinese simply don't believe that house prices could fall, just as the Americans did in 2006 and the Japanese did in 1989.

In fact, the key to the decline in house prices is the collapse of mortgage loans, large and severe defaults forced banks to repossess properties for auction, and the low auction prices crushed property prices. So far, there have been very few cases in China where properties have been confiscated by banks for auction, so the concept of bank foreclosures is relatively indifferent.

When people buy a home through a bank mortgage, both in China and in the United States, because the purchaser has no other assets to put up as collateral, the purchased property is used as collateral for the bank and the bank does not return ownership of the property to the homeowner until the mortgage is fully paid. For home buyers, monthly mortgage payments on time is a continuous process of "redeeming" their property ownership. If repayment is not made in time, then the bank has the right to suspend the homeowner's "redemption" and put the mortgage at auction, which is where the "foreclosure" comes from.

Under normal circumstances, banks are reluctant to hold large numbers of foreclosed properties, which would be costly in terms of human and financial resources and would be more costly than the benefits, and the best option is to auction the properties as soon as possible to recover the funds quickly. Foreclosures tend to be very inexpensive, and they come to the market in large numbers and concentrations, equivalent to the massive and violent sell-offs that occurred in the "4-1-2" gold market, where the flow ultimately determines the stock price. The collapse of foreclosed homes has worsened home price expectations, while the decline in home prices has exacerbated the emergence of foreclosed homes, a vicious cycle that has continued for five years in the United States from 2007 to 2012.

William C. Dudley, president and CEO of the Federal Reserve Bank of New York, worriedly noted at the New Jersey Bankers Association's Economic Forum on January 6, 2012, that since 2006, when home prices peaked, U.S. real estate has suffered an unprecedented 34 percent decline, with homeowners losing $7.3 trillion, more than half of their net worth. The number of new housing starts dropped dramatically from a peak of 1.75 million per year to 360,000 at the beginning of 2009, and remained at only 420,000 in 2012.[27]

By early 2012, although the flood of mortgage defaults had passed, there were still 1.5 million households that had been in serious default for more than 90 days on their home loans, and 2 million households that were already in a state of bank foreclosure. When a bank seizes a property, these foreclosed properties are called REO (Real Estate Owned). If the situation doesn't radically improve, another 3.6 million homes will become foreclosures in 2012 and 2013.

To make matters worse, there are 11 million families in the U.S. with total mortgages in excess of the value of their homes, and these "drowning property" debtors have a strong incentive to "abandon" their properties and join the defaulting army at any time, bringing the total number of potential foreclosures in the bank to tens of millions!

Imagine that the banks hold tens of millions of foreclosed properties, into batches and continue to hit the fragile real estate market, U.S. house prices will be inevitable again in a major collapse situation, difficult to recover within 10 years.

When the economy was booming, American households basically didn't save, and when they needed to spend, the house that was rising in value was the cash machine. When the economy is in recession, it is difficult for people to even keep their jobs, and with negative real income growth, it is even more difficult to want to spend freely. The house is the primary household wealth of Americans, and if home prices

---

[27] William C. Dudley, *Housing and the Economic Recovery*, Remarks at the New Jersey Bankers Association Economic Forum, Iselin, New Jersey, 2012-01-06.

keep falling, the wealth effect shrinks, and consumption pulls the economy along, it's empty talk. Where is the cash flow and tax revenue when consumption is sluggish and the economy is depressed and there is a lack of economic activity? And how can the stock market and financial market bubbles be sustained?

Housing prices continue to fall is the United States most deadly and the most headache economic difficulties, the Federal Reserve's QE policy has been implemented for two rounds, while house prices have been slow to improve.

Suppressing interest rates can easily lead to a boom in bonds and stock markets, but most Americans don't directly own stocks and bonds. The wealth effect of the financial bubble on a large number of wealthy people with financial assets is far greater than the average middle class who are struggling to keep their jobs and make ends meet, so the record high stock market is not enough to stimulate sustained consumption growth, while the Fed's easy money flows mainly into the financial system, stimulating a larger shadow bubble, ordinary Americans can not enjoy the benefits of QE. In this way, the recovery in real estate prices simply does not refer to the already debt-ridden and "stressed" middle class.

By early 2012, the Federal Reserve has clearly seen that relying solely on QE money printing and ultra-low interest rates will not fundamentally reverse the trend of falling house prices, the most effective way is still to use the tried and tested price manipulation in the financial markets.

Once again, it needs to be stressed that real estate, like financial markets, has a common law that the price of flows determines the price of stocks, or furthermore, it is the expectations of the price of flows that play a decisive role.

The U.S. real estate market has a total inventory of 133 million units, with a total value of approximately $23 trillion, and an annual sales volume of 8 million new and existing homes, which means that traffic represents only 6% of the inventory.

In a market where house prices are declining, developers who are ready to start new housing are first concerned about the transaction price of existing homes and judge the competitiveness and profitability of new homes in the market, and the pricing of new homes is in fact swayed by the existing housing market. In the current housing market, nearly a million foreclosed homes sold each year, seriously suppressing the transaction price of more than 7 million units of current housing transactions.

If the average price of a home in a neighborhood is $250,000, all it takes to hang a few bank foreclosed homes at auction for only $120,000 will put all the home sellers under tremendous psychological pressure. The point is that this price differential can sway market expectations, causing buyers to be more patient and sellers to be more impatient.

If traffic determines inventory, foreclosed homes are the incremental part of the traffic, the most critical "point" that determines the overall price.

The Federal Reserve Bank of New York and the U.S. Treasury Department are full of financial market experts who know how to play the market, and since the stock, bond, interest rate and precious metals markets can be artificially controlled, the real estate market can certainly learn from them. What is called "human control" is "managing expectations" in the good sense and "manipulating expectations" in the bad. Whether it is "management" or "manipulation", the basic common denominator is the word "human".

The key to reversing home price expectations is to control the supply and demand for foreclosed homes, forcing them up! To achieve this, it is first necessary to reduce the supply of foreclosed homes.

Foreclosure blockage, house prices stabilize

Keeping homeowners out of the bank is the first trick to reducing the supply of foreclosed homes.

The HAMP (Home Affordable Modification Program) was launched in 2009, with the goal of allowing taxpayers to pay and banks to profit, so that homeowners can continue to "latch on" to homes that have become "drowning assets" in order to delay foreclosures, and the HAMP program is entirely bank-led, and if the bank assesses that it has more to gain from the government, it will notify the homeowner to revise the terms of the home loan, for example, by slightly reducing the monthly payment at the expense of increasing the total loan amount. If the bank feels the government isn't subsidizing enough, it will decide to go straight to foreclosure and auction.

The HAMP program was expected to "save" 4 million households from the "drowning house" swamp, and only 1.2 million households that had already defaulted on their mortgages were processed for loan modifications due to efficiency and standard setting issues. Sadly, 306,000 families are again in default and another 88,000 are on the verge of default, a total of 33 per cent of all participating families! And the longer a family is in the program, the more likely they are to default. The default rate for families who have participated in the program since its inception in 2009 is 46%! When these families defaulted again, they not only faced higher total debt, but also suffered more severe credit harm.

By the end of April 2013, the HAMP program had received $19.1 billion in credits, but had used only $4.4 billion, with losses of $815 million due to further defaults, and the program will be extended until 2015.

In effect, the HAMP program is less of a rescue operation and more of a trap. Families in foreclosure are essentially incapacitated by the loss of their jobs, the extreme depression of the job market has made it difficult for these families to obtain an adequate source of income, while the total amount of home loans has increased dramatically, and there is little suspense that their default rate will increase dramatically over time.

Regardless of the ultimate effect of HAMP or other "bailout" operations, the implementation of these policies has been effective in relieving the imminent supply pressure on foreclosed homes, delaying the explosion of the time bomb of millions of foreclosed homes.

In addition to government intervention, banks have also delayed the foreclosure process.

In November 2010, the sudden revelation of the "robo-signing" scandal escalated again in the troubled banking scandal. While banks issue mortgages, they do not have the manpower or resources to handle the thousands of "chores" of collecting money, making calls or issuing foreclosure notices to defaulters, which are often outsourced to "servicers". When a default occurs, the workload of the "service provider" increases dramatically and their meager profits are quickly swallowed up by the enormous workload of the subsequent foreclosure process. The service provider's staff handles thousands of legal documents every day, including signature and notarization procedures. In the interest of convenience and cost savings, they barely read the specifics of these documents and simply sign them like "robots", sometimes even completing the notarization process haphazardly without witnesses and notaries, and some documents contain numerous errors.

The "robo-signing" incident has set off an uproar in American society, after all, real estate is an important foundation of the "American dream", when a family is about to lose this dream of heartbreak, so hastily handled, the public's antipathy to the bank even stronger. The foreclosure process has been widely questioned by society as a result of the crisis caused by the banks and the "straw man" that followed.

To proceed with a foreclosure, the foreclosure must first be confirmed, and it is usually without completing the foreclosure confirmation that the bank rushes to issue the foreclosure notice, proceeds to evict the homeowner, and completes the auction. The "procedural illegality" of the attorneys' collective victim suit against the bank led to a protracted lawsuit that swept the United States.

This huge mess has paralyzed the bank's foreclosure efforts, and it's never easy to clear out what are the formalized applications from the millions of foreclosures. Unable to figure out the status quo, banks have had to suspend the foreclosure process on a large scale, resulting in a backlog of up to 2.5 million foreclosure cases.

At this point, the Fed and the big banks haven't come up with a brilliant plan to turn around home prices, so of course their mindset is that the faster the foreclosure process goes, the better to cut the banks' losses.

By early 2012, after the U.S. government and banks reached a compromise on "robo-signing" cases, banks suddenly saw the benefits of a massive backlog of foreclosure cases, which slowed the decline in home prices.

The banks have finally realized that foreclosures are the key to reversing home prices!

U.S. foreclosed home supply declined sharply in November 2010 and continued into 2012 shrinking, the result of a deliberate backlog of foreclosure filings at the bank. As a result, even after the lawsuits have been resolved and the foreclosure backlog has been eliminated, banks have continued to hold back on foreclosures, causing foreclosure auctions to hit record lows in 2012 after repeated crises. In New York, the foreclosure process has been stretched to 1072 days, a three-year period, 4.3 times longer than in 2007; in Florida, 858 days; in California, nearly a year; and the situation in other states is broadly similar. Banks have deliberately reduced foreclosure auctions, resulting in real estate investors having to scramble through a much smaller supply, which has significantly mitigated the drastic impact of foreclosure auctions on home prices.

Of course, banks that deliberately stretch out foreclosures will also suffer some losses. When a serious default occurs, the original homeowner, knowing that he or she will be evicted, simply does not continue to pay the bank, and the bank has no right to evict the homeowner until the foreclosure is complete. In the course of the standoff between the two parties, the bank equated the provision of housing to homeowners for free.

However, reducing the supply of foreclosed homes will only serve to slow the decline in home prices and will not be enough to generate momentum for home price increases. To complete the house price reversal, strong buying intervention is needed.

That's the latest rising buyer's mainstay in American real estate – the Wall Street speculation mob!

Wall Street Speculation, the Rhythm of Home Price Reversal

The idea of concentrating superior forces to fight a war of annihilation is equally true in the financial markets. The game of the financial market and the battlefield between the enemy and us, all in order to seize the initiative, that is, to change the expectation of the outcome of the war, the victor to destroy the momentum and the loser to the despair of defeat like a mountain, are all expected to form the consequences of the side down.

On April 12, 2013, Wall Street's thunderous sell-off completely destroyed the gold market's long resistance will is a vivid example of the battle, in early 2012, Wall Street is ready to launch a sharp counterattack in the real estate market, in order to change the market's expectations of house prices in one fell swoop, the main direction of attack is foreclosure housing as a strategic breakthrough, and the main assault force is Wall Street's fierce PE, REITs and hedge funds, among which, Blackstone Group is said to be the main force of the main force, ace in the ace.

The strategic layout of the major real estate counterattack was planned as early as August 2011, and the backlog of foreclosure hearings has created a favorable situation for the slowdown in home prices. From the point of view of market psychology, the expectation of short real estate has been controlled to a certain extent, but if not to take advantage of this favorable opportunity to counterattack, then the future supply of foreclosed homes will continue to pour into the market, and the scale is getting bigger and bigger, the short-selling power will continue to strengthen. Only by concentrating on a sudden bounce back, and with an intensity that must be large enough to shake the market, will it be possible to destroy the will of the short-sellers and send house prices rallying in a big way. Higher housing prices, in turn, will weaken the source of supply of foreclosed homes, fundamentally reversing the trend in real estate.

On February 1, 2012, the U.S. Federal Housing Finance Agency (FHFA), in close coordination with the Federal Reserve, the U.S. Treasury, the Federal Reserve and Insurance Corporation (FDIC), the U.S. Department of Housing and Urban Development, Fannie Mae, Freddie Mac and other agencies, issued a "general mobilization order" to more than 4,000 investment agencies to the real estate counterattack.

Since August 2011, FHFA has been working on an action plan to attract private investors to help address the bank's foreclosure inventory, and on February 1, 2012, the implementation details were released with the overall approach of 1) digesting the foreclosure inventory of Fannie Mae, Freddie Mac, and the Federal Housing Administration; 2) the breach is a real estate disaster; 3) welcoming large purchases by investment institutions at extremely favorable prices; and 4) the condition that the low purchase price be held and rented for a certain period of time.

Funds, companies, investment trusts, banks and individuals with a net worth of more than $1 million can participate in this real estate "feast of the century", and investors may even be able to obtain loans for two homes to expand their holdings. The size of the asset package is roughly 500 to 1,000 individual houses, and the total size of the two-room and FHA foreclosures is about 210,000 houses, which would require about 200 super investors to subscribe if each asset package was 1,000 houses.

How far is the price discounted? The discounted price of an asset package is not more than 30 cents to 40 cents for a $1 asset. It's a

$200,000 detached house with a reduced price of $60,000 to $80,000. If the average investment of 10,000 to 20,000 U.S. dollars per house for renovation and refurbishment, you can change hands to invest 1,000 to 1,500 U.S. dollars in the rental market, even taking into account the vacancy period of rental housing and other factors, the return on investment can be at least 14% to 20%. In a yield-starved Wall Street, such a good thing is just pie in the sky.

Spurred on by the ultra-high yields, Wall Street investment institutions, represented by Black Rock, began killing off the foreclosure market in a big way.

On February 1, the U.S. Federal Housing Finance Agency issued the real estate counterattack of the "general mobilization order", has had an immediate effect. in March, the U.S. real estate industry for five years, the bear breath, ushered in a miraculous turnaround. The effect of financial manipulation of the real estate market has been remarkable and the rebound has been dramatic, far exceeding the expectations of policy designers in advance.

How exactly did Wall Street reverse its fortunes?

Phoenix, the first test of the speculators

The U.S. real estate bubble began to burst in the summer of 2006, with house prices initially swooping high, followed by a shock plunge, and until early 2012, real estate was an area that frustrated everyone. It was like a stock market lacking a major player, wasting nearly six years in a disillusioned, pessimistic trance.

When Wall Street strong funds suddenly and violently killed into the real estate market, inspired by the magic of the "eel effect", pessimistic, tired, discouraged, lazy atmosphere suddenly disappeared, large and small real estate speculators like an electric shock generally active. Wherever Wall Street's "eels" swim, the market begins to boil.

Of the top five areas in the U.S. with the most real estate injuries, Phoenix (Arizona), Southern California, Las Vegas (Nevada), Florida and Atlanta (Georgia), Wall Street money chose Phoenix first.

Phoenix is the capital of Arizona and one of the important industrial centers, with a population of 4.3 million in the metropolitan area that even surpasses that of the Capital District of Washington. Phoenix is also the seat of state government, with Intel's research and development center and chip manufacturing facility, numerous high-tech and communications companies, Apollo Group headquarters, Honeywell's military engine manufacturing plant, and Luke Air Force Base, all of which employ large numbers of well-paying people, as well as many universities and research institutions that attract talented people to Phoenix. Due to the warm winter climate, the tourism and golf industry is well developed. As long as there are high income earners, there's no worries about a stable rental market.

Phoenix was hurt badly by the financial crisis, with bank foreclosures dropping 57 percent from peak real estate prices. Phoenix's real estate market is a wretched, miserable place.

The Rothschilds had a famous saying: when the streets are full of blood, make sure to buy assets!

A crisis is an opportunity in the midst of danger.

One of the first people to spot an opportunity in Phoenix was Steve Schmitz and his partners. They formed an investment company, American Residential Properties, in 2008 and began buying a dozen bank foreclosed homes in Phoenix with their own funds. Since most of these homes are products of the real estate bubble days of a few years ago, the houses are new, basically maintenance-free, and can be rented out quickly. Steve became interested in the "foreclosure-rental" business model after his initial acquisition, and in order to get to know the tenants, he went door-to-door and found that the tenants were a typical middle-class American family, a husband and wife with two children and a dog who had lost their homes for various reasons, but whose love and dedication to the house was no different from other homeowners.

In 2010 Steve decided to set up a REIT (Real Estate Trust) to raise funds from the capital markets to replicate the foreclosure-rental business model on a large scale. The so-called REIT fund is a trust set up to avoid the problem of double taxation of companies and individuals, its profits are almost entirely distributed to investors, i.e. the profits are only "pass-through" companies, but directly into the investor's account, so that the investor only has to pay personal tax, but the company does not have to pay tax.

In the traditional real estate market, the "foreclosure-rental" model is mainly the behavior of retail investors, while the REIT funds will be the capital market of large-scale capital into this market, guerrillas encountered the regular army, retail investors are difficult to fight against the capital strength of institutions, the ecological environment of the market has changed dramatically.

Steve and his "American Residential Real Estate Corporation" are recognized in the industry as pioneers of the "foreclosure-rental" model. From 2010 to the summer of 2012, Phoenix's institutional funding expanded from 15 percent to 26 percent of property sales.[28]

As Phoenix's economic recovery has been slow, more families have lost their homes, leading to a significant increase in the share of the detached housing market used for rentals, which jumped from 8 percent before the crisis to 22 percent in 2013. The number of properties available for rent has increased dramatically, but competition has become more intense.

Beginning in the summer of 2012, Phoenix's local institutional investors began to face a tough challenge from PE giants like Black Rock and Wall Street's more fierce hedge funds, as the mighty dragon and the groundhog took on Phoenix. By the summer of 2013, Wall Street money had snapped up 11,440 of Phoenix's 230,000 rental detached houses, not a large number, but the "eel effect" of Wall Street had activated the entire Phoenix housing market.

The massive influx of funds led to a fierce housing grab, with house prices skyrocketing and the rapid decline in the rate of return on investment, and by 2013, the rental rate of return on investment in Phoenix real estate fell to a mere 5% to 6%. Foreclosure inventory has dried up and the ultra-low-priced homes are gone.

The Wall Street speculators no longer clung to Phoenix, they swooped like locusts on Las Vegas (Nevada) and North and South California in the Northwest, then turned around and headed straight for Florida, Georgia and North and South Carolina on the southeast coast before moving on to the hard-hit Midwest real estate areas of Chicago, Detroit, Denver and Ohio.

Vegas, Las Vegas, rent $1117, home price $109K.

---

[28] Morgan Brennan, Wall Street Buying Adds to Housing Booming, *Forbes*, 2013-06-24.

The Vegas Bounty

In early 2012, the Wall Street speculation mob crossed over to Las Vegas and pounced directly on Phoenix. That's because while home prices have fallen deeper and are cheaper in Vegas, the city's economic model is too homogeneous, with a 10 percent unemployment rate. During the recession, the number of people coming to Vegas to spend money is far less than it used to be, and its rents are less sustainable than Phoenix's.

When the supply of foreclosed homes in Phoenix dried up and home prices skyrocketed, it didn't take long for prices in Vegas to become much cheaper. Wall Street speculators began making a big push into Vegas in late 2012, and by November Black Rock had joined the city's speculation army, with Wall Street slamming $8 billion into the city's real estate market for a bumper bet.

In the Vegas real estate market, Nevada's legislation (Assembly Bill 284) overprotects homeowners' interests, making foreclosures nearly impossible, and making it difficult for any more severely defaulted homes to appear on the market, artificially creating the illusion that the market is in short supply. At least 64,000 homes are vacant, and up to 45,000 families have been in serious default on their mortgages for more than 90 days, but only 8,000 homes are listed for sale in the entire Las Vegas housing market, according to local power company data.

Las Vegas has seen an influx of homes vacant and unable to sell, while the existing inventory of properties is experiencing a frenzied home grabbing battle by institutional investors. A Las Vegas realtor preparing to sell a foreclosed property for $86,000 spent about $20,000 on repairs and renovations, and as soon as the ad went up, it immediately drew 41 bidders, 39 of whom paid all cash. The broker had never seen such a frenzied rush for homes, even at the height of the real estate bubble, with such a high percentage of cash bids that his home ended up selling for $135,000, more than half the price he had expected.

On the one hand, tens of thousands of vacant foreclosed homes are being held back from entering the market, and on the other, billions of dollars are being snapped up to grab 8,000 scarce existing home inventory, the natural result of which is not only driving up existing home prices, but also directing purchasing power to the new home market. in 2013, new home sales in Las Vegas soared 87% and the number of permits to start jumped 52%.

In the second half of 2012, when the Wall Street speculators began to enter the Las Vegas market, a total of 19% of Las Vegas' annual real estate sales were eaten up, and if you translate that, nearly half of the properties were swept away by the Wall Street speculators in the last few months of the year. With cash payments accounting for as much as 60 percent of total home sales in Vegas, home prices in the city soared 30 percent year-over-year in 2012, thanks to a combination of massive amounts of money and concentrated firepower.

However, even after the price increase, home prices in Vegas are still 56 percent lower than their pre-crisis peak.

Turn to Southern California

Southern California Inland Empire Riverside County, home prices $172K, foreclosed homes $156K, tops 60% drop

The Inland Empire, located in the Los Angeles metropolitan area of Southern California, has a population of 4.3 million and is the second largest metropolitan area in Southern California. Southern California has a comfortable climate with sunny seasons, pleasant winter temperatures, and a uniquely rich natural landscape. Here, one can surf to the beach in the morning, then take a trip to Disneyland and finally enjoy the tranquility of skiing in the snowy mountains of San Bernardino City. With close proximity to Los Angeles, San Diego, and Las Vegas, Disneyland, Hollywood, Universal Studios, Palm Springs, beaches, deserts, snowy mountains, and other recreational activities, there's everything. Such an alluring location and natural beauty naturally attracts immigrants from the United States and around the world.

However, the Inland Empire unfortunately became the center of a real estate crash in the Southern California region when the financial crisis hit in 2008.

By the time the Wall Street speculators drove into Southern California in April 2012, their operations were well on their way to an assembly line operation. They organized a modular way of handling, every morning at 6:30 a.m. began to prepare for the day's foreclosure sale of the house snatching action plan, they took out the energy of Wall

Street analysis of stocks, an average of 1,000 foreclosed houses a week to analyze the conditions of the various, dozens of LCD screens in turn, voluminous display of Wall Street trading room atmosphere.

The first thing that needs to be determined is the criteria for housing selection, and since it is an investment, it is not the pursuit of housing comfort, but the control of costs to ensure the stability of the rent. If the house comes with a pool, which would have been an advantage of a normal house, it is a fatal disadvantage in the eyes of the speculators, because a pool requires higher maintenance costs, and raising the rent without covering the corresponding expenses makes it more likely to make it difficult to rent. Good law and order, good school district, convenient transportation and proximity to shopping malls, these four criteria are the only way to recruit tenants.

Based on these criteria, the speculative group quickly sifted through the auction house to snatch up the list, then the assembly line began to rumble up. Fieldwork team immediately set off to the housing site, interviewing homeowners, assessing the cost of repair and renovation; housing assessment team began to calculate a variety of taxes and fees, inquiring whether the ownership of the house is clean, such as whether the homeowner has other creditors have the right to claim the house as a mortgage, if the ownership of the house there are other creditors may be tainted, the purchase of the house must also be repaid after the related costs of other creditors; housing transfer, maintenance team immediately follow up, they need to contact the local contractor to complete the shortest time to repaint the walls, replace curtains, cleaning carpets, mowing the lawn, kitchen renovation and other specific matters; finally, the marketing team started, using various channels to release rental information, receive tenants to see the house, investigate the tenant's background, and sign the contract.

In the Inland Empire, from mid-2012 to early 2013, 52% of foreclosed properties were swept away by Wall Street speculators, properties that weren't even publicly advertised on the market. The news of Wall Street's foreclosures has caused panic among local investors, who previously feared that home prices would continue to fall if they bought, but now fear that they will not be able to get a home if they are late. Even more frightening were the stories in the local newspapers of home buyers who submitted 200 consecutive bids for a home with no success, which caused even more panic and desperation among loan buyers who went out of their way to look around and submit bids when they saw a home. The wave of house grabbing has pushed up house prices in the Inland Empire by 18% to 25%.

In Southern California's Orange County, Wall Street speculation accounted for 22% of total home sales in 2012, with 10,600 homes listed for circulation in 2011 and only 3,300 left in early 2013, and a fierce rush mentality pushed home prices up 10%. In Orange County's foreclosure market, institutional investors accounted for no more than 10% of the market in 2008, while Wall Street speculators accounted for nearly half of the market in 2012.

The Inland Empire as the representative of Southern California's soaring home prices, not because of the economy's dramatic improvement, but Wall Street speculation in the market created by the "eel effect", the actual economic situation in Southern California is far from optimistic.

In data from the U.S. Census Bureau's survey of cities with a population of 65,000 or more, unemployment rates in several California cities have declined after 2011, but still hover around 15 percent, almost twice the rate before 2008. Although the unemployment rate declined in 2011 and 2012, some jobs are only low-wage or part-time jobs. While the recession ended in 2009, many Southern California cities became even poorer in 2012. California's poverty rate increased by 3.6 percentage points from 2008 to 2012. Poverty in Los Angeles County increased to 19.1 percent from 15.5 percent in 2008, while the average annual household income decreased to $5.3001 from $59,196 in 2008.

Phoenix, Las Vegas and Southern California in the southwest of the United States, once the birthplace of the subprime mortgage crisis, since March 2012, but has become the most popular "investment mecca" for Wall Street speculators, who swept the three areas, respectively, 38.6 percent, 48.5 percent and 27.3 percent of total home sales. Among them, Las Vegas was once the most sought-after, with 50.2 percent of buyers who didn't show up at all for a home sale in October 2012 – they didn't even bother to look at the house they were buying and just paid for it. A whopping 52.5% of all transactions were all-cash lump sum payments.

Just as the Wenzhou real estate speculation group in China's provinces set off a wave of wildly rising house prices, Wall Street speculation group from the beginning of 2012 began to sweep the United States east and west coast and the central region, where the inventory of foreclosed homes has been significantly reduced, all over the tourist capital to move, the battle for housing intensified, local house prices should rise sharply.

The US manipulation of the real estate market by means of financial markets has indeed had immediate results.

Black Rock, the largest landowner in the United States

Among the Wall Street speculators, BlackRock is sitting at the head of the pack.

For many PE funds, hedge funds or asset management companies, speculative housing is to buy and hold a lot of cheap housing, first hold and rent for a period of time, such as house prices rise to the right price to sell to cash out and leave. But BlackRock's ambitions are clearly much greater, and its aim in snapping up real estate is to create a "tenant empire" that will consolidate rental markets scattered across the United States and even around the world, with a standardized product that will supply rental housing in bulk and in an industrialized way. Instead of trying to sell individual properties when house prices are high, Black Rock is trying to finally walk away from the capital market in one piece.

In February 2012, the U.S. Federal Housing Finance Agency (FHFA) issued a general mobilization order for a house price counterattack, and in April, BlackRock Group formed its own "tenant empire" (Investment Homes) and began an unprecedented housing merger in the real estate industry.

Having originally been involved in the real estate industry as well, but with no direct experience of managing large and decentralised rental properties, Blackstone was prepared to run things in-house from the outset in order to get first-hand information. The "tenant empire" employs thousands of full-time staff, which is huge for a fund, in addition to targeting more than 5,000 outsourcing providers. When entering a market, Empire employs local market analysts, an M&A team for the purchase of properties, a maintenance and renovation team to oversee the local construction team, a property management team for day-to-day operations, and a rental team that works closely with local brokers to solicit tenants.

The "empire" mainly buys foreclosed homes from banks, or cash-out homes from small investors, and in individual cases also buys resale homes in bulk from other companies. After receiving the house, the repair and renovation work takes about 2 to 3 weeks and costs about 10% of the purchase price. The most standard template is a three-bedroom, two-bath, two-garage house with a lawn, which usually attracts the most "sticky" families who rent.

In one community, Empire-managed properties are often very visible, the exterior of the house is often repainted and the green lawn is mowed to a crisp. Inside the home, the master bedroom tub is one size larger than normal, the kitchen countertops are all brand new marble, and the new carpet and walls are light brown, which is the custom standard for black stone. The rent for such a house is approximately $1,750 per month, with a rental rate of over 80 per cent and a net yield averaging approximately 6 per cent of all detached houses held by the Empire.

With such high standards, "Empire" has taken the nation by storm.

In July 2012, Empire announced that it had acquired 2,000 detached houses at a cost of $300 million, focusing on five major areas of the United States where real estate had been hard hit.

In September, the Empire landed in Tampa Bay, Florida, and dropped a $1 billion "heavy bomb", hiring a large number of local realtors and targeting homes between $100,000 and $175,000. The "empire" "mercenaries" have been "sweeping" the entire Bay Area in droves, printing a large number of leaflets with shocking words such as "all cash", "no assessment", "pay now", "quick deal" and so on, and these "small ads" can be found everywhere along the streets of the city. The "Empire" is eating into foreclosures at the rate of hundreds of houses per month, and its goal in Tampa Bay is to take down 15,000 single family homes in 3 years!

Florida Tampa Bay area, $1210 rents, $93K homes, $89K foreclosures, 53% top drop

With home prices in Florida down 45% since their peak in 2006, and a large number of homeowners forced to start renting after being swept out of their homes, the statewide rental market has rapidly ballooned to $100 billion, making Florida a fertile ground for the rental market to be exploited due to low prices and high rents. Since most of the tenants were originally homeowners who knew how to take care of everything in the house, and had a strong sense of community and were the standard tenants that investors liked so much, the "Empire" in

Florida focused on sweeping up the strategic layout that could be described as quite visionary.

In October, Black Rock claimed that they were sweeping the U.S. foreclosure market at a rate of $100 million per week.

In November, Black Rock turned to Las Vegas to join the Wall Street speculators who had arrived earlier to scramble foreclosed homes for a whopping $8 billion.

In April 2013, Black Rock made a significant one-time acquisition of 1,400 homes in Atlanta from another institution, setting a record for the largest single transaction in the foreclosure-rental model.

By September 2013, Black Rock had invested $5.5 billion to capture 12 major US real estate markets, including 32,000 detached houses.

In addition to acquiring detached houses for rent, Kuroshi also wants to complete the product chain of the "tenant empire," of which rental apartments are an integral part. The Wall Street Journal claimed on August 13 that "Black Rock takes over GE's apartment assets." The report says, "The PE firm, Black Rock Group, is making a big bet on the post-financial crisis apartment rental market." BlackRock Group is set to spend $2.7 billion to acquire a major stake in GE Financial Corp.'s 80-unit apartment portfolio, which spans Atlanta, Texas and the southeastern states and totals up to 30,000 residential units. Of the $2.7 billion acquisition funding, Blackstone is prepared to pay $1 billion out of its own pocket and rely on capital markets for the rest. The controversial deal is one of the biggest deals in the property industry, with Black Rock eyeing a record number of people who can't and won't buy a home after the crisis and who must have a place to live, with apartments clearly the best option to satisfy young people who can't afford to buy. Rising apartment rents and declining vacancy rates indicate that the apartment rental market is becoming the hottest segment of the U.S. real estate industry.[29]

The Moody's Index, which tracks rental apartments across the U.S., shows that rental apartments have risen 59 percent from their 2009

---

[29] Craig Karmin, Blackstone to Buy Stakes in Apartment Complexes From GE Unit, *Wall Street Journal*, 2013-08-12.

lows, while overall real estate is up 35 percent. Apartment rents rose by 2.3% in 2010, 2.4% in 2011 and 3.8% in 2012. Meanwhile, the apartment vacancy rate fell from 8 percent in 2009 to 4.3 percent in 2013, a 12-year low.

Black Rock's "tenant empire" not only holds a whopping 32,000 individual houses, but if you add in 30,000 apartment units, it's the largest landowner in America!

In addition to Black Rock, members of the Wall Street Speculation Group have also made their mark, and as of September 2013.

In addition to the main players of these speculative groups, there are countless small and medium-sized financial companies, overseas hot money, individual speculators, and even sovereign wealth funds have jumped on the chariot of the Wall Street speculative groups, they try to make a killing in the real estate bubble 2.0 frenzy.

In August 2013, there were approximately 5.6 million U.S. real estate sales, of which the percentage of all-cash purchases was as high as 45%, much higher than the 30% in August 2012, compared to 10% to 20% in the normal real estate market. In metropolitan areas with a population of 1 million or more, the highest rates of all-cash home purchases were found in Miami at 69%, Detroit at 68%, Las Vegas at 66%, Jacksonville, Florida at 65%, and Tampa at 64%.

There is no doubt that speculation has become a major driver of rising home prices in the United States.

Who are the victims of the Wall Street speculation?

In the US real estate market, one can clearly see what is happening in the stock market, where the rally in prices is not due to improving fundamentals, but is directly driven by money. In the stock market, nearly $2 trillion in huge share buybacks by big companies blew up a new stock market bubble; in the real estate market, Wall Street speculators played the role of the originators of Bubble 2.0.

Surprisingly, the tens of billions of dollars of Wall Street money, can be in such a short period of time, pry up the $23 trillion real estate market, and the magnitude is so large, which is unprecedented in the history of American real estate.

Goldman Sachs sees cash buying nearly 60 percent of homes.

Three times as many as before the financial crisis.

In early 2012 alone, the CEO of the Federal Reserve Bank of New York was still worried about the real estate market, when almost everyone thought that real estate would go through an 8 to 9 year recession like the previous recession that began in 1989, considering that the 2008 crisis was much more severe than the 1990 recession, the real estate downturn would last for more than 10 years. If that is true in a normal economic cycle, it remains to be seen whether the proliferation of currencies will alleviate the extent of the crisis or shorten the cycle of its outbreak, as there have been so many anomalies this time around, especially the unprecedented one in monetary policy.

Clearly, the abnormally high percentage of all-cash home purchases is indicative of the extreme dysfunction of the real estate market, which according to Goldman Sachs estimates, has reached nearly 60% of all-cash home purchases, three times as high as before the financial crisis! If this data is to be believed, it suggests that most players in the real estate market are speculators, as it is extremely rare for the average American middle class to be able to buy a home all cash. If the real estate market is investment-driven and characterized by upselling for profit, then this is a classic case of a housing bubble.

This is a market with a severe lack of homeowner participation, not that they don't want to participate, but that the Wall Street speculators have denied them the opportunity to participate.

On February 16, 2013, the *Los Angeles Times* reported the story of how a typical average home buyer was squeezed out of the real estate market. The protagonist is a 28-year-old home buyer with a stable skilled job, fully meets the terms of the loan, and has received a pre-approved home purchase loan from the bank. He began looking at homes in the Inland Empire region of Southern California in August 2012 and submitted 200 bids, none of which were successful.[30] After the crash in the Inland Empire, expensive homes became relatively inexpensive, and many potential homebuyers now became qualified buyers who took advantage of the opportunity to prepare for their

---

[30] Alejandro Lazo, Inland Empire housing is more affordable but still out of reach, *Los Angeles Times*, 2013-02-16.

"American dream" of owning a home of their own, but they soon found out that the home was cheap, but not for them.

In the foreclosure market, Wall Street speculators have taken a good chunk of homes right out the back door. In the general market, all-cash buyers not only make high bids, but also pay in a lump sum, and for home sellers, of course, are willing to choose cash buyers, avoiding the time and risk of waiting for bank approval for loans. This is tantamount to keeping real homeowners out of the doorstep of home buying, while speculators have the leverage for short-term arbitrage. Paul Leonardo, director of the California Center for Responsible Lending, said helplessly,

> "For those who play by the rules and rest on their laurels, they really are missing out on an opportunity to try to get home ownership."[31]

Definition of the new "American Dream": from the basement of your parents' home: Move out and live in Black Rock's "tenant empire."

In the Inland Empire, the average homebuyer needs at least 20 to 30 fierce bids to have any hope of success, and often goes way over budget, forcing many to cut back on other consumer spending, while the lucky ones are always in the minority. Most people can only watch home prices rise to heights they can't afford, then are forced to give up the dream of owning their own property and return to the reality of renting, awaiting them in the form of the Wall Street speculators' rental ads.

This is not a phenomenon that happens all over Southern California; similar stories happen every day in all corners of America.

It is no wonder that the "American dream" of the younger generation is to move out of the basement of their parents' house and live in the "tenant empire" of Black Rock.

---

[31] Ibid.

Is real estate awake or sleepwalking?

To figure this out, one must first look at the full picture of American real estate.

The total U.S. real estate inventory is 133 million residential units housing 310 million people, and as of 2013, the total value of U.S. real estate was $2.37 trillion. The total number of owner-occupied homes is 78.9 million dwelling units, of which 48.4 million dwelling units still have outstanding mortgages.

Of those mortgages, a total of 3.3 million were in serious default for more than 90 days, and they were supposed to be auctioned off by banks, but instead were backlogged by the slow foreclosure process, directly contributing to the severe shortage of supply in the nation's housing market in 2012. There are also 2 million loans that have defaulted between 30 and 90 days, and they are the back-up for foreclosed homes. Apparently, out of 48.4 million mortgages, 5.5 million have already defaulted, which is a whopping 11.4% default rate! This is already a breathtaking number.

The total number of homes in default and "negative equity" in the United States reached 11.1 million in 2012. In addition to this, there are 5.8 million "drowned homes," where the total amount of mortgages exceeds the price of the home, and where the likelihood of the homeowner walking away is usually very high and they are a potential source of foreclosures. When defaulted and drowned homes are added together, the "shadow inventory" of foreclosed homes is a whopping 11.1 million!

The Wall Street speculators traveled through 12 major U.S. real estate markets for a year and a half between 2012–2013, taking a total of less than 100,000 properties, and the "shadow inventory" was 111 times higher than the total Wall Street ate up!

The desperate pressure of "shadow stocks" can only be mitigated by a further sharp rise in house prices!

While the rebound in house prices that occurred after 2012 helped to weaken the scale of "drowning house" conversions to foreclosures, and while banks deliberately delayed the pace of foreclosure listings and were able to create supply shortages and house bidding, the problem was only exposed by the delay but not eliminated.

Foreclosed homes are inherently asset poisoning junk, and shadow inventory is a time bomb that banks temporarily cover up on their balance sheets, but the inner panic and anxiety speaks for itself. The Basel III Agreement is about to be implemented, the interest rate rise is unavoidable, the repurchase market outside the loose inside, the danger of liquidity shortage follows the shadow, foreclosed houses are not disposed of one day, the bank's day is always in the torment of hanging upside down.

Bank of America (BOA) acknowledges the staggeringly large inventory of foreclosed homes that must be addressed over the next few years, with mortgage loan strategists predicting that 6.6 million foreclosed homes must be disposed of over the next five years. It's only after 2016 that the foreclosure scale will gradually return to normal. As mentioned earlier, 5.5 million defaulted houses are largely destined for foreclosure, and another 5.8 million "drowning houses" need to be rescued with at least a 30 per cent increase in house prices, and even then, some 600,000 "drowning houses" will still be foreclosed. If house prices in 2013 have driven most real home buyers out of the market, a continued 30% rise means that I'm afraid more than 80% of property transactions are speculators.

Banks must dispose of 6.6 million buildings by 2016. Under normal real estate conditions, the average number of homes foreclosed on by banks is 21,000 per month, for a total of about 250,000 a year. Even by Bank of America's most optimistic estimates, banks will have to dispose of 1.32 million foreclosed homes per year by 2016, more than five times the normal state!

No wonder the Fed won't move its benchmark interest rate until 2016, because when interest rates go up, asset prices go down and liquidity goes down, not only pushing up the cost of buying a home and weakening the purchasing power of real estate, but also simultaneously driving down the price of toxic assets that banks have yet to dispose of, leaving them undercapitalized.

It's just the Fed and the banks' wishful thinking that the eruption of the interest rate volcano won't necessarily be on their schedule.

The footsteps of real estate sleepwalking with the aid of the crutch of the speculative mortgage group, can also last for some time, but the speculative mortgage is not the way, there must be new purchasing power to support real estate prices, otherwise the speculative mortgage group will also be high hedge.

Where are the additional home buyers that follow? It's up to the younger generation, of course. However, the situation for America's younger generation is rather bleak.

A new trend for young people: moving back home to "eat the old"

Over the past 30 years, the median age group of first-time home buyers in the U.S. has ranged from 30 to 32 years old, and the underlying trend in home prices over the next five to 10 years will be the affordability of the younger generation in their 20s and 30s.

And the most notable trend of the current generation is this – moving home to "gnaw at the old age"! The percentage of American millennials moving home to "eat their old age" is increasing dramatically

The traditional "American dream" of owning your own home by the age of 30 or so has been destroyed by the financial crisis. A more realistic dream would be to move into the "tenant empire" of Black Rock, but it seems that a strong financial position would be required to make this dream a reality. The reality is that since the recession, more and more young people are moving back to their parents' homes to "eat their old age". In the five years following the financial crisis, 14.2 per cent of young people between the ages of 25 and 34 returned to their parents' homes, compared with 10.5 per cent before the crisis, while 54.6 per cent of young people between the ages of 18 and 24 went home.

For the younger generation, most of the new job opportunities are mall cashiers, McDonald's, bartenders, hotel waiters and other positions, these young people of all sizes earn only $25,000 a year, after tax monthly salary is only about $1,700, and there is no health insurance and social security benefits, Black Rock's "tenant empire" often start at $1,750 to $2,000 a month, the younger generation is afraid that the only way to continue to "eat the old" at home.

Americans grew up with an emphasis on independent living, and it's true that young people in the past were rarely dependent on their parents, and living with them after college was a rather humiliating thing to do among their peers. Five years after the financial crisis, young people who have graduated from university not only find it difficult to find a job, but also have generally low wages and have to repay high student loans.

The pressure to pay off student loans is something that few young people of the same age in China experience. As tuition continues to rise rapidly, the pressure on students to repay their loans at graduation continues to rise

The financial crisis and the economic downturn have not slowed down the rate of tuition increases at American universities. The average debt for undergraduates is as high as $40,000 (including student loans carried by their parents) once they leave school, compared to $55,000 for graduate students.

Still want to start a business right out of college? I'm sorry, it's not the Bill Gates and Steve Jobs era anymore, when tuition at public universities was super cheap, private universities were worthless compared to today, students had a wide variety of federal and state scholarships, and student loans were under too much pressure, and the entrepreneurial drive of the young American generation of the 21st century was moribund with debt. The Wall Street Journal conducted a survey on August 13, 2013, which found that "the stress of student loan debt is the single largest factor in depressing the entrepreneurial spirit".[32]

Student loans have surpassed the $1 trillion mark, surpassing credit card and auto loans combined, with nearly 40 million people borrowing and nearly half of all student debt concentrated in the 25-something age bracket, the most dominant group of potential home buyers.

Will they be able to pay off their student loans on time in a recession? Unfortunately, the default rate on student loans is at a worse level than it has been in 30 years.

Of the 40 million young people who owe student loans, a portion of those students receive loans from commercial banks, while the majority receive loans directly through the federal government, with a total of 27.8 million receiving government loans. Of these, 7.9 million are still in school and they don't need to pay back their loans for a while. Only 10.8 million people will be able to repay their loans on time, and

---

[32] Ruth Simon, *Student-Loan Load Kills Startup Dreams*, Wall Street Journal, 2013-08-13.

the remaining 9 million are either already in default (more than a year behind) or in a state of delay and forbearance. In other words, there are almost as many people who can't pay their debts on time as there are people who do! And half of the 7.9 million students in school will struggle to pay their debts as soon as they leave school, just like the seniors.

Of the 27.8 million student (government) borrowers, only 10.8 million are repaying their loans on time. 7.9 million people are in school and another 9 million are not paying their loans on time.

When commercial bank loan defaults are added to the mix, the overall default rate for student loans is simply abysmal, with a high rate of serious defaults of more than 90 days among those under 30 years of age with student loans at 35 percent. Of the 40 million future homebuying mainstays, 14 million could have their credit collapse and they will be priced out of the picture, as this severely defaulted credit history inevitably leads to denial of loan applications when banks approve mortgage loans.

The number of new home sales is well below normal market levels. (Source: Case-Shiller Index)

In the United States, not only to buy a home to apply for a mortgage to check credit history, but also to rent a home to check credit, for 14 million potential homebuyers under the age of 30, it is not only difficult to get a loan to buy a home, but also not easy to find a rental apartment, to move into the Black Rock "tenant empire", is really a new "American dream".

It's no wonder that young people in the United States have no choice but to go home and "eat their old age". In 2012, only 4% of the population in the 25–30 year old age group were willing to sign a mortgage if they had a student loan.

The ability of the younger generation to buy a home has been hit hard, and this is the root cause of the continued sluggishness of new home sales, with only 400,000 new homes sold in the United States in 2013, well below the 1.3 million sold during the bubble and well below the 900,000 sold around 2000, when the U.S. population grew by at least 40 million people and new home sales were less than half of what they were in 2000.

Looking to the future of U.S. real estate, on the one hand the supply of foreclosed homes will continue to skyrocket by 6.6 million through

2016, and the shortage of supply caused by homes that are vacant but not available for auction will spur more new home starts, and the overall supply of properties will grow substantially; and the demand? Of the real homebuyers who can afford a loan, most have been squeezed out of the market by Wall Street speculators, and of the potential 40 million young homebuyers, 1/3 have already been priced out of the market and will only end up with more being abandoned by real estate.

This is the future trend of real estate supply and demand, the lack of real demand, how long can the speculation group support house prices?

Interest rate volcano will burn real estate

On Friday, July 12, 2013, mortgage rates saw the biggest single-day spike in real estate history! If a lender saw a bank 30-year fixed home loan rate of 4.2 percent on Thursday, that rate rose to 4,575 percent on Friday.

In May alone, the 30-year fixed mortgage rate was only 3.25%, and in July it went all the way to 5%! 30-year Mortgage Rates Soar (Source: Federal Reserve Bank of St. Louis)

It was all Bernanke's fault, of course, that he let the wind out of QE in May and re-emphasized his resolve in June, with the result that global financial markets erupted into violent turmoil in June. Emerging markets almost collapsed, Wall Street is still in shock, China made a big "money shortage", reflected in real estate loans, is the most violent mortgage rates in history soared.

This is just a verbal exercise, the Fed's bond purchases have not slowed down in the slightest, and the disastrous impact of the sudden change in market psychology on financial markets is evident.

The rise in mortgage rates naturally means that the monthly repayment amount is rising, if there is a sustained and dramatic spike in interest rates, it will inevitably lead to a "monthly payment panic" for homeowners to be caught off guard, not only the possibility of default has risen sharply, but also house prices will be more than people can afford. As assessed by the real estate industry experience, every 1 percentage point increase in mortgage rates means a 10 percent drop in affordability (Affordability), and the spike in rates between May and July resulted in a 17 percent steep drop in affordability.

If an average family spends a fixed $2,000 per month on a home loan, the amount of money that family can afford to pay will fall as interest rates rise. If the interest rate on a 30-year fixed-rate home loan is 2.5 percent, the family can afford a $500,000 house, and when the rate goes up to 6.5 percent, it can only afford $300,000.

When the 30-year mortgage rate skyrocketed from 3.25% in May to 4.75% in July, the difference in interest rates between the two translates into a drop of about $50,000 in home prices.

As interest rates rise, house prices that can be afforded by fixed monthly expenses will fall. Soaring interest rates are not only putting a lot of pressure on home prices, but also affecting the business of refinancing. The reason why Americans can use the house as an ATM is that whenever interest rates fall, the lenders who lock in interest rates can apply to the bank to readjust the terms of the loan, on the one hand, to lower the level of interest, on the other hand, can take out cash to spend by raising the loan balance, which is also one of the motives of the Federal Reserve to spare no effort to push up house prices to stimulate the economy. If interest rates rise, then refinancing will not allow people to cash out, and with limited savings, people will have to spend less.

In July, Bank of America announced the completion of 20,000 layoffs to deal with bad mortgage loans; in August, Wells Fargo, the largest mortgage lender in the United States, announced 2,300 layoffs; JPMorgan Chase plans to lay off 15,000 people, 3,000 of whom are mortgage lenders; in September, Bank of America announced another 2,100 layoffs in its mortgage lending division; and Citibank announced 2,200 layoffs.

Because new home sales can't keep up, first-time home buyers mortgage lending ability is greatly suppressed, and the old housing transactions in most people belong to the speculative group, they are all cash payment, do not need to apply for a mortgage, the first two years of bank mortgage sector business is booming, profits rolled, relying on the Federal Reserve's ultra-low interest rate policy stimulated by the large-scale refinancing wave. 2012, the size of the U.S. refinancing as much as $1.25 trillion, and 2014 is estimated to be only 388 billion business left.

The interest rate tide is quietly turning, new home loans for existing homes have yet to see an upturn, and refinancing has also been tomorrow, the bank to keep so many mortgage loan people what use is there?

Banks are already seeing interest rates rise and big layoffs are just a rainy day. If the interest rate volcano does erupt, the outlook for real estate will be very bleak. As home prices rise and interest rates soar, American households and monthly mortgage payments are soaring.

The immediate strong hit was, of course, mortgages; the 30-year fixed mortgage rate before the 2007 crisis was 7%, compared to 9% in the late 1990s. From 3.25% in May 2013, to 7%-9% back to normal, interest rates have not only changed dramatically!

The median household income level in the U.S. is $50,000, and after mandatory costs such as taxes and insurance, disposable income is about $35,000, or an average of $2,900 per month. For a family of four, a large part of their income is gone, and they can afford to pay the mortgage at around $1200. In the 7%-9% level of mortgage interest rates, can only afford $160,000–$170000 home loans, they can afford the house price is roughly around 200,000. In August 2013, the median price of a new home in the United States was $257,000, and the median price of a current home was $237,000, and the price has obviously been overvalued, about $30,000 to $50,000 higher, the higher part is the result of QE, if QE exit, this part of the rising prices will be forced to retract.

The interest rate volcano will severely suppress real demand for rising house prices. If 60% of the buyers in the real estate market are paying cash, especially the wealthy Wall Street speculators, is it possible that the eruption of the interest rate volcano will have no effect on them?

The answer is no.

The "tenant empire", represented by Black Rock, has a dangerous model flaw.

The Deadly Trap of "Tenant Empire"

On the face of it, the decline in homeownership in the US means that more people have to rent, and in 2013 the US homeownership rate has fallen to 1980 levels, which should be great news for the "tenant empire" model, but the problem is not so simple.

The "tenant empire" model may seem reasonable, but in reality it is fatally flawed. Homeownership in the U.S. has fallen to 1980 levels.

The growth rate of real income, net of inflation, of American households is on a downward trend, with negative growth in 2013

Families forced to rent, mainly those of average or poorer means, are either former homeowners who have been evicted by the banks or newly formed families who are overwhelmed by student loans and other debts. If renters are represented by the median U.S. household, the rent they can afford if they can't afford the monthly mortgage payment is also limited and has little room to grow.

As a result of Wall Street speculation, the super-cheap rental housing resources have been quickly divided up, and the rapid rise in house prices, so that the speculation group's input-output ratio continues to decline. early in 2012, the speculation group's investment in rental returns as high as 14% to 27%, and in the second half of 2013, the rental rate of return quickly fell to 3% to 4%. Meanwhile, the average occupancy rate for Wall Street speculators is only 50 percent, which is nowhere near as high as originally anticipated. Black Rock is a relatively good performance, early, low purchase price, large capital, the formation of a scale effect, the occupancy rate of more than 80%, but the overall yield of detached house rental is also only 6%, other speculative groups are difficult to exceed Black Rock.

Managing tens of thousands of properties scattered across the country is a stone-pelting, labor-intensive industry, which is completely different from managing a hotel chain with a high concentration of residents. Each house in the "tenant empire" is the equivalent of a mini-hotel, and the costs of daily maintenance and operation are hardly significantly reduced.

"Tenant Empire" tries to industrialize large-scale customized products to meet the needs of customers in different geographic locations, different climatic conditions, different living habits, different ethnic customs, especially the thousands of different personalized preferences, but also difficult to meet all aspects. Unlike eating McDonald's and staying in a hotel, where one meal or one night solves the problem, living in a home is a long-term, individualized process that is tied to everyone's psychological feelings.

There was a wave in the United States in the 1990s of replacing real estate agents with the Internet, which made perfect sense in theory, but did not work in practice. Because one has to walk into that house, touch the kitchen counter, unscrew the bathroom faucet, step on the soft carpet, step out onto the balcony and breathe in the fresh air to be sure if that wonderful chemical reaction called love is going on.

There is a basic condition of all mass-produced things that people do not have, and do not need to have, any special emotional connection to that product, and housing clearly does not fall into that category.

These are simply flaws in the business model, and more deadly are the potential dangers of the financing model.

Indeed, soaring interest rates pose no immediate threat to the properties that Black Rock and other Wall Street speculators have already taken, as they essentially use all-cash purchases. However, yields like 6% are not enough to sustain a promising business model, especially in the early stages of model formation. To successfully realize the ideal of "tenant empire", Wall Street speculation must continue to expand the scale, with a scale effect to reduce costs, to offset the ever-increasing expenses of personnel, it has to face not only the rising cost of home purchase and the bottleneck caused by the limited growth of tenants' ability to pay, but also suffer the severe test of soaring financing costs.

The Wall Street speculators are financed by the capital market and the big banks, and Deutsche Bank is the biggest supplier of funds for the "tenant empire" model. When an interest rate volcano erupts, the repo market, interest rate swaps, and bond stocks all suffer, and capital market liquidity is depleted. The big banks themselves can't protect, hedge funds cry, where are the funds to expand the frontiers of the "tenant empire"?

What is more likely to happen is that the speculative mortgage group within the many institutions broke the financial chain, forced to sell property on a large scale to cash, at this time, homeowners are "monthly supply alarm" forced to large-scale default, the speculative mortgage scattered households are scared to run away, who has the ability to catch at every turn thousands of houses of the dump?

The "tenant empire" is feared to be dead before the next round of interest rate crises can reach scale.

Roadmap to the Great Escape for Victory

At the beginning, the speculative group in order to seize the foreclosure market advantageous position, to strike the atmosphere, the appetite is fierce, no matter how much money renovation. With the rapid rise in house prices, the initial investment in the speculative housing group increased significantly, while the occupancy rate is not satisfactory, the cloud of risk began to gather. interest rates have soared since May 2013, the speculative housing group's bigwigs scared, financing costs rose sharply, competition for housing is becoming increasingly fierce, while the vacancy rate remains high, the rental income potential is limited, the ideal of "tenant empire" more and more like "chicken ribs", tasteless, abandoned pity.

The bigwigs in the Wall Street speculation mob are having to start thinking about backing out.

Carrington Holdings, the first hedge fund to experiment with the "foreclosure-rental" model, took a look at the wrong wind and began pulling back in late May 2013, with the fund's CEO candidly admitting, "We don't see enough return to stimulate further investment." The speculators who are still jumping into the market have been called "stupid money" by him.

However, it is by no means easy for the speculative group to back off in one piece, and the dumbest way is to sell the house directly.

Hedge funds and PEs have no intention of becoming long-term property managers from the start, neither with such an ideal nor with such an interest, and their thinking is to buy low and sell high to earn spreads, and the shorter the time the better. But selling tens of thousands of homes outright in the real estate market is almost entirely unrealistic, and no one in the real estate market can afford to take on a sale of this size.

In addition, the transaction costs of selling a home directly would be staggeringly high; imagine that before selling a home, tens of thousands of homes would have to be renovated again, advertised in the national media and on the Internet, countless people would have to be hired and received by countless home viewers to find potential qualified buyers; then each family's credit history, employment status, criminal record, and bank flow would have to be reviewed to determine whether they would be able to obtain a loan and the interest rate on the loan, which would require the coordination of a large number of banks; then tens of thousands of purchase agreements would have to be signed, and finally local governments would have to register, transfer, and pay taxes, which would involve a staggering amount of manpower and work. From the whole body out of the path to consider, only the financial market can through the speculative group of the sell-off scale.

For the speculative real estate group, the most ideal retreat route is the real estate trusts (REITs) funds to get listed, both to cash out to avoid their own risk, but also in the "tenant empire" game to continue to play, to the shareholders' money to risk a gamble, win the benefits are their own, lose a large number of scapegoats to carry. The bigwigs are in and out, sitting back and watching the clouds roll in.

The first real estate speculator to eat crabs was Silver Bay Real Estate Trust, which was listed in December 2012 and publicly raised funds. It has 2,548 rental properties with a total capital investment of $300 million and an average purchase price of approximately $120,000, with an average rent of $11,266 per building and an occupancy rate of 46 per cent. Of these, 900 were purchased prior to June 2012 and were 91% occupied, with revenues of $4.0 million in the fourth quarter of 2012 and operating costs of $24.6 million for the full year, resulting in a net loss in 2012. With saturated occupancy rates, annual revenues could reach $42 million and are expected to be profitable in 2013.

Silver Bay's planned $245 million public financing recouped 82 percent of the $300 million purchase cost with a 35 percent stake. With an issue price of $18.50, the speculative group's value immediately rose to $455 million. At this point, 82% of the risk of the original investment has actually been passed on to the investor, who himself remains the majority shareholder. If the business model doesn't work, it's much easier for the speculators to pull themselves out of the stock market than it is for them to go door to door in the real estate market and sell the houses that they can't sell to shareholders.

The listing is a wonderful move, and the speculation group is in a good position to fight, defend and move.

However, investors and shareholders are much more vigilant than before the crisis, "Silver Bay" debut did not receive the expected enthusiastic pursuit, the listing price fell below the issue price in six months, since then has not been slowed down.

Silver Bay has performed poorly since going public in December 2012. As we watched Silver Bay go public, other speculative groups were also impatient.

Colony American Homes, which is gearing up to go public in May 2013, has far larger assets than Silver Bay, holding 9,931 foreclosed properties at the end of April, primarily in Phoenix, California, Florida and Texas. It plans to raise $245 million. Just as American colonial real estate excitedly awaited the listing bell, Bernanke came out to talk about preparing to exit QE, the bad news came to Wall Street in a mess, the expectation of rising interest rates made investors immediately lose appetite for real estate projects, Silver Bay and other real estate stocks fell in a mess. Seeing the big picture, American colonial properties had to announce plans to delay listing.

There are unbelievers in the real estate speculation crowd, and American Homes 4 Rent is one of them, which insists on a June listing. American Rental Properties, which is larger than American Colonial Properties, has invested a whopping $2.5 billion and holds 14,210 properties with an average purchase price of $176,000, which is $56,000 more than the purchase cost of Silver Bay. Why does it have to be rushed to the market in June? Because it had splashed $700 million into a house grab in November 2012, when the buy-in price was no longer low, according to industry experience, the best time to go from bulk buy-in, renovation to rental is six months, because tenants have signed up in large numbers to move in, there has not been a phenomenon of tenants moving or surrendering, when tenants are the most stable, the highest rental rates and the best cash flow. If this moment is missed, the financial statements will be hard to tell.

There is a price to be paid for the top wind operation, and going public in June at a time of money shortage is bound to end in tragedy. U.S. rental properties were scheduled to raise $1.25 billion, but ended up with only $700 million, representing a 44% discount to the stock price.

The listing was supposed to be the ideal retreat for the speculative group, and it was also a plan they had considered in early 2012, but who knew that the plan couldn't catch up with the changes and the interest rate spike came too suddenly and beyond their expectations.

The company's boss, Black Rock, is a bit depressed, and its entry into the foreclosure market is to take a quick exit after the bottom of the idea, the superb PE if the long term into the mother-in-law rental affairs, what is the status?

The listing should also be said to be Black Rock's best option, but with the lessons of the past and interest rates soaring, if that path doesn't work for the time being, then you need to start looking for other exit routes immediately.

The second battleground of escape: rent-backed securities

Just as the IPO debut of "American Rental Real Estate" was falling on its face, Black Rock had already started a second battlefield of escape, namely rent-backed securities.

On July 31, 2013, the Wall Street Journal reported that "BlackRock, Deutsche Bank in talks to issue RBS (Rental Backed Securities) bonds," and the news broke that immediately sparked a heated discussion in the real estate and financial industries.

It would be the world's first bond collateralized by housing rents and could be described as the latest play on Wall Street asset securitization. Wall Street believes in the idea that as long as there is future cash flow, make it into securities now and sell it tomorrow.

Theoretically, housing rents are a relatively stable cash flow, while thousands of housing rents can be pooled into a pool of assets, which, through complex separation techniques, will be refined into standardized bond products, which are similar in nature to MBS (mortgage-backed securities) and different in origin, MBS relies on the cash flow of monthly loan repayments, while RBS is the cash flow of rent.

In the wake of the financial crisis, MBS had a stinky reputation, and Wall Street was largely cut off from MBS products made by other investment banks except for Fannie Mae and Freddie Mac, which were indirectly guaranteed by the government to issue MBS. There is an American proverb that the first time you get lied to is someone else's fault and the second time you get lied to is your own fault. No matter how much the MBS publisher has changed its mind, it is hard to see much improvement in a decade. The psychological wounds inflicted by MBS will only truly heal if this generation of traumatized investors exits the historical stage and a new generation of completely untouched investors enters the market.

In the current state of the market, the RBS is at best a miniature version of the MBS, no match for the pre-2007 MBS in terms of size or importance.

MBS is collateralized by the home, as is RBS. Black Rock's first RBS bond issue was modest, about $240 million to $275 million, with mortgaged home equity of about $300 million to $350 million, corresponding to 1,500 to 1,700 rental homes, each of which would need to generate an average of $172,000 in cash flow, or about 10 years of gross rental income if the average monthly rent for each home was $1,500. This means that once the bonds are sold, Black Rock is selling the houses in disguise and the remaining risk is all transferred to the buyers of the investment bonds. If the bond defaults, the foreclosed house is a souvenir that Black Rock left to the investors, and the money is in Black Rock's pocket anyway.

The underwriter of Black Rock's RBS bond issue was Deutsche Bank, the continent's most Wall Street-esque player, which organized a $3.6 billion financing for Black Rock in the first half of 2013 alone, making it the premier provider of financing for foreclosed home acquisitions among large banks.

In order to ensure the success of the RBS debut, BlackRock and Deutsche Bank will inevitably engage in a "grand opening", not only the size of the bond issue is small, but also the quality and quantity of collateral assets will be quite good and abundant, at the same time, there will also be a large concession in price, 10 years of rental cash flow, if sold into 7 years, investors will not be crazy.

Are RBS bonds reliable?

At least this time the rating agencies have learned the lessons of old, and Moody's is being very cautious. Kuroshi believes that the lack of rating is not important for the first business, this time the RBS even without rating will not affect the sales, as long as the return given is attractive enough. After all, the yield-hungry funds in the market are picking their noses through the "garbage pile" of assets, looking for scraps of leftover food to feed their hunger. The prevailing mentality is that it is better to die of poison later than to starve alive now. Blackrock's first RBS is sure to make a green light rise out of their eyes.

On the face of it, the risk with RBS is that it lacks historical data and is difficult to price default risk. But logically analyzed, RBS is not even as good as subprime mortgage-generated MBS. There is a fundamental difference in the psychology of renters and homeowners, and even if a pre-crisis subprime lender buys a home, what they lack is a steady source of income, but not the love and dedication that homeowners have for their property. The tenants are different, the house does not belong to them, careful care of the house is never their focus, so the cost of maintaining the house will be higher. PE and hedge fund managers are insiders in investing, doing Excel tables is easy to calculate, but managing tens of thousands of foreclosed properties is much more complicated.

Fund managers certainly don't manage a property of this size themselves, and specific matters must be outsourced to a local management company. However, there are many issues that are difficult for outsourcing companies to solve. Tenants' credit varies and their financial capacity varies. In the era of the "new normal" where income growth is severely squeezed, finding and retaining qualified tenants is a complex and delicate project that fund managers can't handle and outsourcing companies have nothing to do with it.

Foreclosures are densely populated, often in communities with concentrations of poor people, and are generally characterized by weak economic capacity. The difference between the rent and the monthly payment is not so great that the monthly payment is even less stressful than the rent, and if the tenants are families who have been kicked out of the bank for not making their monthly payments, how much better will they be able to pay their rent on time?

Tenants can sign a one-year rental agreement, or they may prefer to lose some of their deposit and move early, and since the amount and liability involved is much less than buying a home, the default rate on a rental is bound to be much greater than on a mortgage, with the result that the home will be left vacant until the next tenant is found, how long the interval between this is, and how big the rental loss is, again with a lack of data statistics.

Because tenants don't maintain their homes as meticulously as landlords do, there's a chance that if repairs requested by tenants aren't immediately in place due to common problems like clogged sewers, leaky roofs, uncool air conditioning, unheated heat, cockroach infestation, and water in the basement, they could angrily stop paying rent. If a tenant suffers a layoff, serious illness or any accident that results in incapacity, no one can immediately evict them from the house. State laws protect tenants' rights and interests, ranging from a few months to more than a year, and it's anyone's guess how much these accidents cost.

Black Rock's first RBS bond business kicks off a new round of real estate adventures. The total size of the rental market is $1.5 trillion and once the RBS is successful, a large number of new RBS will be listed in bulk and after the principal is recovered, it's a risk-free net profit to keep rolling. the more RBS are issued, the faster real estate prices will rise. However, the rapid rise in house prices will also lead to a rapid decline in rental yields, and in order to maintain sufficient yields, the speculative groups are likely to begin to join forces to push up rental levels, after all, higher house prices, higher interest rates and stricter mortgages will force more people into the rental market, where the speculative groups are already preparing them for the feast of high rents. The ever-increasing squeeze will eventually lead to massive tenant losses and the collapse of RBS bonds.

Under the mentality of "victory on the run", RBS bonds will inevitably overestimate their value and underestimate their risk, again deceiving investors from all over the world, which is what Wall Street is all about!

Expound

The big rebound in U.S. home prices that began in March 2012 is not indicative of a real recovery in the real estate industry, a market that is primarily a market for speculators, not buyers. The average person is vulnerable to a price rebound.

The biggest gainer in rising home prices is still Wall Street.

In the 2008 crisis, the middle class saved Wall Street with their hard-earned money, and Wall Street turned around and used their money to take property that belonged to them, forcing them to become tenants in an "empire of tenants" that continues to feed Wall Street with their hard-earned money, which is tantamount to robbing the middle class three times!

The U.S. government claims to be an elected government that is supposed to represent the interests of its constituents, but its policies on real estate are clearly biased in favor of Wall Street, allowing the wealth of its constituents to be repeatedly looted by Wall Street.

Is there no other solution to the real estate foreclosure crisis than to indulge the Wall Street speculators in their plunder?

Of course not!

The logical and just solution to the bailout is actually quite simple, since Wall Street accepted the government and taxpayer bailout, it rightfully should give up ownership of the foreclosed properties, which have been foreclosed at taxpayer expense, and they no longer belong to Wall Street, but to the taxpayer, who can entrust the government with escrow of the foreclosed properties.

Delinquency is default, default or default, foreclosure owners must be punished and their price is the loss of ownership of the property, the local government just needs to mark the property in the property register as an escrow asset.

The local government can then work out a rent agreement with the foreclosing homeowners to regain ownership of the property, which can be very inexpensive, as long as those homeowners do not default on their rent for several consecutive periods. At this point, rents will replace the original property taxes and continue to provide revenue for local governments to improve the standard of public services such as schools, policing, and hospitals.

This way, foreclosed homeowners don't have to be swept out of the market, and there won't be a lot of foreclosed homes on the market to sell, eliminating a major source of the plunge in home prices. Foreclosed homeowners are still taking care of their homes, the community is free of the security hazards of overgrown weeds and burglars, and the overall property values of the community are naturally stabilized.

With significantly lower rents, the financial strain on foreclosed homeowners is greatly reduced and they will work hard to regain their energy and fight for early redemption of their properties, which will significantly reduce the numerous family tragedies and lower the combined cost to society.

As the economy gradually improves, real homebuyers will be given the opportunity to participate in the real estate recovery, and only their broad participation will gradually pull real estate out of the mire of recession.

Under reasonable policy, there is no need for Wall Street speculators to artificially push up home prices. The trouble now is that there is a resurgence of massive speculation in real estate, and unlike the last widespread retail speculation in real estate, this time the institutions became the main players, who enter the market fast and run even faster if the wind is not in the right direction. Instead of smoother house prices, there are more violent shocks lurking, and real estate is not heading for a recovery, but an accelerated run to the next crash.

CHAPTER VI

Wealth Divided, Broken Wings of Dreams

The so-called "American Dream" is a belief that a better life in the United States can be achieved through personal effort and tireless struggle, not dependent on any particular social class origins, nor on the extraordinary assistance of parents, relatives, friends or other social connections, but rather on one's own diligence, courage, creativity and determination to move towards prosperity.

The American Dream is like a parking lot with only 1,000 spaces but 2,000 cars. Only the hard-working and early risers can grab a parking space and realize their American Dream, while the lazy ones can only park on the far side of the road.

In the U.S. job market in 2007, there were 71.8 million high-paying jobs compared to 138 million total jobs, a ratio of about 1:2. By 2013, high-paying jobs had fallen to 67.6 million, with a net loss of 2.5 million total jobs and a net increase in population of 15 million. It is difficult to get a job.

In terms of income, the vast majority of Americans, who make up 90% of the employed population, have real incomes 1% less than they did in 1970, with real spending power backwards by over 40 years, while the 10% wealthy group sweeps 50% of national income, 17 percentage points higher than in 1970!

For Americans, there are more people waiting to park, but there are fewer spaces in the parking lot, and a tiny minority of 10 percent of people have cars that take up half of the spaces. Statistically, no matter how hard people try, more people are already doomed to be excluded from the parking lot, and that's the inevitable demise of the American Dream.

A vibrant and dreamy society where the "parking lots" for employment should be bigger and bigger, where more and more people will have a better chance to "park" successfully, is a prerequisite for people to believe that they can get a better life through their efforts.

What are the factors that have led to the disillusionment of the "American Dream"? What lessons can today's China learn from this? This will be the theme explored in this chapter.

On Wall Street, the president ate behind closed doors

On September 14, 2009, U.S. President Barack Obama came to Wall Street with confidence, and his purpose was twofold: first, to hammer the big boys on Wall Street, and second, to urge them to support financial reform.

By this time, the President was feeling pretty good about himself, and his campaign slogan, "We must change," was already a household word and a popular one. Americans are struggling with the financial crisis, the blow of unemployment, the torment of debt, can't keep up with the pain of losing their homes, and the culprit of the crisis, Wall Street, actually took the taxpayers' bailout and received an even more exaggerated huge bonus than before the crisis, how can this make ordinary Americans feel at peace? The mood of American society toward Wall Street has escalated from resentment to anger, even hatred. Americans desperately need a heroic president who can change this country, and Obama thinks he's the one they have in mind.

Obama has another reason to be more assertive, as he is the great savior of Wall Street. In the rescue of Wall Street, the U.S. government, headed by him, has spent blood money. Bailout after bailout, taxpayer silver in the treasury, one after another, fills the black hole of Wall Street's immense assets. The scale of the tangible bailout has been unprecedented, the invisible blood transfusion is even more amazing, in the moment of crisis on Wall Street, the Fed's temporary liquidity rescue alone reached $16 trillion, far higher than the financial bailout by orders of magnitude. And then there's the massive QE policy of devaluing the currency and running huge deficits, tantamount to forcing blood on taxpayers to subsidize Wall Street's greed. In Obama's view, Wall Street owes him more than the sky is the limit.

It is also an auspicious day for the President to sell financial reform to Wall Street. He can recall the past, reflect on the past, reflect on the present, forge a consensus and create a reform agenda, while the Wall Street bigwigs will be ashamed, humbled, humbled and ready to start over. With strong public opinion and the mentality of a savior, Obama embarked on the pulpit of Wall Street in high spirits, and his central theme was to make the greed of Wall Street "pay the price".

It turned out to be a big surprise to Obama that none of the Wall Street bigwigs showed up! According to the *Wall Street Journal* that is,

> "Not a single CEO of a major U.S. bank was present (for the president's speech)."[33]

What's going on?

Don't the big boys know the president is coming to Wall Street? Of course not, the notice of the President's speech had long been in the hands of the bigwigs, and the news reports were all over the streets of New York. The bigwigs don't come, but they send a bunch of minions to fill the stage, smiling, clapping and flashing lights alike, but the main audience is missing, and the bigwigs of financial reform don't come and talk to the minions.

Obama's face hangs a little, and that's when he realizes that what public opinion, what presidency, what regulation, what reform, in the eyes of the Wall Street bigwigs, counts as shit! The president came all the way to Wall Street to teach the big boys how greedy they are? Then don't blame the bigwigs for not giving the president face!

Now that he's here, Obama has no choice but to start with his speech, only to have the bigwigs hammer him instead.

> "Listen to me carefully: we will not return to that era of recklessness and lack of moderation, which are at the heart of the crisis, where too many people are simply driven by the desire to make quick money and high bonuses."

Obama knows very well in his heart that words like this sound rather harsh on Wall Street, and it's precisely the bigwigs who hate them that are absent. But Wall Street's greed nearly buried the U.S. economy, and where would the financial markets have rallied if the government hadn't taken taxpayer money to subsidize Wall Street? The arrogance of Wall Street makes Obama's stomach burn.

---

[33] Elizabeth Williamson and Damian Paletta, *Obama Urges Bankers to Back Financial Overhaul*, Wall Street Journal, 2013-09-14.

> *"(Financial markets) are back to normal and cannot afford to be complacent... Unfortunately, some in the financial industry have misread the status quo. The bankruptcy of Lehman Brothers and the financial crisis in which we are still struggling did not teach them the lessons they deserve, and they chose to ignore them."*

The bigwigs are very disgusted with the President's savior mentality, no Wall Street campaign funds, Obama is just an unnamed congressman, it was the bigwigs who put Obama in the White House, and now they're holding up the savior rack! It's outrageous to try to lecture the bigwigs when you can't figure out who the savior is.

> *"In short, we will present the most ambitious financial regulatory reform package since the Great Depression era, But I want to emphasize that these reforms are based on one simple principle: we should have clear rules of transparency and accountability. Only then can we ensure that the market will encourage responsible, not reckless, behavior; and only then can we ensure that we reward people who are completely honest and scrupulously law-abiding, not guys who try to drill regulatory loopholes."*[34]

Obama's vocal push for financial reform is one of the two major political achievements he is prepared to leave behind in the annals. Helplessly, Wall Street, apparently uninterested in his financial reforms, became even more antipathetic to regulation that would limit the greed of the big boys.

Obama hasn't seen the big boys on Wall Street, and the grand scheme of reform needs their participation and support after all. So, on December 14, 2009, the President invited the bigwigs to the White House again for an interview. As a result, several of the major bigwigs were again absent, with the excuse that Washington was in fog that day and there was a problem with their plane coming from New York. In fact, they can also make it to Washington by a 90-minute train, only 30 minutes more than a plane.

Or maybe it's that the bigwigs' time is really precious, or maybe they just don't bother to listen to the president ramble, and anyway,

---

[34] Ibid.

what's supposed to come or not comes, and the president continues to play the one-man show.

The President can't help Wall Street, so can Congress pass legislation to curb Wall Street's greed?

The legislation has produced one, and that is the financial reform bill that the President and Congress have been working on – the Dodd-Frank Act, which is said to be the most comprehensive and severe financial reform bill since the Great Depression, and will be a financial regulatory milestone on par with the Glass-Steagall Act (the Banking Act of 1933).

"The Volcker Rule"

Among the many provisions of the Dodd-Frank Act, the closest thing to the spirit and substance of the Glass-Steagall Act is the so-called "Volcker Rule". They all adhere to an extremely simple principle: banks can't just risk making money and put depositors' deposits at risk!

The essence of a bank is to hold assets in trust for society and to provide monetary services, and its legitimate profits should be derived from the service fees charged for such services, e.g. interest on loans is the monetary service fee paid by the borrower to the bank. Historically and in reality, due to the special nature of money, banks have gradually taken advantage of the monopoly position of money services to gain increasing interests in other areas and eventually to legitimize them.

Before the Great Depression of the 1930s, banks could participate in stock market speculation, and exposing depositors' deposits to a high degree of risk, if the speculation made money, was the bank's profit; if it lost money and went out of business, depositors' deposits would also be wiped out, and the bank's risky behavior actually kidnapped their deposits against their will. The Glass-Steagall Act, which completely separates commercial banks from investment banks, is designed to put an end to the risks to which depositors' deposits should not be exposed. The deposit insurance system was created to induce commercial banks, which are guaranteed by taxpayers, to abandon the temptation of high-risk speculation. Investment banks can continue to take risks, but don't expect taxpayers to come to the rescue.

In the days of the British Empire, bank risk-taking was so costly that if a bank went bankrupt, the banker's personal property was subject to unlimited claims by depositors, and it wasn't until the mid to late 19th century that limited liability banks became popular. But under the strict constraints of the gold standard, banks are generally afraid to take excessive risks. Compared to the conservative tradition of the former British banks, the American banks were more like cowboys of the West.

Since the dollar began its massive overhaul in the 1960s, money has grown, the desire to make money has grown, and greed has begun to rush against all obstacles without a care in the world; the abolition of the gold standard in the 1970s and financial liberalization in the 1980s finally led to the end of the Glass-Steagall Act in the late 1990s.

The 21st century is a crazy time when money breaks through all kinds of regulations, strikes all borders, chases all profits, and the 18th century in Europe, the 19th century in England, and the 20th century in the United States have never seen money have such a huge global power.

Unbridled greed not only led to the financial tsunami that swept the globe in 2008, but was also the source of the next larger crisis. How to keep the crazy money wizards in a cage is definitely a world-class problem.

Obama's financial reform package, which originally contained no provisions to tame the money beast, so-called consumer protection, systemic risk monitoring, orderly liquidation of bankruptcies, derivatives clearing and trading, are all about controlling the losses the money beast ultimately causes, not curbing the source of insane greed. It is the "Volcker Rule" that has the real potential to bind the Money Wraith.

Walker is the early 1980s Federal Reserve's all-powerful iron-fisted chairman, to deal with high inflation dare to use high interest rates of the killer, would rather endure recession, but also to defend the status of the dollar, is quite a bold figure. His claim is that banks must cut themselves off from direct ties to hedge funds, or private equity funds, and that the size of their own deals must be limited.

As Obama's senior financial counsellor, Walker had to accommodate Summers or Geithner on other issues, after all, he has long been a marginalized figure, but in the most important principle issues involving financial reform, Walker is amazingly "difficult",

Obama finally agreed to add the "Walker rule" into the financial reform bill.

Banks are involved in hedge funds or private equity, which of course is like the 1930s when banks were involved in stock market speculation, earned their own, and now even if they lose, there are taxpayers who are the victims, the risk is not taken for nothing, the benefit is not taken for nothing. The issue of proprietary trading (Proprietary Trading) is more complex, and it's the most dominant provision of Wall Street's repeated tug-of-war with the new law. The key to whether proprietary trading complies with the "Volcker Rule" is whether it is done for profit or to hedge risk. If the purpose of self-trading is to pursue profit, then the depositors' deposits are also put at risk, if there is profit, there is loss. Savers lose, taxpayers pay, government picks up the slack?

Wall Street argues that if my proprietary trading is about hedging the risk of the assets I hold, it can only be considered buying insurance, not making money, don't I even have the power to hedge my risk? Then the business won't work!

It's really hard to sort out the rules that separate the purpose of proprietary trading. Congress and regulators have come up with schemes that are so complex that they are headache-inducing as to how exactly this rule should be applied in practice. In fact, the implementation of the Walker Rule has become as complex an issue as global warming, reducing poverty, curing cancer or solving problems in the Middle East.

In fact, it's not the problem itself that's complicated, it's the attitude that solves it. When Walker was asked by an MP to define what self-dealing is, he borrowed a quote from the late Lord Chancellor Potter Stewart: it's like "erotic literature" and "I can identify it when I see it".

It's not a matter of rationale, it's a simple principle, just common sense! In the case of the "London Whale" incident that shook the financial markets in 2012, common sense would suffice to determine whether it violated the "Walker Rule".

The demise of London Whale

"London Whale" is the nickname of Bruno Iksil, a trader at JPMorgan Chase who trades bond derivatives at the company's London Chief Investment Office (CIO), where the mysterious trader has generated staggering profits of hundreds of millions of dollars a year for JPMorgan Chase in recent years.

The CIO of JPMorgan Chase is also a fun place to be, located in the city of London, the most financially free and crazy place to play in the world today. J.P. Morgan Chase is said to be the "balance sheet fortress" of the bank and the "Lion King" in the financial jungle of Wall Street. It absorbed $1.1 trillion in savings deposits, the size of the loan is about $700 billion, the deposit is much higher than the loan, it could have continued to lend to the U.S. real economy, to promote economic recovery, but JPMorgan Chase is reluctant to do so, because there are not many qualified lenders, and lending this old business is not very profitable, but not small risk. So JPMorgan Chase took more than $300 billion of the difference in savings and loans and gave it to the CIO office in London to invest. This CIO is the equivalent of a super hedge fund within JPMorgan Chase, managing a massive $323 billion in assets.

JPMorgan absorbed $1.1 trillion in depositors' deposits and nearly $700 billion in loans, at $423 billion. More than $300 billion of the dollar's savings and loan balance goes to CIOs in London for high-risk investments.

Note that the $323 billion investment fund comes from depositors' deposits, which can create jobs if used for loans, and is safe and secure if invested in Treasuries and quality bonds, all in line with the "Volcker Rule".

But the CIO's "London Whales" have turned into bloodthirsty sharks in JPMorgan Chase's culture of high risk, high reward and high bonuses.

The London Whale did not honestly invest in safe and stable bonds, but instead invested heavily in the bond derivatives Credit Default Swap (CDS) market, the name of which was once very famous in the 2008 financial crisis, AIG, Lehman Brothers, Bear Stearns bankruptcy is closely related to it. Credit default swaps are a type of credit default insurance, the essence of which is that both parties bet on whether a company's bonds will default or not, and the party selling the insurance promises to pay for the loss if a company's bonds default, while the party buying the insurance needs to pay the insurance premium to the party selling the insurance periodically. As AIG sold too much insurance in the market, and the crisis led to a huge increase in bond defaults, AIG lost blood, while the value of contracts plummeted, leading to a huge loss of more than $200 billion, no one but the US government could save AIG from bankruptcy.

A few years before the good times, CDS made a comeback. Greed is not a disease, greed is human nature and there is no cure!

Of course, "London Whale" was not foolish enough to make the same mistake as AIG again, he did not go alone to buy and sell a company's bond default insurance, but found a cheaper and more reliable way, which is to invest in the CDS index, as long as the trend is right, do not have to worry about a company problems.

The "London Whale" entered the market with one of the hottest CDS indexes: CDX. NA.IG.9!

IG9 is the quote of CDS Index CDX Series 9 provided by Markit Group, a financial data service provider, which tracks the CDS prices of 121 North American investment grade companies, including McDonald's, American Express, HP, Disney and other big brands. Previously there were 125 companies in the series, including "fallen angels" such as Fannie Mae and Freddie Mac, and after the financial crisis, four companies were removed from the series.

CDS is already a derivative of bonds, IG9 is a derivative of CDS, and London Whale is playing the square of the derivative!

Why invest in IG9 over other CDS index series? Because this series of transactions is the most active, the volume of money in and out, good market liquidity, the nominal value of the contracts up to $886 billion, the real net value of 148 billion, i.e. the total amount of money involved if all contracts are actually executed.

London Whale bought the 10-year IG9 index in large quantities, while shorting the short term index, but with long positions much higher than short positions, just to hedge its risk. In general, the London Whale is the equivalent of a party selling insurance, guaranteeing that the bonds of the 121 companies will not default, so it can be said that the London Whale is confident that the United States economy will improve. His counterparty, the party buying the insurance, was required to make regular payments to the "London Whale". If the IG9 index is getting lower and lower, it means that the probability of default decreases, the insurance contract of London Whale is more valuable, because the counterparty pays higher premiums than the market level, if the contract is sold at this time, London Whale realizes a profit; if not, the book profit. The risk is that if the IG9 starts to move higher, the London Whale will be less profitable; if it rises sharply, the London Whale will lose a lot of money.

At least until the end of March 2012, London Whale was fortunate that the US economy did seem to be improving, the risk of corporate defaults was naturally reduced, the IG9 index trended downwards and London Whale had a good book of earnings.

Human beings are greedy by nature, and being in a culture of JPMorgan Chase super greed only fuels greed into extreme greed! With profits tied to huge bonuses, who can resist that temptation?

In order to make more money, "London Whale" began to increase its position, and then increase it again, just like AIG back in the day, selling insurance in the market like crazy. He represents JPMorgan Chase, the CIO of the $300+ billion super hedge fund behind it, and as the money invested magnifies, so does his price influence in the market, and the more insurance he sells, the more pressure he puts on the IG9 index, in the same way that big banks selling interest rate swap insurance can suppress interest rate levels.

Finally, London Whale became the most influential super player in the entire market, and when he moved, the price moved with him, and all the hedge funds in the market watched his movements to judge where the market was going. He has evolved into a large whale in a small river that can make waves with a single flutter, and the nickname "London Whale" has gained fame in the CDS market.

However, a problem arose when the behaviour of the "London whales" distorted market prices. In a normal CDS market, the price of buying the IG9 index should be comparable to the combined price of a CDS that buys 121 individual corporate bonds, otherwise there would be arbitrage opportunities; prior to August 2011, the two price curves almost exactly coincided, indicating that market behavior was largely normal. But the end of 2011 saw an increasingly pronounced deviation between the price of IG9 and the price of buying CDS alone, and it was cheaper to buy the IG9 index!

By early January 2012, the cost of buying IG9 to insure a 10-year, $10 million bond against default was about $110,000 per year, while the 121 companies that bought IG9 alone would have paid nearly $139,000 for CDS insurance, making IG9 $29,000 cheaper![35]

This discovery led to a flood of hedge funds into the market, either to reduce the cost of hedging against other asset risks or to make bold bets against the London Whale, with everyone snapping up the cheap insurance sold by the London Whale. As a result, "London Whale" suddenly discovered that he was "alone" in the market, and almost everyone became his rival. Although he still had a profitable book in the first 3 months of 2012, the situation was getting worse and worse, as he was already a dominant player in the market, causing him to have difficulty converting his positions. His escape would inevitably cause the price of the contract in hand to plummet.

If the market reverses, the consequences are even worse! He will be eaten alive by other hedge funds in the market, and while he is a big whale, he can't hold up to the frantic tearing of thousands of smaller sharks.

From late March to early April 2012, the European debt crisis suddenly resurfaced, and the U.S. economic data was far from ideal, and the unfavorable news quickly turned into a violent shock in the CDS market. This is really bad news for CIOs with huge positions. On April 10, the "London Whale" disappeared from the market and the retreat of the bookmakers triggered its own disaster. on that day, the CIO's internal report admitted that the losses reached $6 million a day, and with the plunge in contract prices, after 90 minutes, the losses became 400 million!

In 2012, JPMorgan Chase's CIO division ended the year with a huge loss of $6.2 billion. In late March and early April 2012, the IG9 Index began to shake so violently that the demise of the "London Whale" was inevitable.

Of IG9's total default exposure of nearly $150 billion, JPMorgan Chase alone has hundreds of billions, with full ability to manipulate market prices. It's just that the bigger the bet, the higher the risk, and

---

[35] Katy Burne, *Making Waves Against "Whale"*, Wall Street Journal, 2012-04-10.

unless JPMorgan controls all the index series of CDSs, and the CDS prices of every corporate bond, the manipulation is unlikely to last.

It needs to be made clear that JPMorgan Chase's involvement in the IG9 market with such a high percentage of exposure is no longer at all a hedge against so-called risk, but a targeted pursuit of profit! JPMorgan's hundreds of billions of dollars are at risk both for itself and for depositors' deposits. Upwards of $300 billion of JPMorgan Chase's excess savings has been quietly transferred to the CIO division in London.

Aren't JPMorgan Chase's depositors' deposits in the US? How can this money "fly" to London?

One possible path is to "move" the money through repurchase to collateralization.

JPMorgan Chase has hundreds of billions of dollars in excess reserves on the Fed's accounts, which are not being lent out, they are eating the Fed's meager 0.25% interest rate being "idled" there, which is certainly not in line with the banks' nature of chasing high profits. An ingenious way to do this is to "move the universe" of funds through the repo market.

J.P. Morgan can lend "idle funds" in excess reserve accounts in the repo market and collect treasury bonds as collateral, a so-called "reverse repo operation". Under the accounting standards, "idle funds" remain on the balance sheet of JPMorgan Chase. Since JPMorgan Chase is one of the two major clearing houses in the tri-party repo market, it can "collateralize" the repo collateral, such as sub-collateralizing Treasuries to the CIO sector in London, where there is no cap on the number of sub-collateralizations, and the CIO can use these Treasuries to re-collateralize in the London repo market for cash, and then invest in the CDS IG9 market for risky returns, which is why the CIO is based in London.

In this way, JPMorgan Chase's "idle funds" in the Fed's excess reserve account have not diminished, and from a legal point of view, they are still lying there eating 0.25% of the government subsidies. But that is just the "shell" of money, and its "soul" has long since flown to London to make a fortune by buying back the mortgage chain.

JPMorgan Chase is just one example of a big bank where other Wall Street giants are perfectly capable of following a gourd's drawing board to shift their excess reserves.

Due to the lack of understanding of the essence of the repo market, many scholars mistakenly believe that the U.S. banking system in the Federal Reserve accounts still have $2 trillion in "idle" savings, the financial situation should be quite abundant, but I do not know how much of this money has long since floated across the sea to participate in high-risk gambling went.

To risk these funds is, of course, to risk the depositors' deposits, to make money that belongs to JPMorgan Chase, and to lose it to bankruptcy, which is what taxpayers deserve.

After the "London Whale" incident, J.P. Morgan still asserted that it was not a proprietary transaction, but a risk management, and that the CIO's investment in IG9 was purely to hedge J.P. Morgan's other risks, not to make a profit.

There's a lie called staring and talking blind!

Still, Chancellor Stewart put it so eloquently: it's like erotic literature, I can identify it when I see it.

Lawlessness and lawlessness

There are two kinds of corruption in the world: lawlessness, the illegal appropriation of assets, and lawlessness, the legal plundering of public wealth. Heaven, that is, justice, conscience and righteousness!

The law itself does not necessarily protect justice; it is who is making and enforcing the law that matters. Remember the Rothschilds' famous quote? I don't care who makes the laws as long as I can control the currency issue of a country!

The Dodd-Frank Act, designed to curb Wall Street greed, provides a vivid illustration of this assertion.

The version of the bill that Obama signed when it was first introduced has been expanded from 56 pages as proposed by Representative Dodd, and 77 pages as proposed by Representative Frank, to 848 pages covering nearly 400 provisions in what has been called the most lengthy bill in American financial history.

Prior to that, the U.S. financial act was barely more than 50 pages; the 1864 Act establishing the U.S. banking system was only 29 pages, the 1913 Federal Reserve Act was only 32 pages, and the Glass-Steagall Act, the spiritual model of the Dodd-Frank Act, was only 37 pages, so it is no wonder that the U.S. jurisprudence referred to the Dodd-Frank Act as "a hydra-headed monster".

In the two years since Obama officially signed the Dodd-Frank Act on July 21, 2010, the bill has not been simplified with the controversy, but has been compounded by the constant churning of Wall Street interests; what was 848 pages in July 2010 has ballooned to a breathtaking 8,843 pages by July 2012!

And the implementation details of the bill are only 1/3 complete!

People will eventually see a behemoth of tens of thousands of pages, even tens of thousands of pages.

No wonder Yale Law School professor Jonathan Macey snarked,

> *"The law was supposed to be a rule of conduct for ordinary people, and it's clear that the Dodd-Frank Act was not meant to be for ordinary people, it was a platform for bureaucrats to use to guide those people on how to create more regulations that would create more bureaucracy."*[36]

This is the tactical tactic used by lawyers under Wall Street's aegis, using infinitely complex technical details to interfere with the core issues, create a sea of documents to overwhelm the people involved, and set off an endless wave of controversy to sway the legislative process.

The legal profession has teased that when the full details of the bill are available, only two or three of the best law firms in the United States will really understand what the bill is really about. Financial regulators, enforcement units at all levels of government, compliance officers at financial institutions, and financial practitioners will need an extremely long period of learning and training to figure out what they can and cannot do, and the bill will not be enforced without a decade or eight.

The "Volcker Rule" is even more so.

When Walker filed the motion alone, the rules were a whopping four pages. Walker's original intent was to pass a simple law that would have maximally discouraged large financial institutions from engaging in high-risk activities in proprietary trading. In Walker's definition,

---

[36] The Dodd-Frank act Too big not to fail, Economist, 2012-02-18.

self-dealing is easy to define: "Self-dealing is where you make money for yourself, not for the customer." Walker argues, "This can be seen by tracking and calculating the banks' trading positions."

What Walker thought was easy was met with a strong resistance from Wall Street. The stakes are high, and Wall Street won't budge an inch. If strictly enforced under the Volcker Rule, restricting proprietary trading alone would reduce Goldman Sachs' annual revenue by more than $3.7 billion. And Goldman Sachs could also face additional billions of dollars in losses if the relevant rules set by regulators are extraordinarily stringent. In addition to Goldman Sachs, the Volcker Rule has also hit Wall Street bigwigs like JPMorgan Chase, Morgan Stanley, Bank of America, and Citigroup hard, and if the Volcker Rule in the new law of July 2010 is put in place soon and goes into effect in 2011, it will cost the Wall Street bigwigs a whopping $50 billion in total revenue in 2011.

It is for this reason that opposing, obstructing and delaying the implementation of the "Walker Rule" has become a top priority for Wall Street.

To this end, Goldman Sachs has organized an "all-star" lobbying force in U.S. politics to intervene with government regulators, including a number of high-profile former government figures. Goldman Sachs hopes to persuade these institutions to amend the relevant provisions of the Volcker Rule to ease the severity of the rule.

Goldman Sachs' "lobbying corps", headed by Michael Pease, former vice chairman of the U.S. House Financial Services Committee, includes members of the Senate Banking Committee, the White House and former key members of major regulatory agencies. Through the "revolving door" between the government and Wall Street, these dignitaries are transformed into well-paid "diners" at Goldman Sachs, and they move around desperately to prove that the "good food" they enjoy at Goldman is not for nothing. In addition, Goldman Sachs has hired several additional influential retired members of Congress to be based in Washington to strengthen its ties with the government. Among them are heavyweights such as former Senate Republican leader Lott, former Republican Senator John Blue, and former House Democratic leader Gephardt.

Wall Street and Washington have long been honorable and indistinguishable from each other. Under their close cooperation, the law ultimately consolidated the "Wall Street-Washington Axis" of gold power!

Under tremendous pressure from Wall Street, Obama was forced to compromise, and as a result, various interest groups lobbied and inserted a variety of "exceptions" and "rules" into the "Walker Rule". The rules have become extremely complex with the inclusion of amnesty areas such as "valet trading," "hedging," "stop-loss trading," etc. The original four-page "Volcker's Law" quickly swelled to 298 pages, and even Volcker himself sighed as he watched.

100 exemptions, multiplied by 1000 exceptions, equals 100,000 unintelligible!

Among the many "exceptions" and "exemptions", it is worth mentioning that the "Walker Rule" has opened the net of proprietary trading in US Treasuries and two-room MBS bonds. The reason is simple, U.S. Treasuries and two-room MBS are the most important repo collateral in the U.S. and worldwide repo markets. If the repo financing that surrounds them is outlawed, the entire shadow banking system will collapse and the financial crisis will erupt immediately.

Is the repurchase transaction a "proprietary transaction" of the bank? Of course there's no doubt about it. Many of the bank's transactions in this market are clearly for profit, but such transactions are impossible to prohibit. A broader dilemma would arise, as the "Walker Rule", which does not prohibit United States Treasuries, but strictly prohibits banks from trading sovereign bonds of other countries for profit, would make issuing and trading Treasuries of other countries more difficult, costly and risky, and reduce their market liquidity. The partiality of the United Kingdom, Japan and the EU countries to the "Walker Rule" is unlikely to be amicable, and this inevitably affects the coherence of the rules of the world financial markets.

There is resistance from within and suspicion from outside, and the "Walker Rule" is already a struggle.

Not only Wall Street messed up, the Federal Reserve is "biased" to the big banks. Just as the controversy around the "Walker Rule" rules intensified, a Federal Reserve official released the wind that the "Walker Rule" definition of self-dealing may also be changed according to the different financial institutions. This news has added to the already disfigured "Volcker Rule".

Not only that, the original provisions of July 21, 2012 is the "Walker Law" effective date, but the Federal Reserve suddenly jumped out to inform the major banks, do not have to immediately stop self-dealing, and give two years to carry out "the relevant business compliance audit". According to the most optimistic projections, the "Walker Rule" will not be finalized until July 2014, even later, and the Federal Reserve has the authority to continue to delay its entry into force. Even then, the "Walker Rule" will contain many exemptions or extensions for banks, allowing them to continue to own what is now a private equity and hedge fund investment business for more than a decade, while the proprietary trading rules can only be a long list of exceptions, exemptions to the gray area.

Walker's theory of "pornography" will probably have to be enjoyed by himself. In fact, Walker knows the enormous energy of Wall Street, he mentioned in the rules to prevent the financial crisis in 2024 and beyond, the implication is that the previous foul will be lightly punished, this pole will implement the problem 10 years later.

Obama campaigned on the promise to make Wall Street pay for its own greed, and this promise became an empty phrase during his first presidential term, from the end result, Obama is just "speaking for the poor and working for the rich".

If Wall Street's big banks are "too big to fail", the Dodd-Frank Act is "too complex to enforce", and the draconian "Volcker Rule" looks more like a comical "Volcker Game"!

That's why Wall Street doesn't pay any attention to the bill or the rules, JPMorgan Chase is taking a "London Whale" risk, and Goldman Sachs is turning a blind eye to the new law. Since the passage of the Dodd-Frank Act, Goldman Sachs has raised several new funds, including an energy fund, a yuan fund and a real estate mezzanine fund. Goldman Sachs believes that these new funds will be able to meet the requirements of the Volcker Rule, and even if not, Goldman Sachs can apply for an extension or use other means to keep these funds in existence.

The series of sharp contradictions that have erupted around the Dodd-Frank Act and the "Volcker Rule", and the end result, reveal even deeper issues.

The American people abhor Wall Street greed, and the President and Congress of the United States abhor Wall Street greed, so why is it that the voters, the President, and Congress have all joined together to produce a bill that will actually protect the public wealth?

Why is it that the culprits of the 2008 financial crisis caused billions of dollars in losses, tens of millions of people lost their jobs, millions of family homes were dispossessed, and not a single Wall Street bigwig has been convicted and jailed for it? Why are they not only taking higher bonuses, but greedier too?

The most terrible corruption is not lawlessness, but lawlessness! The most abominable greed is not the greed of one individual, but the greed of the interest group as a whole, the greed that is under the protection of the law, the greed of the system!

Oppression under the protection of the law has led to a fundamental breakdown of the principle of equitable distribution of wealth and to an unprecedented division of society between rich and poor.

Sinking middle and lower classes

On August 29, 2013, a general strike of fast food and retail employees erupted in more than 60 U.S. cities, with employees of McDonald's, KFC, Burger King and other restaurant and mall chains taking to the streets in protest of the federal minimum wage level being too low and strongly calling for higher pay packages for the fast food industry. They shouted, "Seven dollars and twenty-five cents, we cannot survive!" They are protesting the federal minimum wage of $7.25, which has plunged them into a vicious circle of permanent poverty, and the strike is aimed at a minimum "living wage" of $15 per hour.

Traditionally, the fast food, retail, catering, entertainment and other industries are largely unorganized and it is almost impossible to organize a nationwide strike, which is so mobile and temporary that the general strike that swept the country at the end of August was shocking. The South of the United States, in particular, has never been an active area for strikes, and this time the fast food, retail industries in the southern states were actively involved in the national strike, reflecting a strong sentiment and determination that filled the entire lower middle class.

When compared to the salaries of employees struggling to stay near the poverty line, the incomes of fast-food executives who move millions of dollars in bonuses are extraordinarily solid, and even the loose and unorganized fast-food industry can explode with surprising energy when extreme collective discontent turns into intense anger.

There is a general feeling that wages in the fast food industry are not high, but the numbers released by the U.S. Department of Labor still look very surprising; in July 2013, the lowest hourly wage in the U.S. was $7.25, the average wage in the nonfarm employment sector was $23.98 per hour, manufacturing workers were $20.14, and fast food was only $9.

Hourly wages in the U.S. food and entertainment services industry have been declining since 2009 (U.S. Department of Labor).

To make matters worse, their real average hourly wage has fallen 6% since the crisis ended. Just such a meager income does not guarantee enough hours of work. Non-farm jobs work an average of 34.4 hours a week, while data from the Federal Reserve Bank of St. Louis shows that food and entertainment services (including fast food) work no more than 26.4 hours a week, with fast food workers earning just $12,355 a year before taxes and the U.S. poverty line at $11,490 a year, meaning that 3.5 million people employed in the fast food industry are only slightly above the poverty line.

The fast food industry is obviously not a tempting job, but the competition for its jobs is surprisingly close to white-hot. After the crisis, McDonald's jobs have become the meat and potatoes of the job market, in 2011 McDonald's chain in the United States employed 62,000 people, while the number of job applications received surprisingly exceeded 1 million, an acceptance rate of only 6.2%![37] is comparable to Harvard's acceptance rate in the same year, and lower than all other Ivy League schools in the United States! 1 million people vie for 62,000 jobs at McDonald's, whose average wage is only $9 per hour.

The fast food industry is not the age when students used to work for a little pocket money, the average age of fast food employees in

---

[37] McDonald's Hires 62,000 in U.S. Event, Bloomberg, 2011-04-28.

2013 was 28 years old, 30% of them have a college degree and 25% of them have at least one child and they are supporting their families!

At $12,355 a year, even if both spouses work, the total income of a family of four is only $24,700, and the monthly income is only $2,000, before taxes. Think of the black stone "tenant empire" rent of $1500 per month, even the cheapest rent is $1000, the transportation cost to and from work is at least $200 to $300, driving is even more expensive, if the whole family of four people eat fast food every day, that life will not live, people who work in fast food restaurants can not even afford to eat fast food. No matter how frugal it is, a family of four is over $500 a month for food and at least $300 for basic expenses such as utilities and telephones, the salary is already overdrawn. Children can't buy clothes, go online, use cell phones, watch movies, travel, or go to restaurants... Is this the "American Dream"?

The wages in the fast food industry are definitely not a "living wage", not even a "survival wage", and I'm afraid the life of a nanny in Beijing is better. In the United States, even such jobs are available to only 6.2% of competitors.

What the fast food industry represents is the living conditions of a large number of lower-middle class Americans, whose situation has worsened, not gradually, in the wake of the financial crisis.

On July 28, 2013, CBS News hit a shockingly big headline: "Survey: 80% of U.S. adults face near-poverty, unemployment, says survey." The article points out that the accelerating globalization of the U.S. economy, the growing divide between rich and poor, and the exodus of high-paying manufacturing jobs have resulted in four out of five adults in U.S. society today struggling with unemployment, near-poverty, or at least partial dependence on government benefits.46.2 million people are below the poverty line, reaching 15% of the total U.S. population,[38] an unprecedented number of poor people in U.S. history.

By the end of 2012, the number of people receiving government food stamp relief in the United States had reached 47.8 million,

---

[38] 80 percent of U.S. adults face near-poverty, unemployment, survey finds, CBS News, 2013-07-28.

surpassing Spain's national population and jumping 70 percent from 2008 to a record high. The government gives about $133 per person per month in food stamp relief, which buys food, meat, fruit, milk, etc., at the mall. In 1975, the percentage of Americans applying for food stamp relief was only 8 percent, and 37 years later, that percentage nearly doubled. The large increase in the number and proportion of people living in poverty is in stark contrast to US GDP growth, declining unemployment, sharply rising home prices and record high stocks.

Which is the true picture of the U.S. economy when the economy improves and poverty increases?

The root causes of the significant increase in the number of people in poverty and on food assistance are the extremely poor employment situation, which prevents them from finding jobs above the poverty line.

In October 2009, the unemployment rate in the United States was as high as 10 per cent, and in August 2013, the unemployment rate had fallen to 7.3 per cent, so if the unemployment rate was declining, the job market should naturally gradually improve, so how could the number of poor people rise significantly? Unemployment rate falls from 10% in 2009 to 7.3% in August 2013.

The truth about the job market

In December 2007, when the U.S. economy reached its pre-crisis peak, there were a total of 138 million jobs in the U.S. job market, which can be roughly divided into three main categories according to the nature of the work and income level: high paying jobs, middle paying jobs and low paying jobs.

High-paying jobs are the backbone of the U.S. economy, forming the core of U.S. economic vitality and international competitiveness, and are the mainstream jobs of the U.S. middle class, as well as the basis of U.S. spending power, with a total of 71.8 million jobs, accounting for 52% of all jobs, 65% of all income, and an average annual salary of $50,000, which happens to be the median income level of American families, can afford the living expenses of a family of four, although the economic pressure is not small. Well-paying jobs are generally full-time jobs with a 40-hour work week, all with good health insurance, pension or 401K plans. Such quality jobs include those in finance, white-collar professionals, information technology, business management, manufacturing, mining, construction, real estate, government employees, transportation warehousing and more.

Medium-paying jobs include health care, education and training, social services and other industries, with an average annual salary of $35,000 and a total of 28.9 million jobs, less than half of the high-wage jobs and 21 per cent of the total employment. Employment opportunities for middle-wage jobs have been growing, although such jobs are almost entirely dependent on government spending and tax subsidies.

The average annual salary for low-paying jobs is just $19,000 and includes low-paying jobs in food and entertainment, bartending, motels, yoga instructors, gardeners, retail, temp jobs and more. The total number of low-wage jobs was 37.2 million, or 27 per cent of all jobs. These jobs generally do not provide health insurance and other benefits, and if one is still dragging a family with children, one is essentially poor.

This is the general outline of the US job market before the financial crisis. The mystery of the decline in U.S. unemployment after 2009 is hidden in the growth of low-wage jobs. Sixty percent of the 5.8 million job recovery touted by the Wall Street media cheerleaders falls into this category.

In July 2013, the total size of these low-wage jobs reached 37.5 million, 2.8 million "new" jobs, up from 34.7 million at the end of the recession. In fact, this size is almost comparable to the 2007 figure of 37.2 million. In other words, the 2.8 million low-wage jobs are not "created" but "regenerated".

After 2009, low-paying jobs have returned to their pre-crisis levels, and the 2.8 million new jobs are actually "regenerated" with an annual salary of $19,000 just above the poverty line, the fast food industry is a low-paying job, and the income of these jobs can only sustain survival. If you take inflation out of the equation, income from low-wage jobs is actually down 6%, and counting on them to drive the recovery of the U.S. economy is a very unreliable idea.

Well-paying jobs are at the heart of the middle class and the mainstay of market consumption, and the employment situation in this sector is much more dire.

The financial crisis resulted in the loss of 5.8 million high-paying jobs, and over the next four years, only 1.4 million were recovered.

With an average annual growth of just over 310,000, even the natural population growth in the United States is more than 10 times the size!

In 2013, the total number of high-paying jobs was 67.6 million, surprisingly a far cry from the 71.9 million in 2000! If the "recovery" happens at this rate, it will be a quarter of a century before good-paying jobs in the US return to 2000 levels by 2025!

And behind the growth of 300,000+ high-paying jobs a year is a whopping $1 trillion fiscal deficit (government spending), and $800 billion a year in Fed money printing. If you spread the $800 billion printing scale evenly over every job, that means the Fed spent $2.5 million just to create a job that pays $50,000 a year! Its effectiveness is unparalleled!

This only goes to show one thing, the Fed's money printing is not about solving jobs at all! A QE of $800 billion a year, if handed out directly to individuals, is the equivalent of creating 16 million well-paying $50,000 jobs a year! Whether Bernanke is flying a helicopter to scatter money, splitting the money, or simply paying off the foreclosed home debt, the economic effect is far better than giving the money to the bank! The nature of the Fed is clear from the results of its actions; it serves not the government, much less the people, but Wall Street!

Since the beginning of 2000, the number of high-paying jobs in the United States has increased by a negative 4.3 million, while the combined cost of supporting a family has increased significantly, gasoline prices are three times higher than before, college tuition is generally more than double, clothing, food, housing and transportation have all increased significantly, and the cost of health insurance and medical care is much higher than in 2000. At that time, full-time jobs offered extremely cheap health insurance, with employees paying just a few dozen dollars a month to insure a family of young and old, and the cost of medical treatment and medication was typically $1 or $20 out of pocket.

The number of high-paying jobs in 2000 was 71.9 million before the crisis in 2007, which shows that there was virtually zero growth in high-paying jobs throughout the "Greenspan bubble"! The so-called "wealth effect", marked by the real estate bubble, has not created any real economic growth at all, but has instead created a financial disaster that has not existed for 80 years. And the subsequent "Bernanke bubble", which tried to bring economic prosperity again with the real estate bubble, only turned out to be worse than the "Greenspan bubble".

Recovery of high-paying jobs in the United States has been extremely slow, well below the highs of 2000 and 2007. Finally, look at the growth of middle-paid jobs. In the more than four years since the crisis, jobs in health, education and social services have increased by a total of 1.1 million, averaging about 250,000 per year. If we count from 2000, employment in health care, education, and social services in the United States has been growing, and even the financial crisis has not changed the job gains in this area. The "UNESCO Guard" is seen by Obama as a "bulwark" to defend American job growth.

From January 2000 to July 2013, 6.6 million middle-paying jobs were added, bringing the total to 30.8 million by 2013. Of these, the mobile health care component alone accounts for 6.4 million, and the so-called mobile health care is the health care system outside of hospitals, such as doctors' offices, out-of-hospital care for patients, home health agencies, etc. Mobile health care jobs surprisingly surpassed the 5.5 million jobs in the U.S. construction industry and far surpassed the 4.5 million in the consumer goods industry. The hospital system employs 8 million nurses, professionals and administrators.

Overall, the U.S. health care system employs 14.6 million people; in the education system, from kindergarten to college, 14 million people; and in social services, 2.2 million people.

Why does employment in the health care system continue to increase? Because government spending on health care has skyrocketed! In 2000, U.S. government spending on Medicare and Medicaid totaled $300 billion, and by 2012, spending had ballooned to $800 billion, almost double the rate of GDP growth.

At the end of the Clinton presidency in 2000, the U.S. government's finances were in surplus, and since the Obama administration in 2009, the deficit has exceeded $1 trillion for four years in a row, which amounts to a massive government transfer of payments to the health care sector. Health care spending is much higher than GDP growth, meaning that profits in the U.S. real economy are being eroded by industries such as healthcare and pharmaceuticals, the manufacturing base is constantly being weakened, and there is a reason why U.S. manufacturing does not want to return to the mainland.

The abnormal increase in employment in the health sector inevitably leads to a greater crowding out of economic resources, thus suppressing the growth of good-paying jobs. The situation in the area of social services is similar to that of health care, where the government transfers jobs from the real economy to social services through transfer payments.

Much of the job growth in education has come from the rapid expansion of the private school system, with non-public school employment in the U.S. up 45 percent since 2000, while student loan balances have skyrocketed from $150 billion to $1 trillion and are in massive default. Education is supposed to strengthen the country's future, but high tuition fees, huge debts, are draining students' futures and destroying the country's hopes.

Middle-paying jobs are increasing all the time, with government transfer payments being the main cause. The increase in middle-wage jobs, especially in health care and social services, is heavily dependent on the government's fiscal deficit, and the cost of financing the national debt will rise significantly after the interest rate volcano becomes active in the future, the government's ability to service its debt will be severely challenged, and health care job growth will be bottlenecked. Job growth in education, particularly in the private school system, has relied heavily on student loans, which have reached $1 trillion, more than car loans and credit card loans combined, to pay for high tuition to sustain expansion. In the current recession in the job market, there is already a serious delinquency crisis, and if interest rates rise sharply again, an implosion of student loans is imminent, and growth in education employment is already facing a reversal.

The increase in low-paying jobs does not lead to an increase in consumption; they simply survive. Not only will middle-wage jobs face bottlenecks in future growth, but spending power will remain limited. Highly paid jobs, which account for half of the employment, have been hit hard and are far from recovering.

Compared to total retail sales in 2007, five years after the economy recovered, 2013 is still 2 percent lower than 2007 if inflation is excluded, and five years after the three crises of the 1980s, 1990s and 2000, total retail sales were 20 percent, 17 percent and 13 percent higher, respectively, than before the crisis. If we take a closer look at the retail sector's household goods and food categories, the level of real consumption has fallen by 6 per cent compared to 2007, something that has never happened in the recovery process after the successive post-war economic crises.[39] The extent of the internal damage to the job market is evident from this.

The sluggish consumption is rooted in a sluggish job market, which is a key reason why the U.S. economy is having trouble recovering.

Overall, the loss of low-paying jobs from the financial crisis has largely recovered, with only 1.4 million of the 5.8 million high-wage jobs lost, and even with the addition of 1.9 million middle-paying jobs, there is still a net loss of 2.5 million jobs over the pre-crisis period. Over the same period, the U.S. population has increased by more than 15 million, while jobs have declined by 2.5 million, and the pressure on young people to be employed is understandable.

In terms of employment participation rates, the U.S. job market is dismal, with only 63.2 per cent of the U.S. population aged 16 and over employed in August 2013, a significant regression of 35 years from the August 1978 level. The median U.S. household income, after inflation, is 7% lower than it was in 2000!

In August 2013, the U.S. employment participation rate went back 35 years to its August 1978 level and in 2013 the median U.S. real household income (net of inflation) was 7% lower than it was in 2000!

The Wall Street media cheerleaders boast that unemployment is falling, consumer confidence has returned, and economic fundamentals are in great shape, completely distorting the dismal picture of the job market and fictitiously creating a mirage of economic recovery. With such poor employment and income conditions, the stock market skyrocketing, the real estate false fires, and the optimistic projections of economic growth, all end up hitting the cold stone wall of employment!

The House on the Rock, or the Dream on the Sand? The return of American manufacturing is just wishful thinking. In April 2009, shortly after taking office, Barack Obama, in an exuberant bid to "change" American society, delivered a lengthy 45-minute speech at Georgetown University. In his speech, Obama described the U.S. economy as a house in peril, citing a biblical parable that says a house built on sand

---

[39] David Stockman, *The Great Deformation*, Public Affair, 2013, Chapter 32.

is prone to collapse, while a house built on rock stands, "so we can't rebuild our economy on sand, we have to rebuild our houses on rock."

The rock in Obama's heart is the rock-solid real economy, especially the prospect of the return of manufacturing and the revitalization of new energy sources, which most impressed Obama.

More than four years have passed since Obama called for the U.S. manufacturing industry overseas to return home and grow, and manufacturing has become an unspeakable pain in Obama's heart since he first took office in 2013.

In February 2011, over dinner with the late Apple CEO Steve Jobs, Obama had persuaded Apple Group to move its iPhone manufacturing back to the United States, to which Jobs responded bluntly at the time: "These jobs are not coming back."

In fact, the truth is very simple, if even the manufacturing industry that stays in the United States, in the QE flooded currency tide, are not willing to spend money on capital expenditures, CEOs are busy issuing debt financing, and then buy back their own company's stock to make a quick buck, even if the overseas manufacturing back to the United States, they will be exempt?

The policy of cheap money is not encouraging the formation of industrial capital, quite the contrary, it is destroying real capital!

On February 13, 2013, Obama, lingering over the fizzling back of manufacturing, put manufacturing at the center of his first State of the Union address since his re-election in Congress, stating that the top priority was to make America a hub for new jobs and manufacturing. In terms of promoting the manufacturing return trend, Obama cited the 3D printing business, the manufacturing innovation institute established in Youngstown, as an example, and announced the creation of three similar manufacturing clusters whose business partners are the U.S. Department of Defense and the Energy Agency, and asked Congress to help establish 15 manufacturing centers to secure a new generation of revolution in American manufacturing.

It is not true that planning is not ambitious and ambition is not ambitious, but its effectiveness gives the impression that the President is a bit "ambitious and untalented". On the report card for 2013 job growth, Obama is afraid his nose will be pissed off. For the first half of the year, the bartenders are more competitive, up 247,000, and what about the manufacturing sector, which is a high paying job? In total, only 24,000 people were added, not even 1/10th of the number of bartenders, whether they were returning or clustered.

The U.S. government is virtually unexecuted in the economic sphere, and under the influence of long-standing free market economic thinking, Obama wants to move against the money-for-money nature, lacking neither the brains nor the hands to implement policy.

And so the president said, and so everyone listened.

The outflow of high-wage manufacturing is not shifted by the will of national policy, but is driven by the instinct of capital for profit, Obama can not influence monetary policy, nor can he influence the direction of capital flows, let alone the grand blueprint of any industrial cluster.

The President of the United States, the most famous leader in the world and one of the least powerful heads of state, is merely a symbol of power, not power itself.

In 2013, manufacturing jobs increased by only 24,000, less than 1/10th of bartenders. Another important pillar of Obama's "House on the Rock" is new energy, of which the "shale revolution" is particularly hot.

According to the 2012 World Energy Outlook of the International Energy Agency (IEA), the United States will overtake Saudi Arabia as the world's largest oil producer by 2017 under the influence of the shale revolution and will be almost "self-sufficient" in terms of the "net value" of energy production. ExxonMobil's 2013 Energy Outlook states that demand for natural gas will grow by 65% by 2040, and 20% of global production will come from North America, mostly from non-conventional sources, particularly shale gas. The report concludes that the shale revolution will make the United States a net exporter of energy by 2025. The U.S. National Intelligence Council also predicts that the United States will achieve energy independence by 2030.

As for the shale revolution, Obama is clearly convinced, and in 2012 he claimed that because of the shale revolution, "our gas supply will guarantee America's demand for 100 years." Energy experts predict that the shale revolution will create at least 1.7 million jobs, which are no doubt clearly high-paying jobs, with an optimistic estimate of 3 million jobs to be created by 2020.

The plunge in US natural gas prices in recent years also seems to be confirming that a shale revolution is taking place. The Wall Street media cheerleaders are also raising the bar, claiming that the United States is becoming a "new Saudi". Not only that, but if shale gas and shale oil can finally take the place of oil, a dramatic drop in energy costs will directly drive manufacturing back, creating more good-paying jobs and bringing more consumption growth, and an economic boom is just around the corner.

The term "shale revolution" suddenly appeared in 2011. When exactly did the shale revolution suddenly catch fire? The age of big data, still speak with big data.

If you use Google's trending tool, reports of shale gas began to heat up in 2005, followed by a media "boom" after 2011, and the explosive term "shale revolution" began to proliferate. What really happened in 2005? Was it a major breakthrough in shale technology, or was it something else?

The core of shale technology is a combination of horizontal drilling and hydraulic fracturing, in which "fracturing fluids," chemical substances entrapped in large amounts of water and sediment, are injected into an underground well at high pressure, which fractures adjacent rock formations and expands the fractures so that free or adsorbed natural gas from the shale can flow into the well and be collected. The chemicals in fracturing fluids are often toxic and can seriously compromise the safety of drinking water if they penetrate the groundwater.

Shale technology has actually been around for a long time, having been attempted in the 1980s and accounting for a paltry 3% of US natural gas production by 2005, with the main problem being the high cost of extraction. Such costs include both economic as well as environmental and legal costs.

In 2005, the former president of Halliburton, the originator of shale technology, and former U.S. Vice President Dick Cheney, and his allies in politics and oil circles joined forces to

> "liberate" hydraulic fracturing from EPA regulation. In the past, the EPA has strictly regulated the pollution and hazards of hydraulic fracturing under the U.S. Safe Drinking Water Act, a significant reason for the high cost of shale gas. Under the strong lobbying of oil interests, shale production broke the U.S. Environmental Protection Agency strictly prohibited the direct

injection of toxic chemicals into the ground, becoming a high priority of groundwater environmental protection of the United States law, "the only exception".[40]

In 2005, the United States Drinking Water Safety Act shed light on hydraulic fracturing nets, becoming the famous "Halliburton loophole" in the legal community. It can be said that without the "Halliburton loophole", there would be no so-called shale revolution.

It seems that asset appreciation is not difficult as long as human life is devalued! In just six years, shale gas has soared from 3 percent to 40 percent of total U.S. natural gas production, making 2005 the "first year" of the shale revolution.

However, in addition to the side-effects of poisoning water resources, shale technology has another fatal flaw, which is that shale wells cycle too quickly, often plummeting by 75 to 80 per cent in the second year of production and then essentially dying out after five years. Producers have had to continue to invest heavily in new shale gas wells in order to maintain production growth and stock prices, and with a lot of hot money to follow suit, the market has seen a sharp increase in supply and a plunge in prices.

Shale gas wells are failing at an alarming rate, with production falling 75% to 80% in the second year. When Cheney got his EPA pass in 2005, the price of natural gas was $14 per thousand cubic feet; by February 2011, the price had plummeted to $3.88; and in early 2013, it fell further to $3.50. And the average cost of shale gas is about $8 to $9, which means that the vast majority of shale gas wells are at a severe loss.

The negative financial cycle in the shale gas industry has led to a funding woes. By 2013, shale gas producers will have to continue to drill 7,000 new wells a year at a cost of $42 billion to maintain current production, compared to $32.5 billion worth of shale gas output in 2012. If prices do not rise, the entire industry loses nearly 10 billion U.S. dollars a year.[41]

---

[40] William Engdahl, *The Fracked-up USA Shale Gas Bubble*, Global Research 13 March 2013.

[41] Ibid.

Why don't shale gas producers cut production and raise prices?

This has to do with property rights in shale gas. Most of the shale gas wells in the United States are extracted on private land, and landowners have contracts with shale dealers for three to five years; if they do not start work within that time, the right to extract the gas will be recovered and the deposits and other inputs will be lost. And producers are borrowing money from Wall Street, and the sooner they mine, the sooner they see cash flow, the only way to ease the pressure to pay off debt and also boost share prices. Under this vicious circle, the greater the production of shale gas, the more the price falls and the more companies lose.

Numerous companies are already struggling to support cash flow pressures, and they have to make up for them by selling land containing shale gas, while an increasing number are being forced to write down assets on a large scale to reflect their actual financial position. The undercapitalized companies will be the first to be eliminated from this big bet, and even the big players with strong capital will feel overwhelmed.

On October 6, 2013, Shell, the world's heavyweight oil major, had to announce that it had conceded a bet on the shale revolution. In his pre-signature speech, Shell's CEO regretted that he had misjudged the "shale revolution" in the U.S., spending as much as $24 billion on shale acquisitions and extraction in North America, and was forced to make a huge $2.1 billion asset write-down in August. Shell's shale adventure in North America is hopelessly underway, with the CEO confessing that "so you have to acknowledge the devaluation of up to $3 billion in assets that have no revenue".[42]

If Shell, with its position and capital in the world oil industry, is not yet profitable in the shale revolution, the 1.7 to 3 million high-paying jobs in the shale industry that Obama is counting on is another spring dream, I'm afraid.

In fact, all technological and social revolutions have one thing in common, which is that in the early stages of the real revolutions, no one

---

[42] Guy Chazan, Peter Voser says he regrets Shell's huge bet on US shale, Financial Times, 2013-10-06.

realizes that they are revolutions, and the things that are called revolutions in the beginning are often bubbles in the end.

The purpose of the exaggeration is, of course, for the minority to steal the wealth of the majority. Wall Street is primarily a money monger, and the oil and military industrial complex is not only a money monger, it's also a life monger. When interest groups wantonly kidnap policies and laws, group greed alienates into institutional greed.

The division of wealth broke the wings of the American dream

There is no better indicator of systemic greed than the distribution of national income, i.e. the proportion of a country's income that is shared by the rich minority and the poor majority respectively.

If one were to call the top 1% of income earners in the US super rich, then they and only they would be considered the real ruling group in the US. Among them, annual income (including capital gains) is also at least $443,000, while the 0.1% of the top wealthy earn at least $5.6 million. The total population of the super-rich group is about 1.52 million people, and if you count a family of four, the total population of the super-rich is about 6.1 million people, which is only 2% of the 310 million people in the US.

The ruling bloc in the United States not only occupies a leading position in all spheres of society, but also enjoys a great deal of voice and decision-making power, and the country's wealth is distributed in the hands of this bloc. If there is any question as to who has benefited the most in American society after the financial crisis, it is they who have shared the lion's share of the dividends of monetary easing, asset appreciation, fiscal stimulus, transfer payments, dollar minting taxes, and so on, with a whopping 95% of the entire added value of national income to their sole share!

Note that the 1% ruling bloc that swept 95% of the income increment of the entire society would have been God's special favor if not for the deliberate design of policy and law. In other words, there is no rational economic logic that can explain this extreme inequality.

As one British scholar put it: it should have occurred to people that the powerful and the rich do things according to the needs of their own interests, and that is called capitalism.

In addition to those who eat meat, there are those who drink soup.

Below the 1% and above the 10% is the high income class in the US, they are sort of the rich or elite but not the ruling group, they have some voice and influence over the distribution of wealth in society but not the decision-making power. While the use of money as a basis for dividing the various segments of American society is somewhat arbitrary, a few errors do not affect the conclusions. The annual income of the wealthy groups that follow the ruling group is roughly between $127,000 and $443,000, and there are 13.6 million of them, so to be precise, the quality of life of the wealthy groups is the "American dream" that people aspire to.

With the exception of the 1% ruling group and 9% of the wealthy, the remaining 90% count as the lower middle class in America. They number 137 million, many of whom are dual-career workers and, counting family members, a total population of at least 250 million. The average annual income for the lower middle class is only $31,000, with a total household income of about $62,000 for a two-earner and about $50,000 for a median household. Median income is the median, not the average, income of lower-middle-class households and is therefore more representative.

A typical lower-middle-class family of four with an income of $50,000, after paying taxes and deducting mandatory expenses such as social security and medical insurance, the actual monthly income is less than $3,000, the mortgage or rent is less than $1,200, the fuel cost of two cars plus maintenance is at least $500, the food and drink for a family of four is less than $1,000, the Internet, mobile phones, cable TV, utilities, house maintenance and other necessary living expenses are at least $300, all of which are mandatory living costs, basically no room for savings. $50,000 income can only guarantee the most basic living expenses for a family of four, and there is hardly any surplus.

Many families have car loans, student loans, and credit card debt, and if the expenses of going to the movies, going to the restaurant, buying clothes, buying electrical appliances, traveling and vacationing, and celebrating New Year's Day are taken into account, the family is not only unlikely to have savings, but most likely will be in debt. That's why the vast majority of American households have little bank savings and rely heavily on their paychecks.

Instead of growing, real income for the lower and middle classes in the United States, which make up 90 percent of the population, has fallen by 1 percent in the more than 40 years since 1970. This is something that has never been the case in the more than 200 years since the founding of the United States.

One percent eat meat, nine percent drink soup, and 90 percent are eaten, a long-term trend since the financial crisis and even after the abolition of the gold standard in the U.S. in 1971. In 2013, the 400 richest people in the U.S. had more wealth than the 150 million lower middle class combined, which is half the U.S. population!

What do you mean, "The American Dream"? Jobs are the foundation of the dream, income growth is the wing of the dream, and for 90 per cent of Americans, the foundation of the American Dream has been seriously shaken, the wing has long since broken, and the division of wealth has turned the American Dream into a nightmare over the past 40 years.

In September 2011, the United States witnessed the worst class conflict in half a century since the civil rights movement of the 1960s, the "Occupy Wall Street" movement, which lasted for a long time, reached so many cities, and involved an alarming number of people. It is extremely rare in American history for the American public to make a clear political slogan that the 99% of the poor will challenge the 1% of the rich! The protest actions of the Americans resonated strongly in all the developed countries of the world, from London to Paris, from Frankfurt to Rome, from Hong Kong, China to Sydney, there is hardly a major city in a developed country or region of the world that has not been rippled. The strong sentiment of polarization of the rich and the poor and class rivalry, which is unique in the post-Cold War world, is no longer a problem for the United States, but a universal problem in all countries of the world.

Greed and Dream Stealing

Historically, the wealth divide in the United States reached its first peak in 1927, when a 10 percent wealthy group swept 50 percent of the national income, followed by the worst economic depression in American history, and the rationale for the crisis in 1929 was not fundamentally different from 2008. Excessive monetary easing spurred a spike in asset prices and a great shuffle in social wealth ensued, with the rich benefiting most and the poor marginalized.

In 1914, World War I broke out and Europe was plunged into a four-year war, while the United States became the largest supplier of arms to Europe. The cruelty and intensity of the war far exceeded European expectations, and money was consumed to the extent of bankrupting the finances of nations. Sixteen Allied Powers, including Britain, France and Russia, were forced to go into debt with the United States to sustain the war, and as a result, the United States was able to produce on credit and its industrial capacity skyrocketed. In 1918, the militarily victorious Allied Powers became financially defeated "sub-lenders".

The lending of money owed entangled, debt distress, reparations dispute protracted, the European economy is difficult to recover, the United States can not expand exports, the situation stalled until 1922, the British came up with a "monetary easing" method to the pound sterling and U.S. dollar banknotes for the central banks of the currency reserves, foreign exchange to replace gold for currency creation, which is the origin of the gold exchange standard system. The dollar, the pound sterling and gold were equated, the basis for credit creation was greatly expanded and the proliferation of currencies, especially the dollar, gave rise to a "boisterous 20s".

The lower and middle classes in the United States, which make up 90 percent of the total population, did not share in the dividends of prosperity in the 1920s, when their share of national income fell from 60 percent in 1917 to 50 percent in 1927, and the 10 percent of the rich rose from 40 percent in 1917 to 50 percent in 1927.[43] The huge industrial production capacity of the United States is severely troubled by "sluggish domestic demand" and has to rely on "export orientation" towards European markets.

Not only did the United States market surplus industrial goods to Europe, but it also provided cheap dollar credit in large quantities, encouraging Europeans to buy American goods in order to continue expanding American domestic production capacity. The United States, on the other hand, protects the interests of domestic industrial capitalists with high tariffs and blocks competition from European products,

---

[43] Anthony Atkinson, Thomas Piketty and Emmanuel Saez, *Top Incomes in the Long Run of History*, Journal of Economic Literature 2011.

resulting in Europe being increasingly indebted to the dollar without having access to enough dollars to repay the principal and interest on the debt. At the same time, instead of fostering an economic renaissance in Europe, the cheap dollar suppressed industrial production and stimulated asset bubbles. The dollar loans obtained in Germany in the 1920s were heavily used for real estate projects like building swimming pools, movie theaters, stadiums and even opera houses everywhere for the simple reason that assets appreciated faster and it was easier to make money.

In 1928, the Federal Reserve raised interest rates by 1.5 percentage points, interest rates reversed sharply, debt default was imminent, the stock market boomed and the financial crisis of 1929 was no accident.

In the early 1930s, the dollar debt defaulted, the British gold standard collapsed, and the European markets collapsed. The severe surplus of industrial production capacity in the United States, with neither external demand pull nor domestic support, can only implode on a massive scale. Thousands of capitalists have gone bankrupt, thousands of banks have failed, and 13 million people have lost their jobs.

An economy that deprives 90 per cent of its population of its spending power will eventually collapse itself. Greed leads to divided wealth, and divided wealth will eventually bury greed!

The United States also started with monetary easing in response to the economic crisis of the 1930s. From November 1929 to June 1930, the Federal Reserve Bank of New York conducted its first round of QE, steepening interest rates from 6% to 2.5%, pumping $500 million into the banking system to bail out the collapse, and the stock market rebounded strongly by 50% in the first half of 1930.

In February 1932, the Federal Reserve lobbied Congress to allow the U.S. treasury bond as a monetary reserve, thoroughly bundling it with the dollar for the first time. Historically, the U.S. Congress has been deeply wary of the monetary powers of the Federal Reserve, fearing that the Fed might one day monetize the national debt, finance the deficit, rent-seek with monetary power, corrupt and kidnap the government, and subvert the value of the dollar. So U.S. law has strict rules for dollar issuance, behind a $100 note, there must be a $40 gold collateral, and the remaining $60 in collateralized assets are primarily short-term commercial paper. National debt was legally prohibited as a collateral asset for the dollar, so prior to 1932, national debt was not even more important in dollar issuance than commercial paper.

The Fed used the crisis to force Congress to decentralize, the door to monetize Treasuries opened, the Fed was finally able to legally carry out open market operations to eat into Treasuries on a large scale, deadlocking the dollar with Treasuries. Since then, the Federal Reserve and the financial capital forces it represents, the use of monetary power for political power to rent, has become an irreversible trend. In 1932, the Federal Reserve launched QE2, buying $1 billion of treasury bonds, injecting liquidity into the banking system, relative to the total GDP of $58.7 billion in 1932, the scale is equivalent to today's $270 billion QE scale, in the 1930s can be called an unprecedented masterstroke, the United States stock market soared 101%.

In 1933, President Roosevelt came to power, then began the QE3, the dollar's legal gold content, from $20.67 to 1 ounce of gold, a substantial depreciation to $35, equivalent to the base currency expanded overnight by nearly 70%, and Bernanke's QE3 to the Federal Reserve balance sheet to achieve "multiply" the scale of similar.

Monetary easing failed to save the United States economy, as did Keynes's deficit policy, and in 1937 the United States fell back into a severe recession; 13 million people were unemployed when Roosevelt came to power in 1933, and by 1941, when the United States entered World War II, the number was still as high as 10 million; and the failure to solve the employment dilemma after eight years in the 1930s was similar to the difficulty of employment recovery five years after the current crisis.

What really got the American economy out of the woods once and for all was the outbreak of World War II. Thanks to the power of war, tens of millions of the American workforce have been turned to the war machine and the problem of unemployment has been radically solved.

War is always a mechanism for compulsory redistribution of wealth, forcing governments to make massive transfer payments, smoothing out the income of rich groups to the poor sons and daughters of those who participate in war. Both wartime military salaries and post-war tuition and military health benefits for demobilized soldiers attending university provide wealth subsidies and more equal development opportunities for 90 per cent of the children of the poor.

In 1917, 10% of the wealthy group accounted for 40% of the national income, and in 1927 50%.

Beginning in the early 1940s, the 10 percent group of the wealthy dropped dramatically, from 50 percent of national income in 1927 to 35 percent in 1942, and in the 40 years between 1942 and 1982, the 90 percent of the U.S. lower middle class shared about 67 percent of national income, while the 10 percent of the wealthy were suppressed at about 33 percent. This was the 40 golden years of post-war economic prosperity and stability in the United States!

However, the wealthy groups are not happy with this pattern of wealth distribution, especially the growing grievances of the 0.1 per cent of the super-rich, who received only 2.6 per cent of the national income in 1975, compared to the staggering 10 per cent they had enjoyed alone in 1927. The rich are complaining, and the super-rich are furious.

In the 1970s, the ruling group, with the Rockefellers at its core, decided to radically change the rules of social wealth distribution, preparing to fundamentally overturn the welfare state system that had been gradually established since the Great Depression and to remove the restrictions imposed by the State on the expansion of the wealth of the wealthy and redirect the scales of wealth distribution in their favour.

In 1973, John Rockefeller published The Second American Revolution, blowing the bugle on the march to the Great Wealth Distribution Revolution. Rockefeller made it clear that radical reform of government was necessary to reduce its powers and "transfer the functions and responsibilities of government, to the greatest extent possible, to the private sector." In the book, he deliberately selects economic cases that highlight the fact that government regulation of finance and business is unnecessary, that support for social welfare is a waste of money, and that only the unrestricted pursuit of profit, and the financial system that accompanies it, can be the driving force of American development.

The sound of Rockefeller's "second revolution" ignited the long-suppressed desire of the rich to redistribute the wealth of society and set off a wave of neoliberalism in the United States. The wealthy have pointed the way, the writers have bombarded, and the ideological, academic, and journalistic communities have launched a massive campaign of criticism of government, with the hats of inefficiency, incompetence, waste, deficit, and inflation all over the place, and the 10 per cent of the wealthy group has taken advantage of the discontent of 90 per cent of the poor class with the hyperinflation of the 1970s to prepare to break the shackles of government regulation of financial and multinational corporations.

To put it bluntly, the government's redistribution of social wealth and support for public welfare hinders the free seizure of wealth by the rich, who want a pristine forest of the weak and the strong, in a world where the government cannot restrain the rich from squeezing the wealth of the poor, but has an obligation to prevent the poor from rising up against it.

In 1976, the "second revolution" of the wealthy began, when the Trilateral Commission, an elite organization financed by Rockefeller, selected the unassuming Governor of Georgia, Jimmy Carter, as its presidential candidate, and installed 26 Trilateral Commission cadres, most of whom Carter had not even met. It was during Carter's term that financial regulation began to be deregulated, and later President Reagan made deregulation and privatization the focus of his administration, with Bush Sr. following in Reagan's footsteps and Clinton's Financial Modernization Act kicking the can down the road and kicking government regulation out of the heart of the financial industry. Later on, Bush Jr. was more blue than blue and said he wanted to put the government in a cage, while Obama also did not fail to live up to the high expectations of the wealthy groups, and the division between the rich and the poor is at an all-time high since the founding of the United States!

Institutional greed began to break through all constraints, and they have driven government out of all areas of the economy, privatizing the public sector, liberalizing financial regulation, monopolizing transnational corporations, mega-banking, and "deregulation" in all sectors of the economy, with calls rising above the waves.

Whose life did the rich sack? Obviously it's the government and the poor. Over the 40 years from 1978 to 2008, the share of the rich in national income has gradually climbed and once again reached the level of 1927, with 10% of the rich sweeping 50% of national income and the 0.1% of the super rich once again enjoying a staggering 10.4% share alone! At the same time, the country's fiscal deficit is growing, the size of the national debt is skyrocketing, local governments are on the verge of bankruptcy, and the real incomes of 90 percent of the poor are falling back to 1970.

In 2008, 0.1 percent of the super-rich again accounted for 10.4 percent of National income, comparable to 1927. History is strikingly similar, as the tipping point for the division of wealth was breached when the 10 per cent of the rich accounted for 50 per cent of the national income, and an economic crisis of the same magnitude as the Great Depression of the 1930s reappeared! The job recovery is also struggling, monetary easing is equally ineffective, and 2013 is even more polarized than 2007, with the share of national income taken away by the rich increasing instead of decreasing!

Obama's fierce campaign attacks on the injustices of the rich and the poor have touched the hearts of countless American voters, and his determination to fight the divide between the rich and the poor has been so firm and bold, and his vow so loud and clear, that all have been moved by the fact that

> *"the divide between the rich and the poor also distorts our democracy, it gives an extraordinary voice to a tiny minority of the rich through costly lobbying and unlimited political contributions, it sells our democracy to the highest bidder, it makes the vast majority of Americans suspect that the political machine in Washington is being manipulated against the poor and that the politicians we elect do not represent the interests of the American people".*[44]

What kind of a system is this? What was said on stage was the truth, and it was the truth out of the heart, and what was done was so counterintuitive! As the saying goes, "lip service does not pay," and Obama has really set a vivid example.

The ancients said, listen to their words and observe their actions. That's right!

The ultimate criterion by which a government, no matter what institutional label it labels and what reform measures it adopts, will ultimately judge the nature of the divide between rich and poor by whether it is gradually getting better or worse!

---

[44] Obama's Income Inequality Speech, 2011-12-06.

Asset fragmentation is far more severe than income fragmentation

The polarization of the rich and the poor is reflected not only in the gross inequality of income distribution, but also in the great divide in asset ownership.

A post-80s middle-class man living in Beijing with an annual income of $100,000 could have become a homeowner if he had bought a house before 2008; if he hadn't bought a house by 2013, he would have lost the ability to afford one despite his rising income. Real estate is like a class threshold of wealth; step over it and you'll see another world, and if you don't, you'll be forever tangled.

In China, real estate is an important indicator of the wealth gap; in the United States, financial assets are a class barrier to wealth.

When the wealthy launched their wealth distribution revolution in 1976, the first surprise direction was monetary policy. The University of Chicago, the birthplace of monetarism, was originally the ideological home of the Rockefeller syndicate armed with money, and the rise of monetarism contributed to the seizure of social wealth by the rich. Friedman, the monetarist guru, was sent by the ruling group to personally tutor President Reagan, and also to "open a small foxhole" for British Prime Minister Margaret Thatcher, and monetary magic was deified as a panacea for all economic ills.

The super-rich admired Greenspan's monetary irony in 1987 in response to the stock market crash, and the Fed was always the first to swoop in and print money to smooth things over whenever there was a disaster on Wall Street. The liquidity bailout and interest rate cut became Greenspan's masterpiece, the 1987 stock market crash was just a bull's-eye test, the late 1980s savings and loan crisis, the Federal Reserve began a massive bailout of the banking system; the 1990s long-term capital management company (LTCM) crisis, the central bank even bailed out hedge funds, the subprime mortgage crisis after the financial system is all risks.

Bernanke went farther than Greenspan, reaching unprecedented heights in the scale of printing money to save the banks. He got his start by studying the Great Depression, and he lamented most of all that the Federal Reserve did not print enough money to bail out the banks from

1929 to 1933, so thoughtful that the super rich would not nod their heads in approval.

U.S. 10-year Treasury yields have been on a 30-plus year long decline since the early 1980s. Under the careful care of the Federal Reserve, the Wall Street bigwigs are all risk-free, the profit is their own, the loss is the country. Meanwhile, inflation has been suppressed by China's cheap labor for 30 years, low long-term interest rates have become the world consensus, and soaring asset prices have been taken for granted.

In the 1980s, Wall Street investment banks, with only tens of billions of dollars in assets, began to play the ultra-short-term repo and commercial paper financing, and then repeatedly expanded the scale of long-term assets of the "securities" business, before the 2008 financial crisis, investment banks sat on trillions of dollars in huge assets, the size of the expansion of hundreds of times. Hedge funds, money funds, and insurance companies are also participating in the richest asset bonanza in 30 years.

To eat a big meal, one needs a big meal, which is the scale of the debt that has inflated America like a blowing up balloon. Other people's debt is an asset to the financial system, national debt, local debt, corporate debt, consumer debt, mortgage debt, student debt, car debt, credit card debt, all become a delicacy for the rich, interest rates keep falling, bonds keep rising and the big dish becomes more appetizing. There is the Fed guarding zero interest rates, plus the effect of QE debt purchases is equivalent to negative interest rates, asset appreciation is making the rich people smile.

At the turning point in the distribution of wealth in 1976, all the U.S. had was $5 trillion in debt, the total debt that had accumulated over the 350 years since the colonial period in the 17th century and until 1976. And just 35 years after 1976, the total US debt has ballooned more than 10 times! At 1/10th of the time, with 10 times the debt, that's a hundred times faster!

In the 350 years prior to 1976, the United States had accumulated a total $5 trillion in debt, compared to 2008–2009. Debt grew by $5 trillion in just two years.

After the financial crisis, debt is not climbing, it's skyrocketing! In just two years between 2008 and 2009, the U.S. added $5 trillion in total debt, catching up with all the debt accumulated over 350 years!

Indebtedness is a repression of cash flow, and the hyperindebtedness of the state and the population is a huge repression of national income, which changes the flow of wealth in society. Under the strong protection of the Federal Reserve, the rich have plundered the wealth of the poor with reckless abandon.

Under a boom of rapidly expanding debt, the stock market was highly capitalized, companies were freed from government and union constraints, employee benefits were drastically cut, labor costs were further squeezed in the wave of globalization, while huge tax dividends were paid, company profits grew spectacularly, and the 30-year stock market boom and constant dividend distribution inflated the wallets of the rich.

There is an unchanging truth in history that the rich and powerful rarely pay taxes, and the world today is no exception. Not only do the rich have overwhelmingly superior assets and incomes, but more importantly these assets and incomes bear only a very low tax burden, which makes the wealth of the rich expand faster and the power to set the rules of distribution more dominant.

The right to tax is one of the most important powers of all governments and a key means for a society to balance itself. When the tax burden is unfair, the distribution of wealth is unbalanced, and the divide between rich and poor is a corollary. An important sign of the emergence of institutional greed in a society is the breaking of the equilibrium of the tax system, resulting in an irreversible polarization, which is the turning point in the rise and fall of all empires and dynasties from ancient times to the present.

It is not a question of will and won't, but of fast and slow in the corruption of the ruling group. The social system is like a building, weathered by wind, rain, snow and frost, and it will inevitably age, with buildings that are well established and constantly maintained lasting longer, and buildings that are dilapidated or even self-excavated collapsing faster.

When ruling groups and the rich indulge their greed and trample on the interests of the vast majority, the national tax system is bound to be the first to be destroyed. In today's world, the rich hold the power to make the tax system and the mysteries of tax avoidance. For example, the capital gains tax is notably low, from 35 per cent in 1978 before the "second revolution" by the super-rich, to 20 per cent in 1981[45] during the Reagan era, to only 15 per cent in 2012. In addition, the estate tax is a sham for the super-rich, and there are various tax benefits for real estate, even mortgage interest is included in the tax credit. On top of that, there are various tax havens, and of course only the rich are eligible to enter "paradise".

In a variety of tax avoidance methods, the super-rich people widely used is the foundation's "paradise" model, they frequently "naked donation" all or most of the assets, reduce the taxable income. By simply including family descendants as a key vote with one veto in the foundation's constitution, it is possible to avoid almost all tax burdens, such as estate, gift, and capital gains taxes, with peace of mind. Of course, foundations are required to give a portion of their money each year to charitable causes such as scientific research, medical care, and poverty alleviation, but these donations are nothing compared to the progressive income tax, and they are effective in giving voice to the super rich. No wonder Americans often say that the essence of so-called Non-Profit is Non-Taxation.

The earliest pioneers in the Foundation's playbook were the Rockefeller family. The Washington Post has previously disclosed that after two generations of running the Rothschild family, the vast majority of the family assets have been transferred to foundations at various levels and levels, as well as the resulting subordinate, branching, direct or indirectly controlled companies, resulting in a network of foundations on a large scale. The financial reports of each foundation, which are neither audited nor published, have completely fallen off the radar of public opinion and government regulation.

When Nelson Rockefeller ran for president in the 1960s and 1970s and had to disclose his finances, he personally declared $33 million, which of course the public did not believe, and later admitted to being worth $218 million, six times more than he originally was. That's $218 million from the gold standard era, far too many times more than the 21st century dollar is worth. This figure is already staggering, but it is only "pocket money" after the Rothschild family has "nakedly

---

[45] Robert Lenzner, The Top 0.1% Of The Nation Earn Half Of All Capital Gains, *Forbes*, 2011-11-20.

donated" most of their assets. With such a staggering wealth, the Senate found that throughout the 1970s, Nelson surprisingly did not pay a dime in personal income taxes.

One certainly doesn't see a big family like Rockefeller on the world's rich list. But by the time the Rothschild family launched its wealth revolution in 1975, the Rothschild family consortium's team of professionals managing their own foundation's wealth had 154 full-time staff, 15 top financial experts, and $70 billion in assets under management – note, this was $70 billion in the 1970s! The Rockefeller Report reveals that by the 1970s there were more than 200 foundations in the Rothschild family's name, and that, indirectly or derivatively, no less than a thousand, the Rothschild family actually controlled Chase Manhattan Bank (JPMorgan Chase), National City Bank of New York (Citibank) and Hanover Bank, not to mention the old Standard Oil Company. In addition, it controls 37 of the 100 largest industrial companies in the United States, 9 of the 20 largest transportation companies, all of the largest water, electricity and gas companies, 3 of the 4 largest insurance companies, 25 per cent of the assets of the 50 largest commercial banks in the United States and 30 per cent of the assets of the 50 largest insurance companies.[46]

This was all before the super rich people started the wealth revolution!

Today, they capture five times as much of national income as they did that year, and the wealth gap is even more stark as a result of asset appreciation, with the bond market inflated 10 times and equity assets inflated 20 times, while the financial derivatives market, which did not exist then, is now a behemoth of hundreds of billions. The privileges of the super-rich have reached the point where they play with the law and politicians are in control.

The rich and powerful, who are richer than the rest of the world, pay little in taxes, while the American Empire has to maintain huge expenditures, with staggering deficits, mountains of national debt, shrinking welfare, and unsustainable social security and health care, draining 90% of the wealth of future generations of the middle and lower classes, who are under extreme and unreasonable pressure to pay

---

[46] Gary Allen, *The Rockefeller File*, Buccaneer Books.

taxes, while facing diminishing opportunities for development. While the "American dream" is fading away, hope is lost, discontent is breeding, and economic pain is creeping into the social crisis.

The problem of divided wealth that has emerged in the United States, a problem common to the major countries of the world, is both the root cause of the last financial tsunami and the trigger for the next round of economic crisis, and instead of improving, it is getting worse. One does not know when the next round of crises will break out, but one can be sure that it will be not only a financial crisis on a much larger scale, but also a currency crisis and a social crisis.

Use history as a mirror to see the deformity of the present. Is the world economy on the mend? The eye sees a mirage; are the financial markets safer? What was felt inside was the silence before the great break. The air was shaking, as if the sky was burning, and yes, a storm was coming!

Expound

With regard to power, President Bush Jr. made a wonderful speech in which he said: "What is most precious in the 10 million years of human history is not the dazzling technology, the vast classics of masters, the smallpox speeches of politicians, but the realization of the taming of the rulers and the dream of keeping them in a cage by democratic means. I am standing in my cage right now to address you."

President Bush Jr. is right that America does put power in a cage, but it is not a cage that represents the interests of the voters, it is a cage of money and capital!

The right question should be whether it is the state that controls capital, or capital that controls the state. The form of democracy is important, but the essence of democracy is more important, and the whole point of people in charge is to get a fair distribution of wealth! Without the end result, the meaning of the process is lost.

Both Clinton and Barack Obama are considered sons of the common man who, through their personal efforts, finally realized the President's dream, which is seen by many as a symbol of the "American Dream". Their story is indeed inspirational, but can a president who comes from a civilian background change the fate of 90% of civilians? Clinton's repeal of the Glass-Steele Act, which had maintained financial stability for 60 years, resulted in a huge financial disaster that hurt the class he came from the most. Obama vowed to curb Wall Street's greed, but his proposed Dodd-Frank Act was tampered with by Wall Street, and he was determined to fight the wealth injustice to the end, with the result that the gap between rich and poor has worsened like never before in his two terms in office.

Civilian presidents must serve the interests of the ruling group, which contradicts their origins and personal ideals, and they can only ultimately submit to the will of the super-rich. Clinton hurt the interests of the common man and Obama did not change the situation of blacks, would he be more friendly to China if a future American elected a Chinese president? I'm afraid it can only get worse because he has to stay politically correct, and the super rich define what it means to be politically correct. Putting the government in the cage of money and capital is the political correctness of the United States, and the political correctness of the United States to sell to the world, and whoever supports this idea will win applause internationally.

The ideological struggle in today's world is no longer a struggle for doctrine, but a struggle for the distribution of wealth, and the world's super-rich are uniting in their determination to collectively dominate the fate of 99 per cent of humanity, as the greed of the 1 per cent grows and the resistance of the 99 per cent inevitably escalates, and the Occupy Wall Street movement, which spread across the globe in 2011, is just a prelude.

Historically, institutional greed, once entrenched, has spontaneously generated irreversible trends of wealth consolidation and the attendant worsening of tax imbalances, which in turn have led to structural deficits in fiscal revenues and forced Governments to raise taxes significantly, which has stimulated popular discontent. If tax increases reach the limits of social stability and still do not meet the demands of fiscal spending, then currency over-issues will be inevitable. The inflationary fires ignited by the devaluation of the currency, in turn, exacerbate the impulse of the rich to annex wealth, exacerbate the tax burden and the fiscal deficit, and induce a new round of devaluation until the population, unable to tolerate the vicious inflation and harsh taxation, resists until a new dynasty is formed.

Figuratively speaking, institutional greed is like a cancerous cell that, when it expands to a tipping point, will break through all restraints and constraints and expand itself infinitely, frantically plundering the resources of other cells until vital organs fail and life stops.

Some argue that the devaluation of the currency is the result of the fiscal deficit, when in fact, the underlying cause of the fiscal deficit is that the rich have half the wealth and rarely pay taxes. Thus, currency devaluation is rooted in the institutionalization of greed among the rich and the irreversibility of the trend of wealth consolidation.

What is happening in the United States today has long been repeated throughout history and is nothing new under the sun. Empires flourish and decline, dynasties fluctuate, both ancient and modern, there is no way out.

The future, in fact, is in history!

CHAPTER VII

Rome's Rise and Fall, Bloodthirsty Path of Greed

The first six chapters are a microscopic look at the current state of America, a look at money from the gold market, an analysis of the economy from the stock market, an understanding of capital from the bond market, an exploration of finance from the repo market, a glimpse into the crisis from the interest rate market, an insight into the bubble from the housing market, a screening of the recovery from the job market, and, ultimately, greed from the distribution of wealth.

Why dissect America in depth? For it is the overlord of the world today, and the living fossil of empires in their prime. If America in the 18th century was juvenile, America in the 19th century was youthful, America in the 20th century was robust, then America in the 21st century is old age.

The aging of the human body begins with the slowing down of metabolism, and the decline of empires lies in the solidification of class mobility. Opportunity, the wealth of the future, is the dream of rising up the social ladder; the drying up of opportunity means that wealth is no longer spreading to the lower and middle classes and that the empire has reached the inflection point of its flourishing and decline. Beyond this inflection point, the odds will turn negative, the so-called doom, with wealth creation diminishing and wealth distribution intensifying, and the greed of the few trampling on the well-being of the many, thus exacerbating the resistance, violence, bloodshed and war of the many until the empire collapses.

The United States is near the inflection point of the empire's prosperity and decline, its future fate, can be seen from similar cases in the past, but also will provide a historical reference system for today's "China Dream".

This chapter will select ancient Rome during the first monetary economic explosion of mankind as a control sample, use the main line of wealth distribution as a scalpel, and dissect the extreme greed of the Roman ruling group, which led to land annexation, tax imbalance, fiscal depletion, currency devaluation, economic depression, asset inflation, class conflict, military degeneration, civil strife and external problems, the fall of the empire, and then make a specimen of civilization, reminding people today of the path we will choose.

Death of the Civil Protector Gracchus

Tiberius Gracchus's fierce confrontation with the Senate in 133 BC, the year he was elected Roman tribune, was well known in Rome and his claims were enthusiastically embraced by the Roman people. Meanwhile, the Senate's nobles' hatred for Gracchus was unabated, and attacks and even physical threats against him were gradually escalating.

The atmosphere in Rome is growing tense, Gracchus has been intimidated more than once, one of his close friends has just been murdered, could it be himself next?

A strong sense of foreboding hung over Gracchus's heart. In order to keep Gracchus safe, the Roman masses spontaneously organized themselves to guard around his home day and night. On this day, the Senate convened to discuss Gracchus's reform bill again, and hundreds of supporters escorted Gracchus to the venue.

The nobles of the Senate had also assembled a large number of slaves, clamoring with sticks and blocking Gracchus's access to the meeting place. The scene grew increasingly chaotic, with Gracchus shouting for help, but angry curses and heated arguments drowned out his voice. Realizing that danger was imminent, he immediately pointed to his head and sent a distress signal.

Immediately someone on the scene shouted viciously, "Gracchus will wear the crown, he is a dictator!"

Someone immediately rushed into the meeting to report to the Senate, "Gracchus demands a crown for himself, he is a dictator!" The patriarchs immediately exploded the nest, and angry curses resounded through the venue. A large number of patriarchs, armed with their slaves who had long been waiting for their turn, rushed out of the meeting hall with sticks and slammed their heads into Gracchus and his supporters. Outside the venue, the slaves of the patriarchs immediately surrounded from all sides and swung sticks to kill them. Gracchus died instantly!

In the end, the mob dragged the body of Gracchus through the streets and the body of the famous Roman politician was thrown directly into the Tiber without a funeral.[47]

On this day, Gracchus and more than 300 of his supporters were beaten to death alive with reckless sticks, the first mass bloodbath in the 400 years since Rome abandoned its monarchy, and its horror and gruesomeness shocked all of Rome.

Gracchus was no ordinary Roman commoner; he was as prominent a Roman nobleman as the man who murdered him in the Senate. His grandfather was the famous Roman general, Hercipus the Great, who defeated the unparalleled Carthaginian commander Hannibal in the Second Battle of Buena Vista and was called "the conqueror of Africa" by the Romans; his grandmother's family produced another famous Roman general, Paulus, the hero of the Illyrian War and the "conqueror of Macedonia" whom the Romans admired; and his father was the consul of the Roman Republic, equivalent to today's president. After his father's death, his mother even rejected a marriage proposal from the Egyptian king Ptolemy, raising the three siblings to adulthood, and the story of this unfailing love affair between the Gracchus parents is well known throughout Roman history. His brother was later also a prominent Roman politician, and his sister married Little Zephyria, who eventually conquered Carthage.

How could such an important aristocrat, who came from a prestigious family, was well-loved by the people, and was in a high position in the Roman Republic, end up in a tragic situation, being publicly massacred by a group of Roman nobles belonging to the same camp, and dying without a place to die?

Even more incredible is the fact that the patriarch who led the massacre of Gracchus was his cousin, the former Roman consul and current high priest, Scipio Nasica.

---

[47] Daron Acemoglu, James Robinson, *Why Nations Fail*, Crown Business, 2012, Chapter 6.

What happened to Gracchus was very similar to that of President Kennedy of the United States, who belonged to the ruling elite, were from a prestigious family, and were determined to do practical things for the people, but in the end they all ended up in a bad way because they challenged the bottom line of the powerful and the rich!

Gracchus upbringing

In the tradition of his family, Gracchus was born with great ambition to rise to the political arena of Rome, as his ancestors and predecessors had done, step by step, with his military and political accomplishments. Roman tradition revered martial arts, and Gracchus's path to politics began with a military career. During the Third Punic War, he followed his brother-in-law Little Zephyr to Africa for a final showdown with the Carthaginians, Rome's century-old enemy.

Carthage (which ruled the territory of present-day Tunisia) was once Greece's main rival in the Mediterranean, famous for its powerful navy and dominance of the Western Mediterranean. Carthaginian agriculture was well developed, navigation was highly skilled and trade was highly prosperous, and Carthaginian currency was once a strong currency in the Mediterranean.

With the rise of Roman power, the rivalry between the two sides in the Mediterranean became increasingly white-hot. After 23 years of fighting the First Buenos Aires War (264 B.C.-241 B.C.E.), Rome finally captured Sicily, but the losses on both sides were unprecedented, and the war's casualties even exceeded the total losses of Alexander the Great's sweep across Eurasia. The Second Punic War (218 B.C.-201 B.C.E.) lasted 17 years, when Hannibal, the Carthaginian commander, led an army that swept across the Italian peninsula, hitting the Roman army continuously and even directly threatening the security of the city. In the famous Battle of Caney, Hannibal annihilated more than 70,000 Roman legions, making it one of the largest single-day casualties in the history of human warfare. The entire war cost Rome 1/5 of its adult male citizens, and while Rome ultimately won, the losses were extremely heavy.

The threat of Carthage left the Romans restless, and taking advantage of the weakness of the Carthaginian state, Rome launched the Third Battle of Buensis (149 B.C.-146 B.C.E.) in order to finally destroy Carthage. The Roman army laid siege to the city of Carthage for three years unbroken, and Gracchus took part in the final battle of the siege, following the Roman army under the command of Zephyrsia Minor. In battle, he charged and fought valiantly, being the first to climb the walls of Carthage, earning the high love of the Roman army.

In order to put an end to this, Little Zephyr razed the city of Carthage to the ground, 200,000 Carthaginians were killed and the remaining 50,000 were reduced to slavery, and Carthage was finally exterminated. Witnessing the tragic end of the war, little Zephyr could not help but shed tears, fearing that the city of Rome would one day suffer the same fate. History is surprisingly similar, after all, and it was from these ruins that the Vandals, who founded the state at Carthage in 455, sacked and sacked the city of Rome.

It was during the battle against Carthage that Gracchus rose to fame and was later appointed diviner of the Order of Priests. It was a very high honor, and it was from this position that later Caesar and Octavian began in their youth and eventually became the supreme rulers of Rome. The former consul and ombudsman, the chief patriarch of the Roman Senate, Apis Claudius, attended the inauguration of Gracchus and took an instant liking to the young and promising Gracchus. The chief patriarch was thrilled to offer his daughter to him on the spot, which Gracchus happily accepted, and the engagement was finalized on the spot.

With the help of his father-in-law, Gracchus was so pleased that he was appointed treasurer at a young age and followed the Roman consul on his expedition to Spain. It was this long journey that opened Gracchus's eyes to the great crisis latent in the Roman Republic.

Passing through Etruria in central Italy, Gracchus saw vast tracts of barren land and dilapidated and dilapidated farmsteads, farmers going bankrupt under the double blow of heavy debt and oddly low food prices. Aristocrats and merchants from Rome seized the opportunity to annex land, leaving large numbers of landless peasants wandering about without support.

Gracchus was shocked at the decline of the countryside. He knew that the soldiers of the Roman army had to be Roman citizens with family property, mainly from peasants who had property. They usually take care of their own land, and when the country is in trouble, they bring their own weapons to fight. They had a country to love, property to protect, a tradition of sharing rights granted by law, defending their own interests and honoring their honor, and together they inspired the

Roman army's strong fighting force, a magic weapon that enabled Rome to defeat its enemies repeatedly. The reason why the merchants founded Carthage and ultimately lost to the predominantly peasant Roman Republic was the mental strength of the army, which was a key factor, and with comparable military skills, the merchants were far less able to withstand losses than the peasants.

For the Roman peasants, the loss of land meant a loss of dignity as a free Roman citizen; for the State, it meant a reduction in the number of qualified soldiers and a reduction in combat power. Only a few years after the destruction of Carthage, the invincible Roman legions suffered repeated defeats in Spain.

The military's defeat stems directly from low morale. When the soldiers heard the news that their wives and children back home were forced to sell their land in debt, when they watched the rich people of Rome take their homes at their peril, when they thought of their own nine dead lives returned from battle without a home, which soldier would still have the will to fight to the death?

In the Republic of Rome, the gap between rich and poor is rapidly worsening, land annexation is growing and popular discontent is growing. At the same time, as Rome's wars of conquest abroad expanded, more and more prisoners of war and plundered human beings were sold into slavery, and they flooded all corners of Roman society, and the harsh oppression and punishment stirred up strong feelings of revolt among the slaves. Veterans who had been discharged from the army and were homeless due to the loss of land had to wander the streets and alleys of the Roman city. Discontent, resentment and hatred are spreading rapidly and a serious social crisis is on the horizon.

Upon his return to Rome, Gracchus witnessed the grave crisis facing the Republic and resolved to run for the office of Protector, to carry out agrarian reform, to curb annexation, to revitalize agriculture and to consolidate the nation.

The Gracchus Brothers' land change law

Gracchus has the gift of an orator. His gentle and serene appearance and self-assuredness, and his speeches, which hit the heartstrings of the country's ills, struck a chord with every listener. During his campaign for the office of Protector, Gracchus's fierce speeches were a thrill to the people; after his successful election, his speech on the change of law was even more exciting:

> *"The beasts of the mountains and the birds of the woods have their nests, but the Roman citizens who fought and died for their country have nothing but air and sunshine: no house, no land, and wander about with their wives and children. When the commanders called on the soldiers on the battlefield to defend the temple of God and the graves of their ancestors from the enemy, they were deceiving the soldiers. It is important to know that many Romans did not have a father's altar or ancestral tombs, but rather they fought to the death to make others live a life of luxury and to make others rich. People call them the rulers of the world, but they don't even have a small piece of land."*[48]

To the enthusiastic cheers of the public, he introduced a land reform bill: to set a limit of 500 Roman acres (about 1,890 acres) for the individual possession of public land by Roman citizens, and a limit of 1,000 Roman acres (about 3,780 acres) for family land, limited to two sons; to repossess all land beyond this limit, to be subdivided into 30 Roman acres (about 113 acres) each, to be distributed among the landless peasants; to establish a three-member commission to make laws, and to give it the power to restore peasant land.

The news came out that the Roman Senate immediately blew up its nest, and the aristocrats and tycoons of the upper class jumped to their feet, and according to the new law, their vast fields would be confiscated and their wealth would be severely reduced.

How serious is it?

After the Second Buenos Aires War alone, Rome looted as much as 4 million Roman acres (about 15.12 million acres), adding to the staggering amount of land confiscated by successive expansions. These land titles belong to "State land", but have long been occupied by aristocrats and tycoons.

There were land acts in Roman history restricting individual possession of public land to no more than 500 Roman acres, and the new law of Gracchus was merely a reiteration of the old law. But the

---

[48] Plutarch, *Life of Tiberius Gracchus*, Loeb Classical Library edition, 1921.

aristocrats and tycoons used to ignore land restriction bills at all. The Roman historian Apian recorded,

> *"The great and powerful occupy most of the unallotted land, and as time goes on, they are emboldened to assume that their land will never be taken away from them. They annexed adjoining lots and poor neighbors' share of the land, partly by persuasion and partly by violent appropriation. As a result, they began to cultivate vast tracts of land, rather than a single field, using slaves primarily for agriculture and grazing."*[49]

In Gracchus's time, aristocratic possession of land was already staggering; Crassus Mucianus alone owned 100,000 Roman acres (about 378,000 acres), Pompeii's ally Domiticus owned at least 60,000 Roman acres (about 227,000 acres), and Caesar, Crassus, Cicero, and other aristocrats, none of whom were super-large landowners, derived much of their land from encirclement of public lands.

Gracchus's new law dared to move the earth on the head of the Taiyan, directly challenging the most sensitive nerves of the aristocrats and powerful business interests, no wonder the aristocrats were quick to kill. Gracchus, being a nobleman, betrayed the collective interests of the aristocracy, so the Senate took violent and extreme measures to purge the class of dissidents.

Little Gracchus continues to push for land change.

However, this tactic angered the Roman public, as well as Gracchus's brother, Tiberius Gracchus. Extreme grief and a strong sense of justice led him to inherit his brother's ambition to change the law. Elected to the office of Protector in 122 B.C. with the overwhelming support of the Roman masses, and successfully re-elected in the first 121 years, little Gracchus continued to push for land conversions, and to a greater extent than his brother's.

As a result, Little Gracchus and a large number of his supporters were bloodily suppressed by the nobles of the Senate, Little Gracchus was beheaded, more than 3,000 Roman citizens who supported the land change were slaughtered, and the blood stained the entire Tiber.

---

[49] Appian, Roman History: The Civil Wars Book I-I p. 7–13.

After the failure of the Gracchus-Brothers' reforms, institutional greed became more rampant in the Roman Republic and the process of privatization of public lands accelerated significantly. "The rich are again annexing the poor's share of the land, or finding excuses to take it unjustifiably, so the situation of the farmers becomes worse than before." When greed in human nature converges into the mass greed of interest groups, it is never something that a few reformers and loosely organized populations can deal with.

Stavrianos, author of *The Globe*, laments:

> "Tiberius Gracchus and his brother, Tiberius Gracchus, courageously campaigned for a reform that sought to use their elected position as tribunes to implement a moderate land distribution scheme, but the rulers of the oligarchy resolutely opposed it and spared no violence to achieve their ends... The fate of the Gracchus brothers shows that moderate and orderly reform is not likely to succeed."

The Roman Republic missed the opportunity to preserve democracy at last. The failure of the Gracchus brothers' reforms sounded the death knell for the Roman Republic, kicking off nearly a century of bloody violence, brutal revolutions and massive civil wars, and leading to its eventual march toward empire.

The greed of the ruling group was an important catalyst for the disintegration of the Roman Republic.

Hard work built Rome, greed destroyed the republic

Since the founding of Rome, based on the clan, with clan unions as civil societies, members of civil societies as citizens, and the land of each civil society as territory, Roman sovereignty naturally belongs to the Roman civil society and Roman citizens. The king was the head of the Roman Civil Society, the Senate was derived from the clan elders, the Senate was the regent of the vacant throne, the citizens could run for king, and the right of the citizens' assembly had been over the king since ancient times. The main obligation of citizens is to perform military service, since the right to join the army belongs only to citizens.

Early Rome had a system of communal farming, where arable land was publicly owned and private property was limited to "slaves and livestock". Roman law did not recognize private property rights in land, so that Rome formed a strong nucleus of the Trinity based on citizens, public lands, and citizen armies. The Roman army was strong because every soldier knew they were fighting to defend their own interests. Cato, who served as consul of Rome, in his biographical work, The Agrarian Chronicle, discusses the nature of the Roman army in this way:

> *"The bravest men and the strongest soldiers are of peasant origin, who seek an honest and steady income, and rarely incur jealousy, while those who engage in this profession rarely have bad ideas."*

It is no exaggeration to say that early Rome was a peasant state. The Romans saw the land as life, and there were few slaves in Rome at that time, and the landowners took such good care of the land that they were called "good farmers" by other peoples. What they bring after their daily hard work is a joyful and fulfilling rest. The farmers went into town four times a month to engage in trading and other affairs. The real rest was confined to the festive days, when the ploughs were stopped according to the divine order, and not only the farmers rested, but also the slaves and cattle enjoyed their leisure. Roman society revolved around farmland, and even Roman literature began with the theory of farming.

Throughout history, many peoples have defeated their enemies and plundered vast tracts of land, but none have preserved the land won by the Gracchus with a plough and blood and sweat as the Romans did. The Romans fought many losing battles, but they never ceded land for peace. The perseverance of the Romans was rooted in the love of the land, which was the spiritual root of Rome's ability to finally triumph over the merchants of Carthage who founded the nation.

Rome's territory expanded as the wars went on, but the number of citizens dwindled, and the growing number of non-citizen civilians, who were free to share communal land without the restrictions of Roman law and without military service, led citizens to want the obligation to perform military service to be shared among all landed inhabitants. With this reform, Rome re-established a census of land, and the cadastre became a register of conscription, in which peasants with different amounts of land, and with different equipment, participated in combat. Citizens were not friendly to non-citizens, but there was complete equality of rights between citizens, two basic principles that the Romans strictly enforced, with the distinction between their own and outsiders being extremely clear.

The economy grew steadily, Roman wealth grew by the day, and human greed began to sprout. The first to start breaking the rules were the kings and hereditary aristocrats who had become lifelong, who not only used the public lands for private purposes, but also forced citizens to work unpaid for more profit, and the inequitable distribution of social wealth began to occur. The expansion of the commons could not keep up with population growth, there was a shortage of land to be divided, and Rome began to divide the commons among private individuals, while the nobility benefited greatly. After the aristocracy had gained its wings, it took advantage of citizens' anger over the unfair distribution of land to abolish the monarchy in 509 B.C.E., and went to the Republic instead.

The greatest highlight of the republican system is the two consuls elected each year, while the Senate has been able to expand the number of civilians and there has been little institutional change in other countries. When evaluating a political system, it is not by what label it is put on, but by how it works and who is better served by the end result of that work. The essence of the political system is to ensure how the country's wealth is distributed. The abolition of the monarchy was due to the gross inequity of the distribution of wealth, and if viewed by this standard, the republic did not change the social situation in the slightest.

The consuls represented the interests of the aristocratic group, and the republic established a typical aristocratic politics in which the power of the state no longer rested with the king individually, but was administered by the entire aristocracy. This is more solid than kingship, but if the greed of the noble group as a whole even exceeds kingship, then the problem of inequitable distribution of the nation's wealth will become even worse.

The reform of the political system led to a dramatic change in Rome's finances and economy, where the power of capital gradually overtook the state. In the past, the kings of Rome did not want the capitalist power to become too inflated and even tried to increase the number of farms as much as possible to balance the power of the capitalist interests, but the new aristocrats of the republic were more greedy and their policies from beginning to end carried out the purpose of destroying the peasant middle class, and the aristocratic rule, with the big landowners and tycoons at its core, tried desperately to oppress the peasant class, which was on the verge of bankruptcy.

The Government began to buy and sell grains, the salt was monopolized, and the State transferred all indirect tax payments and transactions to "contractors", requiring them to have financial resources secured in kind, which undoubtedly benefited the tycoon aristocracy. Thus, a large class of charterers and contractors rose rapidly.

Taxation law, whereby the State contracts fiscal revenue to a tycoon for a specified amount, and after the tycoon pays this amount, the remaining revenue goes to the tycoon. As for the designated amount, it is a matter of "matchmaking" between the rich merchants and the aristocrats themselves, the water is deep. Within a few years, the class of charterers had become so rich in Rome, and the business was so lucrative, that "every rich man in Rome took part in the business of chartering taxes, either as a signed or anonymous shareholder".[50] It is clear that their huge profits are derived from the exploitation of the entire population's taxes, and that the damage done to the State's finances by the tax system is far-reaching and extremely harmful.

The class of Roman tax collectors, the first generation of financial predators of the Roman Republic, in the process of eroding the country's tax revenue, they tied themselves to the aristocracy and their political influence expanded dramatically, quickly rising to become a power group that could influence national policy. Having won the "first bucket of gold", they were ready to take over the public lands.

During the Wang regime, the harmful "land-occupation system" was introduced, whereby the land was ceded to the most powerful and powerful households, and could be inherited from generation to generation, with no formal property rights but special rights of use, requiring the land-occupier to pay 10 per cent of the grain harvest or 5 per cent of the output of olive oil and wine, but in practice taxes could not be collected at all, which was equivalent to the powerful and powerful households occupying public land for nothing.

Since the republic, the policy of land privatization had turned the "right to occupy" these fields into a "freehold", a huge benefit that the ordinary Roman citizens, except for the nobility and the powerful, could not share, and these permanent "fields" could not be expropriated. With

---

[50] Theodor Mommsen, *The History of Rome*, Vol 3, JM Dent and Sons Ltd, 1920, Chapter 12.

the massive reduction of public land and the serious shortage of sources of taxation, and the failure to tax the public land occupied by the powerful and large families, the national tax burden can only be placed on the small farmers. More and more farmers are being forced into debt by the pressure of taxation, and the usury lenders are the same class of tax packagers who are exploiting the tax money from small farmers.

Roman law was known for its ruthless enforcement, allowing private borrowing despite the law's prohibition of land mortgages. Private debts are in effect secured by the person, and if they cannot be repaid, the creditor even has the right to put the debtor to death and cut him up, or to sell him and his children abroad into slavery, without any governmental inquiry.[51] Later, the usury class, which evolved from the underwriters, simply used the military to directly arrest the debtors in default.

The usury class, as creditors, had a great deterrent effect on the indebted peasants, and, compelled by despair and fear, the small peasants had no choice but to transfer their land to their creditors, and sorrow and despair spread throughout the Roman peasant class. There is an old Chinese saying that killing to pay for one's life and borrowing to pay for one's money. The importance of repaying a debt is surprisingly comparable to paying a life.

In just over a decade of republicanism, the division of wealth in Roman society was already so severe as to provoke civil unrest. In 495 B.C., as war approached Rome, the government strictly enforced the debt laws, arousing the public anger of the peasantry at large, and the citizens of Rome refused to be drafted to fight, a blatant refusal to fulfill their obligations unprecedented in the history of Rome.

The consul was forced to suspend the application of the debt law, release peasants imprisoned for debt and prohibit further arrests. It was only then that the citizens of Rome took part in the battle and defeated the strong enemy. However, when the war ended and the debt laws became strict, a large number of peasants were again thrown into prison. The government had broken faith with the people and the Roman peasants were angry to the core. The following year, war broke out

---

[51] Theodor Mommsen, *The History of Rome*, Vol 3, JM Dent and Sons Ltd, 1920, Chapter 11.

again, the lies of the consuls had been debunked, and no one wanted to work for such a government anymore.

In the end it was the old clan leader, trusted by the people, who became dictator and vowed to reform the debt laws so that the Roman citizens could return to the battlefield and win again. As a result, the motion to change the law was rejected by the Senate, and the enraged citizens of Rome, led by the tribunes, marched into Rome and prepared for an armed insurrection, with civil war on the verge of breaking out.

The nobles of the Senate were driven to the wall of war, which made them realize the seriousness of the problem. Without any compromise, the enormous drain of civil war alone will lead to financial bankruptcy. Add to this the serious situation of a divided citizenry and a possible fall of the army, and the Senate has finally compromised with the fact that the republic will be bankrupt only a decade after its opening, with all vested interests at great risk of being liquidated.

This major victory galvanized the citizens of Rome for a hundred years, and the Civilian Protector was the main result of that struggle.

The repeal of the cruel debt laws only eased the end of the farmers' worst fears, but did not eliminate the cause of that end. Land annexation and tax injustice are at the root of all farmers' woes. The struggle around wealth distribution is still being fiercely contested.

Spurius Vecellinus was a three-time consul and two-time triumphalist super-weight nobleman, none of the patriarchs of the dynasty older than him, and he was the drafter of the first Roman Agricultural Law, whose contribution to the Roman Republic was profound. His insight into the roots of the division of wealth, the monopoly on fiscal taxation by the underwriters, is at the heart of the nation's woes.

The tax-paying system has led to a serious loss of national tax revenue, while at the same time, the unfair tax burden has been pressed on the peasants, who have thus become heavily indebted and lost their land, while the tax-paying class has both embezzled tax revenue and annexed land, making a fortune on both ends, how can it not be rich?

He then attacked the root of the ills of fiscal monopoly by introducing a reform bill in 486 B.C. to inventory the country's communal land and lease part of it to peasants at rents that would increase the treasury's revenue; the other part of the communal land would be distributed directly to landless peasants. The key to this reform is that the state increases revenue, the people reduce taxes, and squeeze the profits of tax packagers from both ends. A good law that benefits the country and the people will inevitably be detrimental to the interest groups that wreak havoc on the country and the people. As a result, Veselinas, who was a great father of the nation, was convicted of coveting royal power and treason, publicly beheaded, and his residence was razed to the ground.

Even the most important people in the country who have violated the greed of the interest groups will die without being buried! The cruelty of the class struggle in the Roman Republic is evident from this.

Wealth drives people crazy, greed makes people brutal!

After more than 50 years of republicanism, the division of wealth had intensified to the brink of civil war, and finally, in 451 B.C., a compromise was reached with the Law of the Twelve Brass Tables. The problem of land annexation was not cured and was a civilian compromise; the draconian debt laws were eased to a lesser extent, and the concessions were made by the powerful.

Under the new law, a 30-day period is allowed after a debt is adjudicated or acknowledged; if the debt is overdue, the debtor will be sent to the magistrate. Unless the debt is forgiven, the creditor may detain and imprison the debtor, but must provide food and drink; several creditors may jointly possess and divide the property of a debtor. If the creditor demands interest on the loan in excess of the legal limit of 8,333 per cent, a fine of four times as much is imposed, and the penalty for usury exploitation is greater than for theft.[52]

From the compromise of the distribution of wealth between the powerful and the citizens of Rome, achieved by the Twelve Brass Tables, to the outbreak of the Buenos Aires War, the two ills of land annexation and heavy debt, caused by the division of the rich and the poor, were relieved to a considerable extent and the Roman republic was gradually stabilized. Rome began to free up its hands to consolidate the state, and the gradual unification of Italy was achieved, and the stability of Rome lasted for nearly 200 years.

---

[52] Sydney Homer and Richard Sylla, *A History of Interest Rate*, John Wiley & Sons, 2005, Chapter 4.

In 264 B.C., the outbreak of the First Punic War once again upset the balance in the distribution of wealth in Rome, which lasted 23 years and was followed by an equally protracted war, in which the Roman peasants had to fight for long periods of time away from home, unable to take care of their farmland and relying only on women and the elderly to tend it. With up to a fifth of male citizens killed or wounded in the second war, agricultural depletion has become an irreversible necessity. By 146 B.C., the end of the Third Punic War, Roman agriculture was on the verge of bankruptcy.

The massive bankruptcy of the Roman countryside and the proliferation of land-grabbing greatly stimulated the long-suppressed greed of the powerful and powerful in Rome, with land annexation in full swing, growing tax injustice and a growing debt burden. The second great division of wealth in the history of the Roman Republic was far more violent than the first.

From the end of the Punic War (146 B.C.) to the beginning of the reformation of the Gracchus brothers (133 B.C.), however, in the short span of 13 years, the Roman Republic was plunged into an extremely vicious frenzy of wealth division, the greed of the powerful and powerful had been thoroughly indulged, the anger and hatred of the peasants had become unstoppable, and the republic was accelerating its slide into the abyss.

By 121 B.C., the land reforms of the Gracchus brothers had failed utterly and Rome was plunged into a century-long uprising, riots, bloodshed, chaos and civil war. The first three giants vied for power and attacked for years; the latter three fought for supremacy and blood flowed freely.

The Roman Republic died in 27 B.C. in the midst of the sword.

The big twist: inward exploitation to outward expansion

Rome finally emerged not from an internal equilibrium in the distribution of wealth, but from a shift in the direction of institutional greed, from inward-looking exploitation to outward-looking expansion.

After the unification of Italy, Rome finally defeated its rival Carthage in three fierce battles over a hundred years and captured Africa; it conquered Macedonia and swept the Greek city-states in an easterly direction; it then conquered Asia Minor and annexed Syria; it finally crushed Gaul, invaded England, conquered Spain, captured Egypt and established a super empire spanning Europe, Asia and Africa.

During the era of great Roman expansion (150 B.C.-50 B.C.E.), it was the Roman aristocracy that benefited first, with vast quantities of booty, coins, tribute, slaves, livestock, grain, gold and silver jewelry, pouring into Rome from all sides, mostly into the purses of the nobles. The conquest also transformed the Roman aristocracy into international landowners, and large tracts of conquered land were incorporated into the Roman landscape, leaving untold valleys, pastures, forests, lakes, fisheries, mines and quarries to their domination.

Another who reaped great benefits was the powerful merchant class, which reaped enormous profits from the operation, appropriation and appropriation of Roman state assets. During the war, they supply the army with food, clothing and weapons at high prices, and then buy the spoils of war from the government, generals and soldiers cheaply to make a fortune. The expansion and conquest made the great merchants of Rome look at the world for the first time, and they found the super fat pie of the newly established provinces. The governors of the provinces appointed by the Senate were originally the old relations of the tycoons, and the governors had almost unlimited power over the provinces.

Marcus Tullius Cicero, the famous Roman statesman, had charged the Roman governor of Sicily:

> *"By a new and unprincipled administration, countless sums of money have been extracted from the peasant's pockets; treating our most faithful allies as if they were the mortal enemies of the nation... Famous ancient artifacts, some of which were also gifts from wealthy kings, were all plundered by this governor. Not only did he do this to the statues and works of art of the city, but he also plundered the holiest and most venerated shrines; and if an idol was made with more than the average of antiquity and had a certain artistic value, then he would never have left it to the people of Sicily."*

The lawlessness of the governors is intertwined with the vicious greed of the tycoons, like dry wood on fire. The giants and governors shared a super lucrative business of provincial tax wrapping, providing land mortgages to farmers who ran their fields, and high-interest lending to city states and individuals who were behind in their tax payments. Marcus Junius Brutus, for example, lent the city-state as much as 48 percent interest, and Cicero was shocked to hear it.

They also monopolized all government outsourcing, outsourcing mega-construction projects such as public buildings, road bridges, sewerage lines, stagecoaches, garden nurseries, and large squares in Rome and the provinces. As with the tax bracket system, as long as the relationship is in place and the amount is good, the Roman government is not bad for money. Huge profits rolled in, making the tycoons laugh themselves awake in their dreams. The giants eventually formed the knightly class of the Roman Empire.

With the aristocracy and the knightly class in possession of unprecedented wealth, it was in their bones that the safest asset was land and fields, and larger land annexations were in full swing. With the privatization of publicly owned land, the call for the protection of private land rights grew, and Cicero was a leading representative of the protection of private property rights, stating that "the first concern of administrative officials must be that the owner should be the owner of his property and that the private property rights of citizens should not be violated by the actions of the state." "Be aware that the main purpose of the establishment of a constitutional state and self-government is to secure the right to private property." "Those officials charged with looking after the interests of the nation should put an end to the forms of plundering one man and enriching another... They should do all they can so that envy does not stand in the way of the rich."

Unlike the early republican era, Rome now had a huge number of slaves from various countries who became the main labor force in the lands of the Roman Empire. As the empire expanded, hundreds of thousands of the country's landless people were colonized in the newly conquered provinces of Asia and Africa, and the remaining farmers were reduced to tenant farmers. In the last 30 years B.C. alone, the Roman colonies abroad numbered as many as 100, with a collective emigration of 250,000 adult males, almost one-fifth of the Roman adult male population. The poetry and literature of the imperial era often contained a sentiment about the extinction of the Roman peasant class, the foundation of the Roman republic having disappeared.

Around the whole of Italy, the city was inhabited by some rather wealthy and powerful families, many of them large landowners, who owned thousands of hectares of good land in the provinces of Italy and Rome, with endless pastures, thousands of slaves working for them and professional stewards of slave origin overseeing huge estates for them. Others are the big and powerful property owners of the city, who enjoy a lavish life by renting out houses, shops, warehouses, etc.

The tax-paying classes and contractors had developed into Roman financiers, who shuttled between Rome and the provinces of the Empire, building a vast network of people from the emperor, the senate to the governors of the provinces, running tax-paying, usury, banking, investment and other financial businesses, and the huge flow of money of the Empire was constantly flowing in their financial network day and night, and even in their sleep the money was working for them constantly.

The public square near the temple of Castor in the Roman city was daily filled with speculators of all kinds, who bought and sold stocks and bonds of tax-packed companies, traded goods of all kinds for cash and credit, and bid for the farms, estates, shops, ships, and warehouses of the empire, as well as slaves and livestock from various countries to be auctioned.

The streets around the square were lined with shops of all kinds, crowded with thousands of craftsmen, shopkeepers, slaves of the rich, and agents from all parts of the country, who competed to sell to their customers a variety of handicrafts and agricultural products.

Just behind the prosperity, there were also shadowy corners where a small class of knights, made up of the super-rich, emerged in Rome, and where a large group of itinerant people was born.

In the large ghettos of the remote streets of Rome lived hordes of peasants who had lost their estates, unemployed proletarians, retired soldiers without a single roof over their heads, living in a state of discontent, frustration and resentment, ready to sell their votes and their fists if anyone would pay. In Cicero's words, they were "a poor, starving rabble, an exploiter of the treasury".

It was these rabble, who later joined the Roman legions in large numbers and changed the nature of the army, evolving from itinerant groups to mob groups and becoming the most dangerous subversive force in the Roman Empire.

The imperial age of the monetary economy

Rome's great military expansion also stimulated a great explosion of the monetary economy.

The Roman republican era, with its agricultural state, traditionally had a clear tendency to value agriculture over commerce, and the monetary economy was not well developed, as the Roman monetary evolution illustrates.

In the earliest 300 years of Rome, except for the Greek colonial city in Italy, there was no minting in Rome, and the earliest medium of commodity exchange was cattle and sheep, ten sheep being worth the value of one cow. As the metal was mined, copper replaced cattle and sheep as the benchmark for all Roman values, and copper was measured in Roman pounds, also known as As, weighing about 328.9 grams per pound. Compared to Greece, where commercial civilization was highly valued, the early Roman currency appeared crude and was minted by the regions themselves. Since the scale of trade and market transactions is far less than Greece's, society does not demand as much precision and sophistication of money as Greece does.

The most common currency in early Rome was bronze ingots of ace, which often weighed as much as 5 ace (about 1.6 kg), and the inconvenience of the currency reflected the fact that Roman commerce was far less prosperous than in Greek times. With the gradual development of commerce, the use of money became more frequent, and the heavy currency began to become smaller, lighter and more precise to accommodate the small transactions of daily life, and the heavy As in bronze became the mainstream currency, weighing between about 272 and 341 grams each. Until the First Punic War (264 B.C.-241 B.C.E.), the heavy Asiatic coin was the most popular currency in the Roman Republic.

The outbreak of the Punic War (264 B.C.-146 B.C.E.) completely changed the economic landscape of Rome, with prolonged and massive wars that forced the Roman peasantry to be disengaged from land production for long periods of time, which forced the establishment of a formal and costly military pay system. The payment of military rates accelerates currency minting on the one hand, and promotes the unification of the domestic currency on the other. In fact, the war was even more of a driving force for the monetary economy than for commerce, and at the same time the war created a huge domestic unified market, with a unified currency circulating in a unified market, and Rome began its transition from a physical to a monetary economy.

The most significant change in the monetary system was the replacement of the silver standard with the copper standard, and the silver dinar (Denarius) gradually eliminated the bulky copper ace. Silver coins also existed in Rome at one time, but were minted and circulated mainly by Greeks in the colonies of southern Italy and Sicily, which, although geographically close to Rome, were psychologically more Greek, including the fact that their minting also followed the delicate Greek silver coin Drachma, not at all like the bulky Roman copper ace.

The early Romans minted copper ace instead of silver, not because they didn't like silver, but because of the lack of silver mines in north-central Italy. But when the Roman legions defeated Carthage and gradually took control of the Carthaginian colonies in Spain, the great silver mines of Spain made the Romans rich.

Due to the urgent need to pay military salaries, the Romans overhauled the currency in 211 B.C. and began to issue silver dinars uniformly throughout the country. The dinar contained 4.5 grams of silver (equivalent to $1/72^{th}$ of a Roman pound), the value of which was set at 1 silver dinar equivalent to 10 Roman pounds of bronze money, from which the dinar became the most important currency in circulation in Rome.[53]

By the time of Julius Caesar (49 BC-44 BC), Rome began to issue the gold coin Aureus, containing about 8 grams of gold and worth the equivalent of 25 silver dinars, but the gold Aureus was so valuable that it was used less as currency in circulation and more for large amounts of trade and reward.

Rome's legions went head to head with Rome's silver dinar, sweeping across the Mediterranean. Whenever the Roman army occupied an area, the first thing it did was to close the local mint, or simply allow the minting of small coins. The Roman Mint became the largest mint in the entire Mediterranean region, and other minting

---

[53] *The New Deal in Old Rome*, HJ Haskell, Alfred K. Knoff, New York 1939.

houses were authorized by Rome to produce silver coins, which had to be minted in accordance with the Roman coinage.[54]

From 150 B.C. to 50 B.C., during the 100 years of Rome's great expansion, the amount of money in circulation in Rome soared tenfold, much of it silver dinars. Driven by a rolling torrent of money, Rome's commodity flows and economic model changed profoundly.

Wheat, flax, and reed paper from Egypt, grain from Carthage and Sicily, wool, timber, and carpets from Asia Minor, grain, meat, and wool from Gaul, various minerals from Spain and Britain, amber, furs, and slaves from the Baltic region, ivory, gold, and slaves from sub-Saharan Africa, and spices, precious stones, spices, and Chinese silks from Asia, flocked to Rome from all sides. Stimulated by the great exchange of commodities, Rome's economic model underwent a profound transformation from a productive society based on agriculture to a more and more pronounced shift to a consumer economy based on commerce and industry.

The high efficiency and low cost of overseas food supplies kept prices alarmingly low in Rome, where the city's population was once as high as one million people, along with hundreds of thousands of standing armies and a huge bureaucracy, and deliberately low food prices became a necessity for the stability of the Roman Empire. For Italian agricultural production, such extremely low food prices are tantamount to the fundamental destruction of food production in the country. Small land farmers have all but lost their market competitiveness, and with grain prices at an all-time low, the massive bankruptcy of farmers has provided a godsend for land annexation by the tycoons. The large landowners had adopted large-scale improvements in slave production and farming techniques that had reduced the cost of food production and, even so, had been unable to compete with the low prices of food overseas.

So, in many parts of Rome, grain was grown just to meet the needs of the laborers of the great estates, and the great landowners ignored the unprofitable grain in favor of the highly profitable cash crops and livestock. Italian wine, olive oil and wool production became the most

---

[54] Theodor Mommsen, *The History of Rome*, Vol 3, JM Dentand Sons Ltd, 1920, Chapter 12.

competitive products of the Roman Empire's monstrous price system. In general, in the Roman agricultural economy, livestock was more profitable than planting, while vineyards were more profitable than vegetable and olive gardens, and grain fields were the least profitable. It is estimated that the value of wheat production per Roman acre in the larger estates is only 38 dinars (about 10 dinars per acre).[55]

If the price of silver is calculated at 4 yuan per gram, one dinar in the early days of the empire is equivalent to about 15 yuan today, and the value of a grain acre is only 150 yuan.

Since agriculture was overwhelmed by competition for food from abroad, Rome used only wine, olive oil and competitive wool products to balance trade, as well as handicrafts, which were gradually becoming more dominant.

Italy's red-glazed pottery monopolized all the markets; the emerging manufacture of glassware, especially the beautifully colored and carved pieces, almost defeated Syria, the country of origin of glass; the north-western part of Italy became the center of metallurgy, the bronze and silver products were highly competitive, and the production of agricultural implements and iron weapons were marketed throughout the Empire. In addition, Italian-made hardware, oil lamps, jewelry, balm, etc. are also popular in the market.

Although Italy's industrial goods have a certain advantage, they are still far from sufficient to cover the inflow of goods from the provinces and abroad. Rome is becoming more and more like a mega-consumer metropolis, and Italy is its suburb. Rome's aberrant consumption stemmed not from its own strong production capacity and rational market transactions, but more from its reliance on the squeezing and exploitation of the provinces.

Rome's consumer boom also spurred many high-margin emerging industries. The wealthy people of Rome had a great demand for exotic beasts. It is recorded that one owner raised a large flock of chickens, ducks, geese, peacocks, wild boars, etc., and made an annual profit of 1,250 dinars, which far exceeded the income from running a farm. In his On Agriculture, Varro mentions that a professional bird breeder

---

[55] Ibid.

raised 5,000 birds at a price of 3 dinars each, making an annual profit of 1,500 dinars on the birds alone, twice the profit of a larger farm operating 200 Roman acres (about 756 acres). The profits from raising rare birds are even greater, with a peacock selling for 50 dinars, a peacock egg for hatching for as much as 5 dinars, and the annual income from the breeding of small peacocks alone, out of a total of 100 peacocks, amounting to 15,000 dinars.

The huge profits from taxation, tribute, usury, construction and trade monopolies, concentrated from the provinces to Rome and then to the land, created a large number of super-rich people in Rome. Like Crassus, the former Big Three, he owned properties worth 400 million dinars, making him the richest man in Rome. He used to say that a man who could not afford to maintain a legion with his own possessions was not considered a rich man, and the cost of maintaining a Roman legion for a year was 1.5 million dinars. Caesar was also a great landowner, and before going out on the expedition to Africa, he promised the soldiers,

> "When all the wars are over, I will surely distribute the land to all the soldiers, not as Sulla did, taking the land from the existing land-holders and distributing it to the soldiers ... but distributing the communal land and my own land to the soldiers, and at the same time, I will surely give them the necessary tools to purchase."

What is 400 million dinars a concept? That's about 4 million to 5 million tons of wheat! The richest man in Britain in the 17th century was worth about 21,000–42,000 tons of wheat, and the richest man in Rome was hundreds of times the richest man in Britain over 1,000 years later!

The division of wealth in Rome was so severe as to be appalling!

The importance of food production in the agricultural era was comparable to the manufacturing status in the industrial era, and the shrinking of agriculture meant that the economic base of the country was disintegrating. To sustain the empire, Rome had to become more dependent on the provinces of Asia and Africa for food and other subsistence supplies, while at the same time failing to compensate with equivalent commodities, which could only create resentment among the people of the provinces. Violent and brutal conquests have intensified the fierce resistance of the frontier barbarians, and large-scale military conflicts have become a commonplace. The extreme land annexation has filled the big cities with disgruntled and angry stragglers. The cruelty of slavery filled the entire empire with the dark currents of riots in repression.

A dysfunctional economy and unstable politics have made a superficially prosperous Rome sit like a crater, having to rely on a supersized standing army to bring some sense of security. However, excessive dependence on the military is bound to lead to financial paralysis and a crisis of the regime.

Fragile monetary cycles

In the early years of the Roman Empire, the average Roman soldier was paid about 225 dinars a year, the standard configuration of a Roman legion was more than 6,800 people, and it took 1.5 million dinars a year to feed a legion, and the total size of the standing army in the early years of the Empire was about 200,000 or so people. To feed such a large army, the government spends at least half a billion dinars a year on the military. The cost of resettling veterans is equally staggering, with the latter three giants having to pursue a policy of dispossession against the original landowners in order to resettle veterans, resulting in political unrest and discontent throughout Italy. In order to avoid repeating the same mistakes, in 30 BC, Octavian used state money to buy land for veterans, which cost the treasury 150 million dinars in just two years, an outrageously high cost.

To feed the imperial government bureaucracy is a huge expenditure, the Roman city of the emperor has a complete set of government team, dozens of provinces of the governor will need dozens of sets of provincial officials to match, and the empire thousands of cities also need officials to govern.

The financial strain on the army and government bureaucrats was already so great that in order to maintain the stability of the city of Rome, the government had to provide free food to 200,000 Roman citizens, and 150,000 tons of grain had to be imported from Egypt each year to meet this demand. This "entertainment" alone costs tens of millions of dinars, and the "cost of maintaining stability" is another heavy financial burden on the Government. What if the supply of free food stops? Then the city of Rome would have hundreds of thousands of unproductive, unemployed stragglers rising up and rioting the next morning. No emperor dared to take such a risk, and the free food system continued until the empire's demise.

Figuratively speaking, the Roman Empire was like a giant machine that seized gold and silver from the Mediterranean coastal areas through military expansion and minted them into currency, feeding a huge standing army and bloated Rome. Currency is concentrated in the capital and in the border areas where the military is stationed, and government spending and military payroll consumption inject money into the economic cycles of the empire. Imperial law, in turn, encouraged and even forced the ruled people to use money in their daily lives, and then taxed the money back from the imperial provinces to the capital and the army, and with it, of course, the rolling wealth.

The biggest flaw in this monetary circulation system is that it cannot naturally cycle infinitely. As a result of the endogenous economic imbalance of the empire, which consumed more than it produced and squeezed more than it created, money was concentrated in Rome and its daily wealth was siphoned off, thus leading to a growing productivity trap. In an era of military expansion, in which money could be plundered from outside and supplemented from within, the economic function of the empire remained largely in balance. But as the frontier deepened into the barbarian land, the intensity of barbarian revolt increased dramatically, causing the cost of imperial expansion to rise sharply while the benefits of plunder declined by the day. Eventually, the frontiers of the empire stabilized, which was the break-even point at which the Roman Empire's finances could be supported.

However, once the expansion stops, the cycle of money is bound to go wrong.

Rome's major wars of foreign expansion were largely complete during the republican era, when the empire's first emperor, Augustus (Octavian) (27 B.C.-14 A.D.), had abandoned his ambition to rule the world. Augustus, who had long been in battle, thought long and hard about it, that a little concession to the unconquerable barbarians could still preserve the dignity and security of Rome.

At that time the generals of the empire were still feverishly preparing to fight the Parthians for the supremacy of Asia, to Yemen at the southernmost tip of the Arabian Peninsula and southward to annex Ethiopia. They marched thousands of miles into the desert region, and as a result, the heat and heat defeated the unbeatable Roman legions. In the dense forests of northern Europe were inhabited by Germanic barbarians, who, although difficult to deal with the Roman army's head-on blows, exhausted the Roman legions with their indomitable spirit of resistance. In the extreme cold north of Great Britain's "Antony's Wall" were the wild and unruly natives, who could not be defeated, whose allies were the cold and the blizzard, whose barrier was the steep mountains and the pristine dense forests, and whose veterans of the Roman legionaries' divisions were too tired to make an inch.

The Roman Empire had expanded to the limits of its national power. Ultimately, Augustus left a legacy: the boundaries of the Roman Empire extend west to the Atlantic Ocean, north to the Danube and Rhine rivers, east to the Euphrates, and south to the deserts of Arabia and Africa, with nature's geographical limits as the permanent boundaries of the empire.[56]

In Augustus' will to the Senate, detailed data on state taxes and disbursements were listed, which has unfortunately been lost. In his History of the Decline of the Roman Empire, Gibbon states that the annual recurring revenues of the Roman provinces were not less than 15–20 million pounds (pounds on the gold standard), or about 343–458 million dinars, which included a 1% property tax, a personal tax, and the expropriation of grain, wine, oil and meat. The military expenditure of the entire Roman Empire, not to mention the various levels of government, as well as the infrastructure and daily expenses of all the cities, is not yet sufficient to be supported by the revenues of the provinces alone.[57]

Ever since Augustus was emperor, he was deeply under pressure to spend financially, and he constantly implied that the courtiers' tributes were insufficient and that it was necessary to increase the tax burden on Rome and the Italians. Faced with the discontent of the Roman citizens, the Emperor prudently chose to begin with the introduction of a tariff, followed by the establishment of an excise tax, followed by an inventory of the private property of the Roman citizens and the completion of the preparation of the property for taxation. By

---

[56] Edward Gibbon, The History of the Decline and Fall of the Roman Empire, Northpointe Classics, 2009, Chapter 1.

[57] Ibid.

this time, the powerful and wealthy groups in Rome had not paid their various taxes for over 150 years.

Augustus insisted on pushing for tax code reform despite strong opposition from the powerful. The GST is around 2.5-12.5 per cent and no matter what the law says, it is never the tycoons who end up buying, but the final consumers.

Another major tax item is the consumption tax, which, although fully levied, is still relatively modest, rarely exceeding 1 per cent. Taxes are levied on everything from market transactions and public auctions, from large purchases and sales of land and property, to everyday items of daily living, even if they are of negligible value. The excise tax spreads the bulk of military spending.

Nonetheless, Augustus found that the finances were still out of reach, and in order to cover the deficit, he decided to finally take advantage of the wealthy group in Rome by imposing a 5% inheritance tax.

The wealthy groups in Rome, who valued money more than freedom, immediately blew up their nests at the news of the inheritance tax, and opposition was widespread in the streets. Although the Emperor Augustus, with his military power in his hands and his experience in a hundred wars, and the power of his empire, is far from the strength of the Gracchus brothers, he must be very careful to challenge the institutional greed of the wealthy groups.

Augustus was very strategic in bringing the estate tax proposal before the Senate for collective discussion, and it was clear that the nobles of the Senate were by no means buying it. Augustus can only strongly suggest that the patriarchs, if they remain obstinate, will be forced to propose a land tax and a man's tax, which would clearly be a deadly threat to the noblemen, who have vast land assets and many slave servants.

The Senate's nobles, as representatives of the wealthy group, hated the inheritance tax, but there was nothing they could do about Emperor Augustus, who was beloved by the army and held great power, after all, the inheritance tax was not high, it was much milder than the nasty land and people tax. The lesser of two evils, the aristocrats had to acquiesce to the new tax law.

In addition to reforming the tax code, Augustus also began to devalue the currency by lowering the silver content of the dinar from

4.5 grams to 3.9 grams in the Republican era. By raising taxes and devaluing the currency, the Empire's initial revenues and expenditures were roughly equal.

The economic crisis in dormancy

The heyday of Rome was from 50 B.C. to 50 A.D., when the dividends of military expansion lingered and peace brought about a natural economic recovery. The Roman Empire's coffers, however, were increasingly struggling to meet its ever-inflated expenditures. By the reign of Nero (54–68), the silver content of the dinar was reduced to 90%; by the time of Trajan (98–117), it was 85%; while Marcus Aurelius (161–180) continued to devalue it to 75%; by the end of the 2nd century, the dinar was only 50% silver.

Obviously, there's a big problem with the empire's currency cycle. The roots of the monetary problem are in the economy, and the roots of the economy are in agriculture.

The early dynamism of the empire was driven by expansion, which was halted by recovery and, once completed, by increased productivity, but Italian agriculture was on the verge of bankruptcy, rather than being able to increase productivity. In an era in which the economy is based on agriculture, if agriculture is weakened, all urban civilization and commercial prosperity based on it will be a source of no water.

The main reason for the disintegration of the agricultural base is the overly low price of food, which, in the old Chinese saying, is that low grain hurts farmers. The main reason for the deliberate suppression of food prices in the Roman Empire was to feed the large urban population, especially the large number of peasants who flowed into the cities after bankruptcy.

With the great impetus of Emperor Augustus and his successors, a staggering number of city clusters emerged within the Roman Empire: 1,197 in Italy, about 1,200 in Gaul, 700 in Spain, 650 in the four provinces of Africa, and about 900 in the East, including Greece. The Roman Empire had a high rate of urbanization unparalleled in human history before the Industrial Revolution.

Between the capital and the major cities is the world-famous "Road to Rome" road network, starting from the Piazza della Roma and traversing Italy through all the provinces and ending at the borders of the Empire. From the Antonine wall to Rome and back to Jerusalem, this great transportation system stretched 4,080 Roman miles from the northwest corner of the empire to the southeast border. Mountains can be chiseled through, rapids build bridges, roads are made high enough to overlook the surrounding landscape, the roads are layered with sand, cement and boulders, and the roads to the vicinity of Rome are all granite, and Rome's roads are so solid that after more than 2,000 years, parts of them still function as transportation.[58]

It is a miracle that an urbanization movement of this magnitude took place more than 2,000 years ago, and it is an unimaginable economic burden. The overreaching urbanization movement has placed a heavy burden on the empire, and the agricultural economy in particular has suffered greatly.

Why did Emperor Augustus place so much importance on the urbanization movement that he even went so far as to hit the state hard?

When Augustus came to power, his greatest dilemma was very similar to that of Qin Shi Huang, that while the empire was militarily powerful enough to conquer large swathes of land, the government's organizational capacity was not sufficient to effectively navigate a vast empire of vast size, population, cultural complexity, economic variation and inaccessibility.

In the early years of unification, the Roman and Qin empires were not productive enough, their technological base, their economic level, their ideological system, their political structure, to meet the demanding requirements of direct imperial rule in all corners of the territory. Qin Shi Huang's hasty and forceful introduction of the county system, in an attempt to immediately achieve centralized vertical rule throughout the country, was actually far beyond Qin's own ability, and the faster he went, the harder he fell. It took nearly a hundred years of repeated attempts from Qin Shi Huang to Emperor Wu of Han to form the grand mold of centralized power, while the vertical management of the countryside in the Chinese feudal empire was never really realized, and the emperor's centralized power had to rely on the vast class of village squires to radiate the energy of rule to the vast peasant class.

---

[58] Ibid.

Augustus was equally unlikely to achieve the vertical management of the population by the empire, and the path he chose was one of urbanization, with the empire controlling numerous city federations, and the city federations controlling the population under their jurisdiction, cramming as much of the population as possible into the cities, in order to achieve indirect rule.

Thus, the urbanization of the Roman Empire was by no means the result of natural economic development, but a helpless political choice to rule a vast empire. The established state policy of urbanization also fits perfectly with the insatiable demand for land annexation by the powerful elite. Rome's agrarian economy was the double casualty of imperial state policy and the greed of the powerful.

The provinces of Egypt, Sicily, Afrikaner, Spain, etc., whose natural good soil and climatic conditions make their food prices much lower than the cost of cereal production in Italy, should have raised tariffs to protect Italian agriculture in order to consolidate the country's capital, but the Roman government has mistakenly abandoned indigenous food production. In the eyes of the powerful, land is the ultimate and most reliable expression of wealth, and low food prices have caused the value of Italian farmland to plummet, making it unsustainable for small and medium-sized farmers, who are bound to go bankrupt in large numbers, providing the powerful with a good opportunity for large-scale land acquisitions.

When farmers lost their land, they flocked in large numbers to the cities and became unemployed vagrants, where handicrafts were still quite primitive and crude and the division of labour was far from refined enough to provide adequate employment. Rome, with a population of one million, does not represent an urban economic boom, only a status quo of agricultural bankruptcy; 200,000 adult male citizens are eligible for free government relief food, meaning 600,000 families are on the verge of starvation. The greater the number of jobless migrants in cities, the greater the need for the government to "stabilize" food prices by keeping them down, thus exacerbating the agricultural insolvency in Italy and stimulating larger land annexations, leading to a greater influx of bankrupt farmers to the cities.

The Roman economy was caught in a vicious cycle that was hard to break out of. The agricultural crisis that occurred in Italy during the republican period, and which occurred during the imperial period, came together in all the provinces. Gaul (France), which was originally rich in cereals, turned to extensive grape cultivation during the urbanization movement. The foundation of modern, world-renowned French wine was laid during the Roman Empire. Spain, on the other hand, had a prevalence of olive tree cultivation, followed by Africa as an olive kingdom, and traditional cereal production gradually shrank. At the same time, the winds of land annexation are burning like a blazing fire in these areas, which is unstoppable. By Nero's time (54–68), six large landowners had half the territory of Africa! Throughout the Empire, as the urbanization movement advanced, land was rapidly concentrated in the hands of the powerful and powerful.

These mega-property owners operated with a completely different mindset from the small and medium landowners, who lived in Rome or in the big cities of the provinces, rarely came to their land to check on agricultural production, and who cared neither for nor for the output of the land, not even as much as the large landowners of the republican era who used slave labour on a large scale. Since the cessation of the Empire's expansion, there has been a severe shortage of slaves from foreign plunder, the price of slaves has risen, and the era of the large-scale use of slaves for agricultural labour is over.

For large landowners, the most economical way to make money is to rent the land to tenants and sit on the rent. As for the construction of water, improve the quality of the soil, the selection of good seeds and other sundry things better not, invest in the land is like investing in real estate, the preservation of value is the main purpose, save heart for the biggest principle, spend money to fine farming is not their specialty, and even less their intention. Ordinary tenants, on the other hand, neither put up the money to improve other people's land nor lack the capacity to invest. A decline in the agricultural output of the empire has become inevitable.

Food supplies were gradually becoming a major problem for the Empire. Greece and Asia Minor are supplied by South Russia, where production is declining; Italy was dependent on Egypt, Sicily, Spain and Africa for grain, and as a result vineyards and olive groves are taking over the grain fields, which are declining in productivity and output, and Italy is facing a growing food crisis.

Although the city of Rome enjoyed special rights of supply without food shortages, other cities were not so lucky. Nearly all imperial cities face a shortage of food, and it is those in the most fertile areas that are no exception. Whenever a famine hits, there is usually a serious riot in the society, with the people denouncing the government and parliament for being ill-considered, and the government accusing the big landowners and big businessmen of hoarding. Thus, the "grain collector" became the most dangerous position on the official path of the Roman Empire, who not only had to ensure the availability of food, but also had to be responsible for low food prices.

When Spain began to grow olive trees on a large scale, it quickly became the best quality olive oil exporter, selling well in Gaul, Britain and elsewhere, and the Italian olive oil was robbed of the high-end market, eating away at even the local market. The olive oil of Afrikaner was not as good as the Spanish product in quality, but it was very good in price, so it was widely used in lamp oil and cosmetics, and was marketed throughout the empire, so that the Italian olive oil lost its low-end market, and even the olive oil of Asia Minor and Syria came to divide the Italian market.

Gaul, Greece, and Asia Minor were vigorously cultivating grapes, and the wine market was so competitive and so severely oversupplied that the Emperor Tecumseh (81–96) decreed that the production of wine and olive oil should be restricted, that no new vineyards should be opened, either in Italy or in the provinces, and that half of the existing ones must be destroyed.

The deliberate depression of food prices in the Roman Empire resulted in a series of severe resource mismatches, with the agricultural crisis manifested in shrinking cereal production due to land annexation, a severe surplus of cash crops, stagnant sales of agricultural-based consumer goods for handicrafts, declining commercial viability, and a taxing of the country.

During the republican era, Italy's most important products, apart from wine and olive oil, were many industrially manufactured products that had a clear advantage in the market. With the advent of the imperial era, Gaul (France) had become more industrial and commercial than Italy, with good harbours to the south, west and north of the sea and inland rivers that were easily accessible. Gaul was also exceptionally rich in natural resources and, having accepted the proliferation of Italian industrial technology, quickly became the centre of manufacturing and commerce, with its products covering the vast markets of Gaul, Africa, Britain, Spain, Germania, and Italian industrial goods being squeezed out of Western European markets.

At the same time, the East of the Empire was similarly free of Roman products and merchants. Among the high-end products, Asia Minor and the Syrian provinces of dyed linen, fine woolen fabrics, fine leather products, fine tableware, high-end cosmetics, perfumes, condiments and pigments beat the empire, while Italian products are difficult to penetrate the markets of the East. Not only did Italian merchants cease to appear in the East, but they also disappeared into the West.

By this time, Italy's dominance in agriculture, manufacturing and commerce has been lost, and the monopoly of the financial sector is at stake. With the hollowing out of the Italian economy, land annexation intensified, and after the loss of land, unemployed peasants moved into the cities in droves. The cities of the empire are filled with stragglers who have lost their industries, who hate the government, and hate even more the wealthy groups who have taken their industries, who are dissatisfied with their lives and desperate for the future, with only the vicious fire of revenge burning in their hearts.

In the republican era, the Roman army was filled with pure and productive peasants; in the imperial era, it was filled with proletarians who hated the rich and powerful. The metamorphosis of the army has triggered a more sinister regime crisis.

The economic nature of military dictatorship

Gibbon, in his book *The History of the Decline of the Roman Empire*, succinctly summarized the highly organized and combative nature of the Roman army. In his view, 100 armed men might not be able to deal with 10,000 riotous peasants, but a well-trained Roman legion of 10,000 men could terrorize millions in the capital, while a standing army of 450,000 could firmly rule over an imperial population of over 50 million.

The number of Roman emperors who were abolished by their armies was so great and so frequent that it is feared to be a rarity in the history of the world. This illustrates the simple fact that it is not the emperor who is leading the army, but the army that is controlling the emperor, which is especially true in the later years of the empire.

In China, there is a saying that "the government forces the people to revolt". When the conflict over the unfair distribution of wealth becomes so intense that it is impossible to reconcile it, it is often the peasants who revolt and overthrow the entire ruling group and then change the dynasty. The "peasant uprisings" of the Roman Empire, however, took place within the system, with the frequent change of emperors in the army and the outbreak of civil war being its main features.

The armies of the republican era were based on landed citizens who fought valiantly to protect their own interests, but the armies of the imperial era came mainly from the proletarian exiles of the Italian cities, who formed a highly organized group of exiles, who represented the vast majority of the imperial underclass. Instead of sharing in the benefits of economic growth during the empire's boom, they were deprived of a place to settle down by the powerful and wealthy groups. As a whole class, they are the subservient underclass, while the powerful and wealthy groups are the rulers, whose entire duty is to support the high and sophisticated civilized life of the city with taxes on servitude. No matter how industrious and diligent they may be, they are ultimately inexorable from land annexation and displacement, and their anger and discontent are festering and spreading among the Imperial army.

When the Roman emperors had power struggles with the powerful and wealthy groups represented by the Senate, the army became the main force on which the emperors relied. The civil war of 69–70, which broke out after the death of Emperor Nero, made the army suddenly realize itself to be a powerful force for the transformation of Rome, and their long-standing discontent and anger against the powerful and wealthy groups took out in the civil war in an extremely brutal and vicious manner. The armies of both sides of the Civil War, whoever won and whoever lost, all went on a rampage in Italy and in the cities of Rome to slaughter the powerful and the rich, and many of the noble families of the patriarchs of the republican era were exterminated by the mad soldiers, and the whole empire shuddered for it!

This was merely a prelude to the army declaring war on the powerful and the rich. Emperor Vespasian (reigned 69–79), who had started out in the army and was more aware of the Roman army, was deeply concerned about its political tendencies and ambitions. After ending the civil war, he began to cleanse the army, no longer recruiting soldiers from the proletarian exiles on Italian soil, but hoping instead to build a new Roman army with the provincial proletariat as its backbone. This strategy had maintained the internal stability of the Roman Empire for nearly a century.

But it was also during this period that the land annexation frenzy that had taken place in Italy began to spread in all the provinces, and to a greater extent, the proletarian exodus that had once filled Italy now spread throughout the Empire. The Roman army was once again reduced to a violent group of hatred.

The Roman emperor's ruling power came from two foundations, the economic power of the powerful and wealthy groups and the armed power of the army. But when these two forces are caught in irreconcilable and sharp conflict, the Emperor can only be inclined to rely on the latter.

Another military-born emperor, Severus (reigned 193–211), saw this very clearly, and after he had seized the throne by force to quell civil unrest, he had seen a second civil war far more bloody and protracted than the one that followed Nero's death, the essence of which was a fierce contest between the powerful and wealthy groups and the underclass, represented by the army, for the right to distribute the wealth of society. It was not the Senate that he relied on for his ascension to the throne, his power base was the support of the soldiers, and it was only under pressure from the army that the Senate was forced to acknowledge the fait accompli of his ascension to the throne.

His will, which he left to his sons, says it plainly: "Keep yourselves united, as long as it pleases the army, and the rest need not look upon it." He dramatically increased the army's pay, bestowed various privileges on retired soldiers, and bribed the military by extorting the wealth of wealthy groups. This, of course, provoked a fierce confrontation between the Senate and the wealthy, while Severus took on the powerful groups with a more brutal military crackdown.

Severus' son Caracalla (who reigned 211–217) went farther than his father when he came to the throne, even declaring publicly that the foundation of his imperial power was not in the upper classes of the empire, but in the lower classes and their representatives, the army. He unabashedly expressed contempt and hostility towards the aristocracy, taking a systematic approach to the extraction of wealth from the wealthy groups, while the taxation of the lower classes remained unchanged.

In order to strike a spiritual blow at the aristocracy, Emperor Caracalla, in 212, proclaimed a famous edict granting Roman citizenship to all inhabitants of the Empire, which not only de facto deprived the powerful classes of their political privileges, but was widely supported by the army and the underclass. The essence of the so-called class contradiction is the contradiction in the distribution of wealth in society. Caracalla used and even provoked this contradiction to consolidate imperial power, demonstrating that the Roman Empire was no longer engaged in valuable wealth creation, but was instead embroiled in an internal conflict of harmful and unhelpful class rivalry.

In the history of Rome written by the nobility, Caracalla was more hateful than the murderous tyrant and could be called the worst emperor in Roman history.

Since the murder of Caracalla, the army has become more debauched. In the following 40 years, at least 57 emperors were replaced by the light of day, and all but a few of them died a normal death. The army had completely lost its patience, and their disruption of the order of noble rule had reached an incalculable degree, and the warlike emperor's policy of incurring the slightest displeasure from the army was immediately followed by the scourge of death.

The wealthy groups that had made their fortunes from land annexation were finally caught in the crossfire and brutally cleansed. The attempt to defend the interests of the powerful and the rich, who are unwilling to lose their privileges, has led to a series of civil wars. The military dictatorship of Rome made not only the imperial power heavily dependent on the army, but also the entire empire's survival.

If there is more than internal turmoil, then external trouble is bound to come. The barbarians around the empire were originally shocked by the power of Rome and did not dare to act rashly for nearly a century. But as Rome's economy waned, civil wars continued, and the people's hearts fell apart, it began to harass the frontiers of the empire from all sides, which led to a massive invasion.

The emperor had to strengthen his army in order to consolidate his power, and the empire had to increase its military spending in order to repel the invasion. At the beginning of Augustus's empire, the Roman standing army was just over 200,000, with a salary of 225 dinars per person per year, which already ate up most of the coffers; more than a hundred years later, under Caracalla, the empire had to maintain a standing army of 450,000, and the salary soared to 750 dinars per person, a financial burden more than six times higher, while the economy was severely shrinking. By the time Diocletian (284–305) came to power, after nearly 50 years of civil unrest, the imperial economy had nearly collapsed while the army expanded to over

600,000, taxes were high, currency devaluation was commonplace, and hyperinflation was building.

Currency devaluation and hyperinflation

Historians say that the 2nd century was the golden age of the Roman Empire, with the "Five Wise Emperors", political clarity, high price stability, subordination of the army to the state, and the barbarians not daring to provoke. In fact, the political, economic, social and military crises of the empire in the third century all stemmed from this so-called "boom" period.

After the cessation of the Empire's military expansion, the agricultural productivity of the time was not originally sufficient to sustain a large and complex urban civilization, and the Empire's forcible urbanization movement had to rely on the excessive squeeze on agriculture. The result of the "low grain hurt the peasants" inevitably led to the gradual bankruptcy of the imperial agricultural economy; the laissez-faire policy of "no suppression of annexation" condoned the plundering of peasants by wealthy groups, forcing peasants who had lost their land to flood into the cities, increasing the cost of government "stabilization", further depressing food prices and intensifying land annexation; the conscription of proletarian exiles throughout the empire changed the composition of the Roman army, and armed mob groups with resentment and discontent eventually endangered the stability of the regime.

The urbanization of the provinces, which was vigorously pursued by the "Five Wise Emperors", was not based on the laws of natural economic development, but on the political needs of imperial rule, and was favoured by the wealthy groups. When this negative cash-flow monetary cycle is unsustainable, exorbitant taxes grow and economic vitality shrinks.

One of the "five sages", Trajan (98–117), succeeded in annexing Thrace, the buffer state of the Danube, but was caught in a strategic dilemma between the Germans in the north and the Iranians in the east, and the situation on the northern border was suddenly complicated. His military adventures in annexing Mesopotamia in the East did not pay dividends of peace, but instead stirred strong national hostility. Although Trajan won militarily, it suffered a financial defeat, and the Roman Empire almost lost its fortune.

Agriculture is in decline, commerce is in depression, the rich and the poor are divided, tax sources are depleted, and the gap in the daily expenses of the empire is widening.

In 117, Trajan had to reduce the silver content of the dinar, from 95% in Augustan times, to 85%, and the currency was devalued by as much as 10.5%, which amounted to a 10.5% hidden currency tax on the cash-holding population of the entire empire, to cover the huge fiscal deficit.

Trajan's successor, Hadrian (reigned 117–138), another world-recognized "Five Wise Emperors", had to clean up the mess left by Trajan. The barbarians on the northern frontier had again gone on the rampage, new wars had broken out in Britain, the fighting in Mauritania was raging, the Jews of Mesopotamia, Egypt and Palestine were waging bloody riots, and a new series of wars were imminent. Ultimately, Hadrian was forced to abandon Mesopotamia, not because he was not courageous or bold enough, but because the empire's financial resources were no longer sufficient to sustain the war of conquest.

By the time Marcus Aurelius (reigned 161–180) came to power, the situation in the Empire continued to deteriorate. He is one of the most respected of the "Five Wise Emperors" in Roman history, and wrote the famous book "Meditations" during the years of war and horse poverty, which is still widely circulated today. The scale of his war against the Sabbaths was no less than that of Trajan's, and when the elite Roman troops were all transferred eastward, the barbarians of the Danube Valley again broke ranks, forcing the emperor to turn back and march westward. Several battles came down and the Roman Empire was once again on the verge of financial ruin.

The emperor had vowed not to add new taxes, claiming he would rather sell his property to keep the empire running. The financial crisis drove the emperor to his knees, and he literally started auctioning off his family's assets, which lasted for more than two months. But trains are not pushed, bullocks are not blown, and empires certainly cannot be sustained by emperor sellers. In the end, the emperor still broke his promise and began to raise taxes and taxes.

When the soldiers overcame the barbarians' demand for an increase in the army's pay, Marcus Aurelius replied sourly: "If you want anything more than your regular pay, it is only to extract the blood and sweat of your parents and relatives. As for the throne, only the heavens can make the call." It is clear that the emperor deeply understood the extent of the crisis in the empire's finances, preferring to face the exasperation of the soldiers and the ferocity of a potential mutiny.

Even though the emperor was militarily victorious, the provinces had reached the limits of their financial power, Spain refused to send soldiers on several occasions, while Gaul and the other western provinces were filled with desperadoes, who broke out in increasing numbers and even openly broke out into regular war with the Roman army. In Egypt, large numbers of people fled from their villages to avoid military service, servitude, and taxes, and took refuge in the marshes of the Nile Delta, later forming an army to start a rebellion.

The Roman Empire under Marcus Aurelius was already in crisis and in peril. By 180, the emperor had to devalue the dinar's silver content to 75 percent, a devaluation of 11.8 percent over the Tularecan dinar.

It was only thirty-five years after Marcus Aurelius that the Empire's finances were once again on the verge of collapse. The military dictatorship of Emperor Severus, who relied on family plagiarism, confiscation, and forced donations, and the wealth he obtained from the nobility, was reduced to what was left by his son Caracalla. Caracalla, deeply influenced by his father, firmly rooted the foundations of imperial power in the army, and military spending finally drained the treasury of revenue.

The only solution to the urgent financial crisis was to further devalue the currency, but instead of making it too obvious, as Marc Aurelius had done, Caracalla made a major "innovation" and began issuing new silver coins, the "Antinori", in 215.

In 215, Caracalla issued "Antony", the Roman version of "Fold Two". The Antinori silver coin is slightly larger in size than the dinar and contains 1.5 times as much silver as the dinar, but has a face value equivalent to two dinars, which amounts to a disguised one-time devaluation of 25%, more than double Marcus Aurelius's devaluation!

It was the first "sovereign credit currency" in Roman history! The essence of the Anthem is to compensate for the missing silver content of the new currency with a 25% national credit. This legal approach to the value of money has fundamentally broken with the traditional method of devaluing silver, and is no less important than the "leap" from "ape to man".

The advent of the "Antinomian coin" signified a qualitative change in the viciousness of imperial finances. The people of Rome were not foolish, and began to stock up on old silver dinars and silver ingots, while merchants increased the prices of their goods according to the silver content of the new coins, and the price increases began to accelerate.

To make matters worse, the Roman trust in the government had been greatly undermined, and everyone was complaining about the new currency, and resentment against the government pervaded the landscape.

Rome was powerless to plunder gold and silver, the original Spanish silver mines had been depleted, and silver and gold had disappeared from the market without a trace, and the panic in the market was like a spasm, stimulating commodity prices to rise in turn. In modern terms, it's a sudden shift in market expectations of prices.

The silver content of the "Antinori" rapidly depreciated from 40% in 240 years to 4% in 270 years. By the time of Galenus (253–268), the Empire's finances were not on the verge of bankruptcy, but were bankrupt. Under his rule, Rome suffered its worst crisis since its founding, when hundreds of thousands of Germanic barbarians fought their way under the city for the first time in over 600 years. At the same time, the Roman Empire faced a major crisis of disintegration with the secession of Gaul, the independence of the East, the secession of Egypt, and the rebellion of the Africans.

The emperor was left with the only way to over-issued money. The Roman silver coins saw the worst devaluation in history, with the silver content of the Antinori coin plummeting from 40% in 240 years to just 4% in 270 years![59]

In addition, the emperor also issued a large number of crude copper coins, these so-called copper coins are actually only thin sheets of copper, weighing only 2.48 grams, even the banks refused to accept such poor coins.

Gracchus has devalued the currency to its physical limit!

---

[59] Glyn Davies, *History of Money*, University of Whales Press, 2002, p. 97–98.

In the end, Gracchus died at the hands of a rebellious army.

It was not Emperor Aurelian (who reigned 270–275) who really triggered the super-inflation of the Roman Empire after Gracchus. Aurelian was a military genius who, during his short five-year reign, recovered two-thirds of Rome's territory, crushed the barbarian invasions and internal divisions in Europe, Asia and Africa, and became known as the "Restorer of the World". However, as far as the devaluation of the currency was concerned, he was the "point man" of the Roman Empire's hyperinflation and played a decisive role in the eventual collapse of its currency.

In 274, the famous monetary reform in Roman history began with the introduction of the "Coin of Aurelian", a new coin with a silver content of 5% and a weight of 4.04 grams.

For the sake of credibility, the back of the new coin was minted with the Roman numeral "XXI", which stands for "20:1", i.e. 20 new Orleans coins containing 5% silver, equivalent to one dinar from the Augustan period. The silver content of the new coins seems to have the promise of national credit, and in the future the purity of silver coins will be restored to the Augustan era. However, all of this is nothing more than a flip-flop.

The change in the curve of the silver content of the Roman Empire's currency, the "thermometer" of economic, political and social health.

In fact, the value of the new coin is similar to the 4% silver "Antinori" coin, which is abundant in the market, but the emperor has played it even harder than Caracalla by stipulating by law that one new Orleans coin = two old Antinori coins, which is tantamount to the government depreciating the new coin by 100% once again on the basis of the already depreciated Antinori!

The people of Rome were in such a hurry, who would dare to take such currency? People rushed out into the streets and alleys and began a mad rush to buy. To be precise, not shopping madly, but throwing away the currency madly! The modest price rise of 250 years, immediately like a wild horse off the leash, all the way to the dust. Food shortages, commercial paralysis, banditry, and a plummeting population brought the Roman Empire's 3rd century crisis to a climax!

The price of wheat in Egypt increased two to three times from the 1st century to the middle of the 3rd century, basically reflecting the devaluation of the currency. However, from 250 years later, wheat prices began to accelerate, and by around 280, they were 100,000 times what they were 30 years ago!

This is the first time mankind has ever seen hyperinflation!

The collapse of the currency sounded the death knell for the empire

Emperor Diocletian (reigned 284–305), took over a monetary system that had collapsed and an empire that was about to collapse.

In order to save a monetary system that had completely lost the trust of the people, Diocletian first set about issuing new gold, silver and other coins of high purity. He was full of hope that the new currency would cure hyperinflation and at least relieve the pressure of soaring prices.

Without money there is no economy and ultimately no empire.

To his great distress, his new coins were of comparable quality to those of Nero's time, but were hundreds of times more valuable. The reason is actually very simple, the proportion of new coins in the total amount of money in circulation in the whole empire is too low, and whenever both good and bad coins are in circulation at the same time, good coins are always collected, and only when absolutely necessary will they be taken out for payment, such as the state tax must be paid for good coins; while bad coins are like hot potatoes, everyone can't help but use them immediately after getting them, so that the flow of bad coins will be faster, thus increasing the price of goods.

Diocletian's new coin was like a mud cow in the sea, swallowed up by the inferior coin in an instant without a word.

The root cause of the continuing spike in prices is that the Roman Empire's system of production, transport and commerce has been paralysed and purely monetary policy has been unable to undo the economic debacle.

Efforts to save the currency have finally failed and inflation continues to worsen.

Diocletian had to rely on administrative means to directly control prices, as in the famous Royal Decree on Prices of 301. In the royal decree, Diocletian blames the root cause of inflation on speculation and hoarding by businessmen, rather than economic collapse and currency devaluation. The royal decree establishes price ceilings for thousands of goods and services, which are punishable by death. However, the officially set price, far below the cost to the producer, if enforced, would no longer exist for the commodity in the market.

This doomed price controls to failure.

After the failure of price controls, Diocletian relied only on rationing, completely isolating the military and government supply from the market, taxing it in kind to ensure the military and government supply, and leaving the common people to fend for themselves in hyperinflation.

The empire's productivity has collapsed, more and more land is deserted, irrigation and drainage projects are abandoned, the agricultural economy is bankrupt, famine and pestilence have begun to spread, the population has been drastically reduced, banditry is rampant on the sea routes, international trade is virtually cut off, urban commerce has fallen into the abyss, the former prosperity is gone, the majestic public buildings are beyond repair, and the roads are overgrown with weeds.

The wealthy groups that remained of the empire began to move out of the cities in large numbers, moving to huge estates in the countryside, while also taking with them large numbers of craftsmen, the centres of industrial activity were no longer in the cities, and demand for their products was limited to estates or localities. The Empire's star-studded city clusters were turned into lifeless economic ruins.

Hyperinflation led to the death of the imperial monetary economy, leaving behind a fractured belt of self-sufficient, feudal, secular economies.

In 292, Diocletian divided the Roman Empire in two, with four emperors. After surviving for over 100 years, the Western Roman Empire perished.

Expound

It is often said that Rome was not built in one day, nor did it collapse in one day, and that the end of the Roman Empire in 476 was only the end result of two centuries of disintegration.

The question of why Rome fell has fascinated countless scholars over the millennia, who have pondered it with great pain, but still have not come to an accepted conclusion. Montesquieu, in his *Treatise on the Causes of the Rise and Fall of Rome*, concluded that the "loss of liberty" was the key to Rome's demise; Gibbon, author of *The History of the Fall of the Roman Empire*, argued that the emperor's centralized political system was the main cause of the fall of the Roman Empire, i.e. "Rome's enemies were within it: tyrants and armies"; Stavriano, author of *The General History of the Globe*, pointed to the "instrumental" diseases of the Roman Empire's economy as the root of its decline, and slavery as the root. In addition to the political system and economic issues attributed to it, there are religious, barbarian, slavery, climate, geotechnical, military, and other views.

The purpose of this chapter is not to draw conclusions about how the Roman Empire declined, but to raise the new question of whether the great division of social wealth caused by the excessive greed of the powerful and wealthy groups of the Empire was also a cause of the rise and fall of Rome.

Human activity through the ages has ultimately been about two things – wealth creation and wealth distribution – and everything else has been derived from these two basic activities. Wealth creation is premised on increased productivity, and the principle of wealth distribution is fairness. While economics tends to study the former, political science often focuses on the latter, and only political economy can do both.

As long as wealth is involved, it is impossible to circumvent greed. To the rich, covetousness is a trickery; to the poor, greed is a vice. Fundamentally, covetousness is a desire to acquire wealth that is not one's own by all means.

Greed is not a disease, greed is human nature!

Buddhists define greed, anger and infatuation in human nature as the three poisons that are the source of all suffering on earth. In other words, whether people like it or not, greed will always be with human society and cannot be cured. This can also be understood as the ultimate reason for the decline of all empires in history; the decline of the Roman Empire was nothing more than a duplication of human nature.

A good system is never one that avoids greed, but one that restrains it to the greatest extent possible. In any society, there must be a situation in which the rich few rule over the poor majority, and we have not found the opposite in human history. At the heart of curbing greed is the strong urge to restrain the tricky and desperate actions of the wealthy groups, who have the power, strength, motivation and determination to change the rules of social distribution of wealth. Such restraint is at best self-restraint by the rich group, which of course has rarely been the anomaly in history, and at worst the forces of the poor's revolt can force the rich group to restrain itself. A good political system is one that is able to control the social vibrations of conflict between the two sides without breaking the lower bound of bloodshed and revolution.

The Law of the Twelve Brass Tables, the compromise of the fierce conflict between the poor masses and the rich groups during the Roman Republic, did not break the bottom line, civil war was averted, and the stability of the Roman republic was guaranteed for the next 200 years. The Roman Republic of this time, with its institutional capacity for self-correction, was, in the final analysis, the political and economic system of the trinity of citizens, communal land, and civil army in the Roman Republic was in line with the fundamental interests of Rome at the time, and therefore had a vigorous vitality.

After the outbreak of the war of Buenos Aires, the citizens of Rome took to the battlefield, eventually suffering heavy casualties and bankrupting their wealth, and losing effective leverage on the political scales against the greed of the wealthy groups, resulting in a situation in which the wealthy groups carried out crazy wealth mergers without serious consequences. The division of wealth thus accelerated abruptly, the power of the wealthy groups surged, and the social balance was completely reversed. In this state, the reforms of the Gracchus brothers have been doomed to failure. A hundred years of bloodshed and civil war ensued, and the Roman Republic was powerless to return.

The ensuing Roman Empire was in fact a monstrosity spawned by the great dividends of Rome's military expansion, and although it was militarily powerful enough to conquer the Mediterranean littoral states, its organizational capacity was not sufficient to effectively navigate a vast empire. As a result, the Roman Empire had to push hard on the urbanization movement, with the aim of indirect rule by means of an imperial control of numerous urban federations, with urban federations controlling the population under their jurisdiction and incorporating as many people as possible into the cities. The urbanization movement of the empire was by no means the result of natural economic development, but a helpless political choice to rule a vast empire.

The highly deformed process of urbanization has had extremely serious economic consequences, with deliberate suppression of food prices, unprofitable cereal crops, deformed development of cash crops, misallocation of agricultural resources, a false boom in industrial products, a false boom in commercial trade and an ubiquitous asset bubble. A worse consequence is that the greed of the wealthy conglomerates, under the established urbanized state policy, is once again out of control, land annexation has reached unprecedented proportions, and the contradictions in the distribution of social wealth are unprecedentedly acute.

Ultimately, the division of wealth led to the rise of the exiles, the deterioration of the army, the confrontation of the rich groups with the mob groups, the constant civil war, the bloodshed, and the irreversible fate of the empire's demise.

The phenomenon of the collapse of empires due to the excessive greed of the powerful and the rich is not unique to Western society, and the same problem can be found in the overthrow of successive dynasties in Chinese history.

CHAPTER VIII

The Rise and Fall of the Northern Song Dynasty

From a military point of view, the Northern Song was a feeble and nurturing dynasty; but from an economic point of view, it was a period of high wealth and extreme prosperity. The Northern Song Dynasty was not only the pinnacle of monetary economic development in China's feudal history, but also a beacon of global urban civilization in the Middle Ages.

The economy of the Northern Song Dynasty was four times larger than that of the Sheng and Tang dynasties, with more than 1,800 cities, an urbanization rate of nearly 12 percent, and a degree of monetization unprecedented in the feudal era. More importantly, the high degree of urbanization and monetization in the Northern Song Dynasty was not based on the need for political domination and military garrisoning, as in the Roman Empire, but was a natural result of increased productivity and economic expansion.

The rise of urban civilization brought about the flourishing of science and technology, culture and art. Three of the "Four Inventions" of ancient China, six of the "Eight Masters of Tang and Song", were born in this great era. The monetary civilization of the Northern Song Dynasty also created the world's first sovereign credit notes, the first financial note exchange market, a thousand years ago Kaifeng Financial Street is no less dominant than today's Wall Street in the United States.

Although the civilizations of China and the West are markedly different, with vastly different histories, politics, cultures, languages and religious traditions, one thing is common, and that is humanity.

Rome's heyday was nearly a thousand years removed from the peak of the Northern Song dynasty, but the disparity between rich and poor that destroyed the Roman Empire was also a fatal source of disintegration. The failure of the reform of the Gracchus brothers and the abortive change of law by Wang Anshu illustrate the failure of the political system's ability to correct itself.

As a result, both Rome and the Northern Song had similar problems, with land annexation, unfair taxation, fiscal deficits, currency devaluation, internal and external disturbances, and even the outbreak of crises in the exact same order.

The history is strikingly similar, stemming from the strikingly similar humanity behind it!

The Northern Song Dynasty, the pinnacle of mankind's second monetary civilization

After the collapse of the Roman Empire, European civilization fell silent for a thousand years, just as the darkest era of the Western Middle Ages was setting the second wave of monetary economies in human history on the Asian horizon.

In 960, the Northern Song Dynasty was established, and a great era was kicked off.

If the civilization of the Roman Empire was based on the force of iron blood and conquest, the prosperity of the Northern Song Dynasty was the result of progress and peaceful development based on productivity.

During the Northern Song Dynasty, the most dazzling productivity revolutions first broke out in the energy and iron smelting industries.

Although China was able to make iron as early as the Spring and Autumn and Warring States periods (or even earlier), until the Northern Song Dynasty, the cost of iron smelting was high, production was low, quality was poor, and the price of iron was so high that China's agricultural economy could not afford its massive popularity, the main problem being an energy bottleneck, iron smelting required the use of charcoal, which was extremely expensive and limited in heat. By the Northern Song Dynasty, coal developed to the stage of large-scale mining and began to be used heavily for industrial energy, coal replaced charcoal, and the energy revolution gave rise to the explosive growth of the iron smelting industry.

By 1078, during the Song dynasty, the iron production in the Northern Song Dynasty had reached 75,000 ~ 150,000 tons, about the same as the total iron production in Europe in the 18th century (including Russia) before the industrial revolution! If you compare it to the Sheng and Tang dynasties, which were known for their wealth and power in Chinese history, the Northern Song Dynasty produced three to four times as much iron as the Tang.

The highly developed iron smelting industry of the Northern Song Dynasty was not only astonishing in total, but also increasingly refined in its division of labor. For example, steel knives from Shinju, agricultural tools from Yanzhou, stools from Yuanju, tableware from Leizhou, scissors from Taiyuan, castor knives from Heshan, needles from Leiyang, nails from Hangzhou, etc. In the local "fist product", the more detailed division of labor has given birth to a wide variety of iron products, with huge production. For example, Hangzhou has a brand store specializing in selling iron pins and "nail hinge" specializing in iron nails, and the annual supply of iron nails to the manufacturing industry alone reaches 600,000 kg.

The rapid progress of the iron smelting industry has also driven the unprecedented development of the steel industry, steel irrigation, 100 steel, copper steel and other steel smelting methods have been widely used. The technological revolution in production in the iron and steel metallurgy industry, in turn, has led to great advances in the tools of agriculture and a broad increase in agricultural productivity.

The Northern Song Dynasty began to popularize steel-bladed farming tools on a large scale, such as steel swords and side knives to promote the cultivation of wasteland, and the regulating plow became the regulating plow to facilitate deep plowing and detailed work. In terms of mu of grain production, the Song Dynasty reached 460 kg, more than twice as much as during the Sheng and Tang dynasties and more than four times as much as during the Warring States period.

The increase in the production of agricultural acres and the expansion of the total scale of cultivated land was directly reflected in the substantial increase in the population of the Northern Song Dynasty. Compared to the previous generations, the population of the two Han dynasties peaked at 50 million, and at around 60 million during the heyday of the Tang dynasty, these population increases created the heyday of the Han and Tang dynasties. The population of the Northern Song Dynasty has exceeded that of the two Han dynasties since Song Renzong, and is comparable to that of the Sheng and Tang dynasties, peaking at over 100 million, almost double that of the Han and Tang dynasties. In the Northern Song Dynasty, the number of "teeth" was unprecedented.

The huge food production not only led to a huge increase in population, but also contributed to the first wave of urbanization in Chinese history.

The proportion of urban dwellers in the entire population of the Northern Song Dynasty reached 12 percent, bringing the total number to more than 12 million, far exceeding that of the previous dynasties in successive generations. The total number of cities in the Song Dynasty reached more than 1,800, and compared with other countries in the world at that time, Nanjing, Yangzhou, Chengdu, Wuchang, Changsha, Fuzhou, Guangzhou and other cities were mega-cities with hundreds of thousands of people, and Kaifeng, the capital of the Northern Song Dynasty, and Hangzhou, the capital of the Southern Song Dynasty, were mega-cities with millions of people.

The surging urban population had to rely on a massive supply of commodity grain, which led to the rapid rise of the monetary economy in the Northern Song Dynasty. During the Middle Ages, the world's largest urbanization paved the way for the Northern Song economy to become a global power.

The way of life of the urban population is very different from that of the rural population, and after being freed from the closeness and narrowness of working at sunrise and resting at sunset, they have been given unprecedented freedom of choice, specialization is a prerequisite for their survival in the towns, and market trading is a daily necessity. The social division of labor led to a deeper intellectual grasp of the city people in the Song Dynasty, while market exchange accelerated the flow of information, and the aggregation effect of population stimulated new thinking, new inventions, and new needs.

During the Song Dynasty, Bi Sheng invented the art of printing with movable type, which was called the "information revolution" of the Middle Ages, greatly reducing the cost of information and indirectly increasing the productivity of various economic activities of the whole society.

Higher productivity, creating more exchangeable goods, stimulates a wider range of consumer demand.

The urban population is no longer satisfied with eating enough produce, but more importantly, eating well. In the pursuit of higher profits under the impulse of the Northern Song Dynasty, the rapid development of cash crop cultivation, such as citrus, lychee took the lead in breaking away from traditional agriculture, becoming an independent branch of cash crops, "a mu of orange than a mu of field profit several times"; as many as 32 species of lychee, only Fuzhou, there are 25 kinds of a place, "so merchants selling a wide range of benefits, while the townspeople kind more, a year out, I do not know hundreds of millions of dollars".

Vegetables are a necessity for people in the city, and the economic benefits of vegetable gardens are much higher than farmland, known as "one mu garden, ten mu field". The Song poet Yang Wanli once passed through Dingjiazhou, Jiangxin Island in Tongling, Anhui Province, and found that the island is "three hundred miles wide, and only radishes are grown and sold to Jinling", so he wrote: "The island is not a place to smile for three hundred miles, and the vegetables will live for ten million people." It can be seen that vegetable cultivation in the Song Dynasty was highly intensive and often supplied remotely.

In addition to eating well, the townspeople put a premium on dressing well. Cotton became popular from the Song Dynasty onwards, and cotton products became popular among the townspeople; linen continued to expand the market among the lower and middle income groups; and silk was a necessity for the high and rich. From the point of view of the government, silk is the mainstay of fiscal revenue, in the government levies taxes on 10 kinds of cloth, silk products account for 8 kinds.

In 1086, the revenue of the Northern Song Dynasty was as high as 24.45 million horses, more than three times that of the Sheng Tang Dynasty. The production of silk cotton and linen products on this scale requires a finer division of labor. The Northern Song Dynasty emerged to specialize in the textile industry as the main "machine", before the professional division of labor, a weaver both to spinning, and to weave cloth, the annual output of about 20 horse. When the locomotives appeared, they began to hire workers to divide the work between spinning and weaving, and the output of weaving was up to 40 hp and productivity was doubled. There were three or five looms for each family, and as many as six or seven hundred, and the total number of families reached 100,000.

The increase in productivity is reflected not only in the increase in the number of products, but also in the improvement in quality. The quality of silk weaving in the Tang, Song and Yuan dynasties was compared and it was concluded that "the Tang silk was thick and thick, the Song silk was thin and fine, and the Yuan silk was similar to the Song silk but slightly uneven". The townspeople of the Northern Song Dynasty wore the best fabrics in the world at the time.

After being fed and warmed, the city people of the Northern Song Dynasty were more attentive to their taste in life.

Porcelain is not only an indispensable kitchen item for daily life, but also a decorative appreciation item for home furnishings. The practicality and beauty of Song porcelain at the same time achieved a high level of achievement. As far as productivity is concerned, the Northern Song Dynasty was a rapid advance, not only improved the production process of porcelain, but also a more detailed and specialized division of labor. The geotechnician, baker, glazier, box worker, kiln worker became independent, porcelain making process is constantly optimized. In the past, porcelain fired using the "sagger method", a porcelain in a sagger box burned to do, while the Northern Song people invented the "cover burn method", will vary in size, different patterns of the bowl and plate components, in contrast to the combination of the sagger placed by the gasket box fired once, porcelain production was explosive growth.

In addition to porcelain, which is a consumer product for both the masses and wealthy groups, special handicraft products such as carved lacquer, root carving, jade tooth bone, gun, gold, gun and silver, and conch inlay are specifically designed to meet the needs of the luxury market.

A series of production breakthroughs in the manufacturing of consumer goods in the Northern Song Dynasty led to an unprecedented boom in the number and variety of commodities, which was matched by an unprecedented specialization in the social division of labor. During the Sui and Tang dynasties, society was roughly divided into 112 rows, and by the Song dynasty it had reached 414 rows, an increase of nearly three times! There is a Chinese proverb called "Three hundred and sixty rows, and a scholar comes out of every rows", which is probably from the Song Dynasty.

The prosperity of commodities and the rise of the monetary economy gave rise to the formation of four regional markets in the country, namely, the northern market centered on Beijing (Kaifeng), the southeastern market centered on Suhang and Guangzhou, the Sichuan-

Shu market centered on Chengdu, and the Guanlong market centered on Shaanxi. These regional markets, in turn, consist of a series of cities, towns and marketplaces that form a cross-overlapping, top-down, left-right cobweb of commodity and currency flows.

In terms of national commodity flows, agricultural and sideline products are in a "centripetal" movement, concentrating from markets and towns to cities, while handicraft consumer goods are in a "radiating" movement, spreading from cities to rural areas. The nation's taxes and goods converged in Beijing from south to north and from west to east, while the currency flowed back from the capital to other markets.

The large-scale movement of goods throughout the country, centered on the Beijing market, relies heavily on the inland waterway shipping system, and thus, there is a great demand for the manufacture of watercourse vessels. In the early years of the Northern Song Dynasty, the total size of the channel ships reached 3,337, and overseas trade and maritime transportation also developed rapidly due to the economic prosperity. The tonnage of ocean-going vessels can be over 500 tons and carry five or six hundred people. At the same time, the productivity of the Northern Song shipbuilding industry is very amazing, only Wenzhou, a government-run shipyard, with a fixed number of 252 people, the annual output is actually as high as 340 ships, almost 1 ship a day!

The prosperity of the shipbuilding industry gave birth to many generations of shipbuilding tycoons, and the Northern Song government liberalized full market competition in the shipbuilding industry, and the production of private ocean-going giant ships far exceeded that of the government shipyards.

The tea, silk, silk and silk yarn, gold, silver, jewels, porcelain and lacquer treasures, pavilions and pavilions, poetry and wine paintings.

The city of the Northern Song Dynasty was full of goods, material supplies were abundant and spiritual pursuits were at an all-time high. The Northern Song economy, driven by the locomotive of the soaring productivity of the iron and steel industry, also made a major breakthrough in the field of agricultural tools, and agricultural productivity doubled, triggering the concentration of agricultural population in the cities. The convergence of the three currents of urbanization, commodification and monetization has stimulated a finer social division of labour, a broader increase in productivity and a greater demand for consumption, which has led to the overall development of various industries such as cash crops, textile printing and dyeing, food processing, construction and shipbuilding, mining and smelting, porcelain lacquerware, paper printing, and salt, tea and wine, creating more urban jobs and accelerating the further transfer of the agricultural population to cities.

The monetary economy not only made the Song people richer, but also made them more independent in their thinking. Six of the eight Tang and Song dynasties, three of China's four ancient inventions, all appeared in the Northern Song Dynasty. The period of unprecedented intellectual activity in Chinese history, the Spring and Autumn Period and the Warring States Period, was also the period of the first great development of the monetary economy; in ancient Greece gave birth to the great era of Socrates, Plato and Aristotle, and it was also the era of the explosion of the monetary civilization of Lydia in the Aegean Sea.

The monetary economy is inseparable from the currency, and the driving force that keeps the huge economic machine of the Northern Song Dynasty running is the constant flow of copper money.

Currency overshoot and inflation

Although the Northern Song Dynasty did not have a statistical system of GDP, when comparing the major economic indicators of the Northern Song Dynasty and the Sheng Tang Dynasty, it is clear that the Northern Song Dynasty had nearly twice the population and doubled the productivity of the Tang Dynasty, and its total economy was roughly four times the size of the Sheng Tang Dynasty. Considering that the Northern Song Dynasty was more urbanized and commodified than the Tang Dynasty, the money supply in the Northern Song Dynasty should have been no less than four times that of the Tang Dynasty.

Yet the truth is even more shocking.

The amount of new money added each year in the Northern Song Dynasty gradually increased from 800,000 Guan in 995 to 1.25 million Guan around 1000, 1.83 million Guan in 1007, 3 million Guan in 1045, and peaked at 5:06 million Guan in the third year (1080) of Yuanfeng, the Song Godzong!

This is just copper money, the Northern Song Dynasty at that time there were more than 1 million guan of iron money minted each year, as well as paper money in the Sichuan region (the total circulation at the beginning was 1.25 million guan).

The annual minting of coins during Tang Xuanzong Tianbao's reign (742–756) was about 320,000 Guan, and during Tang Xianzong Yuanhe's reign (806–820) was 135,000 Guan. If the Yuanfeng years of Song Shenzong were the turning point of the Northern Song Dynasty from prosperity to decline, then the Tianbao years of Tang Xuanzong were in the same position as the Tang Dynasty, meaning that the amount of new money added during the Northern Song Dynasty's extreme prosperity was at least 19 times the amount of money added during the same period.

By 1085, the total amount of coins minted in the Northern Song Dynasty over a hundred years was about 140 million to 150 million Guan, and the total stock of currency, together with the private coins minted and the copper money still in circulation in the previous dynasty, was about 250 million to 260 million Guan. If you count the number of copper coins (770 in the Song Dynasty), it is around 200 billion.

In the Western Han Dynasty, there were only a handful of rich people with tens of millions of dollars in family assets, while the capital of the Northern Song Dynasty was full of "ten millionaires". The reasoning is simple, the purchasing power of Northern Song copper money has seen a significant devaluation compared to the Han and Tang dynasties.

In its heyday, the Northern Song Dynasty had an economy four times the size of the Tang Dynasty, yet over-issued 19 times as much currency, and it was clear that the currency problems of the Northern Song were quite serious.

The first effect of a currency overhaul is naturally inflation.

> *"Between the early Song Dynasty and Song Renzong, prices went from low to high, and the price index rose from 100 in the early Song Dynasty to 1150, or to 11.5 times. By the reign of Song Shenzong (during the period of Wang Anshi's change of law), prices had fallen, but then increased from low to high by Song Huizong, with the indices of wheat and rice increasing to 1,200 and 1,500, or 12 and 15 times respectively."*

Ye Shi, a famous writer of the Southern Song Dynasty, lamented when comparing the price changes in the two Song dynasties, especially the soaring prices in Jiangsu and Zhejiang:

> "The land of Wu and Yue, half the population of the world, but less than half the land, and the price of rice, cloth and silk has been three times the previous (late Northern Song Dynasty), chicken, pork, vegetables, timber, coke has gone up five times, the land of fields and houses has soared 10 times, and the golden lot of homes and fertile fields, it is very difficult to get people to compete, their prices are hundreds of times the past."

One important detail in Ye Sui's description of prices in Jiangnan at the end of the Northern Song Dynasty and the beginning of the Southern Song Dynasty is that real estate prices rose the fastest, with house prices in prime locations surprisingly soaring dozens and hundreds of times! This illustrates the second serious consequence of the currency overshoot, where asset inflation is far more violent than the CPI rise!

The monetary over-issues of the Northern Song Dynasty were not evenly distributed to everyone, but were rapidly concentrated to a few through the expansion of assets, and in addition to land and property, financial assets were also extremely important components.

The "Tokyo Yumehwa Rok" chronicles the luxury and grandeur of Nantong Street, the famous "financial street" of Bianliang. On the "Financial Street", there were many financial institutions, the fashionable name at the time was the "Jiao-yin Shop", where various securities such as various currencies, "salt money", "salt money" and "tea money" were traded in an unprecedented manner. "Nantong a lane, and is a place of gold, silver and silk trading, the house is majestic, the facade is wide, look at it, every transaction, move is ten million, horrifying."

If each transaction is ten million bronzes, i.e., a transaction at the level of 10,000 Guan, which is equivalent to 5 of the Northern Song money supply (200 billion bronzes), and if China's money supply M2 in 2013 is 106 trillion, 5 is 53 billion, which means that the single transaction size of the Northern Song bankers reached 53 billion, which is quite appalling indeed! With such a level of capital transaction scale, the price of the "Financial Street" in Beijing can only be sky-high.

Back then, the financial streets of Beijing were as big and influential as Wall Street in the United States today.

Apparently, the bankers of the Northern Song Dynasty were not the average rich people, but the super rich. How was it possible for banking in the Northern Song Dynasty to be so incredibly profitable?

In fact, they made money with a very similar mindset to bankers on Wall Street today, with the most profitable profit model being financial transactions, with the traditional lending business (usury) still a close second.

The Northern Song bankers traded not ordinary commodities, but typical financial bills, that is, the government monopoly on the monopoly of salt and tea financial derivative products – cross-lingual (salt, tea) and salt bills.

The rise of the banker

The bankers of the Northern Song Dynasty gradually expanded their business from coin exchange, which in the early days was also called "exchange shop". The Northern Song Dynasty was both a time of high monetary economic development and the most complex monetary system in China. The currency circulation in the country is fragmented and fragmented, with different currencies in circulation in different regions.

In the main currency, first of all, there is the difference between metal money and paper money, metal money and copper money, iron money, and copper money and iron money itself has the difference between big money and small money, plus gold and silver in the circulation of the growing status, especially the importance of silver in the Northern Song Dynasty has far exceeded the Tang Dynasty. When the country's commodities move across the four major markets on a large scale, regional currencies need to be converted, and inflation patterns such as gold, silver, copper, iron and paper need to be converted, which constitutes the most basic banking business of the exchange shop.

Exchange shop owners are engaged in daily is the low buying and selling of the currency between, to earn the spread, in today's words is short-term arbitrage trading. As the circulation of money in the Northern Song Dynasty skyrocketed, they soon evolved into the most important market makers in the Northern Song financial market, providing liquidity for currency exchange. They are super-sensitive to market fluctuations, and even the spreads of every single hour can't escape their eyes, and they make a meager spread. Like the market makers in the U.S. bond market, they have gradually developed their own customer base and established strong sales channels, and the profits from currency trading are derived from the spread between wholesale and retail prices. The owners of the exchange shops had become the most sensitive to market transactions during the Northern Song Dynasty, gradually evolving into the first generation of bankers.

In the second year of the Yongxi Dynasty (985), the bankers of the Northern Song Dynasty suddenly discovered a new arbitrage trading opportunity, and far more profitable than the currency exchange, which is the "cross-in" arbitrage.

The Song Taizong Zhao Kuangyi from 985 began secretly planning a three-way army north of Liao, trying to recapture Yan Yun sixteen states in one fell swoop, and in the following year launched the battle of Qigou Pass, which ended in a fiasco. Yang Ye, the famous general of the Yang family, was killed in the Chen family valley after the defeat of this battle.

As the saying goes, before the troops and horses are moved, food and grass come first. In order to transport grain to the north, the government mobilized merchants to participate in military logistics, a model of outsourcing government operations unprecedented in the history of feudal China, and only possible in the highly developed monetary economy of the Northern Song Dynasty. The commercialization and privatization of governmental functions is entirely consistent with the idea of American neoliberalism, and more accurately, the Northern Song is the originator of neoliberalism.

Merchants need to buy large quantities of grain themselves, and also responsible for hiring people to transport grain and grass thousands of miles to the border areas, of course, the government is a relief, but merchants do not have the benefit of the early, without the temptation of generous profits, who will work for the government. When the frontier receives the grain, it is valued according to the local market price and the proximity of the merchant's transport route, on the basis of which there is a certain preference, namely the merchant's profit. After valuing the money, the officials in the border area gave the merchants a receipt for the money, called a "delivery guide", and the merchants returned to the capital with the guide to collect the money from the officials. The government did not have enough cash and substituted some of the cash payments with salt tea notes, which the merchants had come for.

Salt is a necessity of life, and tea began in the Tang Dynasty and rose in the Song Dynasty, the wealthy urban middle class of the Song

Dynasty demand for tea was enormous, so the government monopolized the supply of salt tea, becoming an important source of national tax revenue. Salt and tea belong to the super profiteering government monopoly commodities, the price of each catty of salt is only 2.5 yuan, that is, two and a half copper coins when the government buys it, and sells it in the market at a high price of 26 yuan, "the government has nine times the net profit"! And tea sales have a super profit margin of 100% to 300%. Merchants can legally buy and sell franchised goods as long as they have the official salt and tea bills, the "salt guide" and "tea guide", which means huge profits at their fingertips.

The official government in Beijing does not have salt tea in stock, businessmen need to take the salt tea bill to the competent department for "approval", in current words, the official seal. The competent authorities indicate the place to receive salt or tea, and the area designated for sale, and the salt is generally collected in Xiechi, Shanxi Province, while tea is mostly found in Jiangnan Province. After receiving the salt tea, the merchants must be transported to an area designated by the government for sale, and must not cross the border to sell it, or be severely punished. The government's land-limit sales policy is, of course, designed to ensure a monopoly on the high profits of salt tea.

For the smart businessman, there is a greater oil and water in the government outsourcing business of transporting grain and grass. They were able to overestimate the cost of delivering rations by "taking care" of local officials in the border areas. To what extent is it overestimated? For example, a bucket of barley is only 30 yuan in the mainland, and the border officials added the price, freight and concessions together, and the valuation reached 1 Guan 254 yuan, which is as much as 30 times the price difference! There are many "reasonable" explanations for this from border officials, such as distance, bad road conditions, banditry, floods, bridge collapses, mudslides, earthquakes, fires, whatever makes sense. After all, the frontier had made great sacrifices for the war, so who would want to work for the court without giving some oil and water?

In this way, the salt tea note is worth a lot more.

So the merchants, on hearing the wind, rushed in droves to the frontier to deliver food and grass, responding to the call of the government to contribute to the imperial court and make money for themselves.

When the bankers in the capital saw the great value of the salt tea bills, they began to lobby the relevant departments of the imperial court, saying that these foreign businessmen were from unknown sources and their credit was very problematic, in case they bought and sold the salt tea bills backwards, or sold them across the border illegally, would it not mess up the market and undermine the country's general policy policy?

Businessmen must have a banker's guarantee in the capital, otherwise the relevant authorities refuse to "approve" them. Merchants from all over the place, who were carrying grain, had to run to the capital to forge ties with the bankers.

The banker took this opportunity to instruct the businessman in a bitter way: you earn too much money, take the salt tea bill and run across the mountains to Shanxi to get salt, or travel a thousand miles to the south of the Yangtze River to fetch tea, and then spend time and effort to transport salt tea to further areas to sell, and encounter bandits on the way do? What about poor quality salt tea? What about salt tea when it gets wet from a rainstorm? It's not worth it to run for half a year, to go around China, to make a hard-earned buck, and to be scared. Instead of earning money so hard, sell us bankers the salt tea bills at a discount, you make quick money, it's easy and hassle free, the profit is good, and then you can go back to hauling grain and grass and sell us the bills again, speeding up the money, which is good for both of us.

The merchants, upon hearing this, felt that it made sense, and painfully sold the salt tea bills in their hands at a discount to the bankers. Thus, the bankers in the capital began to buy and sell bills, and the exchange shop became the "gold and silver exchange shop", the exchange banker evolved into the "exchange banker", became the second generation of bankers in the Northern Song Dynasty.

What if some businessmen are just dead set on their minds, or find it too much of a loss to cash in on a discounted salt tea note? Then the bankers of the capital joined forces to refuse to give guarantees to such merchants. In this way, they could not get the "approval" from the government, and the salt tea note could only rot in his own hands. Even the most powerful businessman has to bow his head at the door of a banker in the capital. As for a few discounts, that's an internal negotiation between the bank bosses, whether it's two or three discounts, depending on how greedy the bosses are.

Of course, there will also be disgruntled businessmen to complain to the government, the bigwigs have deep ties with the government, and the maintenance of financial market order is justified, such a lawsuit can not win. From then on, the bank bigwigs banded together to block such a prick, and the businessman was never going to do salt tea again.

The more "chips" bankers have in their hands, the more control they have over market prices. They are also generally in the financing business such as usury and pawnbrokers, and have a direct influence on the capital city's capital supply. When they are ready to buy notes, they can tighten the silver root by raising the cost of financing in the capital, and then sell the notes in large quantities in the field to trigger a price avalanche, on the one hand to deter the government, and on the other hand to absorb at low prices. If they need a high sell-off, they will pull up the price of the note, luring profit-seeking speculators in for a bite to eat. This is not dissimilar to the modern approach of JPMorgan Chase and Goldman Sachs.

The imperial court wanted to use merchants to transport grain and grass for the borderlands in order to save financial expenditure, so they were tempted by the huge profits of salt tea, but did not want the merchants to be tricky, took care of the borderland officials, sold grain and grass to the borderlands at an average price of 6 times the market price, and swept the southeast of the imperial court 3.6 million Guan tea profits tax.

But the wise merchants meet the more intelligent and ruthless bankers of the capital, and the big bankers halfway out, again robbing the merchants of their ill-gotten gains.

In the age of the monetary economy, only those who play with money can play with the market. Northern Song Dynasty literati officials, in the fierce impact of the currency can not help but lament, "buy up (buy grain) only 500,000, and 3.6 million tea in the southeast to the merchants. In other words, businessmen and bankers robbed the country of 3.6 million kyat in taxes at a cost of 500,000 kyat! In fact, this is entirely consistent in nature with the Roman republican class of tax-payers who, through the outsourcing of government finance operations, embezzled state taxes and exploited Roman citizens on a grand scale. The literati government of the Northern Song Dynasty and the aristocratic regime of the Roman Republic were in no way rivals to the merchant and banker classes in terms of "wealth", and they even joined forces with them to divide the public wealth.

The fight between gold and power

Since bankers control the huge stock of salt tea bills, they can become both big salt merchants and big tea merchants, thus making a fortune again in the commercial circulation of salt tea. Having amassed vast wealth, the financial bigwigs are even more powerful. They were able to spend huge sums of money to get more officials in order to influence the policies of the court. Many have even climbed the ladder and risen to the ranks of the bureaucracy.

A famous story has been circulating in the Northern Song Dynasty. After Song Renzong abolished Empress Guo, a large tea merchant in the capital paid heavy money to bribe powerful people in the harem, sent his daughter into the palace, wanted to become the Empress of Song Renzong, and obtained the support of the Empress Dowager, Song Renzong confusedly agreed to come down. Later, an old eunuch reminded the emperor that the merchant was just a slave of a minister. It was only then that Song Renzong came to his senses and hurriedly sent the woman out of the palace. A tea merchant surprisingly has the energy to buy the support of the Empress Dowager who lives in the deep palace for a long time, can see how amazing the influence of money in the Northern Song Dynasty.

In 1023, the imperial court finally resolved to rectify the tea service, accepted the advice of the Minister Li consultation, curb the wastage of tea profits, abolished the salt tea bill "to guide" system, the implementation of the "see money law".

At its core, the "see money law" replaces the self-evaluation of transport costs by frontier areas in the form of central financial subsidies. In the first year of implementation of the new law, the total increase in revenue and decrease in expenditure of the state treasury amounted to 6.5 million kyats! The fiscal tax savings from the abolition of the salt tea note surpassed the peak of the total amount of money issued in one year in the Song Dynasty (5.06 million Guan). If you compare that to China's monetary increment in 2013, it's equivalent to a fiscal increment of over 13 trillion yuan!

The mega-money grabbing of the salt tea bill shocked the imperial court.

The new law has clearly dealt a serious blow to the vested interests of businessmen and financial interests, which has now stirred up a hornet's nest, resulting in "businessmen losing out and slander swarming". After only three years of implementation, the new law for the benefit of the nation and the people has come under frenzied attack from vested interests both inside and outside the country. The Minister of Reform, Li Cun, was demoted, and his men were even assassinated and exiled, and the system was restored again.

Apparently, the power of the Northern Song super-rich group has been able to sway the dynasty.

In 1036, Song Renzong once again resolved to reform the tea law, re-enabled Li consultation. Since the last time he was relegated to the rank of official, Li had some palpitations, and this time he put the ugly words in front of the first. He stated to the emperor that if he repealed the citation again, "the fear of inconvenience to the rich and powerful merchants, rely on the powerful and noble, in order to move the imperial court", Li Tuan asked the emperor must have a firm attitude of support. With the direct support of the emperor, Li Tuan again abolished the old tea method. But the good times did not last long, and soon there were more fierce attacks from the tycoons, and the new law did not hold.

The Northern Song tea law repeatedly changed until the end of the Song Dynasty, the focus of its dispute is the golden power and the regime to compete for huge amounts of tea profit attribution. In a highly centralized feudal dynasty, the power of finance was already strong enough to compete with the regime for state tax revenue, something that was unthinkable before the Song Dynasty.

Not only have the tea law changes met resistance from the financial bigwigs, but the salt law reforms are no exception.

Fan Xiang, the Minister for Salt Law Reform, suggested that the "salt money" law be replaced by a "salt-boot" law, in which merchants pay cash to obtain "salt money", eliminating the drawbacks of overestimating the cost of transporting foodstuffs to the border areas. In addition, the Salt Institute, a special salt price levelling institution in the capital, is dedicated to the manipulation of salt prices by the financial bigwigs, to control the fluctuation of salt prices between 35 and 40 yen per catty.

The bigwigs certainly have to fight back. The result was Fan Xiang's demotion. After his comeback, Fanxiang once again resumed the salt bill method. Later, during the financial crisis of the late Northern Song Dynasty, the salt banknotes had to be severely over-issued, resulting in a significant depreciation of their value.

The financial bigwigs fought a salt-and-tea battle with the imperial court until Cai Jing came to power. The financial bigwigs have all defected to the Caijing Group, Caijing once again changed the method of salt and tea, and the financial bigwigs have followed suit to make a fortune. The Wei Bo Rou, whom Caijing relies on, are all in cahoots with the financial bigwigs of the capital. Under the auspices of Wei Bojou, merchants had to deal with bankers and pay a 40% "fee" to exchange old notes for new ones. And when the old and new exchange, you also have to "clip the new with the old", otherwise you will not get salt tea. Caijing's frequent replacement of old and new banknotes has forced businessmen to repeatedly pay staggering "fees" to bankers.

The wool comes out of the sheep, and the merchants' "fees" are naturally passed on to the salt and tea farmers, as well as to the consumers in the market, which ultimately translates into a loss of state revenue.

After repeated battles, the Jin power and the regime gradually became a community of interest, the financial bigwigs mingled with the bureaucratic class and became one with the big tea and salt merchants. In the tide of the monetary economy, financial capital consolidates the interests of bureaucrats, big businessmen and big landowners into one, gradually solidifying into a wealthy and powerful class of powerful and powerful people, evolving into a kind of institutional greed that whales the wealth of society.

After sweeping through the country's taxation, they began to transfer huge amounts of wealth to the land, becoming the main force in large-scale land annexation and becoming the great landowners of the Northern Song Dynasty.

6–7% of the wealthy have annexed 60%-70% of the land

The land annexations of the Northern Song were strikingly similar to those of the Roman period, with both empires experiencing the culmination of two annexations, and the latter on a much larger scale than the former. The first land annexation will hit the country's coffers hard, leading to severe social polarization and tax injustice, and without reform the regime will gradually fall into crisis. The second land annexation will be even crazier than the first, and the extreme division of wealth will destroy all hope the poor have of government, leading to a vicious hatred of the rich and the aristocratic. If the last efforts at reform fail, it will quickly lead to bloody violence, continued civil war, or invasion by foreign enemies, and ultimately the collapse of the empire and the overthrow of the dynasty.

The Roman land annexation began with the rise of a class of tax collectors, who seized the universal tax, the "first barrel of gold" of the Roman land annexation; the Northern Song Dynasty was a time when the bankers coincidentally took the government's salt and tea profits through the salt and tea bill trade, which was also the universal tax and the starting capital for their land annexation.

The first great tide of land annexation in the history of the Northern Song Dynasty occurred during the reign of Song True Emperor and Song Inzong.

The military conflict between Northern Song and Liao lasted until Liao's Ninth Southern Expedition in 1004, which ended in the "still abyssal alliance" of Song and Liao. It was because of the great demand for food and grass in the war in the north that the system of transportation flourished, thus allowing the financial power groups in the capital to reap huge profits and make a fortune from the national disaster.

The Salt Tea Note appeared from 985, with a brief interruption in between, and lasted until the end of the Western Summer War around 1050. For more than 60 years, merchants and bankers swept through the government franchise of uncountable tea, salt and sherry, thus gaining access to substantial funds to carry out massive land annexations.

"The rich have the capital to buy land and the powerful to occupy it", while the imperial court has given the land annexation a complete free hand, the so-called "non-repression of annexation" State policy. Or rather, there was never any economic policy in the Northern Song. From the point of view of government intervention in the economy, the Northern Song Dynasty can be described as a pioneer in the adoption of the neoliberal economic model.

At the beginning of the Northern Song Dynasty, due to the collapse of the system of equalization of land, the original belongs to the state regulation of wasteland, uncultivated land, anyone can occupy the wasteland, as long as the official registration for the record, then taxation according to chapter can be. As to who owns the land and how much is in possession, the Crown neither cares nor intervenes. As long as the buyer and the seller voluntarily enter into a transaction, they only need to send the deed to the government for the record, stamp it with the seal of the government (the so-called "red deed"), and pay the tax on the deed, the transaction is completed, and the new owner is responsible for the handing over of the land.

If the transfer of land does not go through the government, the deed is not stamped with the seal of the government, this is the so-called "white deed", the government does not recognize its legality. In the case of the White Covenants, the Crown simply insisted that the transaction be reported, not intervened in the transaction itself. In the case of state-owned land, those who rented the land did not have land ownership, but had "field rights", the Northern Song version of "small property rights", and the land could also be bought and sold and circulated.

In the feudal dynasties that regarded land as life, the Northern Song policy of complete laissez-faire on land purchase and sale, can be called a feudal history of the "oddball". Even in the Tang Dynasty, which was known for its openness, the sale of one mu of "mouth divided field" is subject to 20 whips, the sale of Shiye ancestral fields will be strictly limited by the government.

In 966, the Song Taizu just won the world, on a high call: "the long official, the Oracle people, there is a wide range of planting mulberry dates, reclaiming barren fields, and only the old tax, never check." In the early years of the Northern Song Dynasty, the booming economic growth, the rapid reproduction of the population, and the huge land reclamation all showed that the early free land policy was effective. But when the reclamation of wasteland is gradually completed, the contradiction of more people and less land is becoming more and more prominent, no longer adjust the policy, land annexation is inevitable, the contradiction between rich and poor is bound to intensify.

The first to set off a tide of land annexation is of course the powerful officials and noble relatives, who belong to the "powerful occupation of the field", the common people's fields are seized by trickery, "select fertilizer and devour it", even the state-owned land, such as state-owned pastures, government-run school fields, public mountains and forests have also become their targets of forcible occupation, even the "blessed fields" of monasteries are not spared. In the year of famine, the people were in a difficult situation and had to mortgage or sell their land, while the powerful and noble relatives fell on their hands and took advantage of the situation to annex. A small number of powerful and powerful families even sabotaged dams and created floods in an attempt to seize people's land on the cheap. The first land annexation of the Northern Song dynasty, the momentum of the fierce, crazy means, unseen for all dynasties.

Under the impetus and stimulation of the bureaucratic class, the financial bigwigs, big businessmen and big landowners with huge amounts of money were not willing to lag behind, they belonged to the "rich have the capital to buy the land" generation, and in the tide of land annexation later came to dominate. The descendants of the noble and wealthy officials also mortgaged or transferred the thousands of hectares of their ancestral land to them because of their excessive spending. In the Han and Tang dynasties, the "annexationists", who had been called the "hao-min" and severely suppressed by the government, became the envy of the world in the Northern Song dynasty, but became the "lord of Daitian".

The powerful and wealthy groups of bureaucrats, bankers, big businessmen and landowners make up 6% to 7% of the population, but they cover 60% to 70% of the country's land and half of its wealth.

The government has to fight wars and keep the country running, and the financial consumption is not enough to make the national treasury empty. The rich group has to pay less taxes, the poor class has to pay more. As a result, the quality of life of the middle class in the Song Dynasty deteriorated as a result of the increasing number of exorbitant taxes and disguised exploitation.

The destruction of the Song Dynasty dream

In 1067, when Song Shenzong ascended to the throne room, he found himself sitting less like a dragon chair and more like a pile of dry firewood that could be ignited by a single spark. He knew that without reform, the foundations of the Song Dynasty would fall. He had his eye on a bold minister to implement the New Deal, namely Wang Anshu.

Wang Anshi has long seen the serious predicament that exists in the country's economy, which is the accumulation of poverty, financial depletion, economic depression and uneven tax burden. So, how serious is the problem?

First of all, the quality of life of the common people is much less than before. A typical landed farmer with a family of five, with two labourers and three children, a family with farming cattle and complete means of production, needs 28.8 stone of food for a year's ration, 1.2 stone for salt, 3–4 stone for clothing and 3–4 stone for fodder. In addition, there is also a demand for agricultural tool repair and fertilizer from time to time. At the end of the day, a farming family needs at least 36 stone to 38 stone of food a year to maintain the most basic subsistence and reproduce.

Due to the increase in population, the land of a typical peasant family has dropped from an average of 95 mu in the early Northern Song Dynasty to 50 mu in the Song Dynasty. In the Northern Song Dynasty, the average grain yield was about 2 stone per mu of farmland, taking into account that Ping, Feng, and the year in arrears each accounted for 1/3, the average grain yield was about 1 stone. Thus, the family harvests about 50 stone of grain a year, and after setting aside 5 stone for seeds, about 45 stone of grain is left (about 92 kg per stone). After a family's meal was consumed, 7–9 stone (644–828 catties) remained, with a monetary value of about 2,100–2700 yen.

That's 1,000 coins, which at the time were about as good as 276 kg of grain or 33 kg of salt.

The two taxes (summer and autumn taxes) that the family had to pay to the government were about 500 yuan, which made it possible for the family to live relatively well when the taxes were not heavy. However, by the time of the Song dynasty, land annexation caused a sharp increase in the people's share of the tax burden.

The government increasingly uses disguised means to covertly increase taxes in the collection of the positive tax on land grants. For example, the so-called "discounting method" is the arbitrary exchange of this kind of discount for that kind of discount, or the discounting of that kind for cash at a highly unreasonable price. In Chenzhou, the local government stipulates that the summer tax only collect money not grain, large wheat discount money 100, plus a variety of fees, the official price is set at 140 yuan per bucket, while the market price is only 50 yuan, forcing farmers in the market to sell nearly 3 buckets of wheat in order to pay a bucket of tax; at the same time, the official government in order to ensure the profits of the salt franchise, forcibly distributed to the people to buy salt, the market price of 30 yuan per catty of salt, the official hard sell 100 yuan, a disguised blackmail 3.3 times; then the official again converted the salt into wheat, farmers were once again exploited; things are not over, the official again converted the wheat into cash, the final 1 catty of salt sold to 350 yuan, while the market price is only 30 yuan. After repeated "folding", the taxes of farmers have soared more than tenfold! Although the other states were not as greedy as Chenzhou, the "change of law" did cause the tax pressure on farmers to increase dramatically, and instead of the state's 500 yuan, farmers spent several times as much on their fields.

In addition to the national positive tax of land tax, disguised taxes also emerge in a variety of ways. In order to stockpile military grain in the north, the Northern Song court compulsorily distributed the purchase of grain in various places, the purchase price of only 300 yuan per stone government, farmers have suffered a lot of losses. Not only that, the government paid only 1/4 of the cash for a stone of grain, i.e., 75 kyat, the remaining 3/4 was converted into tea, while the market value of rationed tea was only 37 kyat, a stone of grain was converted into 112 kyat. What is even more ridiculous is that even the 37-week-old tea is not present, but is a "tea guide" that farmers have to go to distant tea-producing areas to collect. In desperation, farmers had to sell their "tea" to merchants. In the end, the farmer sold a stone of grain for only 100 kyat. If two or three stones are distributed, the farmer will lose 400 to 600 yuan of income.

In addition to these hidden taxes, other successive generations of exorbitant taxes were also collected by the local government in an eclectic manner. In the original Southern Tang rule of the Jiangnan region, as many as 17 taxes, the sale of cattle and sheep, grain, fields and houses have a tax, build your own house to pay the "wood tax money", cattle alive have a tax, dead also have to pay taxes ("cowhide money"), the population has to bear a variety of servitude, separation of family life is to pay a "fine"; as for artemisia money, shoe money, foot money and so on is a variety of ways. As Zhu Xi said, "The ancient method of carving and stripping is available in this dynasty".

The root cause of the increasing exorbitant taxes is land annexation!

Large-scale land annexation by the big and powerful is extremely detrimental to ordinary farmers, and the land occupied by the big and powerful is rarely taxed. The "Ziping Accounting Record" had calculated: "Count its rent to know the number of hectares and mu, while the tax does not add ten of its seven." That means that up to 70% of the land is not taxed at all! The vast majority of them are naturally occupied by the powerful and powerful. In the early years of Song Renzong, land annexation began to heat up, the powerful and powerful bought a lot of land but tried very hard to hide, often 15 mu ~ 20 mu of land only to pay 1 mu of tax. By the later years of the Song dynasty, "the official Fu surname occupy unlimited fields, annexation and counterfeiting, and habitual, heavy grace can not be forbidden". The extent of tax evasion in the hidden fields of the big and powerful families reached an alarming level, with the fields registered with the government plummeting from 5.24 million hectares under the Song dynasty's True Emperor to 2.28 million hectares under the Song dynasty's Renzong, and nearly half of the land of the Song dynasty "disappearing"!

The sharp decline in farmland was forcing the government to make up for it in other ways, and the farmland that should have been borne by the powerful and powerful was passed on to the ordinary farmers in various ways.

The ordinary people's life is supposed to calculate tea, rice, oil and salt for these households, and so on, where can farming life can still go on. In a good year, it's just barely enough to maintain subsistence, and in the event of a natural disaster, you can only mortgage the land and are forced to borrow at interest rates as high as 100% to 300%, and once you owe the loan sharks, the farmers will definitely lose their land.

50 acres of land per capita, how can be considered the Northern Song middle class, under the heavy oppression of exorbitant donations and taxes, more and more people were forced to sell their land and act as sharecroppers for the powerful and powerful. The land taxes paid by the big and powerful tenants came from the rent of the tenant farmers, who thought that selling their land to the big and powerful tenants was a way out, but eventually found that it was an even more tragic desperate path.

For farmers, owning land was the biggest dream of their lives, and now the "Song Dynasty Dream" has been completely shattered.

The economic prosperity of the Northern Song Dynasty depended on the labor and creation of thousands of ordinary families, who were originally enthusiastic, inventing and creating, consuming more and more, living a prosperous life and full of hope for the future. But as the land annexation intensified, they found that no matter how hard they had worked, life was getting harder and harder. They depressed, they lost hope for the future.

The day the people's dreams are shattered is the day the country goes down the drain!

Under the three mountains of land annexation, tax injustice, and currency devaluation, the economy of the Northern Song began to lose its vitality, going from prosperity to decline. Civil power is on the verge of depletion, while government spending is skyrocketing.

The number of officials at the imperial court rose sharply from 3,000 to 5,000 during the Song dynasty to more than 20,000 during the reign of Song Emperor Renzong, causing a serious "redundancy" problem. At the beginning of the Song Dynasty, there were only 220,000 troops, and by the time of the Song Emperor Renzong's Qing Dynasty, there were 1.25 million! The military expenditure alone amounted to a staggering 48 million kwangs, accounting for 70 to 80 per cent of the court's revenue, and it was caught in a huge dilemma of "redundant troops" and "redundant expenditure". The largest standing army in the world at that time created the "myth" that there was no victory in foreign wars.

Since the Song Dynasty, the national fiscal deficit has been as high as 3 million Guan per year. By the year of Huang You (1049–1054), the main taxation of the successive dynasties – Tianfu, has been far from being able to meet financial expenses, the monetary income of Tianfu is only 5 million Guan, a shortfall of 22 million Guan; silk income of 3.8 million, a shortfall of 5 million; grain income of 18 million stone, a shortfall of 887 million stone.

The imperial court rushed the tax like a rush, local officials were forced into a hurry, only to play "folding", the field quietly doubled several times, all kinds of exorbitant contributions and taxes, labor and service heavy burden seriously frustrated the Song people's labor enthusiasm, shaking the country's financial resources. At the same time, the imperial court also made great efforts to expand the collection of commercial taxes, the Song dynasty was indeed more developed than the Han and Tang dynasties, the economy reached four times the size of the Sheng and Tang dynasties, but the commercial tax was more than 10 times higher than the Tang dynasty. During the Song Dynasty, the total revenue of the Northern Song Dynasty reached 100 million Guan, and the commercial tax alone accounted for 56% of the total revenue, which exceeded the tax on Tianfu for the first time in Chinese history.

The land was also overburdened by the peasants, which led to a loss of enthusiasm for labour, and the "heart" of wealth creation was on the verge of collapse; commercial taxes were abnormally high, which inhibited the circulation of goods, made it difficult for the economic bloodline to flow smoothly, and the physical condition of the dynasty became weaker; currency devaluation and asset inflation created "high blood fat", "high blood sugar" and "high blood pressure" in the economy, and the "three highs" aggravated the economic condition of the Northern Song Dynasty.

The "money shortage" is worsened by the snow

The devaluation of the currency in the Northern Song Dynasty became more and more serious, and the assets of the big and powerful households needed to be preserved and increased in value, and the conversion of the currency in circulation into physical assets became the inevitable choice of the big and powerful, which gave rise to the problem of "money shortage", which was even more destructive to ordinary farmers.

The first time the term "money shortage" appeared in the Northern Song Dynasty and attracted the attention of the court during the Qing Dynasty (1041–1048), the root cause was also the war with the Western Xia. 1040–1042 Songxia three major wars ended with the defeat of the Northern Song Dynasty, the huge war depletion forced the court to begin to devalue the currency, not only the Sichuan Jiaotzu paper currency 600,000 Guan increased issue, but also began to depreciate the value of copper and iron money, which is the Qing Dynasty for eight consecutive years only issued "one for ten" copper and iron big money.

The standard copper money of the Northern Song Dynasty was called "small flat money", "when ten money" is bigger than "small flat money" one, but far from small flat money contains 10 times the amount of copper, but by the imperial court with 10 small flat money equal to the value of the law, this behavior and the Roman Empire's "Antony coin" "Orleans coin" is simply a master trained. To put it bluntly, pawn ten is a blatant devaluation of the currency, which of course causes market panic. The clever merchants began to hoard more copper in the small flat money, while the greedy merchants made huge profits by stealing and minting dang ten coins, the effect of bad coins expelling good coins occurred automatically, and there was an increasing shortage of small flat money in circulation.

The court was shocked, the benefits were not reaped, but the ills were piled high, and the draconian law of headbanging and exile could not stop the greed of humanity. In order to curb piracy, the imperial court had to announce that the "ten pounds" had been changed to "five pounds". The frenzied speculation still could not be quelled, later changed to "pawn three", still difficult to work, the theft of castings still has huge profits. In the end, the imperial court had to "discount two", that is, one big money for two small money, which stopped the urge to speculate. It's not easy to fight human greed, but it's not easy to get a harsh sentence. Fortunately, the Song and Summer War ended for the time being, and this "dang ten" money did not continue to be distributed indiscriminately, the Xiao Ping money returned to circulation, and the money shortage problem eased.

Later, with the continuous deterioration of the fiscal, the imperial court again issued "pawn ten" money, due to the fierce market reaction, piracy cast serious, inflation worsened, then again "pawn three", finally "fold two". However, "Folding two" copper money gradually became the practice of currency minting, the large-scale weight loss and serious over-issuance of copper money became a long-term monetary nightmare of the Northern Song Dynasty, the problem of money shortage began to worsen.

At the time of the flood of ten, five, three and two-fold money, Xiao Ping money became a sought-after commodity. Merchants hoarded small amounts of flat money in large quantities, then re-melted cast bronze and changed hands for a 5x windfall. In the process of severe currency devaluation, Northern Song bronzes, like today's Wada jade and jadeite, became a hot commodity for capital speculation. In the face of the lucrative and profitable molten money casting, even the officials have been involved in the middle, joined the ranks of the "traitorous people", the imperial court could not help but exclaim that "the official shall not cast bronze".

There is an implicit condition to the principle of expelling good coin by bad coin, and that is that the law provides that bad coin and good coin are equal in value, otherwise who in the free market would be willing to accept bad coin? It is by the power of the State that bad currency is expelled. After withdrawing from circulation, fine coins always converge toward places that value them. The copper in the good coin has been given its due market value recognition, and sometimes, under the psychological expectation of asset inflation, the wind of speculation fuels the price of copper, which is the essence of the molten money maker.

Another outlet for good money is outside the country.

The Western Xia, Liao and overseas countries all respected the true value of copper more, so the Xiao Ping money of the Northern Song dynasty went down like a torrent. The Northern Song Dynasty adopted the so-called "money ban" to deal with the money shortage, strictly prohibiting the private casting of money, the destruction of copper money, the outflow of copper money, and the over-storage of copper money, the focus of which was to prevent the outflow and destruction of copper money. Even has always been "benevolent" known as Song Renzong on the money ban are exceptionally harsh, "copper money out of the outside world, always above, the head of the execution", and Song Renzong before the death penalty standard is to carry copper money 5 Guan out of the country. The end result was that neither Liao nor Western Xia had to mint their own coins, and the Northern Song coinage circulated freely there in such large quantities that even Japan and Vietnam were desperate for it. "Pan Yi got Chinese money, divided into treasuries and stored it as a treasure for the state. Therefore, into the Fan, not copper money does not go, and the Fan goods are also not copper money does not sell."

In the face of human greed, even the threat of death pales.

No wonder Su Zhe, the great writer, lamented about the exodus of copper money: "Where there is profit, there is no end to it."

Various kinds of big money, which contained a serious shortage of copper, were in vogue, but the small flat money was increasingly in short supply, the bigger the issue of big money, the faster the small money disappeared, the serious inflation eventually caused the production of small flat money into a loss-making business, the supply of copper money in the Northern Song began to decline rapidly. Because the court was short of money, big money was cast; because of the casting of big money, small money disappeared; because of the casting of big money, things became more expensive, and the production of small money lost money; and the supply of even less small money exacerbated the issuance of more big money, so that the money supply of the Northern Song was caught in a terrible vicious circle.

Money shortage, to be precise, is the rapid withdrawal of small flat money from circulation under the interaction of currency devaluation and asset inflation. The more economically developed Jiangsu and Zhejiang, the more money shortage, this is not only because the circulation of small flat money in economically developed areas is greater, but also because the big and powerful households in these areas have stronger incentives to melt money casters.

Farmers in Jiangsu and Zhejiang are far more dependent on the monetary economy than people in other underdeveloped regions, and are dependent on the government's exorbitant taxes and the "folding" of all kinds of land grants to get cash payments from the sale of agricultural products. Small flat money shortage, resulting in an odd lack of market liquidity, farmers are forced to sell agricultural products at a reduced price, for the ordinary farmers who are already in deep trouble, is no different from adding to the frost.

The land annexation has led to an increase in the tax burden of ordinary farmers, the run-off of land grants and the expansion of government spending, resulting in fiscal incomes exceeded, serious deficits forced the government to devalue the currency, currency devaluation stimulated asset inflation, asset inflation accelerated the land annexation, and at the same time induced a money shortage, while the land annexation and money shortage exacerbated the plight of farmers, such a vicious cycle, the people are not able to live.

This was the great economic and social crisis facing the Northern Song before Wang Anshu changed his ways.

Why did Wang Anshi change his ways and why did he fail?

In 1069, with the strong support of Song Shenzong, Wang Anshi began the famous movement for a change of law.

Wang Anshi's insight into the root causes of the economic ills is also very perceptive, and his thinking hits the nail on the head: "Those who have not yet done anything nowadays should use their money as a matter of urgency." Fiscal depletion is an imperative for law change, and the solution is to cut costs.

Open source is what Wang Anshi calls "wealth management", which is based on developing production and creating wealth. Wang Anshi once stated his views in his advice to Song Renzong, "Therefore, I think that wealth management is the first priority for today", and "wealth management is an emergency for agriculture". Wang Anshi was quite accurate in taking the pulse of the country's condition, the foundation of the Northern Song economy was agriculture, and a lack of agriculture would lead to depression. And how to stimulate agricultural production? Wang Anshi even said, "Farming is a matter of urgency when it comes to removing illnesses and suffering and suppressing annexation."

Wang Anshi's economic thought of "suppressing annexation" is where it shines most brightly. The hardships of farmers, the low enthusiasm for labor, and the inconvenience of production conditions are the root causes of land annexation! A more reasonable order should be to "prevent mergers and acquisitions" first, before "eliminating diseases and hardships" and "tending to agriculture" can be achieved.

From the viewpoint of the key measures to change the law, Wang Anshi is to "remove the ills and sufferings" as a breakthrough, indirectly solving the "suppression of merger" of the hot potato. For example, the "green seedling law" stipulates that all states and counties, before the annual summer and autumn harvest, can go to the local government to borrow cash or grain to subsidize farming. In those years, the loan was returned with the spring and autumn taxes, and the interest rate was 20% to 30%. At the time of the decline, the government's agricultural credit to alleviate the plight of farmers, without the government's "low-interest" loans, farmers would have to borrow from the financial bigwigs, the government's 30% interest rate sounds high, but the financial bigwigs' usury has reached 100% to 300%. Borrowing at usury meant mortgaging the farmer's land, and once the money wasn't paid, the land was annexed by the big boys. The purpose of the "green shoots law" is to counteract the exploitation of usury with loans from the government, so that farmers can "always preserve their land during the "bad years" and not be annexed by large families".

The law of exemption from service is based on each family's wealth level, the number of acres, the number of small and strong to determine the monetary value of the service, the rich more share, the poor less share, the people can choose to pay "exemption money" instead of the service of the service. Since ancient times, the labor service is a heavy economic burden of farmers, garrison, repair palaces, build mausoleums, digging drains, for the official government when a job, a month or more, not only delay the family's agricultural production, but also weakened the handicraft and commercial labor supply, more unfair is the government officials do not take grain, not to be a job is the common practice, the burden of national service all fell on the ordinary farmers.

The exemption law broke down this unreasonable mechanism of the distribution of hard labour, the powerful and large households had to bear the main economic burden of hard labour, while the "hardships" of the farmers were relieved to some extent. More importantly, "free money" and the number of acres of land linked, the more acres of land, "free money" the heavier, which is just like the modern property tax on "house sister" "house uncle" will have a huge inhibiting effect. Therefore, while the exemption law directly alleviates the "hardship" of ordinary farmers, it also indirectly inhibits land annexation. When the news that a powerful and powerful family in Zhejiang was forced to take out 600 Guan "free money" reached the capital, the imperial court was shocked. Wang Anshi told Song Shenzong, "Give six hundred Guan or unwillingly, and then destroy the annexation, as such!"

The Fangtian equal tax law is a powerful tool to inhibit land annexation, "Fangtian" is to re-measure the national land, "equal tax" on the basis of the measurement of "Fangtian", according to the size of the acre of land and the poor fertilizer for the regrading of the field assessment. The Fangtian equalization tax was resolutely resisted by powerful and powerful families and local authorities throughout the country and was eventually introduced only in parts of the north. The five northern provinces account for only 20% of the country's total area, while the fields identified accounted for 54% of the country's tax land, so it can be seen how serious the situation of the big and powerful households hidden land tax leakage. If the policy of equal taxation of square fields is spread across the country, it is bound to deal a fatal blow to the frenzied momentum of land annexation.

The implementation of the Law of Equalization and the Law of Exchange focuses on curbing "mergers" in commercial circulation and breaking the price monopoly formed by financial bigwigs and tycoons, leaving room for the free competition of small traders, while increasing the revenue of the Treasury and easing the burden on the people.

In addition to open source, the new law also emphasizes cost savings. In response to the "redundancy", the reformists merged and reduced the number of states and counties nationwide, abolishing 38 state, military and supervisory bodies and 127 counties. During the five years after Wang Anshi's change of law, the Northern Song finances were in great surplus, the wind of land annexation was hit hard, and the taxation pressure on ordinary farmers was relieved.

Although Wang Anshi did not directly introduce policies to curb land annexation, this may be his political strategy, lest the enemy face too wide, triggering a strong backlash from vested interests, making it difficult to implement the change in law. But his measures hit the nail on the head of the land annexation, and the wealthy group saw it in their eyes, hated it in their hearts, and suffered from it.

Most of the officials in the Northern Song court were "speaking for the poor and working for the rich". Wang Anshi so moved to "speak for the poor, but also to do things for the poor", not only broke the rules of the officialdom, but also directly touched the bureaucrats and gentlemen and the powerful and large households of the vital interests, they have long formed an indestructible community of interests, one loss, one glory and glory, the change of law is bound to provoke the madness of institutional greed backlash.

And Wang Anshi's only backer was the ill-intentioned and unyielding Song Shenzong. The fact that the five-way attack on Xia was defeated shows that the emperor's talent was mediocre, with no ambition to rule and no determination to kill or attack. In the face of the overwhelming criticism of the literati led by Sima Guang, and the open resistance and dark struggles of the bureaucratic powerhouses in the imperial court, and even the enormous pressure from relatives of the emperor, including the Empress Dowager and Empress Dowager, Song Shenzong, who began to worry about the stability of the throne, finally beat a retreat.

Less than five years after the change of law, Wang Anshi stepped down in disgrace. Although the Song dynasty maintained the provisions of the change of law, but lost a large number of change of law ministers of strict supervision, from the central to local officials to see the loss of the change of law faction, where is the mind to seriously implement the details of the change of law. After Wang Anshi stepped down, the law was changed in name only.

The last reform of the Northern Song dynasty to check and balance the powerful and powerful finally failed, and when Sima Guang came to power in 1085 and repealed the new law, the Northern Song dynasty began a larger expansion of greed.

In China's history, there have been few cases in which reforms have finally succeeded because they were not powerful enough to break through the institutional greed that had been entrenched. The root cause of Wang Anshi's failure was that he wanted to challenge not only the few powerful and powerful who had annexed land, but also the greedy desires of various interest groups inside and outside the country. Without the iron and steel will of Qin Xiaogong, it would be difficult to change the law.

Reform and change is, in effect, a second revolution, and one that moves the knife on itself.

The final madness of greed

Cai Jing was called the head of the "Six Thieves of the Northern Song Dynasty", which is an apt comment. Cai Jing started his career as a powerful general who changed the law with Wang Anshi, and was good at seeing the wind and the rudder. Sima Guang, in the "General Guide to the Rule of Qi", had very profoundly defined the gentleman and the villain, he believed that the virtue is greater than the talent is the gentleman, and the talent is greater than the virtue is the villain. However, even people like Sima Guang, who sees through history, have to rely on the little people to do things.

Sima Guang's antipathy to Wang Anshi's change of law was well known to all, and once he came to power, he naturally made a complete restoration. Wang Anshi's reformist cadres were all purged, and Cai Jing was no exception. When Sima Guang repealed the new law, the first thing he started was the "exemption from service law", which made vested interest groups very unhappy. As a matter of urgency, he ordered the reinstatement of the former "law on military service" within five days, which meant that all the implementing rules would have to be completely changed, with a wide range of implications, a wide range of personnel involved, and an apparently unworkable workload to convince and even repress the population, with officials at all levels expressing difficulties in completing them on time. However, Choi Kyung, a former general of the law-breaking faction, completed the restoration of all the "law of the Magistrates" within the deadline. In an instant, Cai Jing was transformed from a cadre general of the new party to an able official of the old party. Sima Guang was impressed by Cai Jing's talent and praised him: If everyone acted according to the law like you, how could there be any law in the world that did not work?

Sima Kuang is very discerning when it comes to reviewing history, but you can't really run a business without a capable man like Cai Jing. However, the Qingliu of the imperial court hated both sides of the head and the rat, Sima Guang was impressed with Cai Jing, but could only temporarily put it aside.

The biggest difference between Wang Anshi and Cai Jing is not in the doing itself, but in the purpose of the doing. Wang Anshi changed the law to help the people through the world and serve the country; while Cai Jing, under the banner of changing the law, even by changing the law, seeks to maximize his own interests. For the villain, it does not matter whether it is right or wrong, nor is there justice or injustice; what is wrong is right and what is not right is also righteous as long as it is good for oneself. None of the villains in history are talented, but in the end, the more talented they are, the more harmful they are to the country.

What stands out most about the villain is his super-sensitivity to opportunity, and often his ability to seize the opportunity to change his destiny. Cai Jing's artistic cultivation was extremely high. When he learned that the new emperor, Song Huizong, was a master of calligraphy and painting, he collected rare painting invitations and exotic stones and treasures in Hangzhou, and took the opportunity of Tong Guan, a close minister of Song Huizong, to go south to find treasures for the emperor. Cai Jing went to great lengths to accompany him around the clock, and he befriended him with pearls and treasures, finally allowing Tong Guan to bring his paintings and calligraphy to the capital. The emperor's impression of Cai Jing was greatly improved by Tong Guan's beautiful words. Later, Emperor Huizong of the Song Dynasty called Cai Jing to the capital and became a confidant of the painting and calligraphy.

With the Emperor's recognition and his own ability, Cai Jing soon became a powerful figure in the court. Bureaucrats, officials, financial magnates, and the powerful and powerful came to their aid, forming the "Caijing Group" represented by Caijing, Wang (embroidery), Tong

Guan, Liang Shi Cheng, Zhu, and Li Yan, with Song Huizong as their general backstage.

In order to serve Song Huizong well and secure the emperor's favor, the Caijing Group spared no expense to satisfy Song Huizong's preferences. He built palaces and gardens, built Daoism everywhere, set up the bureau of Yingbong and the bureau of construction, greatly promoted the battle of Huashizhizang, built the Yanfu Palace and the burgundy, costing huge amounts of money. In order to increase his own political achievements, he started the war in the northwest and used troops; in the north, he joined hands with the Golden State to attack the Liao, which eventually led to the wolf's entry. What Caijing is considering is not the strategy of the country at all, but the maximization of his own interests at the expense of the country.

To do all this, the Caijing Group would need to amass a large amount of money. He took the change of law to the extreme as the successor to Wang Anshi. He greatly changed the law of salt tea, the local salt tea benefits of all to the central government, the poor and exhausted local government in order to cope with Cai Jing's harsh "financial management" assessment indicators, only cruel oppression of ordinary people, finally forced Fang La rebellion, Fang La army is the main force in the bankruptcy of the tea farmers.

At the same time, the Caijing Group, with "Xichengzhao" as its core, set off the second and most insane land annexation spree in the history of feudal China.

After Caijing appointed Li Yan, a close friend of Caijing's, to take charge of the Xicheng Institute, the expansion of the official land became a tool for Caijing's group to "enrich themselves". They planned to annex all the vast civilian lands from Xiangsheng in the south to Mianchi in the west and the Yellow River in the north into "public lands".

They passed legislation to compel the owners to produce the deeds of their land and to pursue their claims one after another until a hundred years ago, when they could not recover the original deeds of several generations ago, the land was confiscated and the acres were re-measured, and the original owners were forced to sign a tenancy agreement with Xicheng and pay the rent thereafter.

In the process of annexation, whenever the Caijing Group was interested in good land, it secretly instructed people to report to the government, falsely claiming that the field was originally wasteland and all the deeds were forged, so the whole county land was "confiscated", arousing public discontent. The local government was ordered to arrest the troublemakers and kill thousands of good people and annex 34,000 hectares of land in Henan's Chushan area alone.

In the process of the Caijing Group's crazy annexation of land, Liang Shanbo was also within the encircled land, which only forced the rebellion against the 108 Liang Shan good Han led by Song Jiang.

The second large-scale land annexation resulted in "the southeastern part of the country being exhausted by Zhu, the northwestern part by Li Yan, and the fundamental wealth of the world being exhausted by Cai Jing and Wang (embroidery)".

With the summer expedition in the northwest, the Liao Expedition in the north, the Fang La Rebellion in the south, and the Song Jiang Rebellion in the east, the imperial court was in a state of disarray and the treasury was depleted. The Caijing Group then began to devalue the currency in a frenzy, enriching the world. As a result, the tea cucumber proliferated and the salt bill plummeted. At the same time, the Caijing Group also carried out a large-scale devaluation of copper and iron coins, small flat money, folded two, when three, when five in a row, the money is still far from enough to spend, so when ten money again, the market panicked, businessmen closed their accounts. When the ten money went bankrupt, the Caijing group pushed the super bad coin-jacketed tin money again, and as a result, public discontent boiled over and the court was shocked. In the end, even Emperor Huizong of the Song Dynasty couldn't bear to see it anymore and had to admit that "the harm of the tin money was even greater than the dang ten".

The fate of the currency, and ultimately of the nation. At the critical inflection point between the rise and fall of empires and dynasties, currency devaluation is the most sensitive observation indicator, which directly reflects the state of fiscal deterioration, indirectly showing the sharpness of the polarization of the rich and the poor, wealth consolidation, tax injustice and social conflicts.

The dramatic devaluation of copper and iron money led to a total collapse of the monetary system in the Northern Song Dynasty. As the first country in the world to invent a paper currency system, could the Northern Song Dynasty change the fate of money by replacing metal money with paper money?

This goes back to the origins of the Northern Song paper money.

The world's first paper currency

In 965, the Chengdu area, known as the country of Tianfu, came under the territory of the Northern Song Dynasty after more than half a century of five generations and ten states. After more than 30 years of peace and stability, the formerly prolific Chengdu region has reemerged as the commercial center of western China, second only to the world's two most prosperous regions, Zhejiang and Zhejiang.

However, the rapid economic development of Sichuan at the time was faced with an increasingly difficult trade bottleneck, a currency dilemma.

There is a severe shortage of copper money in Sichuan, and market transactions rely mainly on the extremely inconvenient iron money. A piece of silk sold for 2,000 iron dollars at market price, weighing 130 pounds, and to buy a few pieces of silk one had to pull a wagon to carry the money. At that time, the government stipulated that one copper coin for 10 iron coins and one slab of copper coin weighing about 5 catties would have the purchasing power of 65 catties of iron coin. Jiangsu and Zhejiang people carry 5 pounds of copper money can be casually wandering the streets, while Chengdu people have to carry 65 pounds of iron money "heavy march".

The people of Chengdu were forced to do nothing and came up with a world class financial innovation, the world's first paper currency, the Jiaotzu, which appeared around 1000 years ago.

The world's first paper currency, the Jiaotzu (later changed to the government, and at the end of the Northern Song Dynasty changed its name to Qian Yin)

At that time, 16 wealthy businessmen in the Chengdu area got together to discuss: why are we so stupid, to run around carrying heavy iron money to do business, we might as well put the iron money in the warehouse, using "receipts" for transactions is not simple? Everyone shouted in unison. Sixteen wealthy merchants then agreed to print paper receipts of equal size and material, with seals on the front and back of the house and tree figures, each of which was stamped. In order to prevent forgery, a "password", which can only be identified by each other, has been added, i.e., "Zhu Mo made a mistake and thought it was a private record". The printed delivery is like a receipt, with the amount left vacant, temporarily re-filled.

These 16 wealthy businessmen were called "Jiaotzi households" and became the "Jiaotzi bankers" in Sichuan.

In this way, 16 rich merchants of large and small customers, just in the various branches of the household of the delivery of heavy iron money, the shop staff to verify the amount of iron money in the delivery of the amount of iron money, and then the merchants can get a light iron money receipts, shopping around to purchase it. No matter how far away you are in the areas covered by the 16 major Kotoko branches, the million-kwan-class Kotoko can travel without any hindrance. A person who holds a handover can go to a handover house at any time and ask for the money to be exchanged for iron money in kind, and the handover house immediately cashes it without even frowning, except that a "printing fee" of 30 yen, or roughly 3% of the handling fee, is charged.

At this time, the trade in the Chengdu area was already highly developed, commercial credit was widespread, and the 16 trading households had business dealings with each other, credit trading was also a common occurrence, when their customers carried out large transactions, often completed by funds transfer, and finally by the trading households to clear the difference on a daily basis, only the balance of the iron money needed to be transported between the trading households, transaction costs were greatly reduced.

The iron money warehouse of the 16 large Jiaotzu households constitutes the iron money reserve warehouse in Chengdu, and it is a reserve warehouse of 100% of the iron money for one Jiaotzu. The PTIs were as bullish as JPMorgan Chase and HSBC today, and their iron-money warehouses were like the vaults of the US COMEX today, made up of various warehouses together. Every day, each family had to report to the head of the family on the amount of iron money in stock and the amount of money issued by the family, and the head even had to report to the government.

Such a complete system of currency issuance was an epoch-making revolution in the world's financial history, and the world's first paper money was born, which predated Western paper money by six or seven hundred years!

The emergence of the Jiaotongzi, reducing the cost of transporting iron money in market transactions to nearly zero; the reputable 16 wealthy merchants joint insurance mechanism, which in turn makes the credit risk of Jiaotongzi almost negligible; the significant decline in transaction costs, bringing unprecedented economic and trade prosperity in Sichuan region. Every year in Sichuan silk tea, rice and wheat will be ripe, the merchants carrying lightweight turn to the countryside, go more remote, travel lighter, the trade network spread more open, the circulation of materials is greater, cheaper prices.

Everything is so perfect!

After just over 20 years, Koshiko began to change its flavor. Human greed, especially the greed of the Kotoko bankers as a group, began to quietly eat away at Kotoko's credit.

If you think about it in a different way, if you have the right to distribute the sons, and there is no outside supervision, and you quietly print more sons, or fill in a few more numbers, who will know? After all, only about 1/3 of the people who hold a handicap will come to exchange iron money, people are afraid of trouble, secondly, they believe in the credit of the handicap household, and thirdly, they have used paper money for a long time and have gotten used to this convenience.

Every night, when the families look at the piles of iron money lying idle in the warehouse, it is like a cat scratching the itch, if you move the pen, tomorrow you can buy the neighbor's mansion in your own name, and the day after tomorrow you can buy hundreds of acres of good land in your old home, as well as gold, silver and jewels, jade agate, can easily get their own home. Maybe the Kotoko-chan struggled for half a day this evening, or forget it, credibility is more important. But if you think about it for half a night, for more than 20 years, it's a life sentence of mental torture.

Greed eventually prevails.

When a family begins to reap huge benefits by quietly increasing the number of children, then how can other families not learn? They too were tortured by the same temptation for over 20 years. When groups of interlocutors form interest groups, they can cover for each other while befriending officials to keep the government from interfering with interlocutor issues. As long as there is no mess, the government is happy to be free.

Finally, the sub-bankers found that printing money was far more profitable than risking their lives in the morning, and that the great temptation to go to jail for nothing could not be resisted.

So did the Junzi bankers of the Northern Song Dynasty 1000 years ago, so did the goldsmith bankers of the West 300 years ago, and so do the bankers of Wall Street now.

After more than 20 years of successful operation in the Sichuan region, the problem of flooding with cross-cuts is becoming more and more apparent. The people who hold the crossover are not stupid, they are just half a beat slower to react due to information asymmetry. When doubt and fear began to permeate the market, the credit cost of the transaction skyrocketed. As a result, things finally got big, and a large number of customers took the money to squeeze the money to the account, bankers closed the door, some even carried gold and silver and softness away from home. "Or people came to ask for money, gathered to get the seal of the head, closed the door without coming out, or even gathered in a crowd of quarrels", although after mediation by the government, the households "could not pay the burden and several lawsuits". Finally, the Chengdu government is worried about the collapse of the financial order, and has demanded that the subcontractors close down their businesses and sell their assets to pay off their debts.

After more than 20 years of indifference, the government finally saw that the "financial innovation" of paper money can bring such great benefits. So, the government of Chengdu went to the imperial court and said that it was a good thing for the people to have their own money, and that it was a good thing for them to have their own money.

In November 1023, the 64th anniversary of the founding of the Northern Song Dynasty, Song Renzong approved the establishment of the "Yizhou Jiaozuo", officially launched the first sovereign credit currency in human history.

Sovereign credit, greed as usual

Strictly speaking, the Northern Song government-run jiaozi was not a purely sovereign credit currency, because the government-run jiaozi could exchange iron money at any time, which can be said to be an early version of the Bank of England in 1694, but not the gold standard, but the "iron standard".

The government office of the Jiaotongzi has made a sovereign monetary kingly move, starting with the five chapters of the law between the government and the Sichuan people.

1. The printing of banknote masters by the government must be strictly controlled, with the "Yizhou Jiaozi Service" responsible for printing banknotes and the Yizhou Observer Mission responsible for supervising, exercising mutual checks and balances to ensure justice, fairness and openness.

2. The accounts of the issuance of sons and daughters shall be kept strictly and every sons and daughters issued, from 1 Guan to 10 Guan, shall be registered in full and sealed by the Ombudsman for inspection.

3. Recovered sons are purchased and sold on the issue books and then immediately destroyed.

4. The issuance of sons and daughters must be subject to a reserve for exchange.

5. Every two years, a new replacement will be issued.

The first government-run Jiaozi was grandly launched in November 1023, and a total of 125,630,340 Guan notes were issued, with a reserve of 360,000 Guan in iron money and a reserve ratio of 28.7%. The main area of circulation is restricted to the Sichuan region, while the rest of the country, still dominated by the circulation of copper money.

Obviously, the level of management and social credibility of the government-run consortium far exceeds that of the private consortium. In order to further improve the convenience of the Jiaozi, the government lowered the value of the Jiaozi from 5 and 10 Guan to 500 and 1 Guan banknotes in small denominations in 1069, with 40% and 60% respectively. Not only that, the government also allows the people to pay various taxes, such as Wang Anshi's change of law during the Qingmiao money, free service money can be used to pay for the Jiaotzi. At the same time, the Jiaotzu can also be used to pay the official government for salt tea wine franchise fees, merchants' customs clearance fees, bridge crossing fees, business taxes and other circulation links of taxes, the official government also accept the Jiaotzu to pay. As a result, all strata of Sichuan are not happy to use the Jiaotzu.

Of course, the most fundamental reason for the popularity of Kotoko is that the government maintains an adequate reserve. If the value of the slave is too high, the government will immediately issue more slave to suppress the price. This is exactly the same principle that governed the Bank of England's control of the value of the pound through gold buying and selling during the gold standard era. In fact, the "Ishu Jokko Misa" was the equivalent of the central bank of the iron money circulation area of the Northern Song Dynasty.

For 54 years, from 1023 to 1077, the value of the government-run handover was highly stable, and at times there was even competition from all sectors of society to hold paper money rather than carry iron money. In order to get 1 Guan paper money, Chengdu people were even willing to pay 1 Guan and 100 iron money, the paper money actually appeared a premium price. The British pound during the heyday of the British Empire and the American Empire's post-World War II dollar, there was also a time when the pound and dollar notes were more sought after than gold.

Confidence is more important than gold, and the key to maintaining confidence in paper money is that the issuer of the paper currency must value credibility above life. Unfortunately, the private sector cannot do it, nor can the government.

The first quiet breach of the contract by the official office of Jiaozi occurred in 1044, followed by another breach in 1047 and 1051, due to the war with Xixia.

In 1040–1042, Emperor Yuan Hao of Western Xia personally led a large army against the Northern Song Dynasty and launched three battles: Sanchuankou, Haoshuichuan and Dingchuan, and annihilated the main force of the Song Dynasty with more than 40,000 men. In order to strengthen the strength of the army in the northwest, the Northern Song imperial court urgently mobilized the military, deployed more than 200,000 troops on the northwest front, a large number of military supplies to the northwest continuously gathered.

After the merchants transported the grain to the northwest, the local government could not get enough cash or salt money to pay for it, so the imperial court asked the "Yizhou Jiaotzu Service" in Chengdu to print 600,000 guangs of paper money and urgently transport it to Shaanxi to pay the merchants. However, this batch was not withdrawn at the time of the replacement issue.

This is the first time that the number of copies issued and the circulation of a delivery child have exceeded the legal limit!

From 1023 to 1044, but over 20 years later, both the government and the private sector began to default quietly. However, in the early stages of the default, the size of the additional delivery was not obvious, the market did not notice, so prices did not change significantly. But once a default has occurred, the issuer's moral bottom line has disintegrated and all that is left is the growing desire for greed.

In 1069, Wang Anshi changed the law, in order to increase the revenue, in the paper currency system, adopted the "two parallel" approach, which should have been two years out of circulation of the Jiaotzi and the new Jiaotzi parallel to the market, which is equivalent to the circulation of paper currency over-issued one times.

From 1077 onwards, the value of the kokozuna depreciated significantly, with the market only being able to exchange the kokozuna for 940 to 960 yen, a depreciation of 4% to 6%. Although only in circulation in Sichuan, the devaluation trend in the Jiaotongzi reflects to some extent the general currency devaluation trend in the country.

After the failure of Wang Anshi's change of law, domestic conflicts became increasingly acute. Song Shenzong misjudged the internal and external situation of the dynasty and launched a massive five-way offensive against Western Xia in 1081–1082, which resulted in two unprecedented defeats in Lingzhou and Yongle, with losses of over 600,000 personnel and untold military expenditures. Song Shenzong heard that the dynasty wept and lost its voice, the ministers "do not dare to look up". Three years later, Song Shenzong was exhausted and died.

The war had failed, the country was in disrepair, its finances were in dire straits, the economy was in decline, and the gap between rich and poor was wide. By 1086, the value of the crossover had depreciated by more than 10%. At this time, the government had gradually lost confidence in maintaining the stability of the currency value of the handover, and there was a shortage of money everywhere, and only printing money came the fastest. The greed of the government has crossed the tipping point, and Jiaotzu is beginning to enter the fast lane of currency devaluation.

Cai Jing came to power in 1100 when Emperor Huizong of the Song Dynasty came to the throne. In 1105, Cai Jing's campaign to escalate the Northwest War to demonstrate his political achievements was nearing financial collapse in the Northern Song Dynasty.

The expansion of the war required huge military expenditures, and the Caijing power group began to use the idea of over-issuing paper money in order to cover the financial deficit. However, since the circulation of the sons was limited to the Sichuan region, this greatly hindered the effect of enrichment. Therefore, the Tsai Kyung Group is committed to promoting the Jiaotzu nationwide, "making it more costly to introduce new types of printing. After that, the name was changed to "Qian Yin", and the expenses of the Northwest soldiers were all met by printing bills, and the volume of paper currency issued began to rise sharply. Although the Caijing Group had exhausted all means, the "money" could only circulate in Sichuan and the northwest region, and the rest of the country resolutely refused to do so.

In 1105, the circulation of the money cited as high as 265,600,000 Guan, that year an additional 5.4 million Guan, to 1107, again increased 554,000 Guan, and "two parallel" together with circulation, the total circulation of paper money is 40 times higher than in 1023 when the official handover officially began! When the money lenders changed, the new money lenders received the old money lenders at 1:4, which means a one-time devaluation of 75%! At the same time, the government also eliminated the reserve for the issuance of paper money.

Public confidence in paper money began to crumble, followed by the "sovereign credit" of the government.

After 1110 years, 1 Guan paper currency is not even worth 100 iron money in the eyes of Chengdu people, and the paper currency system is on the verge of bankruptcy.

In 1127, the Northern Song Dynasty perished.

Expound

Water can carry a boat and overturn it, and so is human nature. Moderate greed can stimulate the economy, while excessive greed can destroy it.

The reason why a healthy person may also have cancer cells in their body that do not develop into cancer is that the body's own immune system is effective in suppressing the growth of cancer cells. Once cancer cells break through the immune system's defenses and begin to divide and multiply in large numbers, they will frantically rob other normal cells of their nutrients, leading to organ failure and ultimately life threatening.

When a few in society continue to expand their wealth map to the point of swaying policy and changing laws, it will stimulate them to develop a greater desire to take possession of more of the society's wealth. This anomaly in the distribution of wealth inevitably undermines the ability of the majority of society to access economic resources to develop itself, thereby combating the wealth creativity of society. When the wealth of the few reaches a very high proportion, the majority will lose the basis of wealth creation, the economy will gradually lose its vitality, politics will begin to darken, and people will lose their dreams. Ultimately, revolution and insurrection will come quickly when a few, under the protection of law and the State apparatus, wantonly trample on the interests of the majority and wildly divide the wealth of society.

The reason greed is called human nature is because it is impossible to change. Human knowledge can accumulate, production can advance, technology can be invented, matter can be improved, life can be enhanced, but human greed never evolves.

Not only in the West, but also in China; not only in the past, but equally so now. How similar is the path, process, and outcome of the Northern Song Dynasty's capitulation to the collapse of the Roman Empire! The history is strikingly similar, stemming from the strikingly similar humanity behind it!

The regime of the Northern Song dynasty died not from military but from popular sentiment; the state power of the Northern Song dynasty collapsed not from finance but from greed.

When greed flourishes, there will be annexation; when land is concentrated, there will be taxation; when the national treasury is empty, there will be a depreciation of the currency; when the people's strength is depleted, there will be internal strife and external trouble!

The observation of money reveals greed, and the observation of mergers reveals sorrow.

Those who are politicians must not be cautious in their thinking.

CHAPTER IX

What's not the Chinese Dream?

The first eight chapters of the book focus on a typical sample of civilizations in three historical periods, the Roman Dream, the Song Dynasty Dream, and the American Dream, all of which were once glorious and desirable, about 1,000 years apart from each other, geographically spanning Europe, Asia, and the Americas, and which represent the three monetary economic high points of human civilization.

The "Roman Dream" and the "Song Dynasty Dream" have long since vanished, and now the "American Dream" has broken its wings. There are no long-lasting empires or dynasties in history, and the metabolism of civilization always alternates and never stops.

A new civilization is bound to awaken new dreams, new dreams destined to create new glories.

"The Chinese Dream" is a fascinating realm, which has been elaborated, interpreted and envisioned from various perspectives, and will be added more and richer in the future through practice.

However, the road from the beautiful dream to the ultimate success is not the way flowers bloom and dances, but the rapids are dense and dangerous. History is the best teacher of how to avoid going astray, or getting into danger.

This chapter will try to define the options that should be avoided for the Chinese Dream in the light of the lessons of the fragmentation of the Roman Dream, the Song Dynasty Dream and the American Dream.

If China can successfully avoid the lessons of history, then the "China Dream" will no longer be just a dream.

"The Roman Dream," "The Song Dream," "The American Dream" is broken

There is no doubt that Rome, the Northern Song, and the United States have all made remarkable contributions to human civilization, 50 years of Roman civilization at its peak, 1050 years of Northern Song prosperity in its prime, and 1950 years of American national strength in their respective eras, and their peoples have all had wonderful dreams.

However, when things go badly, they go badly, and the most brilliant moments often breed the shadow of decline. Land annexation and division of wealth due to unbridled greed will always be a major factor in the ruin of the country.

In the history of Rome, the Northern Song, and the United States, there have been two serious land annexations or annexations of wealth.

The first major land annexation in Roman history began with the outbreak of the First Punic War (264 B.C.) and culminated with the end of the Third Punic War (146 B.C.). The Roman peasants were forced to leave their land for long periods of war, their economy became bankrupt with heavy casualties, and the powerful and wealthy groups took advantage of the situation to plunder the peasants' land, creating a serious division between rich and poor in Rome.

The reason why the Roman legions were invincible and invincible, plundering thousands of miles of land and destroying countless countries, was that the Italian peasants were the core strength of the Roman legions. They defended their land, protected their property, shared the rights of the law, loved their country and honor, and they were an impregnable community of interest with the Roman state.

However, the excessive greed of the powerful and wealthy groups destroyed the very foundations of the Roman republic. The failure of the Reformation of the Gracchus-Brothers (133 BC-121 BC) meant that the "immune system" of the Roman republic was crippled and the "cancerous cells" of greed of the powerful and rich were spreading in full force. Ultimately, what ushered in Rome was a century of bloody civil war and the total collapse of the republican system.

The first wave of land annexation in the Northern Song Dynasty began in the latter part of the reign of Emperor Zhenzong of Song (997-1022) and reached a climax in the latter part of the reign of Emperor Renzong of Song (1023–1063). The state's land policy of "not suppressing annexation" stimulated the powerful and wealthy groups to "occupy the land with their strength" or "buy the land with their money", which eventually led to the 6% of the powerful and powerful households in the Northern Song Dynasty to monopolize 60%-70% of the country.

The economic prosperity of the Northern Song dynasty stemmed from the great progress in productivity, the dramatic increase in iron production, the leap in the quality of agricultural tools, the great increase in agricultural efficiency and food production, which triggered the convergence of the three currents of urbanization, commodification and monetization, creating an urban middle class of unprecedented wealth. They are full of freedom of choice, they have a more professional division of labour, they have a strong incentive to innovate, they receive richer social information, they enjoy a more independent mind and culture, and they are full of better dreams.

However, uncontrolled land annexation has resulted in a gross inequity in the tax burden, and the huge financial burden of the country is weighing more and more heavily on the heads of ordinary people. Fiscal deficits induce currency devaluation, which exacerbates land annexation, and land annexation leads to greater fiscal deficits. Economic vitality was stifled, popular dreams were dashed, and the failure of the Wang Anshu Change of Law (1069–1076) meant that the decline of the Northern Song state was irreversible.

The first great annexation of wealth in American history began with World War I (1914) and peaked in 1927. War dividends and dollar dividends have enriched the 10 per cent of the wealthy in the United States, with the rapid expansion of American industrial production capacity and heavy reliance on the European market, while European countries generally rely on dollar credit to repay American war loans and sustain national economic recovery. But American capital interests, in order to make high profits, prevented European goods from being exported to the American market through high tariffs, causing Europe's dollar-indebted countries to over-inflate their debt and inevitably fall into default.

The United States has similarly adopted a policy of "non-merger control" over the distribution of wealth, with the 10 per cent of the wealthy group sweeping half of the national income, and the 90 per cent of the general population deprived of the ability to sustainably expand consumption and the domestic market sluggish. When Europe went into default on its dollar debt, the external market in the United States collapsed while the domestic market could not digest the enormous excess productivity, and with it, the return on investment in American industry deteriorated, bank loans defaulted, financial markets collapsed, factories closed, banks failed and workers lost their jobs. Ultimately, the Great Depression of the 1930s kicked off the bloody Second World War.

The first major mergers of the powerful and wealthy groups in Rome, the Northern Song and the United States always came at the cost of bloodshed, war or a great economic depression.

The climax of the second mega-merger, and often the last insanity of the empire, will destroy not only the economy but also society and the hearts and minds of the people, and lead to the dire consequences of the collapse of the empire, the overthrow of the dynasty and the decline of civilization.

The policy of urbanization that began during the Roman Empire was not the result of natural economic development, but of political and military necessity for domination. Extremely distorted and ultra-low food prices not only brutally plundered the agricultural fruits of Egypt, Africa, Sicily and Spain, but also simultaneously destroyed Italy's grain economy and set in motion a second wave of mega-land annexation.

In this annexation, the imperial aristocracy and wealthy groups not only enriched the land in Italy, but also, in an even more unscrupulous way, gobbled up large tracts of land in the imperial provinces, as in the case of the six mega-owners of Africa, who annexed 50 per cent of the territory, with a concentration of land far greater than in the Republican era.

The hordes of bankrupt peasants in the empire were driven to the cities, where they became dangerous vagrants, mingling with more resentful slaves, and the cities of the Roman Empire were filled with dry wood for vengeance and the flames of resentment. In order to stabilize the urban drifters, the Reich had to supply them with food free of charge, which led to cheaper cereals, a bankrupt agricultural economy and severe suffering for the people of the provinces. Land annexation was in full swing throughout the Empire, and explosive social conflicts were on the verge of breaking out.

Where there is oppression, there is resistance, and the deeper the oppression, the stronger the resistance. As the frontier barbarians raced to revolt and internal stragglers rose up, the Empire had to maintain a large standing army, ready to conquer and suppress. Not only did the war drag down the finances, but it was also extremely short of troops at a time when the empire had no free peasant class, and the Roman legions had to recruit urban vagrants in large numbers, filled with hatred for the wealthy groups, and the nature of the Roman legions gradually evolved into mob groups.

In the repeated battles between the emperor and the wealthy group represented by the Senate, the emperor increasingly relied on the support of the military, while the mob group saw an awakening to power. When the Emperor and the Senate had to resort to force to settle their dispute, the wildness of the army seized up. Regardless of who won or lost the civil war, the armies on both sides began a frenzy of slaughter against the city's wealthy cliques, with the empire's patriarchs, noblemen, prominent clansmen, and tycoons almost slaughtered. The wealthy groups have paid a heavy price for their extreme greed, and the elite of the empire have since been so badly wounded that they can no longer regain their strength.

The Roman emperor was no longer the commander-in-chief of the army, but a hostage to a mob group. The history of Rome since then has been one of regicide and usurpation of the throne, foreign and civil wars, economic deprivation and depletion, until the final collapse of the Empire.

The second land annexation in the Northern Song Dynasty was also a prelude to the destruction of the dynasty, and when Emperor Huizong of the Song Dynasty came to power in 1100 and reused the Caijing Group, the land annexation went into a frenzied phase. The result of the second mega land annexation was that "the wealth of the southeast was exhausted by Zhu Zhou, the wealth of the northwest was trapped by Li Yan, and the fundamental wealth of the world was exhausted by Cai Jing and Wang (embroidery)".

With the depletion of the Northern Song finances, the Caijing Group even sacrificed the currency devaluation of serious legal instruments, as a result of the land annexation, heavy taxes and currency devaluation of the three big mountains of oppression, provoked the Fangla uprising, Liang Shanbo rebellion of civil unrest, which led to the Western Xia, Liao and Jin foreign trouble, the Northern Song was finally destroyed by the Jin people.

The second land annexation took just over 20 years to bury the "Song Dynasty Dream" of 150 years of prosperity and wealth.

The Second Wealth Merger in the United States

The aftermath of America's first annexation of wealth was the Great Depression and war. The outbreak of World War II shifted more than 10 million of the U.S. workforce into the war system, not only solving a decade-long unemployment trap, but forcing a massive tilt of government finances toward the general population. Millions of poor children went to war in Eurasia, and after the war they received huge welfare benefits such as college tuition, vocational training, priority employment, veterans' health care, and a fairer chance to compete. In a word, "World War II" eased the divide between rich and poor in the United States.

From the early 1940s to the early 1980s, the distribution of wealth in the United States was largely rational, with the 10 percent of the wealthy taking about 33 percent of national income and the 90 percent of the middle class sharing the remaining 67 percent. The country's tax burden is also roughly balanced, fiscal health is still healthy, the dollar is still up for grabs under the gold standard, the asset bubble is almost extinct, social class harmony is widespread, and the United States has experienced the golden age of 40 years of postwar economic prosperity.

However, the powerful and wealthy groups in the United States were not satisfied with such a proportional distribution of wealth, and they strongly demanded a greater share of it, which was the wave of "neoliberalism" that emerged in the United States in the mid-to-late 1970s, when the wealthy groups strongly demanded a "second American revolution".

In less than 30 years, the second wealth merger in the United States has worsened to the level of 1927, and the financial crisis of 2008 has exposed the inevitable economic collapse of 50 per cent of national income by 10 per cent of the wealthy groups, exactly as it was in 1927. The "Occupy Wall Street" movement in the United States of America showed sharp social class antagonism.

The U.S. government has also tried hard to correct the system, President Obama said more than once to "declare war" on the division of the rich and the poor, and Congress has been working hard on legislation to create the "Dodd-Frank Act", which aims to curb the pace of wealth consolidation by the Wall Street tycoons. The result is that the bill has been tampered with by the rich and powerful, with a huge and complex content, with numerous obstacles to the core provisions, with "exceptions" to key rules, with no time frame for implementation, and with a worsening gap between the rich and the poor.

Obama's financial reforms have largely failed, and another major initiative, health care reform, has evaded the mark.

The health care bill, of which Obama is proud, does nothing more than force 50 million poor people without health insurance to contribute to insurance companies, and does nothing at all to touch the root of the absurdly high cost of health care. The trio of insurance companies, pharmaceutical companies, and the health care system are no less super greedy than the bigwigs of Wall Street, in whose eyes the human body is an asset, a super ATM that generates cash flow in a constant stream.

Pharmaceutical companies and the food industry have joined forces to make a fortune together, with the food industry supplying high-calorie, high-fat junk food like McDonald's and KFC, leading to a deterioration in public health; Coca-Cola and Pepsi, carbonated beverages that hurt the stomach and ruin teeth, are prevalent; and genetically modified foods, which are ubiquitous, are also dangerous. When the body is sick, the business of the pharmaceutical company comes, especially the high blood lipid, high blood pressure, high blood sugar such chronic disease is the best, life does not stop, take more than medicine, cash flow constantly, every patient has become a long-term "excellent asset" of the pharmaceutical company.

The overall price of prescription drugs in the United States is more than 50 percent higher than similar drugs in Europe and Japan because of the laissez-faire policy of the U.S. government on drug prices, while the vast majority of developed countries regulate the pricing of pharmaceutical companies and limit their profit margins to a certain level.

Not only is medicine expensive in the US, it's even more expensive to see a doctor.

Everyone knows that health care costs in the US are ridiculously high and outrageously expensive, but the February 2013 Time magazine article "Bitter Pills: Why Medical Bills Are Hurting Us" was an eye-opener to read: a fall, a 15-minute visit to the doctor, and a $9,400 bill at the end; an outpatient visit to the hospital with back pain and an $87,000 bill; if it was a serious case like cancer, the bill would be $900,000!

The pricing system in U.S. hospitals is almost entirely black box, directly contributing to the failure of market price discovery. Physicians, while not involved in pricing, show a strong preference for drugs and medical devices, and the kickbacks these companies give doctors are equally smack in the face. "We found that between 2002 and 2006, the four pharmaceutical companies that controlled 75 percent of the artificial hip and knee market paid out more than $800 million to physician consultants under about 6,500 consulting agreements," the Times disclosed. Hospitals charge patients for a variety of drugs, medical equipment, blood tests, CT, surgical gowns and other fees, basically more than 10 times the transparent market price. The so-called nonprofit hospitals in the U.S. have become the largest for-profit institutions, with hospital executives earning millions of dollars a year, catching up with Wall Street and far exceeding the CEO class.

Although doctors may earn up to $200,000 or more, they are working for insurance companies because they have to buy medical malpractice insurance, which costs $80,000 to $140,000 per year, accounting for 40 to 70 percent of doctors' annual salaries. America's first concern for doctors is not how to cure their patients, but to prevent them from being sued by their patients, and one lawsuit down the line can bankrupt the doctor. It is common to see attorneys wandering around the hospital looking for a chance to make a fortune from a medical malpractice lawsuit. As a result, doctors, knowing the cause of the patient's illness, still ask the patient to undergo all kinds of unnecessary tests, take the most expensive drugs, and follow a plan that is ineffective but correct, in order to prevent future problems. If the doctor doesn't treat according to the insurance company's standard process, standard prescriptions and standard doses, all consequences are on themselves.

In the entire medical industry chain, pharmaceuticals, devices and other companies, can not be subject to any constraints to raise the basic cost of medical care, hospital system groping to take advantage of the opportunity to raise the cost of medical care, insurance companies sit on the ground to raise insurance charges. In such a vicious circle, the United States health care industry consumes 60 per cent of federal revenue, far more than 25 per cent of military spending, and less than 12 per cent of environmental, agricultural, energy, education, transportation, housing, etc., with health care costs being the most significant factor in the huge United States deficit.

The U.S. health care system consumes 18 percent of GDP, more than double that of other developed countries, and the end result is the lowest of all developed countries in terms of life expectancy.

Desperately, the U.S. health care costs as a share of GDP have never declined in 40 years, but have continued to climb higher and higher. Of the $10 trillion in hidden liabilities in the United States, the "contribution" of health care spending is the most prominent and will continue to be so.

America's health care system, increasingly resembling the Roman-era system of charterers and contractors, has become the No. 1 hole in the pockets of taxation for all. Without health care reform, U.S. finances will surely be dragged down.

Obama sees the danger of inflated health care costs going down, just as he sees the greed of Wall Street. He can't move Wall Street, nor can he move the health care system.

The United States Government's laissez-faire policy of "no mergers" in the health care system is at the root of the continuing vicious inflation of health care costs in the United States. The Times commented, "U.S. laws not only block the government from limiting drug prices, but also make the largest buyer (i.e., Medicare) non-negotiable, a permanent gift from Congress to pharmaceutical companies (Congress also accepted their rationale that unrestricted drug prices and profits are a necessary safeguard against R&D risk). Congress has repeatedly prohibited the Centers for Medicare and Medicaid under the U.S. Department of Health and Social Services from negotiating drug prices with drugmakers. Medicare simply determines the average selling price, plus a 6% subsidy." It's a modern American version of the Northern Song merchants' practice of transporting grain to the frontier, with frontier officials overestimating costs, coupled with merchant profits.

Such an absurd policy can only mean that the legal system has failed in the face of greed, and that universal taxation has been hijacked by a few powerful and large corporations.

Obama is afraid to touch the interests of pharmaceutical companies, and even more afraid to touch the cake of insurance companies. He tried to announce the creation of a state-owned insurance company to compete with private insurance companies, but was opposed by both liberals and conservatives, and there was a media outcry, accusing Obama of socialism and even labeling him a Nazi. Some have openly announced their intention to assassinate Obama, even going so far as to bring guns to Obama's campaign rallies, frightening him into rushing back from the proposal and evading the most important key measure to reduce health care costs, leaving health care reform in name only.

Simply put, living in the United States without health insurance is no less than a super-adventure, not returning to poverty due to illness, but going bankrupt with one illness. It is because insurance is so expensive that 50 million people in the U.S. can't afford it, and Obama's health care reform won't lower health care costs and can only continue to subsidize the big and powerful with a universal tax.

Obama's health care reform forces these 50 million people to buy insurance, which is tantamount to once again paying tribute to the big and powerful, and the insurance companies can wake up laughing in their sleep.

For a freelancer earning $50,000 a year without health insurance, buying "Obamacare" would cost up to $7,200 a year, four times the price of regular insurance, with $14,000 out-of-pocket for real visits, and upwards of $20,000 for insurance plus visits, or 60% of after-tax income!

Is this insurance? It's a robbery! Instead of serving the people, it benefits insurance companies, pharmaceutical companies and big hospitals.

If you think it's too expensive, you don't want to participate, okay? No way. "Obamacare" is mandatory insurance, refusal to participate will result in a fine and you will receive a fine bill of up to $4000 per year! If you don't pay, first your driver's license is revoked, which for Americans on wheels is the equivalent of chopping off your legs; if you refuse to pay the fine for 24 consecutive months and you happen to own the property, then your property will be subject to a government claim, which means you could lose your property. If you're ready to sell your home in a fit of rage, I'm sorry, but this accumulated penalty and interest will be deducted by the government first.

Limited visits, unlimited liability. That's what Obamacare is all about.

The financial reform is only a skin deep, and the health care reform is even more of an end in itself. The government is no longer able to reverse the pattern of wealth distribution, so the myth of systemic error correction in the United States can go away!

The two major reforms of Obama's presidency were not so much about curbing wealth consolidation as they were about fueling the greed of the powerful and powerful to carve up the wealth of society. The president of civilian origin, but not the aid of the common people, has neither the courage of the brothers of Gracchus nor the character of Wang Anshi.

The second wave of wealth mergers in the United States, which began in the early 1980s, continues to gain momentum after the financial crisis of 2008, and all reforms under normal conditions can no longer stop the pace of wealth mergers, the contradictions between rich and poor will become more acute, and the intensity of the next financial crisis will escalate.

If history is anything to go by, the United States is in a vicious cycle of wealth consolidation, tax injustice, fiscal deficits, currency devaluation, and class antagonism.

What is not the Chinese Dream?

All history is modern history, with Rome, Northern Song, and the United States each representing three waves of the monetary economic explosion that, despite being thousands of years apart and spanning thousands of miles, present fairly similar logical cues. Along this trail, one can not only look at the past and analyze the present, but also look far into the future.

Today's "Chinese Dream" theory should be placed under the historical reference system in order to present a more complete outline.

The prerequisite for knowing what the "Chinese Dream" is is to know what should not be the "Chinese Dream" in the first place.

A society where the powerful are in power and the elite are greedy should not be the "Chinese Dream"!

A society in which wealth is annexed and the rich and the poor are divided should not be the "Chinese Dream"!

A society with an unfair tax burden and fiscal deficit should not be the "Chinese Dream"!

A society with devalued currencies and inflated assets should not be the "Chinese Dream"!

A society with depleted people's power and internal and external problems should not be the "Chinese Dream"!

Are there any big and powerful people in China? Not currently, but possibly in the future.

In 1949, when New China was established, the gap between the rich and the poor was basically eliminated in Chinese society over the next 30 years, which was the first time in China's history that the practice of equalizing the rich and the poor on a very large scale, equivalent to a "zero" distribution of wealth throughout China.

Does equalizing the rich and the poor necessarily mean a prosperous and strong society? The answer is no.

Throughout history, any country, any nation, any era, any system, society has presented the typical pyramidal structure of the elite 10 per cent at the top of society and the ordinary 90 per cent of the population at the bottom, and only this structure can guarantee social stability. Throughout the history of human civilization, there have been attempts to achieve a fully egalitarian society in every era, but this goal has never really been achieved, and even if it appears briefly, it cannot be sustained steadily.

Since everyone has different diligence, different personality, different qualifications, different circumstances and different opportunities, the final gap is a logical necessity. In any society, there will always be around 10% of hardworking and intelligent people who can always rise to prominence quickly in society as long as policies don't suppress their work ethic. Some of them may have taken advantage of their parents, family and social relationships, but more of them relied mainly on their own hard work and intelligence to achieve a superior social status and a large amount of wealth. They are the creators of wealth and the agents of social progress. Any country that suppresses the enthusiasm of this social elite cannot have vitality, drive, opportunity and dreams.

Deng Xiaoping's policy of "letting the few get rich first" has effectively mobilized the great enthusiasm of China's social elite for wealth creation, most of whom dare to be first in the world, take the risk of discouraging ordinary people, use their brains, break conventions and innovate, and obtain the first bucket of gold for career development. Their actions had a clear "eel effect" in a society that had been dull for a long time, stimulating more people to develop the ambition to create wealth, leading to a great leap forward in wealth for the whole society and fundamentally changing the face of poverty in China.

Deng Xiaoping proposed the policy of "Let the few get rich first"

Since 10% of the social elite have created a great deal of wealth primarily through their own efforts, they rightfully deserve the encouragement and protection of society to have a larger share of the wealth-distribution cake, both for the purpose of rewarding hard work and punishing laziness, and as a means of stimulating wealth creation.

The post-1979 reform and opening up of China's society has brought about a return to the historical norm; more than 30 years of rapid economic development have brought about explosive growth in wealth, the re-emergence of social strata, the emergence of powerful and powerful households, the gradual emergence of interest groups, and a significant widening of the gap between rich and poor. This is a critical turning point in society, where on the one hand economic prosperity brings more opportunities and on the other hand wealth mergers are beginning to take shape.

In periods of general prosperity where productivity increases rapidly, the rich get rich faster, the common man gets rich slower, and society's attitude toward the rich is mainly one of envy; when productivity growth slows significantly and prosperity is limited to some regions or industries, the wealth of the rich tends to grow faster, while the real income growth of the common man appears to stagnate, at which point the social mood is one of envy toward the rich; when productivity growth stagnates and the rich begin to reap more amazing benefits through wealth mergers rather than wealth creation, the spirit of enterprise will alienate into excessive greed, the income of the common man appears to decline, and society will generally hate the rich.

The so-called envy, jealousy, and hatred of the rich do not actually occur simultaneously, but unfold gradually. For most of the 1980s and 1990s, the dominant social attitude towards the rich was one of envy; from 2000 until the financial crisis, the element of envy gradually increased; and since 2009, the term "hatred of the rich" has begun to appear with significantly higher frequency, reflecting a sideways shift in the quality and scope of economic growth in China.

Generally speaking, during periods of general prosperity, the rich can acquire wealth in higher proportions, when society is more tolerant; during periods of partial prosperity, the rich need to restrain the infinite expansion of greedy desires and endure the normal proportion of wealth distribution; during periods of economic stagnation or recession, the rich must make compromises, which will not only be conducive to social emotional stability and alleviate the intensification of wealth-hating mentality, but at the same time, the increase in income and consumption of ordinary people will bring more long-term benefits to the rich.

The question is, what proportion of the national income should the 10 per cent of the rich have to be just right?

The historian Huang Renyu, in his book Fifteen Years of the Wan Li, complains that the fineness of digital management in Chinese society lags seriously behind that of the West. His point is not wrong, not only historically, but modern China is still far behind the West.

China's statistics department does not have accurate figures on the distribution of wealth in society, and people do not know what percentage of national income is currently held by the richest 0.1 per cent, 1 per cent and 10 per cent of the country's population, nor do they have a clear idea of the extent of the problem of the division between the rich and the poor, let alone historical data for the past 60 or 100 years. Scholars can only speak by feeling, and precise government decision-making can be compromised.

If the historical experience of the Northern Song Dynasty is taken into account, the approximate proportion of wealth distribution is that by the late years of the Song Dynasty, the Northern Song Dynasty's 6 percent group of powerful and wealthy people held 60 to 70 percent of the country's land and swept half of the national income. It was also after the heyday of Song Renzong that the Northern Song Dynasty began to rectify the crisis of wealth division, which was the Wang Anshi Change of Law. The experience of the United States has shown that if the 10 per cent of the wealthy group accounts for more than 50 per cent of national income, the economy is bound to collapse and society will be in crisis.

As it turns out, if the 10 per cent of the wealthy class swept over the 50 per cent threshold of national income, they would be powerful enough to thwart any reform, the institutional mechanisms of correction would fail and the fate of the country would be near the inflection point of prosperity and decline. After the failure of Wang Anshi's change of law, the Northern Song only remained stagnant for 30 years, and with more violent wealth annexation by wealthy conglomerates, the last 20 years or so saw a rapid socio-economic collapse of the Northern Song.

The United States is another real-life example of what is happening, with the 10% of wealthy groups having passed the 50% national income threshold after 2008. Without the outbreak of a massive war or violent social conflict, the system is powerless to correct its mistakes. The failure of Obama's financial reform and health care reform is clear evidence of this argument. With such a wide disparity between the rich and the poor, any hope of economic recovery can only be the illusion of a mirage. Perhaps the U.S. will remain largely stable for another 20–30 years, while the division of wealth will continue to grow irredeemably, until the final stage of dramatic deterioration.

It can be said that the 10 per cent of the wealthy, who account for 50 per cent of the national income, is the tipping point of a country's fortunes, which is no less significant than the agricultural red line of "1.8 billion acres of arable land", and any responsible government must strictly guard against this tipping point. Breaking through this bottom line, greed will alienate into the cancerous cells of society, and no power can stop them from frantically plundering the resources of other cells until the organs fail and life stops.

China should explicitly enshrine the principles and proportions of social wealth distribution in the Constitution. Anything less would not be sufficient to ensure the country's long-term security.

Real estate and wealth distribution

Neoliberalism emphasizes that government must withdraw from the market altogether or it will distort the market economy. Many people mistakenly believe that the market is flat, when in fact, it is always curved.

History has shown that if a government adopts a completely laissez-faire policy towards the economy, whether it is the no-economic policy of the Roman Empire, the "no-compromise" approach of the

Northern Song Dynasty, or the current "deregulation" trend in the United States, the result is an extreme imbalance in the distribution of wealth. The freer the society, the greater the division of wealth, the result of which will not only destroy economic prosperity, but also lead to a reversal of national fortunes.

The entirety of human activity throughout history has been nothing more than the creation and distribution of wealth, from which all other acts have been derived. The theory of how to create wealth efficiently belongs to economics, while the theory of how to distribute wealth rationally belongs to political science, and only political economics, which combines wealth creation and distribution, can see the whole picture of a country's fate.

Government should intervene in the market as little as possible, but must strongly protect the principle of wealth distribution.

The most vivid example is whether the government should regulate house prices or not, and how it should regulate the real estate market.

Market fundamentalism holds that house prices should be determined by market supply and demand, that no matter how high, as long as someone is willing to offer a higher price, it is perfectly reasonable and any government intervention is completely unjustified.

But if one looks at the principle of wealth distribution, the above assertion must be challenged by historical evidence. Is it in line with the market economy that 6% of the Northern Song Dynasty's powerful and powerful landowners held 60% to 70% of the land, and that the six mega-landowners of the Roman Empire owned half of the territory of Africa? The collapse of the Roman Empire and the demise of the Northern Song dynasty have powerfully countered the idea that the market decides everything.

Distorted house prices have created a widespread inequity in the distribution of social wealth throughout the country, with the greater the distortion the larger the city. "House sister" "house uncle" they occupy dozens of hundreds of housing, and they are only the tip of the iceberg exposed, the widespread phenomenon of high house prices and high rents is the root cause of the phenomenon of insufficient circulation, rather than the absolute stock of insufficient.

There is no property tax, which is equivalent to the Northern Song dynasty occupying most of the land without paying taxes, the rich just hold the property and sit and wait for the appreciation, they have no incentive to rent the property, because the rental income does not arouse their interest; they also have no intention to sell the house, because the currency depreciates and the house price will rise, it is more cost-effective to sell late than early. The large number of vacant houses prevalent in Chinese cities is a clear example of this phenomenon. On the issue of the vacancy rate, once again highlighting Huang Renyu's point, the statistics department surprisingly said that it is not clear how high the vacancy rate is! 15%? 20%? 30%? God only knows!

Since the nation's properties are not online, no one knows exactly what the concentration of property ownership is. This is not really a technical problem, but the result of deliberate obstruction by interest groups, and it is already evident that the mechanism of error correction is frequently failing in the real estate sector.

In the future, the national real estate network will be a major initiative that will be a litmus test of the current system's ability to curb greed.

Housing prices are determined by flow, not stock. In a community of 100 homes, it only takes 1 home to sell to determine how much it will sell for the entire community. In the United States, for example, the annual volume of new and existing housing transactions is only 3% to 4% of the total stock of properties, i.e., the flow is 3% to 4% of the stock. A sudden influx of 500,000 new homes into the market would significantly affect the price of 130 million stock properties. If 5 million new buildings were to pop up, US house prices would collapse in an instant. Similarly, on April 12, 2013, Wall Street reversed price expectations for the world's 170,000 tons of gold stocks with a concentrated sell-off of just 400 tons of gold. In fact, the Wall Street media's carpet bombardment of market psychology has severely shaken confidence in the gold market, with 0.3% of the gold stock smashing into the market in an explosive fashion, enough to cause a price collapse. Simply put, the decisive factor in influencing prices is market psychology, and the media is an important tool to influence that psychology. A sudden and violent concentrated sell-off can create overwhelming price pressure and ultimately gain great price influence with very little trading volume.

It was this strategy that Chen Yun used in Shanghai in the early 1950s, defeating in one fell swoop the speculative forces that had dominated the city for decades in a purely market way. In recent years, the government regulates the root of the ineffectiveness of house prices, lies in the ambush war into an encounter war, the quick war into a protracted war, the annihilation war into a consumption war, the market is expected to completely reverse to the other side, limit the purchase of limited loans and other administrative means are exacerbated by the bullish expectations of house prices.

Property tax is not only an important tool to correct the inequitable distribution of wealth, it is also a necessary path to fiscal sustainability. In order to protect the interests of the vast majority of the general population, property taxes will be completely exempted for the first family home; the second home will be subject to a symbolic levy of 0.1 per cent, which will cover more than 90 per cent of the urban population; the third home will be subject to a general market-based rate of 1 per cent; and the third home will be subject to a punitive multiplier for more than three purely speculative units.

The mere claim of a property tax rollout will have a shocking effect on home prices, much like the Fed playing the psychological game of QE exit. Most homebuyers are buying on expectations, and if price expectations are reversed, a large amount of purchasing power will immediately disappear in favor of a wait-and-see approach. More importantly, have more than 3 sets of "house sister" and "house uncle" they face disastrous tax rate will immediately vacant property into the market, which is equivalent to "four – one two" gold market reappearance, psychological shock and incremental property pressure at the same time burst out, property supply and demand contradiction will be a huge change.

If the implementation of the property tax forces 5% of the vacant housing concentrated into the market, its price destruction force will be no less than a magnitude 8 earthquake; if 10% of the vacant housing mass into the market, except for a few people who are just in need to dare to move against the market, will scare off all the rest of the potential purchasing power; if the property tax finally forced out more than 20% of the vacant housing, five years later city residents will lament: "Who said that real estate is a steady profit without loss?" In fact, there is no serious shortage of absolute property stock in China, but rather a serious injustice of property occupation, which distorts the relationship between supply and demand. How much less arable land, environmental pollution, energy consumption and resource waste would China experience if all vacant houses in all cities were filled with residents?

It is only when the real estate industry spits out the vast economic resources that have been ineffectively occupied that other industries can reclaim those resources, can grow and thrive, can create more jobs, and can bring about real economic prosperity.

A property tax is the most effective and economical way to squeeze out the vacant stock of property, and a significant increase in the cost of ownership will have an immediate effect on improving the contradiction between housing supply and demand and the tension in rental housing. It does not require the huge costly expenditures of mass demolition or the taking of a single cent of arable resources, and its purpose is to redirect the flow of wealth distribution and rebalance the allocation of economic resources through tax policy.

Clearly, at the moment, the real estate market is not flat, but seriously distorted. Just as Obama dared not really challenge the root cause of the high cost of health care in the United States, the difficulty of property taxes, or the lack of regulation, also illustrates the failure of the system to correct errors.

One of the major resistance to the introduction of property taxes is local government. High land prices drive high house prices, high house prices stimulate high land prices, and local governments clearly get the most out of the land gains. House prices go down, land prices don't go up, and local finances go wrong. In recent years, local governments have invested heavily in infrastructure and urban renewal, mostly through debt financing and bank loans, and land sale revenues are an important source of support for local debt.

The financial system is equally reluctant to see house prices fall, fearing depreciation of land collateral on assets and rising default rates on construction loans and mortgages, threatening capital adequacy and affecting profitability and stock prices. At the same time, the upstream and downstream of the real estate chain also connects dozens of industries in which the financial system also has substantial interests, the real estate downturn, the financial system's asset quality in other industries will also take a serious hit.

Real estate developers make their money in the bright and high profile, and rightfully become the focus of social discontent, while hidden behind some local governments and financial systems make their fortunes in silence, forming an iron triangle of interests that is almost impregnable. Housing price control policy in front of the Iron

Triangle repeatedly division veterans fatigue, blunt force to hold on to the city, it was expected to happen.

Covetousness is a human nature, which can be sparse but not blocked. Effective promotion of property tax needs to dismantle the iron triangle of interests, financial innovation may provide some ideas.

The "rent-backed securities" developed by BlackRock are bonded products created by using rent cash flows as collateral, similar in nature to MBS bonds backed by the cash flows of mortgage loans or ABS bonds backed by the cash flows of accounts receivable. Since all cash flows can be securitized, the fixed cash flows generated by property taxes can also be securitized, which are "property tax mortgage-backed securities".

It is true that no country in the world has tried the securitization of property taxes, but to try is to innovate, and this innovation in particular would be an effective incentive for local governments to move forward with property taxes, and a potentially huge source of revenue for the financial system.

If 650 million urban dwellers own roughly 160 million homes on average for a family of four, the total value of real estate in China would be a whopping 16 trillion yuan (the total value of real estate in the United States is about $23 trillion) if each home is worth $1 million. If the average property tax rate of 0.5%, then the total property tax revenue will be 800 billion per year, if financial institutions will be the next 10 years of property tax packaged into bonds, that is, the value of up to 8 trillion financial assets, in the face of such a super cake, banks, securities dealers and other financial institutions will not enthusiastically support the property tax reason?

Sometimes it is more effective to attack the poison with the poison and hedge greed with greed than to simply curb greed. For some local governments, the proceeds from land sales will be like a base salary, while the proceeds from property tax mortgage bonds will be more like a bonus. Of course, since the bonuses are being paid, the base salary will be lowered, but the total income will increase.

Specifically, local governments will generate two types of revenue when they auction land parcels: one is revenue from the sale of land. The other is property taxes on future properties such as commodity houses and commercial properties on the land. The innovation team of the financial system can help the local government to take the future cash flow of the property taxes on that or other parcels of land, estimate, mix, layer, refine, complete the production of standardized bond products, then find a rating company to rate, and finally sell in the financial market, the financing obtained is included in the local government budget, which can be used for all the expenses the government considers necessary. It would be an additional revenue that didn't exist before, and the incentive for local governments to push property taxes would increase dramatically. Currently, local governments do not have the authority to issue credit bonds, and new bonds could help local governments with secured financing.

The essence of a property tax mortgage bond is a one-time discounted realization of local government property tax revenues over the next 5, 10, 15 or 20 years, transferring the future discounted proceeds to investors in the financial markets. Of course, to receive this additional bonus, local governments need to make concessions on land sale revenues, such as $2 in local financing with new bonds, and $1 in land sale revenues, which should be used as a special fund for transfer payments to subsidize farmers who have lost their land or for investment in agricultural infrastructure, either in the hands of local governments or nationally by the central government.

From the point of view of the flow of funds, the transfer fund is equivalent to the financial market rich people and a large number of property owners, to compensate for the three agricultural undertakings, enhance the consumption capacity of farmers and balance the uneven distribution of wealth between urban and rural areas.

Property taxes are different from rent, where a rental property may be vacant with no cash flow, and the property will always have an owner, who holds who pays taxes and the cash flow will not be interrupted. As a result, the quality of the property tax mortgage bonds is naturally superior to the Black Rockers' rental mortgage bonds. At the same time, property tax mortgage-backed bonds can also provide quality products to insurance companies, pension funds, money funds, bank wealth management and other institutions in the financial market that are desperate for safety and high yields, resulting in substantial benefits to the financial system.

More importantly, since land revenues are extrabudgetary, there is a lack of transparency in the use of land by local governments, and supervision is difficult to put in place, there are bound to be problems with investment efficiency. And partially replacing land revenues with financing from property tax mortgage bonds would expand the proportion of revenues on the budget, increase efficiency in the use of funds and create more wealth.

Property tax mortgage bonds will provide an effective mechanism to regulate local governments, bonds are traded in the financial market, its price reflects the market's judgment of local government projects every moment, financial analysts hate to run to real estate projects and go door to door to investigate sales ratios, tax status, actual owners and other information to judge the price of bonds. The success of local governments in one development project will reduce the cost of financing other projects, which will effectively motivate local governments to be cautious about development projects, as the financial markets will score their political performance from time to time. A property tax bond that was wildly dumped on the market and saw its price plummet would expose the extent to which the project had failed and put officials under considerable pressure.

Letting the financial markets oversee local governments and using bond prices to assess the success or failure of projects is far more effective than management by higher-ups.

The key to urbanization is job creation

According to the Chinese Academy of Sciences' 2012 China New Urbanization Report, China's urbanization rate passed the 50 percent mark for the first time in 2011, reaching 51.3 percent, which is the highest urbanization record in China's history, meaning that for the first time, China's urban resident population exceeds the rural population. Here, the urban resident population includes the population with an agricultural household registration that has lived in the city for more than six months. If the 180 million migrant workers in agricultural households are deducted, the actual urbanization rate in China is about 35 per cent.

Many optimistically estimate that a 1 percentage point increase in China's annual urban population share could kick-start more than $5 trillion in domestic demand. A 10 percentage point increase in future urbanization could kick-start domestic demand at 50 trillion, which is equivalent to rebuilding a GDP of current size.

If this logic is followed, all China needs to do to become a developed country is to keep expanding the size of its cities and then move its farmers to live in them, and GDP growth will be there, urbanization will be high, and economic prosperity will be automatic. This line of thinking is guilty of the same fault as the urbanization movement in the Roman Empire, where urbanization was the result of economic prosperity, not its cause.

Artificial urbanization is where people live in the city and many will become a burden on the city, while economic prosperity urbanizes where everyone has a job and everyone is a contributor to the city.

China's urbanization must provide hundreds of millions of jobs, and they should be full-time jobs with social security and health insurance. Without work, there is no income and no possibility of expanding domestic demand. The 180 million migrant workers now living in the cities are basically employed on a short-term and temporary basis, and if they are converted into full-time jobs with benefits, health insurance and social security, roughly equivalent to the security of urban residents, I am afraid that the number of jobs can only be discounted, i.e. cities have created a total of 90 million urban full-time jobs for farmers in the past 30 years or so, an average of about 3 million per year, which is the approximate scale of urbanization of the agricultural population in the context of China's rapid economic development.

If the 2020 urbanization target is 55 per cent, the urban economy will have to create 150 million full-time jobs in the six years leading up to 2020 in order to convert past and future migrant workers into urban employment, which will require an average of 26 million new full-time jobs per year, an impossible task.

In fact, only about 10 million new jobs are created in China's cities and towns each year, and as many as 25 million people are waiting to be employed in cities and towns in 2012, half of them college and university graduates, which means that the target urbanization rate will result in five urban and one rural youth scramble for a job!

In China's employment landscape, 11 million small and medium-sized enterprises (SMEs) create 75 per cent of urban employment, employing an average of 13 people, with an average lifespan of only 2.5 years, and with conglomerates not surviving for seven to eight years; since 2013, the proportion of SMEs going bankrupt or out of business has risen month by month to nearly 15 per cent. Instead of receiving the financial, tax and policy support they deserve, SMEs continue to be reduced to the dustbin of risk transfer by large enterprises. Large enterprises are paying longer and longer accounts, the proportion of promissory notes is increasing, and the accounts receivable of small and medium-sized enterprises have reached more than half of the assets of enterprises, far higher than the international average of 20 percent. The harsh survival environment has reduced the entrepreneurial success rate of SMEs to 1/40, well below 1/7 in the United States.

Whether the urbanization rate will reach 55% by 2020 is not up to the government, nor should it be, but to the 11 million SMEs struggling to reach the death line. The main obstacle to urbanization is not the lack of office and commercial housing in towns, but the increasing difficulty of survival of small and medium-sized enterprises that can afford rent and operating costs. Urbanization without employment opportunities is tantamount to urban gentrification and gentrification.

The pace of urbanization should be premised on job creation, with stable jobs gradually absorbing the agricultural surplus population, a process that could take 30 years or more before China's urbanization rate truly reaches 50 percent. The industrialization and urbanization of a large country with a population of 1.3 billion is unprecedented in world history and can never be achieved in one step, and its complexity and enormity are, I am afraid, far beyond imagination.

It should be clear that, on the road to urbanization in China, it is also necessary to take into account changes in the world economic situation, and even the possibility of abrupt reversals. In areas where the urban economy is oriented towards international markets, there may be a serious reversal, with urban jobs even shrinking significantly and 180 million migrant workers potentially facing a return to the countryside.

China's biggest risk is not knowing the risk, 30 years of rapid economic development, 60 years of lack of financial crisis experience, let everyone think that economic growth is simply linear growth, only the difference between 7% and 10%, so there is no sense of hedging risk at all. In terms of policy, not enough space is left for the huge gap between optimistic judgments and harsh realities.

If one day 80 million out of 180 million migrant workers are forced to return home, how will rural areas adapt and how will cities respond? If Beijing's empty roads, sparse pedestrians, and cold businesses during the Spring Festival are impressive, the recession is. People don't experience depressions and don't believe in depressions, but that doesn't mean that depressions don't exist, or don't suddenly come.

The wisdom left behind by the ancients is ignored by today's people.

Land transfer and farmers' income

Currently, the United States is creating a world-wide super-cheap food price with huge financial subsidies that seems to be a reincarnation of the Roman era.

Under the pressure of U.S. food prices, Chinese farmers are in a similar situation to Italian farmers of that year. Agriculture has had a bumper harvest for 10 years in a row, but farmers generally have the problem of increasing production without increasing income, the increased production is partly eaten up by rising costs, while the price is deadlocked by international food prices.

In the international trade of food, it is actually the small flows that determine the price of large stocks. The United States, which exports 58 per cent, 43 per cent and 22 per cent of world trade in corn, soybeans and wheat, is well positioned to control world food prices. Distorted international food prices had led to problems similar to those of the Roman Empire, where the agricultural base of developing countries had been eroded by low food prices, agricultural economies had been on the verge of bankruptcy, and large numbers of farmers had flocked to cities, creating slums in major cities in developing countries. Poor farmers provide a steady stream of labor for the export industry, ensuring a supply of cheap commodities in the United States and other developed countries.

China's deep historical understanding of the importance of food has enabled it not to follow in the footsteps of other developing countries in their agricultural economic bankruptcy, but to maintain its agricultural economy by abolishing agricultural taxes and strengthening agricultural subsidies, among other means. However, it has become a consensus that farming is not profitable and that land transfer does not fundamentally change this trend.

The root cause of the lack of interest in increasing food production after the massive annexation of land by the Roman aristocracy remained that Rome had deliberately depressed food prices and that farmers did not make money farming their land, and that it was equally difficult to be profitable after annexation. The aristocrats did not pay even as much attention to agriculture as the large field owners who used slave labor on a large scale during the republican era, lived in Rome or other cities, and rarely even patronized their farms. For them, the most economical way was to lease the land to tenants and sit on the rent. As for the construction of water conservancy, improvement of soil quality, selection of good seeds and other sundry things better not, investment in land is like investment in real estate, preservation of value is the main purpose, saving the heart is the biggest principle, spend money to fine farming is not their specialty, much less their original intention. And ordinary tenants, who neither put money into improving other people's land nor have the capacity to invest, used to farm for themselves but now farm for others, with less responsibility and enthusiasm for their labour. The decline in food output in the Roman Empire following the massive annexation of land was inevitable.

The natural consequence of land transfer in China is necessarily a concentration of land and, ultimately, a concentration in the direction of capital intensity. This raises the interesting question, will capital chase the profits of the grain? Or is the profit from putting the land into food production enough to outweigh other uses?

With food prices grossly undervalued, only a fool would continue to produce food. Chinese capitalist tycoons are likely to be like the Roman aristocrats of their day, living in big cities like Beijing and Shanghai, with land and property all over the country. Even if they continued to produce food, they leased the land to the able planters, who willingly transferred it to them as tenants, or because of the lure of capital, which no one could resist. Will the enthusiasm of the able planters, who used to cultivate the land for themselves and now produce it for others, and who also have to pay the rent for the land, increase or decrease?

Capital-based powerful and large households invest in land for the main purpose of chasing real estate appreciation, rather than looking at the profits of food production, they do not care about soil improvement, nor do they care about precision farming, the construction of water conservancy to improve irrigation and other expenses are the less the better. The big farmers are certainly more reluctant to take their own money and subsidize other people's land, all with existing infrastructure, and they may be able to increase per capita returns substantially at the expense of output per unit of land, just as American farmers have higher incomes and lower yields. The result is clear that the concentration of land created by land transfer does not necessarily lead to an increase in total food output; the effect may be the opposite, with the greater the concentration of land, the less guaranteed the total food output.

Historically, the goal of agricultural efficiency in China is very different from that of the United States, which seeks the maximum output per unit of land, i.e., land productivity, while the United States seeks the maximum output per unit of population, i.e., labour productivity, determined by the harsh reality that China has only 7 per cent of the world's arable land, but must feed 22 per cent of the world's population. Whereas Chinese farmers can toughen up on small plots of land with intensive labour, American farmers prioritize labour-saving measures such as agricultural mechanization and chemical fertilizers, which become relatively inexpensive when the inputs are evenly distributed among large per capita occupants of farmland. And with so little land per capita in China, that input becomes unaffordable.

The question is, is China prepared to change its goals for agricultural efficiency? If maximum output per capita is pursued, then China must be prepared to accept the consequences of not being able to feed itself, and the prophecy of who will feed China may well come true. In the event of a military conflict between China and Japan on the Diaoyu Islands one day, the United States would not have to send an army and simply announce a halt to food exports to China, and the potential geopolitical conflict facing China goes far beyond the Diaoyu Islands.

Food security is not only a matter of economic efficiency, but also of national prosperity!

One of Rogers' long-standing reasons for being bullish on agriculture hits the nail on the head, which is that the world's aging agricultural population is far more of a problem than cities.

The average age of the farming population is already 58 in the United States, 60 in Europe, and 62 in Japan, and young people in developed countries likewise love urban life and hate the dullness of the farm. Under the oppression of low food prices in the United States, developing countries have long been suffering from the collapse of their agricultural economies and the serious loss of young and middle-aged workers. Imagine that in 10 years' time, the agricultural labour force in the developed countries will be 70 years old and the rural areas in the developing countries will have long been deserted, and the world population will be 8 billion, a net increase of a full billion! A severely ageing agricultural workforce will inevitably lead to a decline in agricultural productivity while the population continues to grow substantially, the structural contradiction between total food output and aggregate demand is bound to intensify, and it is only a matter of time before international food prices rise significantly.

China should have no illusions that in the next 10 years, 1.4 billion Chinese will be able to live on imported food! That is why the importance of agricultural output per unit of land in China is still far greater than output per capita, and the goal of agricultural efficiency in China cannot be changed.

With this premise in mind, land transfer policy must map out a clear scope for the next 10 years and not unilaterally pursue big agriculture on scale and high concentration on land. The capitalist tycoons can invest in agriculture indirectly through the capital market, but must control the scale of direct land occupation, the red line of 1.8 billion acres of cultivated land can only be rigidly guarded.

This means that farmers will make huge sacrifices for food security, and this sacrifice must be rewarded in excess, most directly through greater compensation for their income. In fact, a significant increase in farmers' incomes can effectively expand the domestic market, promote the realization of economic transformation and ease the degree of wealth fragmentation.800 million farmers increase their incomes by 1,000 yuan each, meaning 800 million shirts, 800 million pairs of shoes or 800 million mobile phones of new commodity purchasing power, their total consumption scale will far exceed the contribution of 8000 billionaires to the economy. In particular, as 800 million farmers increase their consumption, this will trigger a scale effect, stimulating a new social division of labour and new employment opportunities.

"Overproduction" is largely a false proposition; there has never been a surplus of wealth in human history, except for the inability of the vast majority of the population to consume, as a result of the polarization of wealth and poverty. If 800 million farmers are over-incentivized, it will largely replace export-oriented wealth outflows.

Around 1940, based on the outbreak of the "Second World War", the United States imposed subsidies through the war machine on tens of millions of unemployed labourers and millions of poor sons and daughters who went to war, thus reversing the trend of polarization between rich and poor and resulting in 40 golden years of economic development. China's ability to reverse the widening urban-rural divide in peaceful times is key to its continued economic prosperity in the future.

Compensation for farmers' incomes is only a correction of some degree of serious distortion in international food prices. The expansion of farmers' consumption capacity will stimulate an increase in goods and services in the urban economy, leading to steady employment growth, which in turn will absorb the urbanization of the agricultural surplus labour force and put it on a sound and sustainable urbanization path. When international food prices eventually rise with a vengeance, compensation to farmers can be gradually reduced and they will be more profitable from the market.

Farmer compensation should not only be the responsibility of governments, but also the full mobilization of capital markets to direct greedy money where it is most needed, and this is where financial innovation can work.

An important reason for the slow growth of farmers' incomes has been natural disasters and market changes, and Chinese insurance companies have stepped in to cover agricultural insurance, including income insurance for farmers. Income insurance is a link between the loss of production due to natural disasters in traditional agricultural insurance and the loss of income due to price fluctuations in market price insurance. When agricultural production suffers a loss, the gross income of the farmer is calculated by multiplying the actual harvest yield for the year with the average wholesale unit price in the market and comparing it with the income in a normal year, and the resulting difference is compensated and settled by the insurance company.

A good idea for income insurance, but the cost is high. For example, a certain income insurance policy in Songjiang, Shanghai has a premium of 350,000 yuan and a coverage of over 2.6 million yuan. The government must provide a large percentage of subsidies, otherwise insurance costs are too high for farmers to afford.

If the cost of insurance is too low, it will be difficult for insurers to make a profit because natural disasters are becoming more frequent and market changes are difficult to predict. Is there a way to significantly reduce the cost of insurance and stimulate insurance companies to provide large-scale income insurance in rural areas across the country? Financial innovation can also provide ideas.

Natural disasters and market fluctuations cannot occur simultaneously over all regions of the country and over all agricultural products, and a risk-balanced approach across regions and agricultural crops would significantly reduce the average price of income insurance. Insurance companies can pool income insurance policies from different regions into a pool of assets and work with trust companies or investment banks to rationalize their risk and return to form standardized securities products that can be sold in financial markets.

The insurance company only earns a certain amount of fees, spreading all the risks and benefits to investors, rolling back the money and continuing to expand the business scale. Financial markets have credit default swaps (CDS), which are derivatives of bets on corporate defaults, and farmers' income insurance securities, which are derivatives of bets on natural disasters and market changes. By purchasing such securities, the investor is effectively participating in the business of the insurance company, making a profit or loss on a single policy, but certainly making a profit on a composite security that includes different regions and different types of insurance. The more investors who subscribe, the more insurance companies will be able to reduce premium costs and the more farmers will benefit. In effect, insurance companies earn business development fees, compensation and claims are financed by the financial markets, and investors receive a broad probability of a good food harvest.

The securitization of agricultural income insurance also has no precedent in the world, but if it can be achieved, it will effectively increase farmers' incomes and reduce the financial burden, and the effect will be equivalent to direct transfers from the rich to farmers, benefiting themselves and the country.

Only by enriching farmers can domestic demand be expanded, economic transformation be completed and the process of urbanization be promoted.

Only with boundless strength can you let your dreams fly

In the 1980s, the television series Huo Yuanjia was popular, and there was a plot that impressed the audience. Once, Huo Yuanjia crossed the river in a boat, and when the boat reached the middle of the river, it suddenly hit the reef, and he unfortunately fell into the water. Unfortunately, Huo Yuanjia doesn't know water, and if he struggles desperately to go with the flow, he will only end up drowning from exhaustion. Huo Yuanjia was calm and collected himself, held his breath, sank to the bottom of the river, held a large rock, and walked step by step to the shore, finally turning the danger into nothing. This plot is deeply imprinted in the minds of millions of viewers, and in real life, there are even people who have successfully saved themselves using the same method.

The secret to Huo Yuanjia's survival was that he didn't panic or go with the flow, but rather stepped out of his predicament step by step, which required great perseverance.

Ancient people said: for the way of the general, the first thing to do is to cure the heart, Tai Shan collapses in front but the color does not change, and the elk rises on the left but the eye does not change, then can control the benefits and harm.

That's the power of determination and focus! Not only of the great generals, but the outstanding entrepreneurs as well. In China's high-tech industry, Huawei is one such company with determination.

Distinguished entrepreneurs are by no means born with determination, there is faltering and hesitation in every human being, and no entrepreneur is immune in the face of high profits. Huawei has also been tempted by the lucrative profits of real estate, and greedy instincts can torment the nerves of entrepreneurs from time to time. When the size of the company is rapidly expanding, entrepreneurs are most prone to self-inflation, but also most prone to self-loss, the risk of going astray, much higher than when starting a business to kill a way out of no choice and the company is too large to adjust after the trade-offs.

The brutal competition in the telecom industry and the strength of the international giants have forced Huawei to maintain an almost paranoid sense of apprehension, but also fueled his urge to enter the high-margin, low-competition industry. Stress and temptation are the sharpening stones of determination, and once the path is realized, there is no longer any wandering of the will or spirit. In the end, Huawei's family members withstood all kinds of "moose" interference, sank their hearts, hugged the stone of their dreams and led Huawei step by step to glory.

There are many companies that can make money in China, all business owners who put money first can only be considered as bosses, but not as entrepreneurs; those who have entrepreneurial dreams and build a business empire with their own hands can be considered as outstanding entrepreneurs; and those who have deep determination, focused goals and are determined to do only one thing well in life can be considered as outstanding entrepreneurs, and entrepreneurs in this realm are really rare in China.

An outstanding company does not equal a great company, only an outstanding company that has been handed down for a hundred years and has a long history can deserve the word great. Among China's outstanding private enterprises, Lenovo, New Hope, Fuyao, Wanda, Huiyuan and others are prominent representatives, who have always stuck to their main business and never went with the flow through decades of difficult entrepreneurship, and they all have the potential to become great companies.

China needs at least 10 or more great companies, not by the government, not by monopoly, but by their own determination and focus, to break new ground in the international market and be invincible. Without such a great group of companies, it would be difficult for China to become a great country. This is the real challenge of the Chinese Dream!

More than 10,000 companies, three or even five generations, have focused on one area of excellence in Germany's century-old manufacturing industry. Their daily job is to work tirelessly on details and improvements, pushing for process optimization, researching technical upgrades, the endless pursuit of precision and meticulous and unconditional compliance. It is this unparalleled strength in the manufacturing industry that ultimately makes German manufacturing so competitive.

There are also as many as 10,000 centuries-old stores in Japan, which are surrounded by super-corporations, day after day, year after year, working silently and without complaint, as generation after generation of youth passes away and new people continue to work hard. Impeccable service, exquisite and perfect spare parts, and a constant supply of Japanese flagship companies to conquer customers all over the world.

The United States of America now, and the United Kingdom of old, in the Age of Rising, has always created one technological revolution after another with determination and focus, opening up new markets piece by piece. The decline of Britain first of all stemmed from the disintegration of the manufacturing force and the dispersal of focus, the industrial revolution brought huge profits made Britain lose its way, in the tide of money, industry drowned, finance reached, profit-eating capitalism prevailed, easy investment profit, rapid wealth appreciation, the hard work of stone pelting for the Americans to do. As a result, two world wars brought the British Empire back to life.

The United States today is repeating the same old path as Britain did at the end of the 19th century, with higher profits on Wall Street, greater depletion of the economy, more asset bubbles, and a faster loss of industry. Today's American companies are reveling in the euphoria of a tremendous appreciation of assets, with an industrial determination that is not unlike that of the 1970s, and even more unlike that of the early 20th century. The best talent has long since moved away from scientists and engineers, and the most envied professions are bankers and lawyers.

The human heart seeks ease and comfort, while wealth flows to diligence and persistence. In an era when the world is flooded with money and asset bubbles are inflated, the roots of industry have loosened, hard work is ridiculed, thrift is scorned, speculation becomes fashionable, extreme wealth becomes an ideal, greed swallows up public virtue, trickery is admired, entrepreneurs lack perseverance, individuals are unable to focus, and the whole society is going with the flow in a flood of money.

China's dream of a great renaissance depends not on the desire for wealth, but on perseverance and extraordinary concentration, the diligence and perseverance handed down from generation to generation, and the determination to walk towards the shore with a fixed stone even after falling to the bottom of the river.

Can China let its dream of a strong country and a rich people fly?

How deep is the determination, how high can the dream fly!

POSTSCRIPT

It's an exhausting book and a self-discovery. A lot of things you think you've thought through, only to realize there's a problem as soon as you say them; and when you do, you realize there's a loophole as soon as you write them. Thinking is the spark of leaping thinking, speaking is the improvised logical fragment, writing is the precipitated body of thought.

When I started creating with passion, I never expected the work behind me to be so hard. At the beginning of each chapter, I was confident that I had enough data, information and knowledge to accumulate, only to discover that these things don't really belong to me. The richer the accumulation of knowledge, the more severe the paralysis of the mind always leads to, in a mess, I struggle desperately, like a person about to drown, unable to grasp the primary and secondary clues, unable to find the logical source, unable to distinguish the direction of reasoning, only a wave of higher than one wave of information to beat me into a daze, energy constantly drained, confidence repeatedly collapses, anxiety, frustration and despair swallowing the remaining will.

At the critical moment when I was about to give up and prepare to go with the flow, the clear image of Huo Yuanjia falling into the water, sinking to the bottom of the river, holding a stone and walking step by step to the shore always popped up in my mind. At this time, all the surrounding turmoil slowly fell silent, the turbulent thoughts became as still as the water, I seemed to sink to the bottom of the water, no confidence, no will, no struggle, just fixed the mind, internalized the mind. Gradually, critical data began to flicker dimly, important details emerged with clear outlines, highlights and highlights could connect, clues and clues appeared causally, and the source of logic slowly emerged, finally seeing the light at the end of the dark tunnel. Go out and there's a new world of sunshine.

When I finally got the chapters logically sewn together, I suddenly realized that life should be the same. Only a person with a deep sense of determination will be able to navigate the treacherous waters and experience the pleasures that others cannot.

The cure of the heart is the cure of evil. The so-called "healing of the heart" is to give up all distractions, to discard all delusions, to focus all the energy of life on a meaningful and valuable thing, despite all the difficulties, but not shy, and die without regret. Whenever the heart comes to a certain level, the strength of the mind comes to a certain depth. Only a person who has the strength of mind can weigh the real advantages and disadvantages, and only then can he be keen to avoid the disadvantages and advantages.

All people who have achieved something in the past and the present are masters of mind control and determination. In reality, many people are not unaware of their goals, but are simply unable to heal their hearts effectively, and therefore cannot effectively resist temptation, which often results in harm to profit, and life's potential cannot be maximized.

Indeed, it is not easy to resist the temptation, the exclusion of interference is often not in the mind, in the final analysis, or the mind of too many distractions, delusions of grandeur, it is difficult to do the mind's highly focused. In such circumstances, mentors are extremely important.

The editor of *The Currency Wars*, Ying-Yan Zheng, has been a rare mentor in the writing process, not only in planning the books, but also in making the dreams come true. Over the past few years, she has insisted that high quality content and ideas must always be followed through without allowing any "compromise". When I was wandering, she always stressed that "a person has only one thing to do in life and he is an amazing person." The words I heard no less than a hundred times, thought more than a thousand times, but also may not always be able to do, her encouragement and urging me to benefit greatly, many of the many distractions and delusions were stifled in the cradle. The many setbacks she has experienced and the amount of time wasted have repeatedly confirmed her foresight.

What is the shortcut to life? That is, there must be fewer detours. A good teacher and friend is like a bitter pill, and though words are hard to hear, reason works. It would be a great shame not to encounter such a daring friend in one's life.

A good teacher not only helps to block out distractions and suppress delusions, but also often makes one more sober about oneself, "Today's 'currency war' series bestsellers don't mean everything, and twenty or thirty years from now, if your books are still being read by young people, that's what they're about". The alarm bells of my good teachers and friends shocked me with gold stars in my eyes, and I suddenly realized that my time was already quite tight.

During my writing retreat in Beijing this year, my wife and daughter came to visit me in the summer. We huddled in a hut every day, talking and laughing together, and I suddenly felt that life can be extremely simple in material terms, but at the same time have the greatest joy in the world. We took our daughter to the ground stalls at the foot of Fragrant Hill every day, and a few dollars worth of small things could make us happy for half a day. When the skin is peeled off of all substances, the kinship is instead more fragrant and richer.

From late spring to winter, I have been studying and combing through the night every day, and I have gradually formed a basic judgment on the future trend of the world economy. When I walked out of the fragrant mountain, the sun was still shining, looking at the distant horizon, dark clouds were slowly accumulating, the mountain wind had come in gusts.

Song Hongbing
Xiangshan, Beijing,
November 22, 2013

Other titles

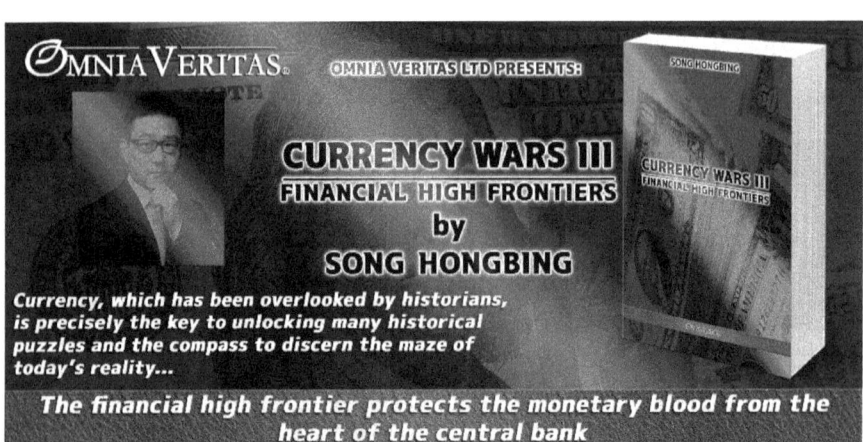

THE COMING RAIN

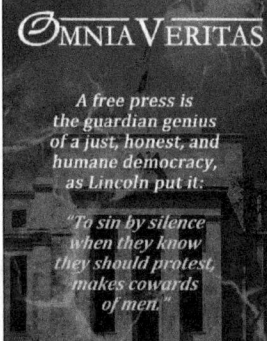
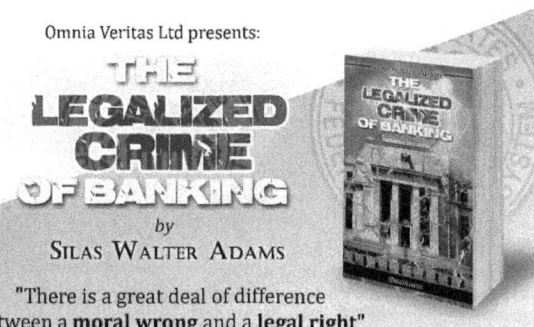

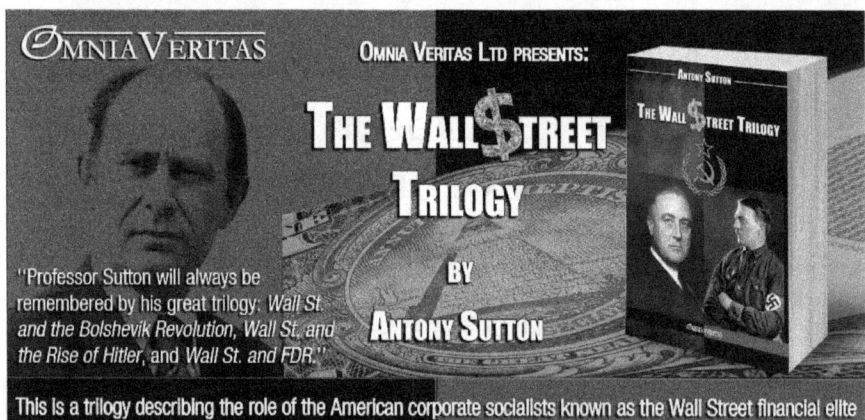

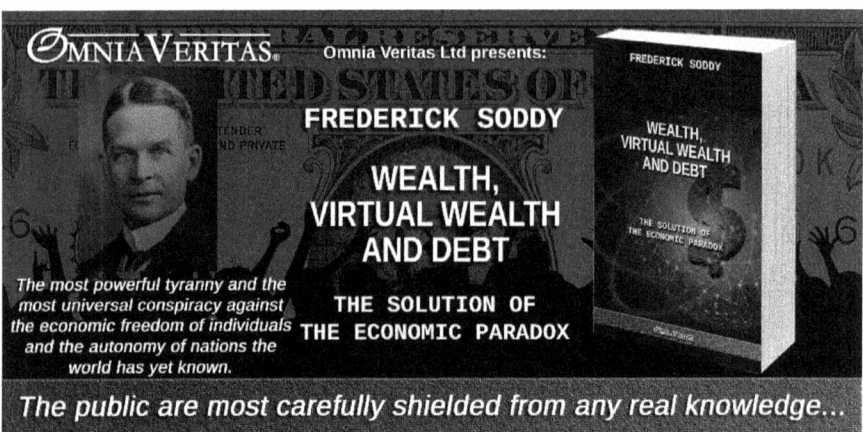
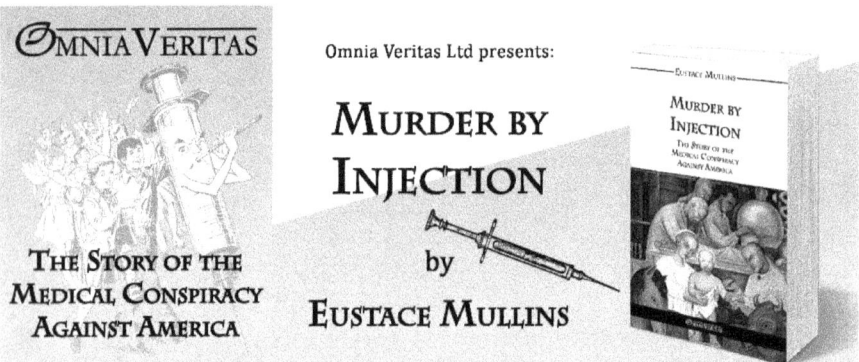
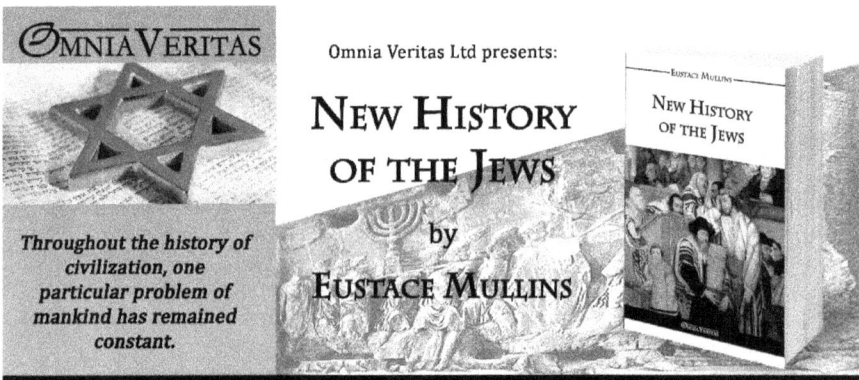

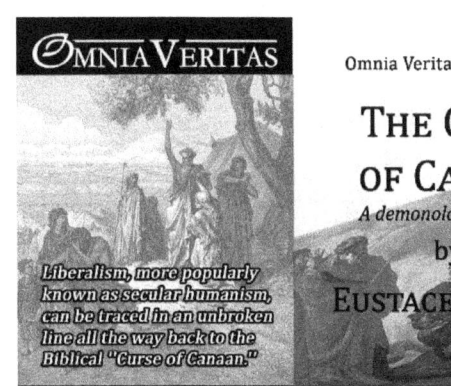

Humanism is the logical result of the demonology of history

American should know just what is going on in our courts

Will we continue to be enslaved by the Babylonian debt money system?

www.ingramcontent.com/pod-product-compliance
Lightning Source LLC
Chambersburg PA
CBHW071310150426
43191CB00007B/575